"This book offers a much-needed global perspective on immigrant entrepreneurship, moving beyond the traditional focus on North America and W[...]nalysis and a rich comparative framework, it illuminates the [...]repreneurs across varied institutional landscapes. It certain[...]ntribution to the field of migration and entrepreneurship st[...]

Professor Nicholas Theodo[...] *Aston* [...]*ngdom*

"This is an excellent resource to get an understanding of immigrant entrepreneurship in different contexts."

Dr Nadeera Ranabahu, *UC Business School, University of Canterbury, New Zealand*

IMMIGRANT ENTREPRENEURSHIP

Analysing immigration around the world, *Immigrant Entrepreneurship: Opportunities, Ventures and Outcomes in a Global Market* illuminates how immigrant entrepreneurs overcome barriers to mobilise resources across diverse socio-economic environments.

Drawing on case studies from Africa, the Americas, Europe, the Middle East and elsewhere, the author explores how contemporary migration patterns, informal economies and digitalisation influence entrepreneurial outcomes. In emphasising entrepreneurial strategies that help adapt to exclusion and regulatory complexity, this book provides a nuanced understanding of the entire field of immigrant entrepreneurship.

The global comparative approach taken by this book sheds light on the vital role that immigration plays in driving entrepreneurial growth in economic development around the world. The result is a resource that is enlightening reading for researchers and advanced students of entrepreneurship, international business and development studies.

Tamaralaiyefa Harold Tiemo, PhD, is a senior lecturer in Global Business and Entrepreneurship at Global Banking School, UK (affiliated with Oxford Brookes University). He is also an economic development consultant focused on policy and enterprise growth in Delta State, Nigeria.

Topics in Entrepreneurship

It has been said that there are as many approaches to entrepreneurship as there are entrepreneurs. This series of accessible textbooks aims to capture the many facets of entrepreneurship in greater detail than general introductory texts are able to.

Topics in Entrepreneurship is a series of textbooks in which each individual book focuses on a particular type or subsection of entrepreneurial activity. Subjects such creativity, innovation, mindset, personality traits and demographics are among the many areas covered in the series.

Aimed at advanced undergraduate and postgraduate readers, as well as lecturers, the books in the series supplement and support the core reading requirements of entrepreneurship courses. With authors and contributors drawn from around the world, *Topics in Entrepreneurship* aims to provide a fuller, more nuanced and colourful picture of entrepreneurship in today's economy.

Immigrant Entrepreneurship
Opportunities, Ventures and Outcomes in a Global Market
Tamaralaiyefa Harold Tiemo

IMMIGRANT ENTREPRENEURSHIP

Opportunities, Ventures and Outcomes in a Global Market

Tamaralaiyefa Harold Tiemo

Routledge
Taylor & Francis Group
LONDON AND NEW YORK

First published 2026
by Routledge
4 Park Square, Milton Park, Abingdon, Oxon OX14 4RN

and by Routledge
605 Third Avenue, New York, NY 10158

Routledge is an imprint of the Taylor & Francis Group, an informa business

British Library Cataloguing-in-Publication Data
A catalogue record for this book is available from the British Library

ISBN: 978-1-032-99609-7 (hbk)
ISBN: 978-1-032-99608-0 (pbk)
ISBN: 978-1-003-60507-2 (ebk)

DOI: 10.4324/9781003605072

Typeset in Times New Roman
by codeMantra

CONTENTS

TABLES

ACKNOWLEDGEMENT

I am sincerely grateful to Professor Alexandros Psychogios for his valuable support and encouragement during the development of this book. His feedback and advice were instrumental in shaping aspects of the ideas presented here. I also thank the wider academic community whose discussions and input have enriched this work.

1

INTRODUCTION

The global landscape of immigrant entrepreneurship

In an increasingly globalised world, immigrant entrepreneurship has emerged as a significant dimension of economic and social transformation. While immigrant entrepreneurs are widely recognised for their contributions to labour markets, innovation ecosystems and transnational trade, their experiences are deeply shaped by diverse institutional structures, migration policies and opportunity environments. Nevertheless, existing scholarship has largely centred on North American and Western European contexts, often neglecting the varied entrepreneurial practices and outcomes emerging across Oceania, the Middle East, Latin America and Sub-Saharan Africa. This chapter first examines global trends and regional perspectives on immigrant entrepreneurship, before turning to conceptual debates distinguishing ethnic and immigrant entrepreneurship, the impact of legal status and migration pathways, the influence of generational dynamics on economic integration and the scope and reach of entrepreneurial ventures. In addition, it situates immigrant entrepreneurship within broader theoretical frameworks that integrate notions of identity, agency and institutional embeddedness. Together, these discussions establish the conceptual foundation for understanding immigrant entrepreneurship as a dynamic, context-contingent phenomenon shaped by evolving global mobility patterns and structural barriers.

Global trends and regional perspectives

To contextualise the emergence and significance of immigrant entrepreneurship, it is important first to outline the foundational role of entrepreneurship in driving economic growth, innovation and market expansion. Entrepreneurship is widely recognised as a catalyst for economic growth, innovation and job creation, and entrepreneurial activity fosters economic dynamism by identifying emerging market opportunities, enhancing productivity and expanding industries (Carree & Thurik, 2010; Reynolds, 2022; Welter et al., 2017).

Within this landscape, immigrant entrepreneurs have played an increasingly pivotal role by bringing diverse skills, global networks and innovative approaches that span both dynamic, opportunity-driven sectors and more traditional, necessity-driven sectors (Kloosterman & Rath, 2001; Welter et al., 2017). Their contributions are evident across industries such as

DOI: 10.4324/9781003605072-1

technology, professional services and innovation-intensive enterprises (often associated with higher opportunity structures), as well as in traditional sectors including manufacturing, personal services and small-scale retail (frequently characterised by lower barriers to entry but more limited growth potential) (Aliaga-Isla & Rialp, 2013; Azoulay et al., 2022; Fairlie & Lofstrom, 2015).

In addition to their economic contributions, immigrant entrepreneurs help address labour shortages, diversify consumer markets and introduce innovative business models (Dana, 2007; Kourtit et al., 2013). However, despite their significant role, they continue to face structural barriers such as restricted access to finance, regulatory complexity and systemic discrimination (Jones et al., 2022; Light & Dana, 2013). These conditions frequently push immigrant entrepreneurs towards informal strategies, community-based financing mechanisms and transnational entrepreneurial activities as means of sustaining and expanding their ventures (Barrett & Vershinina, 2017; Cruz et al., 2020). As a result, immigrant entrepreneurship emerges not simply as a reflection of structural opportunities but as a dynamic and situated process influenced by institutional settings, social relations and evolving patterns of mobility (Bhachu, 2017; Elo & Dana, 2023).

Recent scholarship increasingly highlights the role of digitalisation, transnational networks and hybrid identity practices in shaping immigrant entrepreneurial trajectories (Gurău et al., 2020; Harima, 2022). Digital technologies, online platforms and diaspora linkages have provided new avenues for entrepreneurs to access resources, expand into international markets and negotiate regulatory and institutional barriers (Onyima et al., 2024). These developments challenge nationally bounded models of entrepreneurship by emphasising the transnational nature of resource mobilisation, opportunity recognition and market participation. They also underscore the capacity of immigrant entrepreneurs to exercise strategic agency across multiple institutional and geographic contexts.

Immigrant entrepreneurship in North America and Western Europe has been relatively well-documented. In North America, particularly the United States (U.S.) and Canada, immigrant entrepreneurship has flourished within relatively open business environments and selective immigration regimes that favour skilled migrants (Azoulay et al., 2022; Kerr & Mandorff, 2023). Ethnic networking, transnational resource mobilisation and innovation-driven ventures have been central features in these contexts (Dana, 1997; Kariv et al., 2009). In Western Europe, although immigrant entrepreneurship is also well-researched, challenges such as labour market rigidity, credential devaluation and ethnic stereotyping remain prominent (Ram et al., 2017; Ram & Jones, 2008). Studies show how migrant entrepreneurs, including post-war Polish communities in England (Barrett & Vershinina, 2017) and Syrian refugee entrepreneurs (Refai et al., 2024; Refai & McElwee, 2022), adapt their strategies to navigate complex institutional settings and processes of social and economic integration.

By contrast, entrepreneurial activities in Oceania, the Middle East, Latin America and Sub-Saharan Africa remain underexamined despite growing significance. In Oceania, particularly Australia and New Zealand, immigrant entrepreneurship has been fostered through skilled migration policies and business investment incentives (Collins & Low, 2010), although persistent challenges related to underemployment and skills underutilisation are evident (Duan et al., 2021). Research on former refugee women entrepreneurs in New Zealand highlights how they strategically navigate visibility and invisibility paradoxes to access opportunities while mitigating structural barriers (Ranabahu et al., 2024). In the Middle East, particularly within the Gulf Cooperation Council (GCC) countries, immigrant entrepreneurs operate under restrictive regulatory conditions that limit ownership rights and access to finance (Zahra, 2019), yet many mobilise transnational strategies and informal economic activities to sustain their ventures (Harima, 2022; Refai et al., 2024). In Latin America and Sub-Saharan Africa, immigrant entrepreneurs frequently rely on community-based financing, informal networks and hybrid business models to build resilience amidst widespread informality and political volatility (Fubah & Moos, 2022; Martínez Rivera, 2024; Simba et al., 2023).

Despite growing recognition of the vibrancy and diversity of immigrant entrepreneurship across global contexts, scholarly frameworks continue to disproportionately focus on North American and Western European experiences (Basu & Pruthi, 2021; Beckers & Blumberg, 2013; Chodavadia et al., 2024). This Western-centric orientation risks producing theoretical frameworks that inadequately account for the varied institutional, regulatory and socio-economic conditions shaping entrepreneurial outcomes elsewhere. Emerging research increasingly stresses the importance of examining differentiated entrepreneurial experiences, particularly those shaped by migration regimes, financial exclusion and informal economic structures (Elmassah et al., 2022; Martínez Rivera, 2024). Furthermore, prevailing approaches often generalise immigrant entrepreneurship, overlooking the structural asymmetries embedded in race, gender, migration status and class (David & Terstriep, 2025; Waldinger et al., 1990). Addressing these limitations requires reframing immigrant entrepreneurship not merely as a structural phenomenon but as a dynamic process shaped by the interplay of agency, identity and transnational resource mobilisation. A more nuanced conceptual foundation is therefore essential to situate immigrant entrepreneurship within broader debates on identity, opportunity and embeddedness.

Ethnic vs. immigrant entrepreneurship: conceptual considerations

The concepts of ethnic entrepreneurship and immigrant entrepreneurship are closely related, yet not synonymous, and their distinctions continue to generate debate within the academic literature. Some scholars, including Kloosterman & Rath (2003), Nwankwo (2005) and Ojo (2021), use the terms interchangeably, arguing that both groups encounter similar structural and institutional barriers in establishing and expanding businesses. However, other researchers, such as Blackburn & Smallbone (2015) and Ram et al. (2017), emphasise that ethnic entrepreneurship constitutes a broader category that includes not only first-generation immigrants but also native-born individuals from ethnic minority backgrounds.

Ethnic entrepreneurship is typically characterised by business activities grounded in cultural identity, social networks and community-based resources. Entrepreneurs in this category often establish enterprises that serve ethnically defined markets, drawing on intra-community support systems such as informal financial mechanisms and collective social capital (Daniel et al., 2019; Light & Bonacich, 1988). While these networks can help entrepreneurs overcome initial barriers to entry, they may also result in market segmentation, limiting the potential for expansion into wider economic domains (Ram et al., 2017).

By contrast, immigrant entrepreneurship refers specifically to business activity undertaken by individuals who have migrated to a new country. These entrepreneurs are shaped by migration-specific dynamics, including legal status, access to the labour market and the complexity of regulatory environments (Sepulveda et al., 2008). First-generation immigrants often turn to entrepreneurship as a strategy for economic survival in response to limited employment opportunities, language barriers and the non-recognition of foreign qualifications (Davidavičienė & Lolat, 2016). Research suggests that immigrants are more likely than native-born individuals to enter self-employment, frequently driven by necessity rather than by strategic business intent (Kerr & Kerr, 2017).

Despite their significant economic contributions, immigrant entrepreneurs face considerable institutional challenges, including financial exclusion, restrictive regulatory frameworks and difficulties navigating formal markets (House of Commons Library, 2017). While some immigrant entrepreneurs target co-ethnic consumer bases, others engage with broader markets, depending on their level of integration and the availability of economic opportunities (Ojo, 2021).

Ultimately, the boundaries between ethnic and immigrant entrepreneurship are fluid rather than fixed. They are shaped by a combination of legal status, migration history, generational status and market conditions. Recognising these conceptual nuances is essential for developing more inclusive and context-sensitive frameworks for understanding entrepreneurship among minority and migrant populations.

Legal status and migration circumstances

Entrepreneurial opportunities and challenges for migrants are significantly influenced by legal status and migration pathways. Some individuals migrate voluntarily in pursuit of economic opportunities, while others are forced to flee due to conflict or persecution. These factors shape access to capital, market participation and institutional support, thereby influencing business structures and growth potential. Legal status determines whether an entrepreneur can formally register a business, obtain financing and engage in long-term strategic planning, while migration pathways shape initial access to social and economic networks. Table 1.1 categorises immigrant entrepreneurs based on their legal and migration status, outlining key characteristics and examples of each group.

While legal status and migration pathways influence entrepreneurial opportunities at the outset, other structural factors, such as access to financial resources, regulatory barriers and market entry barriers, shape the long-term viability of immigrant-owned businesses. The legal framework in host countries plays a crucial role in determining whether migrant entrepreneurs can transition from informal survival-based activities to formally registered businesses with growth potential (House of Commons Library, 2017; Kloosterman & Rath, 2018). Policy frameworks must therefore account for the diverse legal circumstances of immigrant entrepreneurs, ensuring that tailored support mechanisms are in place to facilitate their economic contributions and integration.

Generational dynamics and economic integration

Generational dynamics play a critical role in shaping the entrepreneurial experiences of immigrant populations, with first- and second-generation entrepreneurs demonstrating distinct strategies, risk appetites and sectoral orientations. First-generation entrepreneurs, typically foreign-born, often establish businesses in response to economic necessity, prompted by restrictive immigration policies, labour market discrimination and limited access to formal employment channels (Aliaga-Isla & Rialp, 2013; Beckers & Blumberg, 2013). These entrepreneurs frequently adopt risk-averse approaches, drawing upon cultural ties and community-based resources to facilitate business creation and sustainability (Baycan et al., 2012). Their ventures tend to be concentrated in traditional, low-entry sectors such as hospitality, retail and small-scale manufacturing, where they can leverage existing demand and informal support systems (Beckers & Blumberg, 2013).

While ethnic networks provide initial stability, they may also constrain business scalability and integration into wider economic spaces (Ekwulugo, 2006; Ojo, 2013). The entrepreneurial practices of first-generation immigrants are often shaped by a deeply embedded habitus formed through pre-migration experiences, survivalist strategies and socialisation within ethnic

TABLE 1.1 Typology Of Immigrant Entrepreneurs Based On Legal Status And Migration Pathways

Type of entrepreneur	*Definition*	*Key characteristics*	*Examples*
Asylum-seeker entrepreneurs (Barak-Bianco & Raijman, 2015; Fiddian-Qasmiyeh et al., 2014)	Individuals awaiting a decision on their asylum application who engage in self-employment as a survival strategy.	Limited legal rights to work, high uncertainty, reliance on informal business activities.	A displaced professional offering freelance digital services while awaiting asylum approval.
Refugee entrepreneurs (Desai et al., 2021; Newman et al., 2024)	Individuals granted refugee status who start businesses as part of economic reintegration.	Language barriers, financial barriers, reliance on non-governmental organisation (NGO) support and microfinance.	A refugee launching a bakery selling traditional foods from their home country.
Undocumented (irregular) entrepreneurs (Bloch & McKay, 2015; Gold, 2019)	Entrepreneurs operating without legal residency or work permits.	Vulnerability to exploitation, reliance on informal markets, inability to register businesses.	A street vendor selling handcrafted goods without legal documentation.
Temporary migrant entrepreneurs (Dustmann & Görlach, 2016; Witteveen & Alba, 2018)	Migrants on short-term visas who establish businesses within their legal barriers.	Uncertain long-term residency, limited business expansion opportunities, dependency on visa renewals.	A student running an online store while studying abroad.
Skilled/investor migrant entrepreneurs (Elo & Minto-Coy, 2019; Saxenian, 2002)	Entrepreneurs who migrate through investor or skills-based visa programmes.	High financial capital, access to business incentives, engagement in high-growth sectors.	A technology entrepreneur launching a startup under a host country's investor visa programme.

communities. This can reinforce a reliance on familiar, low-risk business models that prioritise short-term security over long-term innovation (Cooper, 2021).

In contrast, second-generation immigrant entrepreneurs are more likely to pursue innovation and seek opportunities beyond ethnic enclaves, benefiting from stronger integration into mainstream economic institutions (Chababi et al., 2017). With greater access to education, broader social networks and institutional resources, they are better positioned to engage in high-growth sectors such as biosciences, digital technologies and professional services (Pruthi & Tasavori, 2022). These entrepreneurs often utilise their bicultural competencies to bridge diverse markets and build transnational networks, allowing for the identification of novel opportunities and the implementation of advanced business strategies (Baycan et al., 2012; Chababi et al., 2017).

Second-generation entrepreneurs are also more likely to access formal funding sources, structured recruitment processes and business development programmes that were often inaccessible to the previous generation (Beckers & Blumberg, 2013). Nonetheless, increased integration and educational capital do not automatically translate into entrepreneurial success. Ojo (2019) argues that second-generation entrepreneurs may face delayed business development, partly due to the complexity of navigating formal startup ecosystems and reconciling the expectations of their ethnic heritage with the norms of mainstream business culture.

Beyond these generational distinctions, the evolving nature of immigrant entrepreneurship reflects broader shifts in opportunity structures, resource mobilisation and urban economic dynamics. Kourtit et al. (2013) distinguish between the *forced entrepreneurship* often associated with first-generation migrants and the *voluntary entrepreneurship* increasingly characteristic of the second generation. These shifts illustrate how changing social and economic contexts influence the motivations and trajectories of immigrant business owners. Second-generation entrepreneurs are more likely to engage in strategic, innovation-driven enterprises that align with contemporary urban growth trends.

The intergenerational transmission of entrepreneurial knowledge and the influence of diaspora networks also play a critical role in this transition. Ojo (2013) highlights how second-generation entrepreneurs leverage tacit knowledge, systemic integration and enhanced market access to redefine entrepreneurial identity (EI) within immigrant communities. Although socio-cultural barriers persist, the entrepreneurial journey of the second generation signals a gradual but significant evolution in the agency of immigrant entrepreneurs, shaped by adaptation across generations and the ongoing reconfiguration of economic participation in host societies.

Business scope and market reach

The scope and market reach of immigrant entrepreneurs shape their business strategies and long-term sustainability. Some operate locally, while others engage in regional or global trade, leveraging transnational networks and investment opportunities. Their market reach is influenced by individual resources, host-country policies and broader economic conditions. Table 1.2 categorises immigrant entrepreneurs based on the reach of their ventures, outlining key characteristics, examples and economic contributions.

The classification of immigrant entrepreneurs by business scope reveals a spectrum of strategic approaches shaped by variations in market access, capital availability and policy environments (Dheer, 2018; Urban & Moti, 2024). Immigrant entrepreneurship is far from uniform. Instead, it encompasses a diverse set of practices that respond to institutional contexts and economic opportunities. Transnational entrepreneurs, for example, forge transnational trade networks and promote cultural exports, thereby strengthening global commercial linkages (Duan et al., 2021). Diaspora entrepreneurs often pursue economic integration within host societies while maintaining community-oriented business models that serve co-ethnic markets and reinforce diasporic solidarity (Syrett & Keles, 2022). Returnee entrepreneurs contribute to development in their countries of origin by facilitating capital reinvestment and knowledge transfer, frequently supporting the modernisation of domestic industries (Kassaye et al., 2025).

The scalability and success of these entrepreneurial forms depend significantly on financial access and the regulatory environment. Some countries support immigrant entrepreneurship through inclusive policies and targeted business incentives. Others impose legal and administrative barriers that hinder entry and restrict growth potential (Organisation for Economic Co-operation and Development [OECD], 2019; World Bank, 2019). These contextual differences highlight the need for nuanced policy frameworks and institutional support systems that can enable immigrant entrepreneurs to realise their full economic potential. For policymakers and business stakeholders alike, recognising the diversity of immigrant entrepreneurship is

TABLE 1.2 Typology of immigrant entrepreneurs based on market reach

Type of entrepreneur	*Definition*	*Key characteristics*	*Examples*	*Economic impact*
Transnational entrepreneurs (Drori et al., 2009; Duan et al., 2021)	Entrepreneurs who operate businesses across their home and host countries, leveraging transnational networks and resources.	Transnational business operations, dual-market strategies, leveraging cultural and trade connections.	An entrepreneur importing and selling home-country goods while running a store in the host country.	Facilitates international trade, promotes cultural exports and strengthens global business linkages.
Diaspora entrepreneurs (Elo & Riddle, 2016; Syrett & Keles, 2022)	Entrepreneurs who build ventures catering to their diaspora communities while integrating into the economic structures of the host country.	Strong cultural ties, community-focused businesses, ability to navigate both home and host markets.	A restaurant owner preserving home-country cuisine while adapting to local tastes.	Strengthens cultural identity, creates employment within ethnic communities and fosters local economic integration.
Returnee entrepreneurs (Gruenhagen et al., 2020; Kassaye et al., 2025)	Immigrants who return to their home country to start businesses, bringing back skills, capital and networks acquired abroad.	Leverage experience from abroad, invest in home-country development, transfer of knowledge and business practices.	A former expatriate launching a tech startup in their home country after gaining expertise abroad.	Drives innovation, contributes to knowledge transfer and supports economic development in home countries.

essential for developing effective interventions that enhance its contribution to both local and global economies.

This book conceptualises immigrant entrepreneurship as a dynamic and adaptive process, shaped by migration histories, institutional settings and socio-economic conditions. It is not confined by legal status, generational background, or geographic location. Rather, immigrant entrepreneurship operates along a continuum of business engagement, influenced by levels of integration, the strength of transnational networks and the nature of the surrounding regulatory systems. Immigrant entrepreneurs navigate complex institutional environments, utilising both ethnic and mainstream economic resources while overcoming policy constraints, social integration challenges and barriers to market entry.

Their business activities contribute to innovation, economic diversification, diaspora engagement and international trade. These contributions reflect a broader *entrepreneurial mobility nexus* that captures the interplay between migration, economic adaptation and enterprise formation. This nexus underscores immigrant entrepreneurship as a transformative process that reshapes economic landscapes within and across national boundaries. By advancing this perspective, the book offers a multidimensional understanding of immigrant entrepreneurship that moves beyond rigid classifications and embraces its complexity within the global economy.

Overview of theoretical frameworks

Understanding immigrant entrepreneurship requires a multidimensional theoretical approach that incorporates access to resources, institutional structures, social networks and identity construction. Bourdieu's (1986) theory of capital offers a foundational lens through which to analyse the resources immigrant entrepreneurs mobilise to establish and maintain businesses. Forms of capital, particularly social, cultural, human and financial, are critical in navigating economic constraints. Many immigrant entrepreneurs draw upon co-ethnic networks and community resources to compensate for limited access to mainstream financial systems (Gold & Light, 2000; Ram et al., 2008). These networks facilitate knowledge exchange, informal financing and trust-based partnerships, illustrating how resource mobilisation helps overcome barriers to entry.

However, capital access alone does not explain entrepreneurial outcomes. Institutional structures significantly influence business opportunities and constraints. North's (1990) institutional theory provides a framework for examining how formal institutions, including legal regulations, immigration policy and financial infrastructure, shape entrepreneurial contexts. Restrictive immigration laws may limit business registration, while financial exclusion often inhibits access to credit (Ram et al., 2017). As a result, many immigrant entrepreneurs turn to informal financial arrangements and co-ethnic investment networks.

Formal institutions do not function independently of informal arrangements. Helmke & Levitsky (2012) broaden the institutional perspective by examining how informal institutions such as unwritten norms, trust relationships and culturally embedded expectations shape entrepreneurial behaviour. Welter & Smallbone (2011) further demonstrate that in institutional voids, where formal support is weak or inconsistent, entrepreneurs develop adaptive strategies that rely on informal systems. This extended institutional framework highlights how both formal and informal mechanisms interact to influence entrepreneurial possibilities, especially in resource-constrained environments.

In addition to institutional dynamics, immigrant entrepreneurs operate within dual--embedded contexts that shape their strategic responses. The mixed embeddedness framework (MEF), proposed by Kloosterman et al. (1999), explains how immigrant entrepreneurs are simultaneously embedded in co-ethnic networks and the broader institutional and market structures of the host society. This dual positioning influences access to resources and affects the degree of market integration. Empirical studies by Berwing (2019) and Solano et al. (2022) show that long-term business sustainability often depends on balancing ethnic embeddedness with broader economic participation.

Yet the original formulation of MEF did not sufficiently address the transnational dimensions of immigrant entrepreneurship. Subsequent research by Bagwell (2008) and Yamamura & Lassalle (2022) incorporates the role of transnational entrepreneurship, emphasising how immigrant entrepreneurs utilise home-country networks, engage in transnational trade and mobilise knowledge across national boundaries. This expanded perspective captures the complex, multi-layered environments in which immigrant entrepreneurs operate, shaped by interactions among ethnicity, institutional settings and global markets.

EI theory adds a further dimension by explaining how immigrant entrepreneurs construct their sense of self, interpret their social positioning and respond to changing institutional contexts. Schiller et al. (1992) argue that identity is fluid and formed through migrants' participation in transnational social fields. These fields involve navigating both host-country expectations and obligations to communities of origin. Work by Barrett & Vershinina (2017), Essers & Benschop (2007, 2009) and Romero & Valdez (2016) highlights the role of narrative and intersectionality in EI formation. These studies show that social structures, including gender, class and ethnicity, intersect with individual experiences to shape entrepreneurial trajectories.

Despite its robust psychological and behavioural foundations, research on EI has often been developed in isolation from structural and institutional analyses. While the MEF incorporates institutional conditions and forms of capital, it has tended to underrepresent the role of identity in shaping entrepreneurial agency. This book integrates EI into the MEF to offer a more comprehensive explanation of how immigrant entrepreneurs navigate barriers and shape their strategies. Identity is not only shaped by context but is also actively employed as a strategic resource. This integrated perspective allows for a deeper understanding of how entrepreneurs simultaneously respond to systemic barriers and craft their business pathways within diverse and complex environments.

Positioning the study and structure of the book

This book theorises immigrant entrepreneurship by integrating cross-regional research on how legal frameworks, economic structures and migration pathways shape entrepreneurial trajectories. It moves beyond dominant narratives by critically examining how immigrant entrepreneurs navigate barriers, mobilise resources, embed within institutional environments and negotiate participation across both ethnic and mainstream economic spheres. The analysis emphasises identity, transnational strategies and embeddedness as key dimensions of entrepreneurial agency across varied socio-economic contexts.

The book is organised into two main parts and a concluding chapter. Part I comprises two chapters that establish the theoretical and thematic foundations of the study. Chapter 1 introduces a reconceptualised mixed embeddedness framework (RMEF) developed through an integration of the MEF, EI, institutional theory and forms of capital. This framework positions identity as a strategic and dynamic mechanism through which immigrant entrepreneurs navigate structural barriers, mobilise transnational resources and negotiate embeddedness across intersecting dimensions such as race, gender, migration status and class. Chapter 2 offers a global thematic overview of immigrant entrepreneurship, documenting common barriers and illustrating how entrepreneurs adapt through informal networks, digital platforms and transnational linkages. Rather than applying the framework directly, this chapter serves as a bridge to the regional case studies by highlighting key themes and findings from the general literature on immigrant entrepreneurship.

Part II presents six regionally focused chapters based on documented case studies from North America, Western Europe, Oceania, the Middle East, Latin America and Sub-Saharan Africa. Drawing on secondary sources, these chapters analyse how immigrant entrepreneurs confront exclusion and implement adaptive strategies within diverse institutional and economic environments. Although not based on original empirical fieldwork, the chapters leverage documented examples of institutional barriers, adaptive strategies and identity negotiation to illustrate the analytical value of the RMEF. The final chapter synthesises cross-regional findings, reflects on theoretical and practical contributions and outlines long-term policy directions and future research priorities for building inclusive and context-sensitive entrepreneurial ecosystems.

References

Aliaga-Isla, R., & Rialp, A. (2013). Systematic review of immigrant entrepreneurship literature: Previous findings and ways forward. *Entrepreneurship & Regional Development, 25*(9–10), 819–844. https://doi.org/10.1080/08985626.2013.845694

Azoulay, P., Jones, B. F., Kim, J. D., & Miranda, J. (2022). Immigration and entrepreneurship in the United States. *American Economic Review: Insights, 4*(1), 71–88. https://doi.org/10.1257/aeri.20200588

Barak-Bianco, A., & Raijman, R. (2015). Asylum seeker entrepreneurs in Israel. *Economic Sociology: The European Electronic Newsletter, 16*(2), 4–13. https://hdl.handle.net/10419/156049

Barrett, R., & Vershinina, N. (2017). Intersectionality of ethnic and entrepreneurial identities: A study of post-war Polish entrepreneurs in an English city. *Journal of Small Business Management, 55*(3), 430–443. https://doi.org/10.1111/jsbm.12246

Basu, A., & Pruthi, S. (2021). From ethnic enclaves to transnational landscapes: A review of immigrant entrepreneurship research. *Foundations and Trends® in Entrepreneurship, 17*(1), 1–153. https://doi.org/10.1561/0300000086

Baycan, T., Sahin, M., & Nijkamp, P. (2012). The urban growth potential of second-generation migrant entrepreneurs: A sectoral study on Amsterdam. *International Business Review, 21*(6), 971–986. https://doi.org/10.1016/j.ibusrev.2011.11.005

Beckers, P., & Blumberg, B. F. (2013). Immigrant entrepreneurship on the move: A longitudinal analysis of first- and second-generation immigrant entrepreneurship in the Netherlands. *Entrepreneurship & Regional Development, 25*(7–8), 654–691. https://doi.org/10.1080/08985626.2013.808270

Berwing, S. (2019). Extending mixed embeddedness. *Historical Social Research/Historische Sozialforschung, 44*(4), 162–185. https://www.jstor.org/stable/26804870

Bhachu, P. (2017). *Immigration and entrepreneurship: Culture, capital, and ethnic networks*. Routledge.

Blackburn, R., & Smallbone, D. (2015). *Sustaining self-employment for disadvantaged entrepreneurs*. OECD Centre for Entrepreneurship, SMEs and Local Development.

Bloch, A., & McKay, S. (2015). Employment, social networks and undocumented migrants: The employer perspective. *Sociology, 49*(1), 38–55. https://doi.org/10.1177/0038038514532039

Bourdieu, P. (1986). The forms of capital. In J. G. Richardson (Ed.), *Handbook of theory and research for the sociology of education* (pp. 241–258). Greenwood Press.

Carree, M. A., & Thurik, A. R. (2010). The impact of entrepreneurship on economic growth. In Z. J. Acs & D. B. Audretsch (Eds.), *Handbook of entrepreneurship research* (pp. 557–594). Springer. https://doi.org/10.1007/978-1-4419-1191-9_20

Chababi, M., Chreim, S., & Spence, M. (2017). Are they really different: The entrepreneurial process from the perspective of first- and second-generation immigrant entrepreneurs. *Journal of Enterprising Culture*, 25(3), 263–295. https://doi.org/10.1142/S0218495817500108

Chodavadia, S. A., Kerr, S. P., Kerr, W. R., & Maiden, L. J. (2024). *Immigrant entrepreneurship: New estimates and a research agenda*. NBER Working Paper No. 32400. National Bureau of Economic Research. https://doi.org/10.3386/w32400

Collins, J., & Low, A. (2010). Asian female immigrant entrepreneurs in small and medium-sized businesses in Australia. *Entrepreneurship and Regional Development, 22*(1), 97–111. https://doi.org/10.1080/08985620903220553

Cooper, G., Blumell, L., & Bunce, M. (2021). Beyond the 'refugee crisis': How the UK news media represent asylum seekers across national boundaries. *International Communication Gazette, 83*(3), 195–216. https://doi.org/10.1177/1748048520913230

Cruz, E. P., de Queiroz Falcão, R. P., & Mancebo, R. C. (2020). Market orientation and strategic decisions on immigrant and ethnic small firms. *Journal of International Entrepreneurship, 18*(2), 227–255. https://doi.org/10.1007/s10843-019-00263-2

Dana, L. P. (2007). *Handbook of research on ethnic minority entrepreneurship: A co-evolutionary view on resource management.* Edward Elgar Publishing.

Daniel, E., Henley, A., & Anwar, M. N. (2019). Contemporary ethnic minority entrepreneurship in the UK: A quantitative exploration of break out and entrepreneurial quality. *International Journal of Entrepreneurial Behaviour & Research, 25*(7), 1410–1432. https://doi.org/10.1108/IJEBR-01-2019-0021

David, A., & Terstriep, J. (2025). Against all odds – Migrant entrepreneurs in entrepreneurial ecosystems with constraints. *Journal of Enterprising Communities: People and Places in the Global Economy, 19*(2), 248–275. https://doi.org/10.1108/JEC-03-2024-0052

Davidavičienė, V., & Lolat, I. (2016). *Migrant entrepreneurship in Europe: Challenges and opportunities.* [Vilnius Tech Repository]. https://etalpykla.vilniustech.lt/handle/123456789/154127

Desai, S., Naudé, W., & Stel, N. (2021). Refugee entrepreneurship: Context and directions for future research. *Small Business Economics, 56*(3), 933–945. https://doi.org/10.1007/s11187-019-00310-1

Dheer, R. J. (2018). Entrepreneurship by immigrants: A review of existing literature and directions for future research. *International Entrepreneurship and Management Journal, 14*, 555–614. https://doi.org/10.1007/s11365-018-0506-7

Drori, I., Honig, B., & Wright, M. (2009). Transnational entrepreneurship: An emergent field of study. *Entrepreneurship Theory and Practice, 33*(5), 1001–1022. https://doi.org/10.1111/j.1540-6520.2009.00332.x

Duan, C., Kotey, B., & Sandhu, K. (2021). Transnational immigrant entrepreneurship: Effects of home-country entrepreneurial ecosystem factors. *International Journal of Entrepreneurial Behaviour & Research, 27*(3), 711–729. https://doi.org/10.1108/IJEBR-05-2020-0300

Dustmann, C., & Görlach, J.-S. (2016). The economics of temporary migrations. *Journal of Economic Literature, 54*(1), 98–136. https://doi.org/10.1257/jel.54.1.98

Ekwulugo, F. (2006). Entrepreneurship and SMEs in London (UK): Evaluating the role of Black Africans in this emergent sector. *Journal of Management Development, 25*(1), 65–79. https://doi.org/10.1108/02621710610637972

Elmassah, S., James, R., & Bacheer, S. M. (2022). Ethnic entrepreneurial success factors: Evidence from the United Arab Emirates. *Heliyon, 8*(6), e09732. https://doi.org/10.1016/j.heliyon.2022.e09732

Elo, M., & Dana, L. P. (2023). Transnational diaspora entrepreneurship as a sub-field of international entrepreneurship: Observations and conceptual remarks. In *Research handbook on transnational diaspora entrepreneurship* (pp. 18–36). Edward Elgar Publishing. https://doi.org/10.4337/9781788118699.00010

Elo, M., & Minto-Coy, I. (2019). The concept of diaspora from the perspective of international business and economy: An introduction to the book. In M. Elo & I. Minto-Coy (Eds.), *Diaspora networks in international business* (pp. 1–15). Springer. https://doi.org/10.1007/978-3-319-91095-6_1

Elo, M., & Riddle, L. (2016). Understanding diaspora investment. In *Diaspora business* (pp. 13–28). Brill. https://doi.org/10.1163/9781848884038_003

Essers, C., & Benschop, Y. (2007). Enterprising identities: Female immigrant entrepreneurs of Moroccan or Turkish origin in the Netherlands. *Organisation Studies, 28*(1), 49–69. https://doi.org/10.1177/0170840606068256

Essers, C., & Benschop, Y. (2009). Muslim business female doing boundary work: The negotiation of Islam, gender and ethnicity within entrepreneurial contexts. *Human Relations, 62*(3), 403–423. https://doi.org/10.1177/0018726708101042

Fairlie, R. W., & Lofstrom, M. (2015). Immigration and entrepreneurship. In *Handbook of the economics of international migration* (pp. 877–911). Elsevier. https://www.sciencedirect.com/science/article/pii/B9780444537683000175

Fiddian-Qasmiyeh, E., Loescher, G., Long, K., & Sigona, N. (2014). *The Oxford handbook of refugee and forced migration studies.* Oxford University Press.

Fubah, C. N., & Moos, M. N. (2022). Immigrant entrepreneurship in South Africa: A review and research agenda. *The Journal for Transdisciplinary Research in Southern Africa, 18*(1), 1160. https://hdl.handle.net/10520/ejc-transd_v18_i1_a1160

Gold, S. J. (2019). Liabilities and benefits associated with the involvement of undocumented immigrants in informal entrepreneurship in the US. In V. Ramadani, L. P. Dana, V. Ratten, & A. Bexheti (Eds.), *Informal ethnic entrepreneurship* (pp. 9–28). Springer. https://doi.org/10.1007/978-3-319-99064-4_2

Gold, S. J., & Light, I. (2000). Ethnic economies and social policy. In P. G. Coy (Ed.), *Research in social movements, conflicts and change* (Vol. 22, pp. 165–191). Emerald Group Publishing. https://doi.org/10.1016/S0163-786X(00)80039-7

Gruenhagen, J. H., Davidsson, P., & Sawang, S. (2020). Returnee entrepreneurs: A systematic literature review, thematic analysis, and research agenda. *Foundations and Trends® in Entrepreneurship, 16*(4), 310–392. https://doi.org/10.1561/0300000096

Gurău, C., Dana, L. P., & Light, I. (2020). Overcoming the liability of foreignness: A typology and model of immigrant entrepreneurs. *European Management Review, 17*(3), 701–717. https://doi.org/10.1111/emre.12392

Harima, A. (2022). Transnational migration entrepreneurship during a crisis: Immediate response to challenges and opportunities emerging through the COVID-19 pandemic. *Business and Society Review, 127*, 223–251. https://doi.org/10.1111/basr.12266

Helmke, G., & Levitsky, S. (2012). Informal institutions and comparative politics: A research agenda. In G. Helmke & S. Levitsky (Eds.), *Informal institutions and democracy: Lessons from Latin America* (pp. 1–30). Edward Elgar Publishing. https://doi.org/10.4337/9781781001219.00011

House of Commons Library. (2017). *Migration statistics.* [UK Parliament Research Briefing]. https://researchbriefings.parliament.uk/ResearchBriefing/Summary/SN06077

Jones, T., Roberts, R., & Ram, M. (2022). Much ado about very little: The dubious connection between ethnic minority business policy and ethnic minority entrepreneurship. *International Migration, 61*(2), 9–26. https://doi.org/10.1111/imig.12959

Kariv, D., Menzies, T. V., Brenner, G. A., & Filion, L. J. (2009). Transnational networking and business performance: Ethnic entrepreneurs in Canada. *Entrepreneurship and regional development, 21*(3), 239–264. https://doi.org/10.1080/08985620802261641

Kassaye, B. D., Bayiley, Y. T., & Alemu, Z. K. (2025). Returnee migrant entrepreneurship: A bibliometric analysis (1993–2024). *Journal of Global Entrepreneurship Research, 15*, 6. https://doi.org/10.1007/s40497-025-00422-x

Kerr, S. P., & Kerr, W. R. (2017). Immigrant entrepreneurship. In J. Haltiwanger, E. Hurst, J. Miranda, & A. Schoar (Eds.), *Measuring entrepreneurial businesses: Current knowledge and challenges* (pp. 187–250). University of Chicago Press.

Kerr, W. R., & Mandorff, M. (2023). Social networks, ethnicity, and entrepreneurship. *Journal of Human Resources, 58*(1), 183–220. https://doi.org/10.3368/jhr.58.3.0719-10306R2

Kloosterman, R. C., & Rath, J. (2001). Immigrant entrepreneurs in advanced economies: Mixed embeddedness further explored. *Journal of Ethnic and Migration Studies, 27*(2), 189–201. https://doi.org/10.1080/13691830020041561

Kloosterman, R., & Rath, J. (2003). *Immigrant entrepreneurs: Venturing abroad in the age of globalization.* Berg Publishers. https://hdl.handle.net/11245/1.221088

Kloosterman, R. C., Van Der Leun, J., & Rath, J. (1999). Mixed embeddedness:(in) formal economic activities and immigrant businesses in the Netherlands. *International Journal of Urban and Regional Research, 23*(2), 252–266. https://doi.org/10.1111/1468-2427.00194

Kourtit, K., Nijkamp, P., & van Leeuwen, E. (2013). New entrepreneurship in urban diasporas in our modern world. *Journal of Urban Management, 2*(1), 25–47. https://doi.org/10.1016/S2226-5856(18)30063-3

Light, I., & Bonacich, E. (1988). *Immigrant entrepreneurs: Koreans in Los Angeles, 1965–1982.* University of California Press.

Light, I., & Dana, L. P. (2013). Boundaries of social capital in entrepreneurship. *Entrepreneurship Theory and Practice, 37*(3), 603–624. https://doi.org/10.1111/etap.12016

Martínez Rivera, S. (2024). Constructing Chinese spaces in Mexico City: The case of the Viaducto Piedad neighbourhood. *Journal of Current Chinese Affairs, 53*(1), 111–129. https://doi.org/10.1177/18681026241242488

Newman, A., Macaulay, L., & Dunwoodie, K. (2024). Refugee entrepreneurship: A systematic review of prior research and agenda for future research. *International Migration Review, 58*(3), 1140–1171. https://doi.org/10.1177/01979183231182669

North, D. C. (1990). *Institutions, institutional change and economic performance* (Vol. 332). Cambridge University Press.

Nwankwo, S. (2005). Characterisation of Black African entrepreneurship in the UK: A pilot study. *Journal of Small Business and Enterprise Development, 12*(1), 120–136. https://doi.org/10.1108/14626000510579680
Ojo, S. (2021). Black African perceptions of entrepreneurial outcomes in the UK. *Society and Business Review, 16*(2), 278–305. https://doi.org/10.1108/SBR-06-2020-0087
Ojo, S. (2013). Diaspora entrepreneurship: New directions in enterprise development. In A. G. Wood & J. W. Roberts (Eds.), *Enterprise development in SMEs and entrepreneurial firms: Dynamic processes* (pp. 42–63). IGI Global.
Ojo, S. (2019). Socialising to entrepreneurship: Issues in diaspora entrepreneurship and multiculturalism in the UK. In M. Elo & I. Minto-Coy (Eds.), *Diaspora networks in international business*. Springer. https://doi.org/10.1007/978-3-319-91095-6_14
Onyima, J. K., Syrett, S., & Sepulveda, L. (2024). Immigrant business in transnational contexts: A multifocal understanding of the breakout process. *International Journal of Entrepreneurial Behaviour & Research, 30*(1), 155–179. https://doi.org/10.1108/IJEBR-02-2023-0190
Organisation for Economic Co-operation and Development (OECD). (2019). *The missing entrepreneurs 2019: Policies for inclusive entrepreneurship*. OECD Publishing. https://www.oecd.org/content/dam/oecd/en/publications/reports/2019/12/the-missing-entrepreneurs-2019_668840b2/3ed84801-en.pdf
Pruthi, S., & Tasavori, M. (2022). Staying in or stepping out? Growth strategies of second-generation immigrant entrepreneurs. *International Business Review, 31*(5), 101997. https://doi.org/10.1016/j.ibusrev.2022.101997
Ram, M., Jones, T., & Villares-Varela, M. (2017). Migrant entrepreneurship: Reflections on research and practice. *International Small Business Journal, 35*(1), 3–18. https://doi.org/10.1177/0266242616678051
Ram, M., Theodorakopoulos, N., & Jones, T. (2008). Forms of capital, mixed embeddedness and Somali enterprise. *Work, Employment and Society, 22*(3), 427–446. https://doi.org/10.1177/0950017008093479
Ranabahu, N., de Vries, H. P., & Basharati, Z. (2024). Entrepreneurial identity and business success: Former refugee women's navigation of (in)visibility paradoxes. *Journal of Management & Organization*, 1–16. https://doi.org/10.1017/jmo.2024.43
Refai, D., Lever, J., & Haloub, R. (2024). Entrepreneurship in constrained immigration contexts: The liminal integration of Syrian refugees. *Entrepreneurship & Regional Development, 36*(3–4), 416–435. https://doi.org/10.1080/08985626.2023.2297388
Refai, D., & McElwee, G. (2022). Refugee subentrepreneurship: The emergence of a liquid cage. *Work, Employment and Society, 37*(4), 1032–1051. https://doi.org/10.1177/09500170211062817
Reynolds, P. D. (2022). *Entrepreneurship and economic development: The global scope of business creation*. Edward Elgar Publishing.
Romero, M., & Valdez, Z. (2016). Introduction to the special issue: Intersectionality and entrepreneurship. *Ethnic and Racial Studies, 39*(9), 1553–1565. https://doi.org/10.1080/01419870.2016.1171374
Saxenian, A. (2002). Transnational communities and the evolution of global production networks: The cases of Taiwan, China, and India. *Industry and Innovation, 9*(3), 183–202. https://doi.org/10.1080/13662710220000034453
Schiller, N. G., Basch, L. G., & Blanc-Szanton, C. (1992). *Towards a transnational perspective on migration: Race, class, ethnicity, and nationalism reconsidered.* Annals of the New York Academy of Sciences.
Sepulveda, R. L., Syrett, S., & Lyon, F. (2008). *New ethnic minority business communities in Britain: Challenges of diversity and informality for the UK business and policy frameworks* (Working Paper No. 1). Social Policy Research Centre, Middlesex University.
Simba, A., Ogundana, O. M., Braune, E., & Dana, L. P. (2023). Community financing in entrepreneurship: A focus on women entrepreneurs in the developing world. *Journal of Business Research, 163*, Article 113962. https://doi.org/10.1016/j.jbusres.2023.113962
Solano, G., Schutjens, V., & Rath, J. (2022). Multifocality and opportunity structure: Towards a mixed embeddedness model for transnational migrant entrepreneurship. *Comparative Migration Studies, 10*, 3. https://doi.org/10.1186/s40878-021-00270-0
Syrett, S., & Keles, J. Y. (2022). A contextual understanding of diaspora entrepreneurship: Identity, opportunity, and resources in the Sri Lankan Tamil and Kurdish diasporas. *International Journal of Entrepreneurial Behaviour & Research, 28*(9), 376–404. https://doi.org/10.1108/IJEBR-08-2021-0658

Urban, B., & Moti, M. (2024). Immigrants as entrepreneurs in emerging economies: Institutional, self-efficacy, and social networking effects on enterprise performance. *Small Business International Review, 8*(2), e670. https://doi.org/10.26784/sbir.v8i2.670

Waldinger, R., Aldrich, H., & Ward, R. (1990). *Ethnic entrepreneurs: Immigrant business in industrial societies*. SAGE Publications.

Welter, F., Baker, T., Audretsch, D. B., & Gartner, W. B. (2017). Everyday entrepreneurship—A call for entrepreneurship research to embrace entrepreneurial diversity. *Entrepreneurship Theory and Practice, 41*(3), 311–321. https://doi.org/10.1111/etap.12258

Welter, F., & Smallbone, D. (2011). Institutional perspectives on entrepreneurial behavior in challenging environments. *Journal of Small Business Management, 49*(1), 107–125. https://doi.org/10.1111/j.1540-627X.2010.00317.x

Witteveen, D., & Alba, R. (2018). Labour market disadvantages of second-generation Turks and Moroccans in the Netherlands: Before and during the Great Recession. *International Migration, 56*(2), 97–116. https://doi.org/10.1111/imig.12411

World Bank. (2019). *Leveraging economic migration for development: A briefing for the World Bank Board*. World Bank Group. https://documents.worldbank.org/curated/en/461021574155945177/leveraging-economic-migration-for-development-a-briefing-for-the-world-bank-board

Yamamura, S., & Lassalle, P. (2022). Extending mixed embeddedness to a multi-dimensional concept of transnational entrepreneurship. *Comparative Migration Studies, 10*(1), Article 14. https://doi.org/10.1186/s40878-022-00288-y

Zahra, M. (2019). *The legal framework of the sponsorship systems of the Gulf Cooperation Council countries: A comparative examination*. Gulf Labour Markets, Migration and Population (GLMM) Programme. https://hdl.handle.net/1814/37966

PART I

Theoretical perspectives and structural dynamics

2

TOWARDS A MULTIDIMENSIONAL UNDERSTANDING OF IMMIGRANT ENTREPRENEURSHIP

A reconceptualised mixed embeddedness framework

Introduction

Immigrant entrepreneurship has become an important focus within migration and entrepreneurship studies, reflecting growing interest in how migrants contribute to economic activity in host societies while navigating structural barriers and transnational ties. A wide range of theoretical frameworks has been developed to explain the emergence and trajectories of immigrant-owned businesses. Structuralist theories initially highlighted immigrant entrepreneurship as a response to blocked mobility and labour market exclusion, where self-employment served as a survival strategy in the face of limited formal employment opportunities (Bonacich, 1973; Piore, 1979). Culturalist and social capital perspectives subsequently emphasised the role of ethnic resources, community ties and co-ethnic networks in shaping entrepreneurial behaviour and resilience (Light & Bonacich, 1988; Portes & Sensenbrenner, 1993). Although these approaches offered robust theoretical frameworks, they often examined structural barriers, cultural resources and institutional conditions in isolation, without integrating their interrelationships.

In response to these conceptual limitations, the mixed embeddedness framework (MEF) emerged as a more integrative framework that situates entrepreneurial activity within the interplay of market conditions, institutional structures and social relations (Kloosterman et al., 1999; Kloosterman & Rath, 2001). Drawing on Granovetter's (1985) theory that economic action is embedded in social networks, MEF links individual entrepreneurial strategies to opportunity structures shaped by regulatory environments and labour market segmentation. This framework has contributed significantly to the field by offering a dynamic and relational understanding of immigrant entrepreneurship. It has been widely applied across national contexts to examine how institutional inclusion, policy regimes and social embeddedness influence business development and outcomes (Brzozowski et al., 2022; Kloosterman & Rath, 2018; Solano, 2021).

Despite its strengths, MEF has been critiqued for its limited engagement with identity and entrepreneurial agency. While it incorporates institutional and structural factors, it often presents immigrant entrepreneurs as primarily reactive to external constraints, with insufficient attention to how they actively negotiate, construct and mobilise identity within the entrepreneurial process (Bagwell, 2018; Lassalle & McElwee, 2016; Wahlbeck, 2018). As a result, MEF risks

DOI: 10.4324/9781003605072-3

underestimating the strategic and performative dimensions of entrepreneurship, particularly the ways in which identity serves as a resource for establishing legitimacy, accessing networks and adapting to complex institutional conditions.

This chapter addresses that gap by reconceptualising MEF through the lens of entrepreneurial identity (EI). Rather than treating identity as a fixed attribute based on ethnicity or migration background, EI is understood as a dynamic and socially embedded process shaped through interaction with institutions, markets and communities (Essers & Benschop, 2007; Zhang & Chun, 2018). It draws attention to how immigrant entrepreneurs use identity strategically to navigate institutional barriers, claim legitimacy and reposition themselves within exclusionary systems. Incorporating identity into the analysis allows for a more nuanced understanding of how entrepreneurs mobilise resources and adapt to socio-political barriers, particularly in contexts marked by discrimination, precarity or legal ambiguity.

A focus on identity also facilitates a deeper engagement with the transnational dimensions of immigrant entrepreneurship. Many entrepreneurs operate across national borders, drawing on diaspora networks, home-country capital and regional policy arrangements to mitigate institutional limitations in the host society (Bagwell, 2018; Drori et al., 2009). These transnational strategies underscore the need for a more expansive understanding of embeddedness, one that captures the multi-sited and multi-scalar character of migrant entrepreneurial activity (Yamamura & Lassalle, 2022). In this context, identity becomes a key site of strategic negotiation, enabling entrepreneurs to assert relevance and credibility across diverse institutional settings.

In addition, the chapter incorporates an intersectional perspective to examine how gender, race, class and migration status interact to shape differentiated entrepreneurial experiences. Intersectionality provides a more comprehensive framework for understanding how access to resources, market participation and institutional legitimacy is unevenly distributed, and how overlapping forms of inequality shape entrepreneurial strategies (Brieger & Gielnik, 2021; Crenshaw, 1991; Romero & Valdez, 2016). Research has demonstrated that multiple systems of disadvantage frequently converge, compounding barriers for marginalised groups within migrant communities.

The chapter is structured as follows. It begins by reviewing the major forms of capital, including economic, social, cultural and human capital, and examines how these are mobilised or constrained within institutionally shaped environments. It then examines institutional theory, focusing on the interaction between formal and informal institutions in shaping entrepreneurial opportunities. The next section critically revisits the MEF, outlining its key contributions and identifying conceptual limitations. This is followed by a discussion of EI, conceptualised through intersectionality, as a lens for understanding the dynamic and socially situated practices of migrant entrepreneurship. Building on these foundations, the chapter develops a reconceptualised MEF (RMEF) that offers a relational and multi-scalar perspective on how immigrant entrepreneurs negotiate their positioning within and across institutional structures and translocal spaces. The chapter concludes with a comparative synthesis of theoretical frameworks and identifies implications for future research and inclusive policy design.

Forms of capital

Theoretical discussions on immigrant entrepreneurship have drawn from a range of frameworks, with early research emphasising how migrants mobilise resources to establish businesses. Bourdieu's (1986) concept of capital provides a foundational lens for understanding how economic, social, cultural and human capital function as strategic assets that individuals leverage to navigate social and economic structures. In the context of immigrant entrepreneurship, capital is not simply a resource but a dynamic mechanism that shapes access to opportunity and the capacity to overcome structural barriers (Gold & Light, 2000).

Empirical studies have shown that migrants often face constraints such as limited financial access, exclusion from mainstream business networks and unequal access to market-relevant knowledge, all of which restrict business growth and scalability (Nee & Sanders, 2001; Ram et al., 2008). The accumulation and conversion of capital are therefore central to entrepreneurial success, influencing whether migrant enterprises remain embedded within ethnic economies or expand into broader markets (Kloosterman & Rath, 2018). However, access to capital is not evenly distributed; it is shaped by institutional frameworks and socio-economic hierarchies. Financial systems, regulatory regimes and labour market segmentation mediate access to credit, professional networks and sector-specific expertise, often reproducing exclusionary dynamics (Bizri, 2017; Cederberg & Villares-Varela, 2019).

The following discussion examines the distinct forms of capital, analysing how financial, social, cultural and human capital influence the strategic practices, adaptability and sustainability of immigrant entrepreneurs.

Financial (economic) capital

Financial capital plays a central role in immigrant entrepreneurship, influencing business formation, growth and sustainability (Kloosterman & Rath, 2003; Rath & Swagerman, 2016). However, access to formal finance remains a persistent barrier for many migrants. Limited credit history, unfamiliarity with host-country banking systems and discriminatory lending practices often lead financial institutions to classify migrant entrepreneurs as high-risk borrowers, resulting in loan rejections, high interest rates and onerous documentation requirements (Bruder et al., 2011; Fregetto, 2004; Kašperová et al., 2022). These constraints persist even for highly skilled and economically stable migrants, as implicit biases in financial systems and strict regulatory procedures restrict their participation in mainstream credit markets (Desiderio, 2014; Ram et al., 2017).

In response, many immigrant entrepreneurs turn to informal financial mechanisms such as remittances, community-based lending and rotating savings and credit associations (ROSCAs). While these practices provide essential startup capital, they often lack scalability, regulatory protections and long-term security (Ibrahim, 2020). As a result, many migrant-owned businesses remain confined to small-scale operations within ethnic enclaves, with limited prospects for expansion into broader markets (David & Terstriep, 2025; Lee & Black, 2017; Smallbone et al., 2003).

For instance, comparative studies across Germany, the United Kingdom (UK) and the United States (U.S.) highlight how national financial systems shape the viability of migrant businesses (Fairlie & Lofstrom, 2015; Kerr & Kerr, 2020; Rinaldi et al., 2023). In financially inclusive contexts, policies such as state-backed loans, targeted microfinance and tailored support services enable migrants to transition into higher-value sectors and contribute more significantly to national economies (Desiderio, 2014; Naudé et al., 2017). Conversely, in regions where financial policy frameworks provide limited support, many immigrant entrepreneurs remain reliant on ethnic financial networks, reinforcing economic segmentation and constraining upward mobility (Ram et al., 2017).

Ultimately, the effectiveness of financial capital is shaped not only by entrepreneurial capacity but also by the broader institutional context, including financial policy regimes, regulatory accessibility and the inclusivity of banking infrastructures. Emerging tools such as digital banking, blockchain-based lending and diaspora-focused investment initiatives offer promising avenues for addressing these disparities and expanding credit access for immigrant entrepreneurs.

Human capital

Human capital, understood as the knowledge, skills and experience accumulated through education and work, is widely recognised as a key determinant of entrepreneurial success among immigrants (Brown et al., 2021; Fregetto, 2004). Educational qualifications, sector-specific expertise and prior professional experience not only enhance the ability to identify market opportunities but also support immigrant entrepreneurs in navigating regulatory environments and institutional barriers (Kloosterman & Rath, 2003; Wang & Altinay, 2012). Studies show that immigrants with advanced education and relevant experience are more effective in leveraging institutional resources, accessing financial capital and reducing operational risks in host-country markets (Basu & Altinay, 2002; Ram et al., 2017). The ability to transfer competencies from the country of origin to the host economy further shapes entrepreneurial adaptability, particularly in industries that value technical knowledge and formal accreditation (Nathan & Lee, 2013).

However, disparities in human capital often lead to divergent business outcomes. Entrepreneurs with strong educational and professional backgrounds are more likely to establish ventures that move beyond ethnic niches and integrate into wider economic networks (Ram et al., 2017; Wang & Altinay, 2012). By contrast, individuals with limited education or industry experience may face compounded barriers, including limited language proficiency, restricted access to professional networks and institutional discrimination (Kloosterman et al., 2016; Ojo, 2021). Language skills influence the ability to interact with regulatory authorities, negotiate with suppliers and build relationships with customers (Gold & Light, 2000; Yasin & Hafeez, 2023). Human capital therefore plays a critical role not only in determining entrepreneurial access and resilience but also in shaping long-term business development and formal economic integration (Aliaga-Isla & Rialp, 2013; Brzozowski et al., 2014).

Social capital

Social capital, understood as the resources embedded within social networks, plays a central role in shaping the entrepreneurial trajectories of immigrants by facilitating access to finance, market knowledge and business opportunities (Bizri, 2017; Portes, 2009). It operates through two primary forms: bonding social capital, which arises from close ties within ethnic communities, and bridging social capital, which connects entrepreneurs to broader institutional and economic networks beyond the enclave (Putnam, 2000; Singh, 2024). Bonding social capital offers trust-based access to credit, labour and an initial consumer base, particularly in contexts where immigrants face barriers to mainstream financial systems (Bizri, 2017; Hu et al., 2021). It also reinforces cultural continuity and collective economic strategies, fostering group solidarity and resilience during the early stages of business development (Ojo, 2021). However, overreliance on co-ethnic networks can lead to market saturation, limited innovation and reduced capacity to scale ventures beyond the ethnic niche (Yang & Girotto, 2024).

Bridging social capital mitigates these constraints by enabling connections with mainstream networks, including financial institutions, government agencies and trade associations (Ram et al., 2017; Stoyanov, 2018). These ties expand access to formal funding, regulatory support and diversified customer bases (Jones et al., 2014; Rath, 2002). Entrepreneurs who cultivate relationships with non-ethnic actors are more likely to navigate complex institutional environments and integrate into broader markets (Light & Dana, 2013; Solano, 2021). Balancing bonding and bridging capital enhances entrepreneurial resilience, allowing migrants to leverage trusted community ties while engaging external opportunities (Duan et al., 2021b). Strategic engagement with both forms of social capital has been linked to greater business sustainability, innovation and long-term success in competitive market environments.

Cultural capital

Cultural capital refers to the socially valued knowledge, skills and dispositions that individuals acquire through socialisation, shaping access to opportunity and often reinforcing social hierarchies (Bates & Connolly, 2023; Bourdieu, 1986). For immigrant entrepreneurs, cultural capital is particularly influential in shaping market entry and differentiation strategies, especially within their ethnic communities. Familiarity with culturally specific consumer preferences enables entrepreneurs to develop tailored products and services, giving them a competitive advantage in niche or segmented markets (Cederberg & Villares-Varela, 2019; Cruz et al., 2020). Beyond market alignment, cultural capital also supports entrepreneurial resilience by fostering trust within ethnic networks, facilitating informal finance and reinforcing collective business practices (Li et al., 2023; Light & Dana, 2013). However, reliance on ethnic cultural capital may constrain entrepreneurs to enclave economies, reducing their ability to engage with broader markets if they lack cross-cultural competencies (Aliaga-Isla & Rialp, 2013). As Anthias (2001) warns, privileging cultural explanations without reference to structural barriers risks essentialising identity and obscuring deeper inequalities.

Cultural capital is also crucial for navigating institutional contexts in the host country. The ability to understand and adapt to dominant norms, business conventions and regulatory systems enhances entrepreneurs' interactions with customers, state agencies and financial institutions (Chen & Chen, 2024; Malerba & Ferreira, 2020). Those with a strong understanding of the host country's institutional environment are more likely to access government support, secure formal credit and integrate into mainstream business networks (Desiderio, 2014; Solano, 2021). In contrast, those with limited cultural capital often face barriers to formalisation, encounter bureaucratic challenges and remain reliant on informal mechanisms such as rotating savings groups or co-ethnic finance systems (Light & Karageorgis, 1994; Ndofor & Priem, 2011). The ability to accumulate and adapt cultural capital is thus a critical factor in shaping economic inclusion, long-term business development and integration into wider market structures (Brzozowski et al., 2014; Ram et al., 2017).

Institutional theory

The ability of immigrant entrepreneurs to access and mobilise economic, social, cultural and human capital is shaped by the institutional context in which they operate. Institutional theory provides a critical lens for understanding how formal rules, informal norms and shared belief systems structure the opportunities and constraints that influence entrepreneurial outcomes (Brzozowski et al., 2022; North, 1990). As Scott (2008) outlines, institutions function through three interrelated pillars: the regulative, the normative and the cultural-cognitive. These pillars determine the legitimacy of entrepreneurial activity, who is permitted to participate in formal markets and how business norms are internalised and reproduced. Together, these mechanisms shape access to markets, financial systems and legal protections, influencing whether entrepreneurs can formalise their ventures or must rely on informal economic arrangements (Fuentelsaz et al., 2023; Helmke & Levitsky, 2012; Welter & Smallbone, 2011).

Supportive institutional environments encourage entrepreneurship by reducing administrative burdens, improving access to capital and fostering inclusion through targeted policies. In contrast, restrictive contexts marked by complex immigration procedures, exclusionary financial systems and bureaucratic inefficiencies can hinder entrepreneurial viability and reinforce socio-economic marginalisation (Duan et al., 2021a; Yamamura & Lassalle, 2022). Beyond formal institutions, informal norms and cultural expectations play a significant role in shaping entrepreneurial strategy and legitimacy. These informal forces influence how immigrant entrepreneurs interpret institutional barriers, build trust and position themselves in relation to mainstream markets or co-ethnic networks (Solano, 2020; Urban & Moti, 2024; Yang & Girotto, 2024).

To examine these dynamics in more detail, the following subsections distinguish between formal institutions, such as regulations, financial policies and legal frameworks, and informal institutions, including societal norms, trust-based practices and culturally embedded expectations.

Formal institutions: regulations, policies and barriers

Formal institutions, including government regulations, legal frameworks and financial policies, play a central role in shaping the entrepreneurial opportunities available to immigrants. These structures influence whether immigrant entrepreneurs can access formal economies by regulating business registration, taxation and legal compliance (Brzozowski et al., 2022; Kloosterman & Rath, 2018). In many host countries, bureaucratic complexity such as extensive documentation requirements, financial guarantees and residency conditions impedes business formation (Aliaga-Isla & Rialp, 2013; Desiderio, 2014). Immigration laws also affect entrepreneurial activity by limiting ownership rights and imposing visa restrictions that create legal uncertainty (Wadhwa et al., 2007).

Financial policies further reinforce these constraints. Mainstream banks often apply rigid credit assessments that exclude immigrants lacking formal credit histories or local financial references (Bruder et al., 2011; Ram et al., 2017; Zhang, 2023). Studies across North America and Western Europe highlight how discriminatory lending practices and collateral requirements restrict access to capital, limiting business scalability and long-term sustainability (Chrysostome, 2010; Fregetto, 2004; Wang & Liu, 2015). As a result, many immigrants turn to informal economies, where ventures remain undercapitalised and exposed to regulatory vulnerabilities (David & Terstriep, 2025; Ram et al., 2017; Smallbone et al., 2003).

Nonetheless, some countries have adopted inclusive strategies to facilitate immigrant entrepreneurship. Canada's Start-Up Visa, for instance, offers a path to permanent residency for entrepreneurs supported by recognised incubators (Government of Canada, 2024). The UK introduced the Innovator Founder Visa in 2023, enabling migrant entrepreneurs to establish businesses under specific residency criteria (UK Government, 2023). Beyond visa reforms, several governments have developed public-private initiatives such as state-backed microfinance, targeted business grants and tailored support programmes. The European Commission and the U.S. Small Business Administration (SBA) fund initiatives that enhance migrants' access to financial resources and business infrastructure (European Commission, 2016, 2024; International Rescue Committee, 2023; Rugaber, 2024).

Comparative studies show that structured institutional support is associated with higher rates of business formalisation, greater integration into mainstream markets and more substantial economic contributions by immigrant entrepreneurs (Baycan-Levent & Nijkamp, 2009; Desiderio, 2014;

Solano et al., 2023). These findings suggest that while formal institutions can present significant regulatory and financial barriers, inclusive policies and targeted interventions can foster more equitable and resilient entrepreneurial ecosystems.

Informal institutions: cultural norms, social expectations and market integration

In addition to formal regulations, informal institutions play a critical role in shaping the entrepreneurial experiences of immigrants by influencing their access to markets, the legitimacy of their ventures and their capacity for social integration (Brieger & Gielnik, 2021; Gomez et al., 2020; Malerba & Ferreira, 2020). These institutions include cultural norms, trust-based business practices and shared social expectations that guide economic behaviour outside legal and regulatory frameworks (Helmke & Levitsky, 2012; Welter & Smallbone, 2011). In many host countries, business success depends on reputational credibility and longstanding personal relationships. Immigrant entrepreneurs, often perceived as outsiders, may therefore struggle to enter mainstream markets and form partnerships with established actors (Aldrich & Waldinger, 1990; Hack-Polay et al., 2020). Research in European and North American contexts highlights that trust and informal networks are particularly important in sectors where contracts are relational and partnerships evolve over time (Brzozowski et al., 2022; Zhou, 2004).

To address these constraints, many immigrant entrepreneurs rely on ethnic business enclaves and co-ethnic support networks. These networks offer access to financial resources, a stable customer base and familiar business practices, particularly for first-generation migrants who face linguistic and cultural barriers (Barrett & Vershinina, 2017; Bizri, 2017). While these structures provide security in the early stages of business development, excessive dependence can limit entrepreneurial scalability, reinforce economic segmentation and restrict integration into broader markets (Cederberg & Villares-Varela, 2019; Light & Dana, 2013).

Nonetheless, in multicultural economies, informal institutions also present opportunities for differentiation. Many immigrant entrepreneurs leverage cultural capital through ethnic branding, bilingual communication and specialised consumer knowledge to establish competitive advantages in sectors such as food, fashion and crafts (Kacar et al., 2021; Rath & Kloosterman, 2000; Tiemo, 2024). Businesses that engage both co-ethnic and mainstream customers through culturally informed strategies often experience greater longevity and commercial success (Aliaga-Isla & Rialp, 2013; Solano, 2021). However, cultural positioning alone does not guarantee inclusion. Societal attitudes towards migrants and diversity significantly influence entrepreneurial outcomes. In inclusive settings, supportive institutional frameworks and consumer openness enhance market integration. In contrast, xenophobic sentiments and exclusionary cultural norms restrict access, limit cross-cultural exchange and reinforce marginalisation (Desiderio, 2014; Light & Dana, 2013; Yang & Girotto, 2024).

Understanding the dual function of informal institutions as both facilitators and barriers underscores the importance of inclusive policy frameworks that address structural inequalities and promote equitable entrepreneurial participation across diverse cultural contexts.

The mixed embeddedness framework

The MEF advances the understanding of immigrant entrepreneurship by integrating institutional contexts, market structures and social networks into a comprehensive analytical framework (Kloosterman et al., 1999). While earlier approaches such as forms of capital and institutional theory illuminate discrete factors, they do not fully account for how regulatory conditions, labour segmentation and structural barriers interact to shape entrepreneurial pathways. Previous theoretical frameworks often presented fragmented perspectives, emphasising either ethnic resources or structural barriers without capturing the full complexity of institutional embeddedness.

Structuralist frameworks, such as Piore (1979), viewed immigrant entrepreneurship as a response to labour market exclusion, framing self-employment as a survival strategy for those with limited access to stable work. Middleman minority theory (Bonacich, 1973) built on this by highlighting how institutional marginalisation and economic segmentation positioned immigrant entrepreneurs in intermediary roles, shaped by power asymmetries and host-society dynamics. Portes & Manning (1986) extended this logic through the concept of the ethnic enclave economy, demonstrating that immigrant businesses often form parallel market systems within ethnic communities. These enclaves provide vital support through shared labour and consumer bases but can also reinforce segregation and limit upward mobility.

Culturalist theorists, such as Light & Bonacich (1988), later focused on ethnic resources and social networks, aligning with social capital theory but overlooking institutional barriers and state policy. These frameworks often assumed that ethnic solidarity alone could drive entrepreneurial success. Interactionist perspectives, including Waldinger et al. (1990), introduced the notion of opportunity structures, recognising that business outcomes depend on the alignment between market conditions and resource availability. However, this framework tended to treat such structures as static, neglecting the dynamic nature of institutional change.

MEF responds to these limitations by illustrating how institutional structures, access to finance and labour market conditions collectively shape entrepreneurial opportunities (Kloosterman & Rath, 2001, 2018; Rath, 2002). It highlights the agency of entrepreneurs as they navigate regulatory challenges and adapt to evolving market conditions. Empirical studies confirm that shifts in policy environments, financial institutions and economic restructuring significantly influence business outcomes, alongside the continued relevance of ethnic networks (Brzozowski et al., 2022; Ram et al., 2021; Solano, 2021).

Although MEF was originally developed to explain entrepreneurship in local economies, it has since been extended to transnational contexts, reflecting the increasingly interconnected nature of migration and economic activity (Bagwell, 2018; Yamamura & Lassalle, 2022). This expansion acknowledges that immigrant entrepreneurs often operate across multiple regulatory and institutional settings, including home and host-country markets, regional trade agreements and global financial systems. As globalisation intensifies, entrepreneurs must respond to institutional fragmentation by engaging flexibly with diverse legal, financial and labour systems (Moghaddam & Weber, 2021; Rusinovic, 2008).

The following subsections examine the core elements of the MEF, namely institutional embeddedness, social networks and human capital, and explore how these components function in both national and transnational entrepreneurial settings.

Core elements of the mixed embeddedness framework

The MEF comprises three key components: institutional embeddedness, social networks and individual human capital. Together, these elements shape the entrepreneurial trajectories of migrants by linking agency to structural and relational conditions. Institutional embeddedness refers to the influence of regulatory frameworks, labour markets and policy environments on entrepreneurial activity (Kloosterman et al., 1999; Solano, 2021). Many immigrant entrepreneurs encounter structural barriers such as limited access to finance, restrictive immigration rules and segmented labour markets, which constrain business formation and sustainability (Kloosterman, 2010; Lassalle & McElwee, 2016). MEF addresses these constraints by connecting institutional arrangements to entrepreneurial choices, illustrating how policies and regulatory regimes affect business viability (Berwing, 2019). This has been demonstrated in studies of Polish entrepreneurs in the UK, where regulatory flexibility enabled them to navigate institutional barriers, underscoring the significance of policy environments in entrepreneurial outcomes (Lassalle & Scott, 2018).

Social networks form another crucial dimension of embeddedness, providing both economic resources and social support. These networks facilitate entry into markets, enable business growth and support the mobilisation of capital, knowledge and customers (Portes & Sensenbrenner, 1993; Ram et al., 2017). Kloosterman (2010) emphasises the role of ethnic networks as alternative economic spaces, particularly when formal access is limited. Case studies of Moroccan entrepreneurs in Milan and Amsterdam show how co-ethnic ties offer informal financing, supplier connections and cultural knowledge that support day-to-day operations (Solano, 2021). However, such networks can also constrain business expansion, reinforcing economic dependency and limiting access to wider markets (Bagwell, 2018; Wahlbeck, 2018).

The third component, human capital, refers to the knowledge, skills and professional experience that migrants bring to entrepreneurial activity. Human capital theory posits that prior education and sectoral expertise enhance the capacity to identify opportunities and manage business operations effectively (Becker, 2009; Kloosterman & Rath, 2018). Yet for many migrants, the transfer of qualifications across borders is hindered by institutional recognition systems and segmented labour markets (Solano, 2021). While highly skilled individuals, such as information technology (IT) professionals, often integrate into high-value sectors, others must rely on informal learning or adaptive strategies to enter low-barrier industries (Wahlbeck, 2018). According to Kloosterman & Rath (2018), the interaction of institutional context, social embeddedness and human capital offers a multidimensional framework for analysing the diverse ways in which migrant entrepreneurs navigate and shape their business environments.

The expansion of the mixed embeddedness into transnational contexts

The MEF has evolved to address the growing prevalence of transnational entrepreneurship, where migrant entrepreneurs operate across multiple institutional and economic settings. Unlike traditional frameworks that emphasise adaptation within a single host country, transnational approaches highlight how entrepreneurs mobilise resources from both home and host contexts to navigate constraints and pursue new opportunities (Duan et al., 2021a; Solano, 2021). Portes et al. (2002) argue that access to transnational networks, capital and regulatory flexibility enables migrants to bypass institutional limitations and construct hybrid business models tailored to diverse market conditions (Drori et al., 2009; Wang & Liu, 2015). Vertovec (2004) further develops this by introducing the concept of transnational social fields, through which entrepreneurs engage in multi-sited activities that transcend national boundaries. These perspectives collectively reinforce the need to move beyond static, location-bound understandings of migrant entrepreneurship (Solano, 2021; Solano et al., 2022).

Despite these conceptual advances, MEF has been critiqued for its continued reliance on a binary home-host framework, which risks oversimplifying the complexity of contemporary migrant entrepreneurship (Bagwell, 2018; Wahlbeck, 2018). Many entrepreneurs operate within multi-scalar networks that span regional markets, digital platforms and supranational governance structures (Solano et al., 2022). In response, Yamamura & Lassalle (2022) propose a multi-level framework that incorporates macro-, meso- and micro-level dynamics, providing a more refined understanding of how economic, political and social conditions intersect. Their study of Polish transnational entrepreneurs in the European Union (EU) illustrates the importance of meso-level factors such as regional integration policies, transnational trade arrangements and community-based support networks in shaping business strategies. Regulatory developments such as Poland's EU accession and the impact of Brexit further demonstrate how migrant entrepreneurs must continuously adjust to evolving institutional environments (Garapich, 2008; Lassalle & Scott, 2018). While these extensions broaden the framework's relevance, they often remain focused on structural contexts and underemphasise the role of identity, agency and strategic positioning.

Entrepreneurial identity

EI is central to understanding how immigrant entrepreneurs navigate institutional environments and economic constraints while actively shaping their business practices. In contrast to structural frameworks such as the MEF, which emphasise external opportunity structures and social networks, the concept of EI emphasises the subjective, socially situated processes through which individuals define their roles, assert agency and adapt to evolving challenges (Essers & Benschop, 2007; Zhang & Chun, 2018). While the MEF elucidates the role of institutional embeddedness in immigrant entrepreneurship, it tends to understate how identity negotiation, cultural belonging and intersecting social positions influence strategic decision-making. Scholars such as Abd Hamid et al. (2019) and Liang & Chreim (2021) argue that these dimensions are crucial for understanding how entrepreneurs respond to exclusionary contexts and establish legitimacy.

EI is not fixed but shaped through continuous interaction with institutional settings, community norms and market expectations. These identity processes influence how entrepreneurs access resources, construct legitimacy and navigate complex economic environments (Choi et al., 2024; Jones et al., 2019). In contexts marked by structural exclusion, including legal barriers and social bias, immigrant entrepreneurs often mobilise identity strategically to access trust-based networks and reach niche consumer segments. However, they may also face role conflict when their entrepreneurial self-concept clashes with restrictive immigration frameworks or market norms (Choi et al., 2024).

The following subsections examine three interrelated dimensions of EI: social identity, cultural identity and intersectionality. These are explored in relation to how they influence the strategies, market positioning and long-term sustainability of immigrant enterprises.

Social identity: community and belonging in the host market

Social identity theory (Tajfel & Turner, 1979) explains how individuals derive a sense of self from group affiliations, shaping how immigrant entrepreneurs relate to host communities and engage with markets. Many entrepreneurs draw on co-ethnic networks to establish ventures that cater to familiar cultural norms and language practices, leveraging shared identity and social capital to overcome institutional barriers such as discriminatory lending or regulatory exclusion (Abd Hamid et al., 2019; Das et al., 2017; Essers & Benschop, 2007; Kerr & Mandorff, 2023). These networks provide access to informal labour, financial resources and initial customer bases, fostering resilience and reinforcing a sense of legitimacy (Pan et al., 2019; Robertson & Grant,

2016). However, dependence on ethnically bounded networks can also restrict scalability, limiting business diversification and integration into mainstream markets (Essers & Benschop, 2007; Yang & Girotto, 2024).

This dual role of social identity presents a strategic tension. While ethnic affiliation can serve as a valuable resource, it may also confine entrepreneurs to niche sectors if not managed adaptively (Brannen et al., 2013; Stoyanov, 2018). Entrepreneurs often face the challenge of maintaining cultural authenticity while appealing to a broader consumer base. Some embrace ethnic branding and cultural storytelling to leverage identity as a competitive advantage, while others downplay ethnic markers to appeal to mainstream audiences (Das et al., 2017; Essers & Benschop, 2007). The effectiveness of social identity in supporting business growth depends on how well entrepreneurs balance these competing demands. Long-term success often requires navigating this dual positioning, aligning community expectations with broader market strategies (Bipartisan Policy Centre, 2023; Pan et al., 2019).

Cultural identity: heritage and adaptation in new markets

Cultural identity plays a significant role in shaping entrepreneurial motivations, branding approaches and customer relationships. It encompasses deeply held values, traditions and social norms, which influence how immigrant entrepreneurs position their ventures within the host economy (Essers & Benschop, 2007; Radu-Lefebvre et al., 2021). Many strategically leverage cultural heritage as a market differentiator, especially in sectors such as ethnic cuisine, fashion and artisanal crafts, where authenticity is a valued commodity (Falcão et al., 2024; Zhang & Chun, 2018). By embedding cultural markers into their business models, entrepreneurs often engage both co-ethnic communities and mainstream consumers interested in diverse products and experiences (Jones et al., 2019; Walsh & Cooney, 2023).

Cultural identity, however, is not a fixed resource. Its effectiveness depends on the entrepreneur's ability to maintain cultural distinctiveness while integrating into broader market structures (Xu et al., 2019). While heritage branding can foster consumer loyalty and community support, excessive reliance on ethnic identity may result in market segmentation, limiting scalability (Verver et al., 2020). Moreover, the commodification of culture raises ethical concerns when symbolic elements are exploited by dominant markets without corresponding benefits for immigrant entrepreneurs (Walsh & Cooney, 2023). This reflects the paradox of cultural entrepreneurship, where identity may serve as both an asset and a constraint depending on how it is deployed in competitive environments.

In addition to branding, cultural identity shapes business practices. Entrepreneurs from collectivist backgrounds often prioritise trust-based, reciprocal relationships and informal agreements, which may conflict with the formal, contract-based norms of host economies (Abd Hamid et al., 2019; Brannen et al., 2013). These normative divergences can lead to legal and financial vulnerabilities, particularly when informal networks lack the institutional protections of formal systems (Essers & Benschop, 2007). Furthermore, regulatory frameworks in host countries often fail to accommodate culturally embedded business practices, requiring entrepreneurs to navigate unfamiliar compliance systems (Verver et al., 2020). Assimilationist policy approaches may exacerbate these challenges by marginalising ethnic-specific models and pushing entrepreneurs to conform to dominant norms (Cortes Immigration, 2023).

Nevertheless, entrepreneurs with strong cross-cultural competencies such as negotiation adaptability, bilingualism and institutional literacy are better equipped to manage these tensions and expand their market reach (Xu et al., 2019). The ability to integrate cultural identity with host-market expectations is therefore central to determining whether immigrant ventures remain within ethnic enclaves or succeed in reaching wider consumer segments.

Intersectionality: the complex interplay of identity dimensions

Intersectionality, as introduced by Crenshaw (1991), offers a critical lens for examining how overlapping identity factors such as ethnicity, gender, class and immigration status interact to shape entrepreneurial opportunities and constraints. Romero & Valdez (2016) build on this perspective by arguing that immigrant entrepreneurship should be understood not through individual characteristics alone, but through the intersecting systems of power that condition access to resources and markets. Immigrant entrepreneurs do not face challenges in isolation; rather, they navigate barriers shaped by the cumulative and interlocking effects of structural disadvantage (Vorobeva, 2022).

Empirical research illustrates these dynamics with clarity in the experiences of female immigrant entrepreneurs. Studies by Essers & Benschop (2007, 2009) show that women often contend with gendered expectations, restricted access to finance and limited entrepreneurial networks, which push many into low-capital sectors such as personal services, food production and retail. Yet, these same contexts can also present opportunities when navigated through co-ethnic networks and informal strategies (Barrett & Vershinina, 2017). Jones et al. (2019) highlight that despite resource constraints, these entrepreneurs contribute meaningfully to local economies through micro-businesses. However, their growth potential is often hindered by the compounded effects of gender, ethnicity and socio-economic status, all of which influence who enters entrepreneurship and under what conditions (Brieger & Gielnik, 2021; Dávila & Mora, 2013; Mindes & Lewin, 2024). For many women from low-income immigrant backgrounds, entrepreneurship is a necessity-driven response to limited access to formal employment and stable income streams (Zhang & Chun, 2018).

Immigration status adds another layer of precarity. Undocumented and temporary migrants frequently encounter restricted legal rights, exclusion from financial institutions and limited access to labour protections (Gold, 2019; Light et al., 1994). These constraints push many towards informal or low-barrier sectors, where entry costs are minimal but structural risks persist (Gold & Light, 2000). Although some entrepreneurs mobilise social capital to offset these disadvantages, intersectionality reveals that such adaptive strategies are unevenly distributed and often constrained by broader patterns of institutional discrimination and policy exclusion (Brieger & Gielnik, 2021; Vorobeva, 2022). While resourcefulness enables a degree of resilience, structural exclusion continues to shape access to credit, markets and growth trajectories (Mindes & Lewin, 2024).

This analysis underscores a key limitation in mainstream entrepreneurship discourse, which frequently centres individual agency without fully accounting for the systemic forces that govern opportunity. Rather than viewing immigrant entrepreneurship purely as a path to economic integration, an intersectional lens reveals how success depends on the capacity to navigate and resist overlapping forms of structural exclusion.

The reconceptualised mixed embeddedness framework: identity, agency and transnational strategies

The preceding section examined EI as a dynamic and situated process through which immigrant entrepreneurs construct legitimacy, mobilise resources and adapt to evolving institutional and market conditions. Building on this foundation, the current analysis reconceptualises the MEF by positioning identity as a central mechanism through which embeddedness is not only experienced but also actively negotiated and reshaped. While recent scholarship has extended the framework to transnational contexts in recognition of the transnational nature of immigrant entrepreneurship (Bagwell, 2018; Yamamura & Lassalle, 2022), such contributions often retain a structural emphasis that focuses on how institutional environments constrain or enable business activity.

This analysis advances the discussion by placing identity at the core of entrepreneurial agency. Identity is conceptualised as a mediating force that interacts with market conditions, institutional structures and transnational networks across intersecting dimensions of race, gender, migration status and class. Immigrant entrepreneurs are regarded as strategic actors who reshape their embeddedness through identity work, navigating exclusionary regimes, mobilising legitimacy and accessing opportunity across spatial and institutional contexts. Transnational resources such as diaspora ties, home-country capital and transnational infrastructures are not external supplements; rather, they are mobilised through identity-based strategies that reposition entrepreneurs within and across multiple systems of regulation and opportunity. By reframing embeddedness as a contested and relational process, this reconceptualisation offers a more nuanced understanding of immigrant entrepreneurship grounded in the interplay between identity, structure and agency.

The following subsections outline the key dimensions of the analytical framework, examining how institutional embeddedness, social networks, economic and cultural capital and intersectionality function not as fixed determinants but as fluid terrains through which identity is negotiated, contested and strategically mobilised.

Institutional embeddedness and identity negotiation

Institutional embeddedness remains one of the most significant structural forces shaping immigrant entrepreneurship, influencing access to capital, regulatory compliance and market legitimacy. While MEF has traditionally emphasised the constraining effects of financial exclusion, restrictive licensing and segmented labour markets, this reconceptualisation shifts the analytical focus towards institutional barriers as arenas of negotiation rather than fixed determinants. Identity functions as a central mechanism through which immigrant entrepreneurs actively mediate their position within exclusionary systems. Rather than being passively shaped by structural conditions, entrepreneurs strategically reconstruct their professional and business identities to challenge institutional barriers, reframe legitimacy and access alternative forms of capital. Through identity-based strategies, they contest regulatory exclusion and reposition themselves within host-country institutions on their own terms.

Empirical evidence reinforces this perspective. Research on undocumented immigrant entrepreneurs in the U.S. demonstrates that, despite exclusion from formal banking and loan systems, many sustain their ventures through community-based lending circles, informal credit arrangements and trust-based partnerships (Gold, 2019). Similarly, highly skilled refugees in the Netherlands, when denied access to regulated professions, redirect their expertise towards knowledge-intensive sectors such as consulting, digital services and innovation-driven industries (de Lange et al., 2021). The transnational dimension further expands these adaptive strategies, as entrepreneurs bypass domestic regulatory barriers by establishing online enterprises or operating across borders, particularly in technology and education markets (Sandoz et al., 2022). These cases highlight how institutional embeddedness is actively contested and reshaped through identity-driven action, demonstrating a shift from viewing structural barriers as deterministic towards understanding them as sites of strategic agency.

Social networks and identity positioning

Social networks play a critical role in shaping immigrant entrepreneurship by facilitating access to financial capital, business partnerships and market opportunities. MEF has traditionally distinguished between bonding capital, which connects entrepreneurs within ethnic communities, and bridging capital, which links them to mainstream networks (Kloosterman, 2010; Ram et al., 2008). However, this binary distinction tends to assume that these networks are fixed and predetermined, overlooking the strategic agency entrepreneurs exercise in constructing and navigating their social relations. Building on a more dynamic understanding, this analysis argues that immigrant entrepreneurs actively reshape their identity positioning to access different forms of social capital, strategically transitioning between ethnic and mainstream networks as their ventures evolve. Identity becomes a resource through which entrepreneurs perform legitimacy, adapt to shifting consumer expectations and expand beyond the limitations of co-ethnic markets.

Empirical studies support this perspective. Research on immigrant entrepreneurs in Northwest Minnesota shows that many initially rely on bonding networks for early-stage financial support and customer bases but later reposition their identity to engage with broader markets and digital platforms (Bhattacharyya & Mukurazita, 2021). Similarly, in Europe, immigrant restaurant owners frequently rebrand their businesses to align with mainstream consumer preferences, allowing them to expand beyond co-ethnic clientele while maintaining elements of cultural distinctiveness (Baycan-Levent & Nijkamp, 2009). The transnational dimension further enhances this strategic agency, as entrepreneurs leverage diaspora ties to import products, attract investment and expand operations across home and host countries (Chen et al., 2024). In export-oriented sectors, cultural authenticity and heritage branding are used to appeal to both diaspora and global markets, positioning identity not only as a cultural anchor but also as a commercial asset (Chen et al., 2024; Sandoz et al., 2022). These examples demonstrate that social networks are not simply inherited structures but are actively reshaped through identity-based strategies, enabling immigrant entrepreneurs to mobilise resources across multiple economic and geographic contexts.

Economic and cultural capital in identity work

Economic and cultural capital are widely recognised as critical to entrepreneurial success, yet existing frameworks often treat these forms of capital as objective resources that entrepreneurs simply acquire and deploy. This perspective underplays the ways in which access to capital is shaped by identity, social perception and structural positioning. This analysis advances a more nuanced understanding by demonstrating that capital accumulation and mobilisation are not only economic processes but also deeply embedded in identity work and legitimacy construction. Research on Moroccan and Turkish female entrepreneurs in the Netherlands illustrates this complexity, showing that beyond regulatory and financial barriers, identity negotiation is central to accessing both mainstream and ethnic markets. These entrepreneurs must navigate gendered, ethnic and religious expectations to position themselves effectively within overlapping cultural and commercial systems, demonstrating how cultural capital can function as a business asset rather than a liability (Essers & Benschop, 2007, 2009).

Similar dynamics are evident across Europe, where immigrant entrepreneurs use cultural capital to shape market entry and consumer legitimacy. Strategies such as ethnic branding, storytelling and heritage-based marketing are employed to access wider audiences and differentiate their offerings in competitive sectors (Cederberg & Villares-Varela, 2019). The transnational dimension further amplifies these strategies. Many entrepreneurs operate across borders, drawing on home-country supply chains, diaspora funding and cultural legitimacy to strengthen their position in host-country economies (Chen et al., 2024). Rather than being constrained by limited access to formal financial institutions, these actors mobilise alternative financial and cultural resources to develop hybrid business models that integrate home and host country networks (Elo, 2016). Diaspora financing, transnational partnerships and heritage branding are strategically employed to enter niche global markets while navigating regulatory and institutional barriers in host contexts (Nkongolo-Bakenda & Chrysostome, 2020). By shifting the analytical lens from structural exclusion to the strategic use of identity in capital mobilisation, this perspective offers a more differentiated account of how immigrant entrepreneurs navigate financial and cultural constraints through agency, creativity and transnational resource mobilisation.

Intersectionality and multi-scalar embeddedness

While MEF acknowledges that structural barriers shape immigrant entrepreneurship, it often treats immigrant entrepreneurs as a homogenous category, overlooking how intersecting identity markers such as race, gender, migration status and class produce differentiated barriers and opportunities. This analysis advances a more differentiated approach by embedding intersectionality within a multi-scalar analysis of embeddedness. It recognises that institutional and market barriers do not operate uniformly but are layered and compounded, shaping access to capital, regulatory inclusion and market entry in distinct ways across socio-economic, legal and geographic contexts. Structural inequalities are not experienced in isolation but emerge through the interaction of multiple identity positions that condition how entrepreneurs navigate both opportunity and constraint.

Empirical research substantiates this perspective. Female immigrant entrepreneurs in the UK often face compounded financial exclusion shaped by the intersection of racial discrimination and precarious migration status, which pushes many into low-capital sectors or reliance on informal economic networks (Barrett & Vershinina, 2017). In Spain, undocumented migrant entrepreneurs encounter legal precarity that is inseparable from class and ethnic marginalisation, further restricting their access to formal markets and regulatory protections (Solano, 2021). A transnational lens further deepens this analysis by demonstrating how intersecting identities shape entrepreneurial possibilities across borders. Research shows that gender, race and migration status influence access to capital and market integration differently in home and host countries, prompting entrepreneurs to adopt transnational strategies to mitigate systemic disadvantages (Vershinina et al., 2019). By integrating intersectionality into a multi-scalar understanding of embeddedness, this perspective provides a more nuanced account of immigrant entrepreneurship that emphasises differentiated agency, systemic inequality and the strategic use of transnational resources.

Synthesising theoretical frameworks in immigrant entrepreneurship

To consolidate the preceding analyses, this section synthesises key theoretical frameworks in immigrant entrepreneurship to clarify their conceptual interrelations and respective limitations. Table 2.1 positions the RMEF as an extension and refinement of existing frameworks,

TABLE 2.1 Extending and synthesising theoretical frameworks in immigrant entrepreneurship

Framework	*Core focus*	*Key limitations*	*Distinctive contribution of the reconceptualised mixed embeddedness framework*
Forms of capital	Emphasises economic, social, cultural and human capital as strategic resources in entrepreneurship	Conceptualises capital as static and does not fully address how access is shaped by identity or structural conditions	Reframes capital as contextually embedded and dynamically mobilised through identity work and transnational strategies
Institutional theory	Highlights the role of formal rules, informal norms and institutional environments in shaping opportunity	Often treats institutions as fixed constraints and under-theorises entrepreneurial agency and identity negotiation	Positions institutions as negotiated spaces where entrepreneurs exercise agency and construct legitimacy through identity-based engagement
Mixed embeddedness framework	Integrates social networks, opportunity structures and institutional contexts	Limited engagement with intersectionality, identity construction and transnational dynamics	Extends mixed embeddedness framework by embedding identity, intersectionality and multi-scalar agency into analyses of structural embeddedness
Entrepreneurial identity	Examines identity formation, role negotiation and meaning-making in entrepreneurial activity	Often lacks integration with institutional, capital and transnational dimensions	Situates identity within multi-layered structures, linking self-positioning to regulatory environments, network access and transnational opportunities
Reconceptualised mixed embeddedness framework	Synthesises identity, institutional context, social networks, intersectionality and transnational strategy	Requires further empirical application across varied geographies and migrant categories	Offers a relational, adaptive framework that positions identity as a mediating force in navigating opportunity, legitimacy and constraint across contexts

highlighting its contribution to a more integrative, relational and adaptive account of entrepreneurial agency, identity and context.

This synthesis reveals a conceptual shift from static, resource- or structure-driven frameworks towards more dynamic accounts of intersectional agency and multi-scalar embeddedness. The RMEF builds on, yet moves beyond, earlier frameworks by conceptualising immigrant entrepreneurship as a negotiated process shaped by identity work, transnational strategies and the active navigation of structural barriers.

Conclusion

This chapter has reframed immigrant entrepreneurship as a socially embedded and strategically negotiated process shaped by identity, institutional conditions and transnational practices. Building on but extending existing frameworks, the RMEF developed here demonstrates how identity functions as a mechanism through which immigrant entrepreneurs engage with and reshape opportunity structures. Through strategic positioning, resource mobilisation and adaptive engagement, entrepreneurs navigate complex institutional environments and structural inequalities. Drawing on forms of capital, institutional theory and intersectionality, the framework offers a multidimensional account of entrepreneurship that reflects the differentiated and dynamic conditions shaping migrant enterprise. While the framework is theoretical in scope, it is applied in Part 2 of the book to case studies based on existing empirical research. These analyses demonstrate how the framework uncovers patterns of identity negotiation, institutional engagement and transnational strategy across diverse entrepreneurial contexts. The framework also provides a foundation for future primary research and inclusive policy development that better accounts for the structural barriers and strategic practices influencing migrant entrepreneurship.

References

Abd Hamid, H., O'Kane, C., & Everett, A. M. (2019). Conforming to the host country versus being distinct to our home countries: Ethnic migrant entrepreneurs' identity work in cross-cultural settings. *International Journal of Entrepreneurial Behaviour & Research, 25*(5), 919–935. https://doi.org/10.1108/IJEBR-02-2018-0097

Aldrich, H., & Waldinger, R. (1990). Ethnicity and entrepreneurship. *Annual Review of Sociology, 16*, 111–135. https://doi.org/10.1146/annurev.so.16.080190.000551

Aliaga-Isla, R., & Rialp, A. (2013). Systematic review of immigrant entrepreneurship literature: Previous findings and ways forward. *Entrepreneurship and Regional Development, 25*(9–10), 819–844. https://doi.org/10.1080/08985626.2013.845694

Anthias, F. (2001). New hybridities, old concepts: The limits of 'culture'. *Ethnic and Racial Studies, 24*(4), 619–641. https://doi.org/10.1080/01419870120049815

Bagwell, S. (2018). From mixed embeddedness to transnational mixed embeddedness: An exploration of Vietnamese businesses in London. *International Journal of Entrepreneurial Behaviour & Research, 24*(1), 104–120. https://doi.org/10.1108/IJEBR-01-2017-0035

Barrett, R., & Vershinina, N. (2017). Intersectionality of ethnic and entrepreneurial identities: A study of post-war Polish entrepreneurs in an English city. *Journal of Small Business Management, 55*(3), 430–443. https://doi.org/10.1111/jsbm.12246

Basu, A., & Altinay, E. (2002). The interaction between culture and entrepreneurship in London's immigrant business. *International Small Business Journal, 20*(4), 371–394. https://doi.org/10.1177/0266242602204001

Bates, G., & Connolly, S. (2023). Different people, different backgrounds, different identities: Filling the vacuum created by policy views of 'cultural capital.' *The Curriculum Journal, 34*(3), 505–520. https://doi.org/10.1002/curj.198

Baycan-Levent, T., & Nijkamp, P. (2009). Characteristics of migrant entrepreneurship in Europe. *Entrepreneurship and Regional Development, 21*(4), 375–397. https://doi.org/10.1080/08985620903020060

Becker, G. S. (2009). *Human capital: A theoretical and empirical analysis, with special reference to education* (3rd ed.). University of Chicago Press.

Berwing, S. (2019). Extending mixed embeddedness. *Historical Social Research/Historische Sozialforschung, 44*(4), 162–185. https://www.jstor.org/stable/26804870

Bhattacharyya, R. A., & Mukurazita, E. (2021). *Immigrant entrepreneurship in Northwest Minnesota: Two case studies of immigrant entrepreneurs*. University of Minnesota Extension. https://conservancy.umn.edu/bitstreams/2c9300a7-c7c0-4651-9def-6e14b1fe3f8b/download

Bipartisan Policy Centre. (2023). *Immigrant entrepreneurship: Economic potential and obstacles to success.* https://bipartisanpolicy.org/event/immigrant-entrepreneurship-economic-potential-and-obstacles-to-success/

Bizri, R. M. (2017). Refugee-entrepreneurship: A social capital perspective. *Entrepreneurship and Regional Development, 29*(9–10), 847–868. https://doi.org/10.1080/08985626.2017.1364787

Bonacich, E. (1973). A theory of middleman minorities. *American Sociological Review, 38*(5), 583–594. https://doi.org/10.2307/2094409

Bourdieu, P. (1986). The forms of capital. In J. G. Richardson (Ed.), *Handbook of theory and research for the sociology of education* (pp. 241–258). Greenwood Press.

Brannen, M. Y., Moore, F., & Mughan, T. (2013). Strategic ethnography and reinvigorating Tesco Plc: Leveraging inside/out bicultural bridging in multicultural teams. *Ethnographic Praxis in Industry Conference Proceedings,* 2013(1), 282–299. https://doi.org/10.1111/j.1559-8918.2013.00024.x

Brieger, S. A., & Gielnik, M. M. (2021). Understanding the gender gap in immigrant entrepreneurship: A multi-country study of immigrants' embeddedness in economic, social, and institutional contexts. *Small Business Economics, 56*(3), 1007–1031. https://doi.org/10.1007/s11187-019-00314-x

Brown, A., Meriton, R., Devinney, T., Kafouros, M., Gerardo, F. S., & Bhandal, R. (2021). Migrant human and political capitals value in entrepreneur enterprise performance: A comparative study of four emerging markets. *International Entrepreneurship and Management Journal, 17*, 665–692. https://doi.org/10.1007/s11365-020-00710-w

Bruder, J., Neuberger, D., & Räthke-Döppner, S. (2011). Financial barriers of ethnic entrepreneurship: Evidence from Germany. *International Journal of Entrepreneurial Behaviour & Research, 17*(3), 296–313. https://doi.org/10.1108/13552551111130727

Brzozowski, J., Cucculelli, M., & Surdej, A. (2014). Transnational ties and performance of immigrant entrepreneurs: The role of home-country conditions. *Entrepreneurship & Regional Development, 26*(7–8), 546–573. https://doi.org/10.1080/08985626.2014.959068

Brzozowski, J., Šimić Banović, R., & Alpeza, M. (2022). Overcoming constraints to immigrant entrepreneurship in Croatia: The role of formal and informal institutions. *Post-Communist Economies, 34*(8), 1109–1136. https://doi.org/10.1080/14631377.2021.1928825

Cederberg, M., & Villares-Varela, M. (2019). Ethnic entrepreneurship and the question of agency: The role of different forms of capital, and the relevance of social class. *Journal of Ethnic and Migration Studies, 45*(1), 115–132. https://doi.org/10.1080/1369183X.2018.1459521

Chen, X., Bandara, D., & Sanford, B. (2024). A literature review on transnational diaspora entrepreneurship: Utilizing a combined approach of traditional and topic modelling. *New England Journal of Entrepreneurship, 27*(2), 136–151. https://doi.org/10.1108/NEJE-07-2023-0048

Chen, Y. H., & Chen, H. S. (2024). Perspectives on necessity-driven immigrant entrepreneurship: Interactions with entrepreneurial ecosystems through the lens of dynamic capabilities. *Societies, 14*(10), 203. https://doi.org/10.3390/soc14100203

Choi, H., Siegel, D. S., Waldman, D. A., Frandell, A., & Kim, J. (2024). Role conflict, entrepreneurial identity, and academic entrepreneurship: The effects of immigration status. *Small Business Economics, 63*, 611–626. https://doi.org/10.1007/s11187-023-00861-4

Chrysostome, E. (2010). The success factors of necessity immigrant entrepreneurs: In search of a model. *Thunderbird International Business Review*, *52*(2), 137–152. https://doi.org/10.1002/tie.20320

Cortes Immigration. (2023). *The importance of cultural integration for immigrant entrepreneurs*. Cortés Immigration Law. https://cortesimmigration.com/importance-cultural-integration-immigrant-entrepreneurs

Crenshaw, K. (1991). Mapping the margins: Intersectionality, identity politics, and violence against female of colour. *Stanford Law Review, 43*(6), 1241–1299. https://doi.org/10.2307/1229039

Cruz, E. P., de Queiroz Falcão, R. P., & Mancebo, R. C. (2020). Market orientation and strategic decisions on immigrant and ethnic small firms. *Journal of International Entrepreneurship, 18*, 227–255. https://doi.org/10.1007/s10843-019-00263-2

Das, D., Kwesiga, E., Sardeshmukh, S. R., & Juma, N. (2017). To be or not to be an ethnic firm: An analysis of identity strategies in immigrant-owned organisations. *New England Journal of Entrepreneurship, 20*(1), 2. https://digitalcommons.sacredheart.edu/neje/vol20/iss1/2

David, A., & Terstriep, J. (2025). Against all odds – migrant entrepreneurs in entrepreneurial ecosystems with constraints. *Journal of Enterprising Communities: People and Places in the Global Economy, 19*(2), 248–275. https://doi.org/10.1108/JEC-03-2024-0052

Dávila, A., & Mora, M. T. (2013). *Hispanic entrepreneurs in the 2000s: An economic profile and policy implications*. Stanford University Press.

de Lange, T., Berntsen, L., Hanoeman, R., & Haidar, O. (2021). Highly skilled entrepreneurial refugees: Legal and practical barriers and enablers to start up in the Netherlands. *International Migration, 59*(4), 74–87. https://doi.org/10.1111/imig.12745

Desiderio, M. V. (2014). *Policies to support immigrant entrepreneurship*. Migration Policy Institute and Transatlantic Council on Migration. https://www.migrationpolicy.org/sites/default/files/publications/TCM_Cities_Entrepreneurship-FINALWEB.pdf

Drori, I., Honig, B., & Wright, M. (2009). Transnational entrepreneurship: An emergent field of study. *Entrepreneurship Theory and Practice, 33*(5), 1001–1022. https://doi.org/10.1111/j.1540-6520.2009.00332.x

Duan, C., Kotey, B., & Sandhu, K. (2021a). Transnational immigrant entrepreneurship: Effects of home-country entrepreneurial ecosystem factors. *International Journal of Entrepreneurial Behaviour & Research, 27*(3), 711–729. https://doi.org/10.1108/IJEBR-05-2020-0300

Duan, C., Sandhu, K., & Kotey, B. (2021b). Understanding immigrant entrepreneurship: A home-country entrepreneurial ecosystem perspective. *New England Journal of Entrepreneurship, 24*(1), 2–20. https://doi.org/10.1108/NEJE-05-2020-0013

Elo, M. (2016). Typology of diaspora entrepreneurship: Case studies in Uzbekistan. *Journal of International Entrepreneurship, 14*(1), 121–155. https://doi.org/10.1007/s10843-016-0177-9

Essers, C., & Benschop, Y. (2007). Enterprising identities: Female immigrant entrepreneurs of Moroccan or Turkish origin in the Netherlands. *Organisation Studies, 28*(1), 49–69. https://doi.org/10.1177/0170840606068256

Essers, C., & Benschop, Y. (2009). Muslim business female doing boundary work: The negotiation of Islam, gender and ethnicity within entrepreneurial contexts. *Human Relations, 62*(3), 403–423. https://doi.org/10.1177/0018726708101042

European Commission. (2016). *Evaluation and analysis of good practices in promoting and supporting migrant entrepreneurship* (EU Guidebook). Publications Office of the European Union. https://migrant-integration.ec.europa.eu/library-document/eu-guidebook-promote-and-support-migrant-entrepreneurship_en

European Commission. (2024). *Cascade funding opportunities*. European Commission Funding & Tenders Portal. https://ec.europa.eu/info/funding-tenders/opportunities/portal/screen/opportunities/competitive-calls

Fairlie, R. W., & Lofstrom, M. (2015). Immigration and entrepreneurship. In *Handbook of the economics of international migration* (pp. 877–911). Elsevier. https://www.sciencedirect.com/science/article/pii/B9780444537683000175

Falcão, R. P. Q., Silva-Rêgo, B., & Cruz, E. P. (2024). Migrant entrepreneurship: Turning challenges into opportunities. *AIB Insights, 24*(1). https://doi.org/10.46697/001c.92943

Fregetto, E. (2004). Immigrant and ethnic entrepreneurship: A U.S. perspective. In H. Welsch (Ed.), *Entrepreneurship: The Way Ahead* (pp. 253–268). Routledge.

Fuentelsaz, L., Maicas, J. P., & Montero, J. (2023). The social status of entrepreneurs: An analysis of informal and formal institutional determinants. *European Management Review*. https://doi.org/10.1111/emre.12616

Garapich, M. P. (2008). The migration industry and civil society: Polish immigrants in the United Kingdom before and after EU enlargement. *Journal of Ethnic and Migration Studies, 34*(5), 735–752. https://doi.org/10.1080/13691830802105970

Gold, S. J. (2019). Liabilities and benefits associated with the involvement of undocumented immigrants in informal entrepreneurship in the US. In V. Ramadani, L. P. Dana, V. Ratten, & A. Bexheti (Eds.), *Informal ethnic entrepreneurship* (pp. 9–28). Springer. https://doi.org/10.1007/978-3-319-99064-4_2

Gold, S. J., & Light, I. (2000). Ethnic economies and social policy. In P. G. Coy (Ed.), *Research in social movements, conflicts and change* (Vol. 22, pp. 165–191). Emerald Group Publishing. https://doi.org/10.1016/S0163-786X(00)80039-7

Gomez, C., Perera, B. Y., Wesinger, J. Y., & Tobey, D. H. (2020). Immigrant entrepreneurs and community social capital: An exploration of motivations and agency. *Journal of Small Business and Enterprise Development, 27*(4), 579–605. https://doi.org/10.1108/JSBED-07-2019-0232

Government of Canada. (2024). *Start-up visa program.* https://www.canada.ca/en/immigration-refugees-citizenship/services/immigrate-canada/start-visa.html

Granovetter, M. (1985). Economic action and social structure: The problem of embeddedness. *American Journal of Sociology, 91*(3), 481–510. https://doi.org/10.1086/228311

Hack-Polay, D., Igwe, P. A., & Madichie, N. O. (2020). The role of institutional and family embeddedness in the failure of Sub-Saharan African migrant family businesses. The *International Journal of Entrepreneurship and Innovation, 21*(4), 237–249. https://doi.org/10.1177/1465750320909732

Helmke, G., & Levitsky, S. (2012). Informal institutions and comparative politics: A research agenda. In *International handbook on informal governance* (Vol. 2, No. 4, pp. 85–113). Edward Elgar. https://doi.org/10.4337/9781781001219.00011

Hu, M., Su, Y., & Zhang, H. (2021). Migrant entrepreneurship: The family as emotional support, social capital, and human capital. *Emerging Markets, Finance, and Trade, 57*(12), 3367–3386. https://doi.org/10.1080/1540496X.2019.1693364

Ibrahim, H. (2020). Structured savings and asset ownership: The role of rotating savings and credit associations among African immigrants in the United States. *Journal of Sociology & Social Welfare, 47,* 29.

International Rescue Committee. (2023). *Building an ecosystem of support: Refugee access to capital.* https://newsroom.paypal-corp.com/2023-06-Building-an-Ecosystem-of-Support-Refugee-Access-to-Capital

Jones, T., Ram, M., Edwards, P., Kiselinchev, A., & Muchenje, L. (2014). Mixed embeddedness and new migrant enterprise in the UK. *Entrepreneurship & Regional Development, 26*(5–6), 500–520. https://doi.org/10.1080/08985626.2014.950697

Jones, T., Ram, M., & Villares-Varela, M. (2019). Diversity, economic development and new migrant entrepreneurs. *Urban Studies, 56*(5), 960–976. https://doi.org/10.1177/0042098018765382

Kacar, S. O., Verduijn, K., & Essers, C. (2021). Questioning opportunity structures from an intersectional perspective. In T. M. Cooney (Ed.), *The Palgrave Handbook of Minority Entrepreneurship* (pp. 87–115). Springer Nature Switzerland AG. https://doi.org/10.1007/978-3-030-66603-3_5

Kašperová, E., Roberts, R., & Ram, M. (2022). *Time to change: A blueprint for advancing the UK's ethnic minority businesses*. CREME, Aston Business School: Centre for Migration and Forced Displacement.

Kerr, S. P., & Kerr, W. (2020). Immigrant entrepreneurship in America: Evidence from the survey of business owners 2007 & 2012. *Research Policy, 49*(3), 103918. https://doi.org/10.1016/j.respol.2019.103918

Kerr, W. R., & Mandorff, M. (2023). Social networks, ethnicity, and entrepreneurship. *Journal of Human Resources, 58*(1), 183–220. https://doi.org/10.3368/jhr.58.3.0719-10306R2

Kloosterman, R. C. (2010). Matching opportunities with resources: A framework for analysing (migrant) entrepreneurship from a mixed embeddedness perspective. *Entrepreneurship and Regional Development, 22*(1), 25–45. https://doi.org/10.1080/08985620903220488

Kloosterman, R. C., & Rath, J. (2001). *Immigrant entrepreneurs: Venturing abroad in the age of globalisation*. Berg Publishers.
Kloosterman, R. C., & Rath, J. (2018). Mixed embeddedness revisited: A conclusion to the symposium. *Sociologica, 12*(2), 103–114.
Kloosterman, R. C., Rusinovic, K., & Yeboah, D. (2016). Super-diverse migrants—similar trajectories? Ghanaian entrepreneurship in the Netherlands seen from a mixed embeddedness perspective. *Journal of Ethnic and Migration Studies, 42*(6), 913–932. https://doi.org/10.1080/1369183X.2015.1126091
Kloosterman, R. C., van der Leun, J. P., & Rath, J. (1999). Mixed embeddedness: (In)formal economic activities and immigrant businesses in the Netherlands. *International Journal of Urban and Regional Research, 23*(2), 252–266. https://doi.org/10.1111/1468-2427.00194
Lassalle, P., & McElwee, G. (2016). Polish entrepreneurs in Glasgow and entrepreneurial opportunity structure. *International Journal of Entrepreneurial Behaviour & Research, 22*(2), 260–281. https://doi.org/10.1108/IJEBR-01-2016-0012
Lassalle, P., & Scott, J. M. (2018). Breaking out? A reconceptualisation of the business development process through diversification: The case of Polish new migrant entrepreneurs in Glasgow. *Journal of Ethnic and Migration Studies, 44*(15), 2524–2543. https://doi.org/10.1080/1369183X.2017.1391077
Lee, W., & Black, S. L. (2017). Small business development: Immigrants' access to loan capital. *Journal of Small Business & Entrepreneurship, 29*(3), 193–209. https://doi.org/10.1080/08276331.2017.1297106
Li, H., Awotoye, Y., & Singh, R. P. (2023). Immigrant entrepreneurs in the U.S.: Firm performance based on entrepreneurial competencies. *Economies, 11*(10), 242. https://doi.org/10.3390/economies11100242
Liang, J., & Chreim, S. (2021). Immigrant entrepreneurs' identity constructions and endeavours: Considering ethnicity and gender. *Academy of Management Proceedings,* 2021(1), 10571. https://doi.org/10.5465/AMBPP.2021.10571abstract
Light, I., & Bonacich, E. (1988). *Immigrant entrepreneurs: Koreans in Los Angeles, 1965–1982*. University of California Press.
Light, I., & Dana, L. P. (2013). Boundaries of social capital in entrepreneurship. *Entrepreneurship Theory and Practice, 37*(3), 603–624. https://doi.org/10.1111/etap.12016
Light, I., & Karageorgis, S. (1994). The ethnic economy. In N. Smelser & R. Swedberg (Eds.), *The handbook of economic sociology* (pp. XX–XX). Princeton University Press.
Light, I., Sabagh, G., Bozorgmehr, M., & Der-Martirosian, C. (1994). Beyond the ethnic enclave economy. *Social Problems, 41*(1), 65–80.
Malerba, R. C., & Ferreira, J. J. (2020). Immigrant entrepreneurship and strategy: A systematic literature review. *Journal of Small Business & Entrepreneurship, 33*(2), 183–217. https://doi.org/10.1080/08276331.2020.1804714
Mindes, S. C., & Lewin, P. (2024). Intersectional dimensions of entrepreneurship among immigrant Hispanic women. *Journal of Small Business Management, 62*(5), 2181–2210. https://doi.org/10.1080/00472778.2023.2208629
Moghaddam, K., & Weber, T. (2021). Immigrants and international entrepreneurship: Transnational dynamic capability and dual social network embeddedness. In V. Jafari-Sadeghi, H. Amoozad Mahdiraji, & L. P. Dana (Eds.), *Empirical international entrepreneurship* (pp. 9–25). Springer. https://doi.org/10.1007/978-3-030-68972-8_2
Nathan, M., & Lee, N. (2013). Cultural diversity, innovation, and entrepreneurship: Firm-level evidence from London. *Economic Geography, 89*(4), 367–394. https://doi.org/10.1111/ecge.12016
Naudé, W., Siegel, M., & Marchand, K. (2017). Migration, entrepreneurship and development: Critical questions. *IZA Journal of Migration, 6*(5). https://doi.org/10.1186/s40176-016-0077-8
Ndofor, H. A., & Priem, R. L. (2011). Immigrant entrepreneurs, the ethnic enclave strategy, and venture performance. *Journal of Management, 37*(3), 790–818. https://doi.org/10.1177/0149206309345020
Nee, V., & Sanders, J. (2001). Understanding the diversity of immigrant incorporation: A forms-of-capital model. *Ethnic and Racial Studies, 24*(3), 386–411. https://doi.org/10.1080/01419870020036710
Nkongolo-Bakenda, J. M., & Chrysostome, E. V. (2020). Dual environments of home and host countries of diasporic transnational entrepreneurs: An empirical study in the Canadian context. *International Journal of Entrepreneurship and Small Business, 39*(4), 455–500. https://doi.org/10.1504/IJESB.2020.106468

North, D. C. (1990). *Institutions, institutional change and economic performance* (Vol. 332). Cambridge University Press.

Ojo, S. (2021). Black African perceptions of entrepreneurial outcomes in the UK. *Society and Business Review, 16*(2), 278–305. https://doi.org/10.1108/SBR-06-2020-0087

Pan, N. D., Gruber, M., & Binder, J. (2019). Painting with all the colors: The value of social identity theory for understanding social entrepreneurship. *Academy of Management Review, 44*(1), 213–215. https://doi.org/10.5465/amr.2017.0504

Piore, M. J. (1979). *Birds of passage: Migrant labour and industrial societies*. Cambridge University Press.

Portes, A. (2009). Social capital: Its origins and applications in modern sociology. In A. Harrington (Ed.), *New critical writings in political sociology* (pp. 53–76). Routledge.

Portes, A., Haller, W. J., & Guarnizo, L. E. (2002). Transnational entrepreneurs: An alternative form of immigrant economic adaptation. *American Sociological Review, 67*(2), 278–298. https://doi.org/10.1177/000312240206700206

Portes, A., & Manning, R. D. (1986). The immigrant enclave: Theory and empirical examples. In S. Olzak & J. Nagel (Eds.), *Competitive ethnic relations* (pp. 47–68). Academic Press.

Portes, A., & Sensenbrenner, J. (1993). Embeddedness and immigration: Notes on the social determinants of economic action. *American Journal of Sociology, 98*(6), 1320–1350. https://doi.org/10.1086/230191

Putnam, R. D. (2000). *Bowling alone: The collapse and revival of American community*. Simon & Schuster.

Radu-Lefebvre, M., Lefebvre, V., Crosina, E., & Hytti, U. (2021). Entrepreneurial identity: A review and research agenda. *Entrepreneurship Theory and Practice, 45*(6), 1550–1590. https://doi.org/10.1177/10422587211013795

Ram, M., Jones, T., Doldor, S., Villares-Varela, M., & Li, H. (2021). What happens to refugee-origin entrepreneurs? Combining mixed embeddedness and strategy perspectives in a longitudinal study. *Ethnic and Racial Studies, 45*(16), 1–27. https://doi.org/10.1080/01419870.2021.1991970

Ram, M., Jones, T., & Villares-Varela, M. (2017). Migrant entrepreneurship: Reflections on research and practice. *International Small Business Journal, 35*(1), 3–18. https://doi.org/10.1177/0266242616678051

Ram, M., Theodorakopoulos, N., & Jones, T. (2008). Forms of capital, mixed embeddedness and Somali enterprise. *Work, Employment and Society, 22*(3), 427–446. https://doi.org/10.1177/0950017008093479

Rath, J. (2002). A quintessential immigrant Niche? The non-case of immigrants in the Dutch construction industry. *Entrepreneurship & Regional Development, 14*(4), 355–372. https://doi.org/10.1080/08985620220000013158

Rath, J., & Kloosterman, R. C. (2000). Outsiders' business: A critical review of research on immigrant entrepreneurship. *International Migration Review, 34*(3), 657–681. https://doi.org/10.1177/019791830003400301

Rath, J., & Swagerman, A. (2016). Promoting ethnic entrepreneurship in European cities: Sometimes ambitious, mostly absent, rarely acknowledged. *International Migration Review, 50*(2), 361–387. https://doi.org/10.1111/imig.12215

Rinaldi, R., Arrighetti, A., Lasagni, A., & Canello, J. (2023). Immigrant entrepreneurship in Europe: A comparative empirical approach. *Econstor*. https://hdl.handle.net/10419/270873

Robertson, D., & Grant, P. (2016). Immigrant entrepreneurship from a social psychological perspective. *Journal of Applied Social Psychology, 46*. https://doi.org/10.1111/jasp.12369

Romero, M., & Valdez, Z. (2016). Introduction to the special issue: Intersectionality and entrepreneurship. *Ethnic and Racial Studies, 39*(9), 1553–1565. https://doi.org/10.1080/01419870.2016.1171374

Rugaber, C. (2024). *Small Business Administration-backed financing rose 7% to $56B in fiscal 2024*. Associated Press. https://apnews.com/article/5c8ab76c0ce11f05fa86a5623480731d

Rusinovic, K. (2008). Transnational embeddedness: Transnational activities and networks among first and second-generation immigrant entrepreneurs in the Netherlands. *Journal of Ethnic and Migration Studies, 34*(3), 431–451. https://doi.org/10.1080/13691830701880285

Sandoz, L., Mittmasser, C., Riaño, Y., & Izaguirre, L. (2022). *Transnational migrant entrepreneurs: Understanding their dependencies, fragilities, and alternatives. Globalisations, 21*(3), 471–489. https://doi.org/10.1080/14747731.2022.2157149

Scott, W. R. (2008). *Institutions and organisations: Ideas and interests* (3rd ed.). Sage Publications.
Singh, M. K. (2024). Forms of social capital. In *Social capital* (pp. 9–31). Emerald Publishing Limited. https://doi.org/10.1108/978-1-83797-587-720241002
Smallbone, D., Ram, M., Deakins, D., & Aldock, R. B. (2003). Access to finance by ethnic minority businesses in the UK. *International Small Business Journal, 21*(3), 291–314. https://doi.org/10.1177/02662426030213003
Solano, G. (2021). The mixed embeddedness of transnational migrant entrepreneurs: Moroccans in Amsterdam and Milan. In R. Zapata-Barrero & S. Rezaei (Eds.), *Diaspora governance and transnational entrepreneurship: the rise of an emerging global social pattern in migration studies* (pp. 109–127). Routledge. https://doi.org/10.4324/9781003195344-7.
Solano, G., Ram, M., & Rath, J. (2023). Regulation of migrant entrepreneurship: The strained conjunction of laws, policies, and practices. *International Migration, 61*(2), 3–8. https://doi.org/10.1111/imig.13128
Solano, G., Schutjens, V., & Rath, J. (2022). Multifocality and opportunity structure: Towards a mixed embeddedness model for transnational migrant entrepreneurship. *Comparative Migration Studies, 10*(3). https://doi.org/10.1186/s40878-021-00270-0
Stoyanov, S. (2018). Enabling social identity interaction: Bulgarian migrant entrepreneurs building embeddedness into a transnational network. *British Journal of Management, 29*(2), 373–388. https://doi.org/10.1111/1467-8551.12235
Tajfel, H., & Turner, J. C. (1979). An integrative theory of intergroup conflict. In W. G. Austin & S. Worchel (Eds.), *The social psychology of intergroup relations* (pp. 33–47). Brooks/Cole.
Tiemo, T. H. (2024). *Opportunity recognition and new venture creation: A narrative inquiry into Black African immigrant entrepreneurs in the urban environment of the West Midlands* (Doctoral thesis, Birmingham City University).
UK Government. (2023). *Innovator founder visa.* https://www.gov.uk/innovator-founder-visa
Urban, B., & Moti, M. (2024). Immigrants as entrepreneurs in emerging economies: Institutional, self-efficacy, and social networking effects on enterprise performance. *Small Business International Review, 8*(2), e670. https://doi.org/10.26784/sbir.v8i2.670
Vershinina, N., Rodgers, P., McAdam, M., & Clinton, E. (2019). Transnational migrant entrepreneurship, gender and family business. *Global Networks, 19*(2), 238–260. https://doi.org/10.1111/glob.12225
Vertovec, S. (2004). Migrant transnationalism and modes of transformation. *International Migration Review, 38*(3), 970–1001. https://doi.org/10.1111/j.1747-7379.2004.tb00226.x
Verver, M., Roessingh, C., & Passenier, D. (2020). Ethnic boundary dynamics in immigrant entrepreneurship: A Barthian perspective. *Entrepreneurship & Regional Development, 32*(9–10), 757–782. https://doi.org/10.1080/08985626.2020.1757160
Vorobeva, E. (2022). Intersectionality and minority entrepreneurship: At the crossroad of vulnerability and power. In L. P. Dana, N. Khachlouf, A. Maâlaoui, & V. Ratten (Eds.), *Disadvantaged minorities in business* (pp. 225–235). Springer. https://doi.org/10.1007/978-3-030-97079-6_11
Wadhwa, V., Saxenian, A. L., Rissing, B. A., & Gereffi, G. (2007). *America's new immigrant entrepreneurs: Part I* (Duke Science, Technology & Innovation Paper No. 23). SSRN. https://doi.org/10.2139/ssrn.990152
Wahlbeck, Ö. R. (2018). Combining mixed embeddedness and transnationalism: The utilisation of social resources among Turkish migrant entrepreneurs. *Sociologica: International Journal for Sociological Debate, 12*(2), 73–86.
Waldinger, R. D., Aldrich, H., & Ward, R. (1990). *Ethnic entrepreneurs: Immigrant business in industrial societies*. SAGE Publications.
Walsh, L., & Cooney, T. (2023). Understanding the interplay between immigrant nascent entrepreneurship and cross-cultural adaptation. *Journal of Small Business and Enterprise Development, 30*(5), 919–946. https://doi.org/10.1108/JSBED-12-2021-0472
Wang, C. L., & Altinay, L. (2012). Social embeddedness, entrepreneurial orientation and firm growth in ethnic minority small businesses in the UK. *International Small Business Journal, 30*(1), 3–23. https://doi.org/10.1177/0266242610366060
Wang, Q., & Liu, C. Y. (2015). Transnational activities of immigrant-owned firms and their performances in the USA. *Small Business Economics, 44*(2), 345–359. https://doi.org/10.1007/s11187-014-9595-z

Welter, F., & Smallbone, D. (2011). Institutional perspectives on entrepreneurial behavior in challenging environments. *Journal of Small Business Management, 49*(1), 107–125. https://doi.org/10.1111/j.1540-627X.2010.00317.x

Xu, K., Drennan, J., & Mathews, S. (2019). Immigrant entrepreneurs and their cross-cultural capabilities: A study of Chinese immigrant entrepreneurs in Australia. *Journal of International Entrepreneurship, 17*(4), 520–557. https://doi.org/10.1007/s10843-019-00261-4

Yamamura, S., & Lassalle, P. (2022). Extending mixed embeddedness to a multi-dimensional concept of transnational entrepreneurship. *Comparative Migration Studies, 10*(1), Article 14. https://doi.org/10.1186/s40878-022-00288-y

Yang, J. J., & Girotto, M. (2024). Exploring the role of ethnic networking ties in immigrant entrepreneurship: A comprehensive review and research agenda. *Journal of Enterprising Communities: People and Places in the Global Economy.* https://doi.org/10.1108/JEC-07-2023-0111

Yasin, N., & Hafeez, K. (2023). Three waves of immigrant entrepreneurship: A cross-national comparative study. *Small Business Economics, 60*(3), 1281–1306. https://doi.org/10.1007/s11187-022-00656-z

Zhang, T. (2023). *Often shut out of the financial system, refugees and other migrants face economic integration challenges*. Migration Policy Institute. https://www.migrationpolicy.org/article/refugees-migrants-financial-inclusion

Zhang, Z., & Chun, D. (2018). Becoming entrepreneurs: How immigrants developed entrepreneurial identities. *International Journal of Entrepreneurial Behaviour & Research, 24*(5), 947–970. https://doi.org/10.1108/IJEBR-07-2016-0214

Zhou, M. (2004). Revisiting ethnic entrepreneurship: Convergencies, controversies, and conceptual advancements. *International Migration Review, 38*(3), 1040–1074.

3

STRUCTURAL BARRIERS AND ADAPTIVE STRATEGIES IN IMMIGRANT ENTREPRENEURSHIP

Innovation, inclusion and institutional engagement

Introduction

Global economic restructuring, migration flows and shifting regulatory environments have reshaped entrepreneurial opportunities while reinforcing barriers to immigrant business formation and market access. Across diverse national contexts, restrictive institutional frameworks, financial exclusion and sociocultural biases continue to constrain workforce integration and entrepreneurial development (Jones et al., 2014; Kloosterman & Rath, 2018; Ram et al., 2017). In response to limited employment prospects, many immigrants turn to entrepreneurship as a pathway to survival and mobility. However, these ventures often emerge in contexts marked by bureaucratic inefficiencies and systemic exclusion, restricting them to low-margin, saturated markets with limited scalability (Kerr & Kerr, 2020; Kloosterman & Rath, 2001, 2018; Light & Dana, 2013). Gendered financial barriers further compound these constraints, limiting access to capital and institutional support for female immigrant entrepreneurs and reinforcing broader structural inequalities (Azmat, 2013; Brieger & Gielnik, 2021; Essers & Benschop, 2007). Moreover, an overreliance on ethnic cultural capital as an explanatory lens risks reinforcing static conceptions of identity while overlooking the broader social, symbolic and institutional resources that mediate entrepreneurial inclusion (Erel, 2010; Vertovec, 2007). Despite these challenges, immigrant entrepreneurs continue to devise adaptive strategies, including the mobilisation of social networks, cultivation of transnational linkages and adoption of digital infrastructures to navigate restrictive conditions.

Although existing scholarship has addressed many of these structural barriers, it often frames immigrant ventures as necessity-driven rather than as sites of strategic adaptation (Aliaga-Isla & Rialp, 2013; Baycan-Levent & Nijkamp, 2009; Waldinger et al., 1990). While research has considered ethnic networks, transnational entrepreneurship and institutional support mechanisms (Desiderio, 2014; Elo & Riddle, 2016; Light & Dana, 2013), the emerging roles of digital ecosystems, decentralised finance and identity-based resource mobilisation remain underexamined. These dynamics increasingly shape entrepreneurial agency, innovation and long-term sustainability, particularly in urban and transnational contexts (Bolzani & Scandura, 2024; Duan et al., 2020). This chapter responds to these gaps by providing a comprehensive analysis of how

DOI: 10.4324/9781003605072-4

structural barriers intersect with emergent practices and how immigrant entrepreneurs develop adaptive responses. Drawing on documented case patterns and secondary empirical evidence, it examines the everyday mechanisms through which entrepreneurs confront institutional, financial and sociocultural barriers.

To develop this analysis, the chapter begins with understanding structural barriers, examining how institutional and sociocultural barriers limit immigrant entrepreneurs' ability to establish, scale and integrate their ventures. It then turns to exploring adaptive strategies, focusing on informal and formal responses such as ethnic networks, transnational mobility, digital tools and supportive policies. The third section, scaling innovation-driven inclusion, considers how social entrepreneurship and collaborative ventures foster long-term resilience and institutional engagement. The chapter concludes by assessing how these strategies contribute to systemic transformation and inclusive economic integration.

Understanding structural barriers

Institutional barriers

Institutional barriers significantly constrain the entrepreneurial potential of immigrants by restricting access to essential resources, limiting business scalability and reinforcing systemic inequities. This section focuses on two interrelated dimensions of these barriers: (i) regulatory and structural inefficiencies and (ii) financial exclusion. Together, they shape an entrepreneurial landscape that hinders the growth and integration of immigrant ventures, thereby impeding broader economic and social development.

Regulatory and structural inefficiencies

Host-country regulatory systems often present complex and opaque procedures that disproportionately affect immigrant entrepreneurs. Licensing, compliance and taxation frameworks can be difficult to navigate without prior familiarity, leading to procedural delays and unclear requirements that deter formal business creation (Brzozowski et al., 2022). Many immigrants are consequently pushed into the informal economy, where legal and financial risks are elevated (Desiderio, 2014). The absence of targeted institutional support further exacerbates these challenges, leaving entrepreneurs without the guidance needed to engage effectively with regulatory environments.

These structural inefficiencies shape unequal opportunity structures, often steering immigrants towards low-capital, oversaturated sectors such as retail and food services. Although these sectors offer relatively low entry barriers, they typically provide limited scalability and long-term profitability, thereby reinforcing patterns of socioeconomic marginalisation (Jones et al., 2014; Kloosterman & Rath, 2001). This trajectory is not driven by cultural preference but reflects structural exclusion, as noted by Barrett et al. (1996), whereby systemic barriers restrict access to diverse markets and limit upward mobility.

The confinement of immigrant entrepreneurs to ethnic niches illustrates this exclusionary dynamic. While such niches may provide initial footholds, they frequently isolate entrepreneurs from mainstream markets and limit opportunities for growth. Kloosterman's (2010) mixed embeddedness framework (MEF) highlights how institutional and socioeconomic contexts jointly shape these restricted trajectories. High-potential sectors, including technology and advanced manufacturing, often remain inaccessible due to substantial capital requirements and the need for specialised knowledge (Daniel et al., 2019; Kerr & Kerr, 2020). Unless institutional reforms are implemented to simplify regulatory procedures, expand access to growth-oriented industries and provide tailored support mechanisms, immigrant entrepreneurs will remain disproportionately marginalised. This ongoing exclusion not only constrains their capacity for innovation and economic contribution but also perpetuates wider social inequities (Daniel et al., 2019; Volery, 2007).

Financial exclusion

Financial exclusion significantly intensifies the challenges created by regulatory and structural inefficiencies, introducing systemic barriers that constrain the potential of immigrant entrepreneurs. Immigrants frequently encounter stricter lending requirements, including demands for extensive credit histories, substantial collateral or familiarity with local banking systems. These criteria often place immigrants at a disadvantage, as many lack the established financial profiles required to access formal credit mechanisms (Brzozowski et al., 2022; Ram & Smallbone, 2002). As a result, their capacity to secure the financial resources necessary for business growth and innovation is severely limited.

In response to these barriers, many immigrant entrepreneurs rely on informal funding sources, such as community savings schemes or personal networks. While these channels may offer initial support, they typically provide limited capital and lack the consistency required to sustain long-term development (Bewaji et al., 2015; Kloosterman, 2010). This reliance on informal finance perpetuates economic vulnerability, as it restricts entrepreneurs' ability to scale and formalise their enterprises. The MEF underscores how financial exclusion intersects with broader institutional and market-level barriers, thereby compounding the marginalisation of immigrant entrepreneurs (Kloosterman & Rath, 2018).

Gendered financial biases further exacerbate these exclusions, disproportionately affecting female immigrant entrepreneurs. Women often face additional obstacles in securing capital, reflecting enduring inequalities in the financial system. Financial institutions may operate on assumptions that female-owned businesses are less viable or carry greater risk, leading to higher rates of loan denial and less favourable terms, even when such businesses demonstrate equivalent potential to those owned by men (Brieger & Gielnik, 2021; Essers & Benschop, 2007). These challenges are intensified by the intersection of gender and migrant status, which together compound barriers to accessing formal financial support (Azmat, 2013; Heilbrunn, 2004; Kacar et al., 2021).

These exclusions are intersectional rather than merely additive, reinforcing systemic disadvantages that emerge at the nexus of gender, race and nationality (Collins, 1998). In the absence of institutional support, many female immigrant entrepreneurs depend on personal savings or community-based loans. Although more accessible, these sources are often insufficient to facilitate meaningful growth or innovation (Brzozowski et al., 2022). Consequently, their ventures remain undercapitalised and structurally disadvantaged. The continued exclusion of female immigrant entrepreneurs from formal financial systems not only constrains individual potential but also represents a broader loss to local and national economic development.

Sociocultural barriers

Sociocultural barriers pose substantial obstacles for immigrant entrepreneurs by hindering their integration into host-country markets, restricting access to key resources and reinforcing marginalisation. This section examines two principal dimensions of sociocultural exclusion: (i) language barriers and (ii) stereotyping and social exclusion. Together, these factors fragment the entrepreneurial landscape, limit opportunities for scalability and innovation and perpetuate broader patterns of economic inequity and social isolation.

Language barriers

Language proficiency plays a critical role in shaping the entrepreneurial capacity of immigrants. Limited linguistic skills can severely restrict access to essential information, including regulatory guidance, market intelligence and professional networks, all of which are vital for business development and sustainability (Brzozowski et al., 2022; Lochmann et al., 2019). A lack of proficiency often results in misinterpretation of legal and administrative requirements, causing delays in business registration and compliance processes. This situation frequently compels entrepreneurs to adopt informal strategies, which expose them to legal and financial vulnerabilities (Hamberger, 2009).

Chiswick & Miller (2002) underscore the strong correlation between language proficiency and economic mobility, while Dustmann & Fabbri (2003) highlight how limited linguistic ability impairs adaptability and reduces competitiveness in mainstream markets. In turn, many immigrant entrepreneurs become confined to ethnically bounded niches that offer limited growth potential and reinforce economic marginalisation (Kloosterman & Rath, 2018; Light, 2000).

Beyond economic constraints, language barriers also impede social integration. A lack of language proficiency can obstruct familiarity with cultural norms and prevent the formation of diverse social and professional networks, which are crucial for market access and collaborative growth (Adserà & Pytlikovà, 2015; Hamberger, 2009). Although ethnic networks may provide initial support, they often lack the diversity necessary for accessing broader markets and sustaining long-term business development (Nwankwo, 2005; Ojo, 2012).

Portes & Zhou (1992) suggest that linguistic exclusion contributes to segmented assimilation by limiting access to mainstream opportunities and reinforcing isolation. Furthermore, poor language skills hinder understanding of consumer preferences and obstruct navigation of complex regulatory systems, both of which are essential for business competitiveness (Collins, 2015; Constant et al., 2009). Barrett & Duffy (2008) note that these obstacles delay integration into formal labour and business markets, thereby prolonging the challenges faced by immigrant entrepreneurs. Without adequate language support, many remain disconnected from mainstream economic systems, limiting their contributions to host-country economies and reinforcing structural divides between immigrant and local businesses.

Stereotyping and social exclusion

Stereotyping represents a significant barrier for immigrant entrepreneurs, fostering perceptions of them as outsiders and obstructing their integration into mainstream markets and professional networks. These biases frequently confine immigrant businesses to low-growth, ethnically bounded niches, which limits their capacity for innovation and scalability (Stephan & Pathak, 2016). The MEF offers a useful lens through which to understand the interplay between institutional and sociocultural barriers, illustrating how these forces jointly reinforce the exclusion of immigrant entrepreneurs from wider economic opportunities (Kloosterman et al., 1999).

Immigrant entrepreneurs often encounter distrust from institutional actors and customers, who may question the legitimacy, quality or reliability of their products and services, particularly in competitive sectors. These perceptions constrain access to vital resources, such as funding, strategic partnerships and client networks. As a result, immigrant entrepreneurs are frequently confined to sectors that are perceived as low value, which further entrenches their marginalisation and limits their contributions to broader economic innovation (Brzozowski et al., 2022; Ram et al., 2017). This dynamic creates a cycle of disadvantage, whereby entrepreneurs are restricted to subsistence-level activities rather than being positioned to pursue growth-oriented ventures (Kerr & Kerr, 2020; Kloosterman & Rath, 2001).

Social exclusion compounds these challenges by limiting access to market intelligence, professional networks and institutional trust, all of which are critical for business sustainability and expansion. Immigrant entrepreneurs may experience cultural misalignment with host-country business norms and expectations, which can hinder the formation of relationships with key stakeholders and limit opportunities for collaboration (Morales et al., 2019). In many cases, entrepreneurs turn to community-based networks for support. While these networks can offer initial resources, they often lack the diversity and market reach needed to scale businesses beyond ethnically bounded niches (Nwankwo, 2005; Ojo, 2012).

Institutional practices often reinforce these patterns of exclusion. Immigrant entrepreneurs are frequently overlooked in competitive procurement processes and denied equitable access to public contracts and financial instruments, thereby perpetuating systemic disadvantage (Stephan & Pathak, 2016). The cumulative effect of these structural and sociocultural exclusions is the confinement of immigrant entrepreneurs to under-resourced ecosystems that limit innovation and economic mobility. Consequently, the potential of immigrant entrepreneurship remains significantly underutilised, not only impeding individual advancement but also limiting contributions to host-country economic development (Brzozowski et al., 2022; Morales et al., 2019).

Exploring adaptive strategies

Ethnic networks

Ethnic networks play a pivotal role in supporting immigrant entrepreneurs by addressing systemic barriers and fostering resilience. This section examines three strategic functions of ethnic networks: (i) transforming financial exclusion through ethnic networks, (ii) overcoming sociocultural barriers through cultural solidarity and (iii) harnessing ethnic networks for market access and workforce optimisation. By offering alternative financing mechanisms, shared resources and culturally embedded support, ethnic networks help reshape entrepreneurial ecosystems. These forms of community-based support not only counterbalance structural barriers but also promote innovation and inclusive economic participation, thereby strengthening the sustainability of immigrant ventures.

Transforming financial exclusion through ethnic networks

Ethnic networks offer an effective response to financial exclusion by establishing community-based mechanisms such as rotating savings and credit associations and co-ethnic microfinance initiatives. These systems operate on trust and collective responsibility, allowing immigrant entrepreneurs to bypass restrictive requirements often imposed by formal banking institutions. These requirements include the need for established credit histories, significant collateral or proof of familiarity with local financial systems (Ibrahim, 2020; Portes, 1995). By pooling resources within the community, these networks alleviate liquidity constraints and support small-scale entrepreneurs who are frequently excluded from mainstream financial systems.

Beyond access to capital, ethnic networks contribute to operational sustainability by providing shared resources, including equipment, workspace and collective knowledge (Chodavadia et al., 2024; Waldinger et al., 1990). These forms of support reduce business costs and improve long-term viability. In addition, ethnic networks foster entrepreneurial adaptability through informal mentorship and peer learning. These interactions help entrepreneurs acquire the skills needed to navigate complex regulatory systems, understand host-country business environments and develop the financial literacy necessary for business growth and diversification (Battisti et al., 2022; Saxenian, 2002).

Ethnic networks also serve as a critical support structure for female immigrant entrepreneurs. Women often encounter compounded barriers resulting from both gender and migrant status. Within ethnic networks, inclusive support systems create accessible and culturally sensitive alternatives to formal financial institutions. Trust-based lending arrangements and community mentorship programmes empower female entrepreneurs to pursue business activities, access resources and build financial independence (Brzozowski et al., 2022; Heilbrunn, 2004). These environments offer not only financial support but also social affirmation, which can be especially important in contexts where gender biases remain prevalent.

Although ethnic networks are highly effective in addressing immediate financial needs and fostering resilience, they are not without limitations. Their informal and often localised nature can restrict scalability and limit access to national or international markets. To unlock their full potential, these networks must be complemented by institutional reforms that improve access to formal finance, support innovation and enable immigrant entrepreneurs to integrate fully into the broader economic landscape.

Overcoming sociocultural barriers through cultural solidarity

Cultural solidarity within ethnic networks serves as a vital mechanism for overcoming sociocultural barriers, including language limitations, stereotyping and social exclusion. These networks foster trust, shared values and a sense of communal belonging, which support immigrant entrepreneurs in navigating unfamiliar regulatory, cultural and institutional environments. Community-led mentorship is central to this process, offering culturally relevant guidance on local market dynamics, consumer preferences and operational norms (Chodavadia et al., 2024; Ryan et al., 2008). This support is particularly effective in addressing language-related challenges by equipping entrepreneurs with the confidence and tools needed to engage host-country institutions and comply with complex regulatory frameworks (Kloosterman & Rath, 2018).

In addition to providing practical knowledge, cultural solidarity functions as a source of psychological resilience. It helps entrepreneurs adapt to the challenges of establishing and sustaining a business in a new and often unfamiliar environment (Brzozowski et al., 2022). These networks offer more than immediate support; they create emotionally sustaining ecosystems that affirm identity and foster persistence.

Cultural solidarity also mitigates the impact of stereotyping by establishing supportive environments where immigrant entrepreneurs can develop credibility and achieve economic stability. Cultural capital within these networks enables entrepreneurs to create distinctive business identities that emphasise authenticity and heritage. For example, ethnic restaurants and artisanal boutiques frequently draw on traditional recipes, visual aesthetics and music to offer immersive consumer experiences that promote emotional connection and loyalty (Bagwell, 2015). This cultural differentiation strengthens reputational trust, particularly within co-ethnic communities, and provides a stable foundation for broader market engagement (Massey et al., 1993; Waldinger & Lichter, 2003).

These networks contribute to dismantling exclusionary narratives by enabling immigrant entrepreneurs to establish connections with a wider range of stakeholders. Through ongoing engagement and demonstration of credibility, entrepreneurs can expand their reach beyond ethnic enclaves and integrate into mainstream economic systems (Drori et al., 2009; Light, 2000). However, exclusive reliance on culturally homogeneous networks may limit long-term innovation and scalability. Businesses embedded solely within co-ethnic markets may struggle to access diverse resources or compete in larger, more dynamic sectors.

To foster sustainable success, immigrant entrepreneurs must balance the advantages of cultural solidarity with deliberate efforts to engage broader institutional and market structures. This balance is essential for transforming sociocultural barriers into platforms for innovation, legitimacy and inclusion within the wider entrepreneurial ecosystem.

Harnessing ethnic networks for market access and workforce optimisation

Ethnic networks offer critical pathways for immigrant entrepreneurs to overcome barriers to market entry and workforce development. These networks provide immediate access to co-ethnic consumer markets, which often serve as incubators for new ventures by fostering trust, loyalty and a culturally familiar customer base (Aldrich & Waldinger, 1990; Bagwell, 2015). Entrepreneurs frequently employ branding strategies that emphasise cultural authenticity, using traditional food, design and services to create distinctive offerings that resonate with co-ethnic communities (Aliaga-Isla & Rialp, 2013; Bagwell, 2015). These strategies support early-stage business stability and help generate the revenue needed for future expansion (Chand & Ghorbani, 2011).

Ethnic enclaves provide concentrated hubs for culturally specific goods and services, including traditional foods, textiles and ceremonial products. Within these spaces, immigrant entrepreneurs can bypass certain restrictive institutional frameworks that often complicate mainstream market participation (Kloosterman & Rath, 2018; Waldinger et al., 1990). By leveraging the supportive infrastructure and consumer base within ethnic enclaves, entrepreneurs refine their operations and business models in an environment where trust and shared cultural norms reduce the risks associated with early-stage ventures. This approach allows for incremental scaling and creates a foundation for extending into broader markets over time (Drori et al., 2009).

In addition to facilitating market access, ethnic networks play a vital role in workforce development. Family members and co-ethnic employees often serve as a core workforce, providing culturally aligned, linguistically proficient and highly committed labour (Edwards et al., 2018; Ndofor & Priem, 2011). This arrangement reduces recruitment and training costs, lowers turnover and fosters operational cohesion. In the early stages of business development, access to a trusted and reliable labour pool can significantly enhance business resilience and efficiency (Battisti et al., 2014).

However, while reliance on co-ethnic labour offers short-term advantages, it may constrain innovation and adaptability over time. Sectors requiring diverse skill sets, specialised knowledge or broader market engagement may challenge the limits of insular workforce models (Chodavadia et al., 2024). To ensure long-term competitiveness, immigrant entrepreneurs must complement co-ethnic workforce strategies with broader recruitment approaches that embrace diversity across cultural, professional and demographic lines. Such integration not only supports innovation but also enhances adaptability within increasingly dynamic and heterogeneous market environments.

By balancing the strengths of ethnic networks with inclusive workforce and market strategies, immigrant entrepreneurs can address immediate systemic barriers while positioning their ventures for sustainable growth and integration into the wider host economy.

Entrepreneurial mobility across borders

Entrepreneurial mobility across borders enables immigrant entrepreneurs to navigate institutional and sociocultural barriers by leveraging connections between their countries of origin and settlement. Entrepreneurs engaged in transnational, diaspora and returnee entrepreneurship mobilise resources, knowledge and networks to sustain and scale their ventures across diverse economic and cultural contexts. This section examines two critical dimensions of transnational entrepreneurial activity: (i) addressing institutional barriers through transnational trade and integrated supply chains and (ii) overcoming sociocultural barriers through market innovation and global networking. By embedding themselves within multiple economic systems, these entrepreneurs develop adaptive business models that foster economic integration, expand market access and stimulate innovation.

Addressing institutional barriers through transnational trade and integrated supply chains

Transnational trade functions as a strategic mechanism through which transnational, diaspora and returnee entrepreneurs address institutional barriers, broaden market access and facilitate economic integration. Through dual embeddedness, these entrepreneurs draw on both home and host country resources to navigate regulatory inefficiencies, financial exclusions and limited market entry (Li et al., 2022). Transnational entrepreneurs engage in global commerce by sourcing, importing and exporting goods, often operating within established supply chains and under formal trade agreements (Drori et al., 2009; Duan et al., 2021).

Diaspora entrepreneurs cater to the cultural and consumer needs of ethnic communities while simultaneously integrating into mainstream markets and formal economic structures (Elo & Riddle, 2016; Syrett & Keles, 2022). Returnee entrepreneurs leverage capital, industrial experience and technical expertise acquired abroad to enhance domestic supply chains, expand production capacity and modernise local industries (Gruenhagen et al. 2020; Kassaye et al. 2025). These transnational engagements enable immigrant entrepreneurs to build resilient supply chains, optimise production processes and differentiate products in competitive markets (Li et al., 2022). Their capacity to bridge distinct economic environments, coordinate trade networks and apply multi-market expertise positions them as key facilitators of global commerce and innovation (Itzigsohn et al., 1999).

Beyond trade facilitation, the sustainability and competitiveness of these business models hinge on effective logistical coordination, regulatory compliance and cross-jurisdictional financial management. Transnational and diaspora entrepreneurs adeptly navigate trade regulations, customs procedures and taxation frameworks to maintain pricing competitiveness and ensure market stability (Drori et al., 2009; Elo & Riddle, 2016). Returnee entrepreneurs contribute to industrial upgrading in their countries of origin through technology transfer, infrastructure development and the localisation of production strategies (Gruenhagen et al., 2020). These strategies enhance economic interdependencies, promote bilateral trade and encourage knowledge exchange across entrepreneurial ecosystems.

The ability to adapt to trade-related complexities strengthens entrepreneurial agility, enabling immigrant entrepreneurs to respond proactively to regulatory changes, institutional disruptions and macroeconomic volatility (Li et al., 2022). Through logistical coordination, mobilisation of diaspora capital, expansion of transnational business linkages and revitalisation of domestic industries, immigrant entrepreneurs transform structural barriers into opportunities for sustainable transnational collaboration.

Overcoming sociocultural barriers through market innovation and global networking

Immigrant entrepreneurs, including transnational, diaspora and returnee entrepreneurs, address sociocultural barriers by leveraging market innovation and global networks. Their ability to operate across multiple cultural contexts enables them to blend cultural heritage with evolving market demands, thereby promoting economic inclusion and challenging dominant stereotypes (Drori et al., 2009; Gruenhagen et al., 2020; Syrett & Keles, 2022). Transnational entrepreneurs develop hybrid products and services tailored to diverse consumer preferences, creating culturally resonant branding and market-differentiated offerings that appeal to both niche and mainstream audiences (Vershinina et al., 2019).

Diaspora entrepreneurs maintain ethnic identity and community embeddedness while extending their ventures into broader economic systems (Elo & Riddle, 2016). Returnee entrepreneurs apply international experience to modernise traditional sectors, introduce global business practices and enhance domestic competitiveness (Gruenhagen et al., 2020; Kassaye et al., 2025). These activities enable immigrant entrepreneurs to bridge cultural divides, reposition heritage products for contemporary markets and foster cross-cultural exchange (Solano, 2021). For instance, immigrant-led enterprises in the beauty and culinary sectors often combine heritage-based practices with current consumer trends, thereby attracting both ethnic and non-ethnic clientele. As Light & Dana (2013) observe, such strategic adaptations not only challenge prevailing stereotypes but also generate brand credibility, market distinction and long-term sustainability.

To scale their businesses and sustain growth, immigrant entrepreneurs cultivate dynamic capabilities that enable them to repurpose resources, extend market reach and navigate institutional barriers. Strategic responsiveness, resource efficiency and the ability to recognise emerging opportunities enable them to navigate rapidly changing market conditions and societal challenges with agility (Wadhwa, 2012). Diaspora entrepreneurs frequently rely on community-based networks to strengthen business legitimacy, financial resilience and consumer confidence, particularly in contexts where systemic barriers limit access to institutional support (Brzozowski et al., 2022).

Transnational entrepreneurs utilise transnational mobility to enter multiple markets, attract international investment and reduce exposure to localised risk (Duan et al., 2021). Returnee entrepreneurs act as cultural and economic intermediaries by integrating foreign expertise, industrial knowledge and technological innovation into local business environments, thereby revitalising sectors such as agriculture, fashion and information technology (Gruenhagen et al., 2020). Through the transfer of expertise and the facilitation of cross-cultural collaboration, particularly in knowledge-intensive and creative industries, immigrant entrepreneurs enhance the cultural relevance of their products, confront stereotypical narratives and expand access to economic participation (Riddle et al., 2010).

By combining market innovation, international expertise and cultural capital, immigrant entrepreneurs reshape sectoral dynamics, contribute to inclusive economic development and position themselves as key agents in global entrepreneurial ecosystems.

Digital platforms and technological advancements

Digital platforms and technological advancements are transforming immigrant entrepreneurship by enabling market access and fostering resilience. This analysis highlights two key aspects: (i) digital market access for overcoming institutional and financial barriers and (ii) building innovation and resilience through digital knowledge networks. By expanding market reach and overcoming geographic and institutional barriers, these technologies empower immigrant entrepreneurs to scale operations, adapt to global markets and innovate. Collectively, digital tools drive inclusivity, enhance knowledge-sharing and unlock sustainable entrepreneurial opportunities.

Digital market access for overcoming institutional and financial barriers

Digital platforms have transformed the landscape of market access for immigrant entrepreneurs. By enabling participation beyond physical and cultural boundaries, these tools offer a means of circumventing traditional institutional gatekeeping. E-commerce platforms such as Etsy, eBay, Alibaba and Amazon provide low-barrier entry points for entrepreneurs to display and distribute products to diverse global audiences, thereby encouraging inclusive trade (Duan, 2022; Taherdoost, 2023). This form of digital inclusion is particularly salient for immigrant entrepreneurs who may lack access to conventional retail channels or face discrimination within mainstream markets.

Duan et al. (2020) argue that digital entrepreneurship offers alternative avenues for accessing customers, capital and legitimacy, while also introducing new risks such as overreliance on platform algorithms and unequal digital competencies. Similarly, Li & Wang (2025) note that digital technologies have become embedded within the entrepreneurial strategies of migrant founders, especially as they navigate structural exclusion and seek to establish legitimacy in transnational settings. Social media platforms such as Instagram and TikTok further support entrepreneurial growth by enabling brand visibility, consumer engagement and storytelling-based marketing strategies (Evansluong et al., 2019). These tools allow entrepreneurs to move beyond geographically concentrated ethnic markets and reach broader audiences, enabling business expansion despite traditional constraints.

In addition to market reach, digital platforms offer practical solutions for addressing financial exclusion. Crowdfunding and peer-to-peer lending platforms serve as alternative financing mechanisms, mitigating the barriers often associated with formal financial institutions such as collateral requirements and credit histories. These decentralised funding models support entrepreneurial growth by enabling investment in product development, marketing and operational expansion (Chaffey et al., 2009). Furthermore, the integration of digital tools supports data-driven decision-making, helping entrepreneurs monitor market trends, streamline logistics and respond flexibly to change. However, the effective use of such platforms requires sufficient digital infrastructure and skills, highlighting the importance of training initiatives that close digital literacy gaps (Sharma et al., 2016).

By adopting digital technologies strategically, immigrant entrepreneurs can mitigate structural disadvantages, enhance business adaptability and unlock opportunities for innovation and economic integration in competitive global markets.

Building innovation and resilience through digital knowledge networks

Digital platforms support immigrant entrepreneurs in fostering innovation and resilience by facilitating access to global knowledge systems and professional communities. Platforms such as LinkedIn, industry-specific forums and entrepreneurial networks connect individuals with experts across sectors, allowing for the exchange of regulatory updates, emerging market trends and innovative business strategies (Andrejuk, 2022). These networks move beyond localised support structures, offering global perspectives that equip entrepreneurs to navigate complex and rapidly evolving markets with greater confidence.

For example, immigrant entrepreneurs can use these platforms to stay informed about changes in legal frameworks, adopt international best practices and improve operational efficiency. This access to timely and context-specific knowledge allows them to remain competitive and responsive. As Evansluong et al. (2023) suggest, such tools help to bridge information gaps and ensure that entrepreneurs are well-prepared to address shifting market conditions while exploring opportunities for strategic growth.

Innovation thrives in digital environments where immigrant entrepreneurs can develop business models that integrate both online and offline components. Platforms that support such integration enable entrepreneurs to expand their product and service offerings, diversify income sources and align with changing consumer behaviours (Nambisan, 2017). For instance, Amazon combines digital retail infrastructure with physical outlets such as Whole Foods, while Shopify offers comprehensive solutions that support both e-commerce and in-person sales. These tools provide flexible pathways for business expansion and consumer engagement.

In addition, digital learning platforms and virtual training sessions offer tailored resources for developing technical and entrepreneurial skills. These educational tools enable entrepreneurs to update their knowledge, refine industry-specific capabilities and sustain relevance in competitive sectors (Dabić et al., 2020). By tailoring products and services to niche market demands, immigrant entrepreneurs can position themselves strategically and differentiate their businesses.

Digital platforms also play a critical role in strengthening resilience by providing tools for market monitoring, operational adaptation and risk mitigation. Real-time data analytics, customer feedback systems and supply chain technologies allow entrepreneurs to respond promptly to external shocks and shifting conditions (Evansluong et al., 2023). Through the strategic use of these digital resources, immigrant entrepreneurs are not only able to manage uncertainty but also to generate innovative responses that address diverse consumer needs. In doing so, they contribute to sustainable business growth and increased participation in global economic systems.

Supportive policies and programmes

Supportive policies and programmes play a crucial role in addressing systemic barriers for immigrant entrepreneurs. This analysis focuses on two key strategies: (i) facilitating institutional integration through startup visa programmes and (ii) enhancing equity with tax incentives and tailored training initiatives. By reducing entry barriers and providing targeted support, these measures enable immigrant entrepreneurs to establish and scale their ventures. Collectively, they promote institutional access, entrepreneurial inclusion and economic resilience, fostering equitable opportunities for growth and sustainable innovation.

Facilitating institutional integration through startup visa programmes

Startup visa programmes have emerged as a key policy instrument for reducing institutional barriers faced by immigrant entrepreneurs when launching and expanding their businesses. These initiatives streamline administrative processes such as residency acquisition and business registration while connecting entrepreneurs with critical resources including venture capital (VC), angel investors and incubators. By embedding immigrant entrepreneurs within national innovation ecosystems, startup visas help to address structural inefficiencies that often limit access to formal economic institutions. These programmes promote entrepreneurial dynamism and innovation by mitigating regulatory complexity and easing resource constraints (Lee & Glennon, 2023; Wadhwa, 2012).

Through participation in startup visa schemes, immigrant entrepreneurs gain access to networks that facilitate knowledge exchange, mentorship and investment opportunities. This institutional connectivity strengthens their capacity to scale operations and contribute to broader economic development goals. Furthermore, by lowering institutional entry barriers and integrating entrepreneurial talent into formal economic systems, these programmes enhance institutional inclusivity and contribute to economic resilience (Desiderio, 2014; Rath & Swagerman, 2016).

However, despite these advantages, many startup visa programmes prioritise high-growth, technology-driven sectors, which can inadvertently exclude entrepreneurs operating in traditional or small-scale industries. Sectors such as retail, cultural production and hospitality are frequently marginalised due to the emphasis on innovation as measured by capital intensity or scalability (Taddei & Solano, 2020). Research highlights the importance of inclusive entrepreneurship policies that address the needs of a broad range of industries, as such approaches are critical for building robust and diverse entrepreneurial ecosystems (Baycan-Levent & Nijkamp, 2009).

Additionally, these programmes often fail to consider the transnational character of immigrant entrepreneurship. Many immigrant ventures span borders, creating value through trade, investment flows and knowledge transfer. The omission of these transnational dynamics limits the potential of startup visa schemes to maximise economic returns (Moghaddam et al., 2018). Programme structures that are misaligned with the heterogeneous profiles of immigrant entrepreneurs may also restrict their contribution to regional economic development. Evidence suggests that sector-specific incentives and policy frameworks that align with regional development goals can support a more balanced entrepreneurial environment. This, in turn, fosters innovation across sectors and deepens integration within institutional frameworks (Baycan-Levent & Nijkamp, 2009; Rath & Schutjens, 2019).

Enhancing equity with tax incentives and tailored training initiatives

Tax incentives and grant programmes play a significant role in reducing financial barriers and supporting entrepreneurial development among immigrant founders. These fiscal interventions alleviate capital constraints, allowing entrepreneurs to expand their operations, invest in technological development and contribute to job creation (Beckers & Blumberg, 2013). By lowering initial costs, tax relief schemes provide a more secure foundation for business formation, particularly for entrepreneurs with limited financial capital. In addition, targeted grants and subsidies promote the uptake of innovative practices, thereby enhancing long-term competitiveness and business sustainability (Audretsch et al., 2020).

These financial measures also serve a broader inclusionary function by addressing systemic inequalities in access to economic resources. By supporting marginalised entrepreneurial groups, such initiatives strengthen the diversity and resilience of local economies. They create conditions in which immigrant entrepreneurs are better positioned to contribute meaningfully to economic growth and the evolution of regional entrepreneurial ecosystems (Portes & You, 2013).

Alongside financial measures, tailored training initiatives provide immigrant entrepreneurs with the knowledge and skills necessary to navigate complex regulatory environments and strengthen operational capacity. These programmes offer formal instruction on essential topics such as financial literacy, strategic planning and regulatory compliance (Andrejuk, 2022; Bhachu, 2017). In contrast to informal mentorship structures within co-ethnic networks, structured training ensures consistent and accessible support that can be delivered at scale.

Culturally responsive training frameworks further enhance the effectiveness of these programmes. By incorporating language support and contextualised learning, such initiatives address key barriers related to communication and cultural adaptation. As Volery (2007) observes, training that reflects participants' cultural contexts fosters deeper market understanding and reinforces entrepreneurial resilience. Programmes that integrate cultural awareness also improve inclusivity and broaden participation in the entrepreneurial ecosystem (Berry, 1997).

When aligned with financial supports, training initiatives help to overcome structural barriers and promote more equitable access to entrepreneurial opportunities. This combined approach not only supports individual business success but also contributes to broader goals of inclusive innovation and sustainable economic development (Portes & You, 2013; Rath & Schutjens, 2019). Together, these measures establish the foundations of a more inclusive, resilient and dynamic entrepreneurial landscape.

Scaling adaptive strategies for innovation-driven inclusion and economic integration

Building on adaptive strategies, this analysis examines how structured approaches strengthen long-term outcomes by promoting economic integration and fostering innovation. Immigrant entrepreneurs are increasingly transitioning from fragmented adaptation towards more formalised participation in mainstream economic systems. This progression is evident in two key approaches: social entrepreneurship initiatives that address societal needs while fostering inclusion and collaborative ventures that enable resource-sharing, cross-sector partnerships and broader market access. These strategies position immigrant entrepreneurs as pivotal actors in advancing sustainable innovation and systemic change.

Social entrepreneurship as a pathway to inclusive integration

Social entrepreneurship provides immigrant entrepreneurs with a strategic approach to overcoming sociocultural and institutional barriers, enabling them to address systemic inequities and foster inclusion. As Dees (1998) argues, social entrepreneurs prioritise the creation of social value through innovative solutions that respond to societal challenges rather than focusing solely on financial gain. Immigrant entrepreneurs apply these principles to confront language barriers, social exclusion and limited access to mainstream resources. These challenges are commonly encountered in transitional entrepreneurship contexts (Jones & Ram, 2021; Raimi et al., 2023). Many of these ventures are grounded in ethnic networks and cultural heritage, functioning as bridges to economic mobility and broader societal integration (Achidi Ndofor & Priem, 2011). Examples such as translation services, cross-cultural training and community-based healthcare demonstrate how social enterprises can simultaneously address unmet needs while operating as viable and sustainable business models.

Immigrant entrepreneurs also bring unique perspectives on the lived experiences of marginalised groups, enabling them to design culturally relevant solutions that build trust, challenge stereotypes and facilitate broader market inclusion (Kerr & Kerr, 2020). By aligning their social missions with policy support such as impact-oriented grants or culturally adaptive training programmes, immigrant-led social enterprises can expand operations and amplify their societal contributions (Rath & Swagerman, 2016). These ventures not only reduce exclusion but also strengthen social cohesion and promote long-term economic participation. In this way, social entrepreneurship serves as a transformative mechanism through which immigrant entrepreneurs drive innovation and contribute to more inclusive and integrated host societies.

Cross-sector collaboration for innovation and systemic change

Collaborative ventures between immigrant and native entrepreneurs offer a strategic approach to addressing institutional and sociocultural barriers, enabling immigrant-owned firms to participate more effectively in innovation ecosystems. These partnerships combine the transnational connections and cultural capital of immigrant entrepreneurs with the local expertise and institutional access of native counterparts. This synergy facilitates the navigation of complex regulatory environments, supports business legitimacy and expands access to diverse markets (Bolzani & Scandura, 2024). By promoting resource-sharing and collaborative problem-solving, such ventures enhance entrepreneurial adaptability and allow immigrant businesses to move beyond ethnic market confines and participate in wider economic systems (Kerr & Kerr, 2019).

These collaborations also strengthen the credibility and institutional visibility of immigrant entrepreneurs, helping to counteract the effects of stereotyping and social exclusion (Bagwell, 2015; Chand & Ghorbani, 2011). Engagement with mainstream business associations, innovation hubs and research institutions provides immigrant-owned firms with access to advanced knowledge and sector-specific resources that support their growth in competitive industries (Bolzani & Scandura, 2024; Scandura, 2016). These connections foster innovation and enhance competitiveness while contributing to broader systemic inclusion. Through collaborative ventures, immigrant entrepreneurs become integrated contributors to dynamic economic systems, advancing sustainable growth, institutional resilience and cross-cultural exchange.

Conclusion

This chapter has demonstrated that immigrant entrepreneurs are not merely responding to structural adversity but are actively reshaping their economic environments through adaptive strategies that foster innovation, inclusion and systemic engagement. Confronted with persistent barriers such as regulatory complexity, financial exclusion and sociocultural marginalisation, immigrant entrepreneurs mobilise embedded networks, cultivate transnational linkages and adopt digital infrastructures to navigate exclusion and pursue growth. These practices reveal a shift from fragmented, survival-oriented adaptation towards more formalised and future-facing participation in mainstream economies. Social enterprises and collaborative ventures with native actors have emerged as particularly effective in enhancing institutional visibility, expanding market access and addressing entrenched inequalities. While ethnic networks and informal strategies remain vital in early stages, long-term sustainability increasingly depends on access to inclusive financial systems, targeted policy support and innovation-driven ecosystems. Immigrant entrepreneurs should therefore be recognised not only as economic actors navigating constraint but as institutional contributors whose practices catalyse structural change and call for more nuanced, responsive and equitable policy frameworks.

References

Achidi Ndofor, H., & Priem, R. L. (2011). Immigrant entrepreneurs, the ethnic enclave strategy, and venture performance. *Journal of Management, 37*(3), 790–818. https://doi.org/10.1177/0149206309345020

Adserà, A., & Pytlikovà, M. (2015). The role of language in shaping international migration. *The Economic Journal, 125*(586), F49–F81. https://doi.org/10.1111/ecoj.12231

Aldrich, H., & Waldinger, R. (1990). Ethnicity and entrepreneurship. *Annual Review of Sociology, 16*, 111–135. https://doi.org/10.1146/annurev.so.16.080190.000551

Aliaga-Isla, R., & Rialp, A. (2013). Systematic review of immigrant entrepreneurship literature: Previous findings and ways forward. *Entrepreneurship & Regional Development, 25*(9–10), 819–844. https://doi.org/10.1080/08985626.2013.845694

Andrejuk, K. (2022). Pandemic transformations in migrant spaces: Migrant entrepreneurship between super-digitalisation and the new precarity. *Population, Space and Place, 28*(6), e2564. https://doi.org/10.1002/psp.2564

Audretsch, D., Colombelli, A., Grilli, L., Minola, T., & Rasmussen, E. (2020). Innovative start-ups and policy initiatives. *Research Policy, 49*(10), 104027. https://doi.org/10.1016/j.respol.2020.104027

Azmat, F. (2013). Opportunities or obstacles? Understanding the challenges for immigrant Female immigrant entrepreneurs. *International Journal of Gender and Entrepreneurship, 5*(2), 198–215. https://doi.org/10.1108/17566261311328855

Bagwell, S. (2015). Transnational entrepreneurship amongst Vietnamese communities in London. *Journal of Ethnic and Migration Studies, 41*(2), 329–349. https://doi.org/10.1080/1369183X.2014.907739

Barrett, A., & Duffy, D. (2008). Are Ireland's immigrants integrating into its labour market? *International Migration Review, 42*(3), 597–619. https://doi.org/10.1111/j.1747-7379.2008.00139.x

Barrett, G., Jones, T., & McEvoy, D. (1996). Ethnic minority business: Theoretical discourse in Britain and North America. *Urban Studies, 33*(4–5), 783–809. https://doi.org/10.1080/00420989650011825

Battisti, M., Jurado, T., & Perry, M. (2014). Understanding small-firm reactions to free trade agreements: Qualitative evidence from New Zealand. *Journal of Small Business and Enterprise Development, 21*(2), 327–344. https://doi.org/10.1108/JSBED-10-2013-0151

Battisti, M., Peri, G., & Romiti, A. (2022). Dynamic effects of co-ethnic networks on immigrants' economic success. *The Economic Journal, 132*(641), 58–88. https://doi.org/10.1093/ej/ueab036

Baycan-Levent, T., & Nijkamp, P. (2009). Characteristics of migrant entrepreneurship in Europe. *Entrepreneurship & Regional Development, 21*(4), 375–397. https://doi.org/10.1080/08985620903020060

Beckers, P., & Blumberg, B. F. (2013). Immigrant entrepreneurship on the move: A longitudinal analysis of first- and second-generation immigrant entrepreneurship in the Netherlands. *Entrepreneurship & Regional Development, 25*(7–8), 654–691. https://doi.org/10.1080/08985626.2013.808270

Berry, J. W. (1997). Immigration, acculturation, and adaptation. *Applied Psychology, 46*(1), 5–34. https://doi.org/10.1111/j.1464-0597.1997.tb01087.x

Bewaji, T., Yang, Q., & Han, Y. (2015). Funding accessibility for minority entrepreneurs: An empirical analysis. *Journal of Small Business and Enterprise Development, 22*(4), 716–733. https://doi.org/10.1108/JSBED-08-2012-0099

Bhachu, P. (2017). *Immigration and entrepreneurship: Culture, capital, and ethnic networks*. Routledge.

Bolzani, D., & Scandura, A. (2024). The role of collaboration networks for innovation in immigrant-owned new technology-based firms. *The Journal of Technology Transfer, 49*(4), 1203–1233. https://doi.org/10.1007/s10961-023-10035-9

Brieger, S. A., & Gielnik, M. M. (2021). Understanding the gender gap in immigrant entrepreneurship: A multi-country study of immigrants' embeddedness in economic, social, and institutional contexts. *Small Business Economics, 56*, 1007–1031. https://doi.org/10.1007/s11187-019-00314-x

Brzozowski, J., Šimić Banović, R., & Alpeza, M. (2022). Overcoming constraints to immigrant entrepreneurship in Croatia: The role of formal and informal institutions. *Post-Communist Economies, 34*(8), 1109–1136. https://doi.org/10.1080/14631377.2021.1928825

Chaffey, D., Ellis-Chadwick, F., & Mayer, R. (2009). *Internet marketing: Strategy, implementation and practice*. Pearson education.

Chand, M., & Ghorbani, M. (2011). National culture, networks, and ethnic entrepreneurship: A comparison of the Indian and Chinese immigrants in the US. *International Business Review, 20*(6), 593–606. https://doi.org/10.1016/j.ibusrev.2011.02.009

Chiswick, B. R., & Miller, P. W. (2002). Immigrant earnings: Language skills, linguistic concentrations, and the business cycle. *Journal of Population Economics, 15*, 31–57. https://doi.org/10.1007/PL00003838

Chodavadia, S. A., Kerr, S. P., Kerr, W. R., & Maiden, L. J. (2024). Immigrant entrepreneurship: New estimates and a research agenda. *NBER Working Paper No. 32400*. National Bureau of Economic Research. https://doi.org/10.3386/w32400

Collins, J. (2015). Migration, language diversity, and education policy: A contextualised analysis of inequality, risk, and state effects. *Policy Futures in Education, 13*(5), 577–595. https://doi.org/10.1177/1478210315581463

Collins, P. H. (1998). It's all in the family: Intersections of gender, race, and nation. *Hypatia, 13*(3), 62–82. https://doi.org/10.1111/j.1527-2001.1998.tb01370.x

Constant, A. F., Gataullina, L., & Zimmermann, K. F. (2009). Ethnosising immigrants. *Journal of Economic Behaviour & Organisation, 69*(3), 274–287. https://doi.org/10.1016/j.jebo.2008.10.005

Dabić, M., Vlačić, B., Paul, J., Dana, L. P., Sahasranamam, S., & Glinka, B. (2020). Immigrant entrepreneurship: A review and research agenda. *Journal of Business Research, 113*, 25–38. https://doi.org/10.1016/j.jbusres.2020.03.013

Daniel, E., Henley, A., & Anwar, M. N. (2019). Contemporary ethnic minority entrepreneurship in the UK: A quantitative exploration of break out and entrepreneurial quality. *International Journal of Entrepreneurial Behaviour & Research, 25*(7), 1410–1432. https://doi.org/10.1108/IJEBR-01-2019-0021

Dees, J. G. (1998). *The meaning of social entrepreneurship*. Kauffman Centre for Entrepreneurial Leadership.

Desiderio, M. V. (2014). *Policies to support immigrant entrepreneurship*. Migration Policy Institute and Transatlantic Council on Migration. https://www.migrationpolicy.org/sites/default/files/publications/TCM_Cities_Entrepreneurship-FINALWEB.pdf

Drori, I., Honig, B., & Wright, M. (2009). Transnational entrepreneurship: An emergent field of study. *Entrepreneurship Theory and Practice, 33*(5), 1001–1022. https://doi.org/10.1111/j.1540-6520.2009.00332.x

Duan, C. (2022). E-platform-enabled transnational e-entrepreneurship: Case studies of Chinese entrepreneurs in New Zealand. *International Journal of E-Entrepreneurship and Innovation (IJEEI), 12*(1), 1–16. https://doi.org/10.4018/IJEEI.290822

Duan, C., Kotey, B., & Sandhu, K. (2020). *Digital entrepreneurship for immigrants: Motivations, strategies, ecosystems, and performance*. In L. M. Camarinha-Matos, M. Boucher, & H. Afsarmanesh (Eds.), *Leadership, management, and adoption techniques for digital service innovation* (pp. 164–187). IGI Global. https://doi.org/10.4018/978-1-7998-2799-3.ch009

Duan, C., Kotey, B., & Sandhu, K. (2021). Transnational immigrant entrepreneurship: Effects of home-country entrepreneurial ecosystem factors. *International Journal of Entrepreneurial Behaviour & Research, 27*(3), 711–729. https://doi.org/10.1108/IJEBR-05-2020-0300

Dustmann, C., & Fabbri, F. (2003). Language proficiency and labour market performance of immigrants in the UK. *The Economic Journal, 113*(489), 695–717. https://doi.org/10.1111/1468-0297.t01-1-00151

Edwards, P., Ram, M., Jones, T., & Doldor, S. (2018). *New migrant businesses and their workers: Developing, but not transforming, the ethnic economy*. In *Intersectionality and ethnic entrepreneurship* (pp. 35–65). Routledge.

Elo, M., & Riddle, L. (2016). Understanding diaspora investment. In *Diaspora business* (pp. 13–28). Brill. https://doi.org/10.1163/9781848884038_003

Erel, U. (2010). Migrating cultural capital: Bourdieu in migration studies. *Sociology, 44*(4), 642–660. https://doi.org/10.1177/0038038510369363

Essers, C., & Benschop, Y. (2007). Enterprising identities: Female immigrant entrepreneurs of Moroccan or Turkish origin in the Netherlands. *Organisation Studies, 28*(1), 49–69. https://doi.org/10.1177/0170840606068256

Evansluong, Q., Grip, L., & Karayianni, E. (2023). Digital ethnicity affordances: From a liability to an asset in immigrant entrepreneurship. *International Journal of Entrepreneurial Behaviour & Research, ahead-of-print(ahead-of-print).* https://doi.org/10.1108/IJEBR-02-2022-0207

Evansluong, Q., Ramirez Pasillas, M., & Nguyen Bergström, H. (2019). From breaking-ice to breaking-out: Integration as an opportunity creation process. *International Journal of Entrepreneurial Behaviour & Research, 25*(5), 880–899. https://doi.org/10.1108/IJEBR-02-2018-0105

Gruenhagen, J. H., Davidsson, P., & Sawang, S. (2020). Returnee entrepreneurs: A systematic literature review, thematic analysis, and research agenda. *Foundations and Trends® in Entrepreneurship, 16*(4), 310–392. https://doi.org/10.1561/0300000096

Hamberger, A. (2009). Identity, integration, and citizenship. *Journal of Identity and Migration Studies, 3*(2), 2–21.

Heilbrunn, S. (2004). Impact of gender on difficulties faced by entrepreneurs. *The International Journal of Entrepreneurship and Innovation, 5*(3), 159–165. https://doi.org/10.5367/0000000041513420

Ibrahim, H. (2020). Structured savings and asset ownership: The role of rotating savings and credit associations among African immigrants in the United States. *Journal of Sociology & Social Welfare, 47*, 29.

Itzigsohn, J., Cabral, C. D., Medina, E. H., & Vazquez, O. (1999). Mapping Dominican transnationalism: Narrow and broad transnational practices. *Ethnic and Racial Studies, 22*(2), 316–339. https://doi.org/10.1080/014198799329503

Jones, T., & Ram, M. (2021). Immigrant entrepreneurship in world-historical perspective: A transitional phenomenon? In T. M. Cooney (Ed.), *The Palgrave handbook of minority entrepreneurship* (pp. 195–221). Palgrave Macmillan. https://doi.org/10.1007/978-3-030-66603-3_10

Jones, T., Ram, M., Edwards, P., Kiselinchev, A., & Muchenje, L. (2014). Mixed embeddedness and new migrant enterprise in the UK. *Entrepreneurship & Regional Development, 26*(5–6), 500–520. https://doi.org/10.1080/08985626.2014.950697

Kacar, S. O., Verduijn, K., & Essers, C. (2021). Opportunity structures from an intersectional perspective. In T. M. Cooney (Ed.), *The Palgrave handbook of minority entrepreneurship* (pp. 87–115). Palgrave Macmillan. https://doi.org/10.1007/978-3-030-66603-3_5

Kassaye, B. D., Bayiley, Y. T., & Alemu, Z. K. (2025). Returnee migrant entrepreneurship: A bibliometric analysis (1993–2024). *Journal of Global Entrepreneurship Research, 15*, 6. https://doi.org/10.1007/s40497-025-00422-x

Kerr, S. P., & Kerr, W. R. (2019). Immigrant networking and collaboration: Survey evidence from CIC. In K. Ganguli, S. Kahn, & M. MacGarvie (Eds.), *The roles of immigrants and foreign students in ^$. and science, innovation, and entrepreneurship* (Working Paper No. 25509). National Bureau of Economic Research. https://doi.org/10.3386/w25509

Kerr, S. P., & Kerr, W. R. (2020). Immigrant entrepreneurship in America: Evidence from the survey of business owners 2007 & 2012. *Research Policy, 49*(3), Article 103918. https://doi.org/10.1016/j.respol.2019.103918

Kloosterman, R. C. (2010). Matching opportunities with resources: A framework for analysing (migrant) entrepreneurship from a mixed embeddedness perspective. *Entrepreneurship and Regional Development, 22*(1), 25–45. https://doi.org/10.1080/08985620903220488

Kloosterman, R. C, & Rath, J. (2001). Immigrant entrepreneurs in advanced economies: Mixed embeddedness further explored. *Journal of Ethnic and Migration Studies, 27*(2), 189–201. https://doi.org/10.1080/13691830020041561

Kloosterman, R. C., & Rath, J. (2018). Mixed embeddedness revisited: A conclusion to the symposium. *Sociologica, 12*(2), 103–114.

Kloosterman, R. C, Van Der Leun, J., & Rath, J. (1999). Mixed embeddedness:(in) formal economic activities and immigrant businesses in the Netherlands. *International Journal of Urban and Regional Research, 23*(2), 252–266. https://doi.org/10.1111/1468-2427.00194

Lee, S. R., & Glennon, B. (2023). The effect of immigration policy on founding location choice: Evidence from Canada's start-up visa program (No. w31634). *National Bureau of Economic Research.* https://doi.org/10.3386/w31634

Li, H., Wang, M., & Zhang, R. (2022). Transnational network ties of returnee entrepreneurs and foreign market diversity. *Cross Cultural & Strategic Management, 29*(4), 824–845. https://doi.org/10.1108/CCSM-04-2021-0066

Li, Y., & Wang, C. (2025). Migrant entrepreneurship in the digital age. In L. P. Zhou & R. Skeldon (Eds.), *Handbook of Chinese migration to Europe* (pp. 405–424). Brill. https://doi.org/10.1163/9789004712140_016

Light, I. (2000). The ethnic economy. In *The Handbook of Economic Sociology* (pp. 354–650).

Light, I., & Dana, L. (2013). Boundaries of social capital in entrepreneurship. *Entrepreneurship Theory and Practice, 37*(3), 603–624. https://doi.org/10.1111/etap.12016

Lochmann, A., Rapoport, H., & Speciale, B. (2019). The effect of language training on immigrants' economic integration: Empirical evidence from France. *European Economic Review, 113*, 265–296. https://doi.org/10.1016/j.euroecorev.2019.01.008

Massey, D. S., Arango, J., Hugo, G., Kouaouci, A., Pellegrino, A., & Taylor, J. E. (1993). Theories of international migration: A review and appraisal. *Population and Development Review, 19*(3), 431–466. https://doi.org/10.2307/2938462

Moghaddam, K., Rustambekov, E., Weber, T., & Azarpanah, S. (2018). Transnational entrepreneurship, social networks, and institutional distance: Toward a theoretical framework. *New England Journal of Entrepreneurship, 21*(1), 45–65. https://doi.org/10.1108/NEJE-03-2018-0005

Morales, C., Holtschlag, C., Masuda, A. D., & Marquina, P. (2019). In which cultural contexts do individual values explain entrepreneurship? An integrative values framework using Schwartz's theories. *International Small Business Journal: Researching Entrepreneurship, 37*(3), 241–267. https://doi.org/10.1177/0266242618811890

Nambisan, S. (2017). Digital entrepreneurship: Toward a digital technology perspective of entrepreneurship. *Entrepreneurship Theory and Practice, 41*(6), 1029–1055. https://doi.org/10.1111/etap.12254

Ndofor, H. A., & Priem, R. L. (2011). Immigrant entrepreneurs, the ethnic enclave strategy, and venture performance. *Journal of Management, 37*(3), 790–818. https://doi.org/10.1177/0149206309345020

Nwankwo, S. (2005). Characterisation of Black African entrepreneurship in the UK: A pilot study. *Journal of Small Business and Enterprise Development, 12*(1), 120–136. https://doi.org/10.1108/14626000510579680

Ojo, S. (2012). Ethnic enclaves of diaspora entrepreneurs: A critical appraisal of Black British Africans' transnational entrepreneurship in London. *Journal of African Business, 13*(2), 145–156. https://doi.org/10.1080/15228916.2012.693446

Portes, A. (1995). *The economic sociology of immigration: Essays on networks, ethnicity, and entrepreneurship.* Russell Sage Foundation.

Portes, A., & Yiu, J. (2013). Entrepreneurship, transnationalism, and development. *Migration Studies, 1*(1), 75–95. https://doi.org/10.1093/migration/mns036

Portes, A., & Zhou, M. (1992). Gaining the upper hand: Economic mobility among immigrant and domestic minorities. *Ethnic and Racial Studies, 15*(4), 491–522. https://doi.org/10.1080/01419870.1992.9993761

Raimi, L., Panait, M., Gigauri, I., & Apostu, S. A. (2023). Thematic review of motivational factors, types of uncertainty, and entrepreneurship strategies of transitional entrepreneurship among ethnic minorities, immigrants, and female immigrant entrepreneurs. *Journal of Risk and Financial Management, 16*(2), 83. https://doi.org/10.3390/jrfm16020083

Ram, M., Jones, T., & Villares-Varela, M. (2017). Migrant entrepreneurship: Reflections on research and practice. *International Small Business Journal, 35*(1), 3–18. https://doi.org/10.1177/0266242616678051

Ram, M., & Smallbone, D. (2002). Ethnic minority business policy in the era of the small business service. *Environment and Planning C: Government and Policy, 20*(2), 235–249. https://doi.org/10.1068/c0050

Rath, J., & Schutjens, V. (2019). Advancing the frontiers in ethnic entrepreneurship studies. *Tijdschrift voor Economische en Sociale Geografie, 110*(5), 579–587. https://doi.org/10.1111/tesg.12398

Rath, J., & Swagerman, A. (2016). Promoting ethnic entrepreneurship in European cities: Sometimes ambitious, mostly absent, rarely addressing structural features. *International Migration, 54*(1), 152–166. https://doi.org/10.1111/imig.12215

Saxenian, A. (2002). Silicon Valley's new immigrant high-growth entrepreneurs. *Economic Development Quarterly, 16*(1), 20–31. https://doi.org/10.1177/0891242402016001003

Scandura, A. (2016). University–industry collaboration and firms' R&D effort. *Research Policy, 45*(9), 1907–1922. https://doi.org/10.1016/j.respol.2016.06.009

Sharma, R., Fantin, A. R., Prabhu, N., Guan, C., & Dattakumar, A. (2016). Digital literacy and knowledge societies: A grounded theory investigation of sustainable development. *Telecommunications Policy, 40*(7), 628–643. https://doi.org/10.1016/j.telpol.2016.05.003

Solano, G. (2021). The mixed embeddedness of transnational migrant entrepreneurs: Moroccans in Amsterdam and Milan. In *Diaspora governance and transnational entrepreneurship* (pp. 109–127). Routledge.

Stephan, U., & Pathak, S. (2016). Beyond cultural values? Cultural leadership ideals and entrepreneurship. *Journal of Business Venturing, 31*(5), 505–523. https://doi.org/10.1016/j.jbusvent.2016.07.003

Syrett, S., & Keles, J. Y. (2022). A contextual understanding of diaspora entrepreneurship: Identity, opportunity, and resources in the Sri Lankan Tamil and Kurdish diasporas. *International Journal of Entrepreneurial Behaviour & Research, 28*(9), 376–404. https://doi.org/10.1108/IJEBR-08-2021-0658

Taddei, L., & Solano, G. (2020). Immigrant entrepreneurship in Europe: A comparative analysis of trends in the member states of the European Union. In Centro Studi e Ricerche IDOS (Ed.), *Report on immigration and entrepreneurship 2019–2020* (pp. 7–17). IDOS.

Taherdoost, H. (2023). *E-Business essentials.* Springer Nature Switzerland.

Vershinina, N., Rodgers, P., McAdam, M., & Clinton, E. (2019). Transnational migrant entrepreneurship, gender, and family business. *Global Networks, 19*, 238–260. https://doi.org/10.1111/glob.12225

Vertovec, S. (2007). Super-diversity and its implications. *Ethnic and Racial Studies, 30*(6), 1024–1054. https://doi.org/10.1080/01419870701599465

Volery, T. (2007). Ethnic entrepreneurship: A theoretical framework. In *Handbook of Research on Ethnic Minority Entrepreneurship* (pp. 30–41). Edward Elgar Publishing. https://doi.org/10.4337/9781847209962.00009

Wadhwa, V. (2012). *The immigrant exodus: Why America is losing the global race to capture entrepreneurial talent.* University of Pennsylvania Press.

Waldinger, R., Aldrich, H., & Ward, R. (1990). *Ethnic entrepreneurs: Immigrant business in industrial societies.* SAGE Publications.

Waldinger, R., & Lichter, M. I. (2003). *How the other half works: Immigration and the social organization of labour*. University of California Press. https://doi.org/10.1525/9780520936171

PART II

Case studies of immigrant entrepreneurship in global contexts

4

IMMIGRANT ENTREPRENEURSHIP IN NORTH AMERICA

Identity, innovation and institutional engagement across urban contexts

Introduction

Immigrant entrepreneurship has become a defining feature of North America's economic landscape, contributing to innovation, employment generation and the revitalisation of both urban centres and peripheral communities. Immigrant entrepreneurs play a central role in responding to labour market shifts, fostering inclusive growth and building community resilience through enterprise (Azoulay et al., 2022; Business Development Bank of Canada [BDC], 2024). While the United States (U.S.) and Canada are both prominent destinations for immigrant entrepreneurs, they differ significantly in institutional and policy frameworks. In the U.S., immigrant-founded companies accounted for 46% of Fortune 500 firms in 2023, generating over $8.6 trillion in revenue (American Immigration Council [AIC], 2024). Immigrants also launched nearly one in five new businesses that year despite comprising just 14% of the population (Azoulay et al., 2022; Tremper, 2024). In contrast, Canada offers targeted policies such as the Start-Up Visa and entrepreneurship support programmes that enable smoother integration into the business ecosystem (BDC, 2024; Lee & Glennon, 2023). These national contrasts underscore the need for a comparative analysis of how immigrant entrepreneurs operate within distinct regulatory and institutional environments.

Despite growing scholarly attention, immigrant entrepreneurship research in North America remains conceptually fragmented. Much of the literature privileges structural and policy-driven explanations, often overlooking how entrepreneurs mobilise identity, social capital and transnational networks to navigate exclusion and uncertainty (Aliaga-Isla & Rialp, 2013; Dheer, 2018). The mixed embeddedness framework (MEF) developed by Kloosterman and colleagues (1999) remains foundational to the field, yet its limited engagement with identity, intersectionality and agency has been widely noted (Dabić et al., 2020). In response, more recent research reconceptualises immigrant entrepreneurship as a socially embedded and negotiated process, shaped by cultural recognition, systemic inequality and relational identity dynamics (Fernández-Kelly & Konczal, 2005; Romero & Valdez, 2016; Zhou, 2004). These perspectives are particularly relevant in a North American context, where the absence of a dedicated U.S. startup visa contrasts sharply with Canada's more coordinated and sector-sensitive support infrastructure

DOI: 10.4324/9781003605072-6

(Kerr & Kerr, 2021; Canadian Federation of Independent Business [CFIB], 2025; Chand & Tung, 2019; United States Citizenship and Immigration Services [USCIS], 2024). These divergences call for an analytical framework that emphasises identity construction, strategic agency and informal institutional engagement.

Building on Chapter 2, this chapter applies a reconceptualised mixed embeddedness framework (RMEF) to show how intersectional identity, social practice and translocal agency underpin immigrant entrepreneurial strategies across diverse urban and policy environments. Drawing on secondary case study material, it examines how immigrant entrepreneurs negotiate identity, engage institutions and mobilise transnational resources to navigate structural constraints. Entrepreneurship is conceptualised as both shaped by systemic conditions and strategically enacted through identity, social capital and diasporic linkages (Light & Dana, 2013; Romero & Valdez, 2016). The framework clarifies how entrepreneurial practices emerge through the interaction of migration regimes, spatial inequalities and multilevel governance structures, aligning with insights from comparative urban policy research (Desiderio, 2014). In the North American context, where national immigration systems intersect with local entrepreneurial ecosystems, the framework provides a critical lens for understanding how immigrant entrepreneurs adapt to and transform their socio-economic environments.

To demonstrate the analytical value of the RMEF, this chapter draws on secondary case studies from Silicon Valley, New York City, Toronto and Vancouver. These cities were selected for their diverse entrepreneurial ecologies, transnational linkages and strategic roles within national innovation systems. Silicon Valley represents a high-capital innovation economy shaped by restrictive immigration policy and intense resource competition (Basu & Virick, 2015; Saxenian, 2006). New York City exemplifies a super-diverse entrepreneurial landscape where informal networks and community infrastructure are central to resilience (Kim & Chandrasekhar, 2024; Morawska, 2004; Rahman et al., 2021). In Canada, Toronto reflects a policy-enabled ecosystem supported by place-based institutions (George et al., 2024; Zhuang, 2021), while Vancouver reveals Pacific-facing dynamics shaped by diasporic capital and spatial restructuring (Golob & Giles, 2017; Li et al., 2016; Teixeira & Salinas, 2024).

The chapter proceeds as follows. It begins with an analysis of immigrant entrepreneurship in the U.S., focusing on the contrasting urban contexts of Silicon Valley and New York City. This is followed by the Canadian cases of Toronto and Vancouver. Then, a comparative section synthesises key differences and shared challenges across the national and city scales. The penultimate section outlines targeted policy interventions, and the chapter concludes with a reflection on the theoretical contributions of the RMEF and implications for future research.

The United States

Silicon Valley's success: how immigrant entrepreneurs drive global tech innovation

Located in Northern California, Silicon Valley has emerged as a global centre for technological innovation, with immigrant entrepreneurs playing a central role in the region's development. Founders from diverse backgrounds have contributed to the formation of its entrepreneurial ecosystem by bringing technical expertise, global networks and cultural perspectives that drive innovation and firm creation (Chodavadia et al., 2024; Saxenian, 2002, 2006). Immigrant entrepreneurship has become a defining feature of the region's economic landscape, embedded in transnational flows of capital, knowledge and people. Despite widespread narratives of meritocracy, access to opportunity within Silicon Valley remains uneven, shaped by broader structural hierarchies common to high-tech economies (Nee & Drouhot, 2020). This study examines the experiences of Indian, Israeli and Korean American female immigrant entrepreneurs, highlighting how they contribute to and reshape one of the world's most competitive and unequal innovation environments.

The glass walls of Silicon Valley: barriers facing immigrant entrepreneurs

Structural exclusion continues to shape entrepreneurial outcomes in Silicon Valley, where immigrant founders often struggle to access capital, institutional support and elite networks. Despite their documented contributions to innovation, many remain sidelined due to implicit biases that favour culturally familiar, native-born entrepreneurs (Azoulay et al., 2022; Kerr & Kerr, 2019; Saxenian, 2006). Indian entrepreneurs, although frequently entering the technology economy with strong technical expertise, face disadvantages when they lack elite educational credentials or insider access to venture capital (VC) communities (Saxenian & Edulbehram, 1998; Varma, 2024; Wadhwa et al., 2007). Israeli founders, with backgrounds in cybersecurity and artificial intelligence, encounter scepticism from investors unfamiliar with Israel's military-industrial innovation ecosystem (Gold, 2018; Saxenian, 2000, 2006). Korean American female entrepreneurs confront multiple barriers related to race, gender and institutional positioning that marginalise them within a VC sector that remains predominantly male (Chen & Lee, 2024; Lee & Lee, 2020). These forms of exclusion not only constrain individual trajectories but also hinder the broader diversification of Silicon Valley's innovation landscape.

Institutional and immigration frameworks further embed inequities by restricting mobility and complicating access to formal entrepreneurial pathways. For Indian entrepreneurs, the H-1B visa system imposes structural barriers by tying skilled professionals to specific employers, creating legal and financial risks that often delay or deter entrepreneurial transitions (Saxenian, 2000; Varma, 2020, 2022). While Israeli entrepreneurs may arrive under more flexible visa arrangements, they encounter regulatory complexity when registering businesses, accessing transnational markets or complying with foreign ownership regulations (Gold, 2018; Saxenian, 2006). For Korean American women, immigration status is less often a direct barrier due to their citizenship or permanent residency. However, they face institutional neglect in entrepreneurial support systems, where the intersection of race and gender is insufficiently addressed. As a result, many lack access to mentorship, capital readiness programmes or public funding initiatives (Chen & Lee, 2024; Lee & Lee, 2020). Across these cases, structural frameworks reinforce unequal access to opportunity, though the mechanisms of exclusion vary.

Financial exclusion remains one of the most enduring challenges for immigrant entrepreneurs. Indian founders often depend on informal capital such as family loans, personal savings or co-ethnic investor networks, which rarely provide the scale or strategic support necessary for growth in high-technology sectors (Basu & Virick, 2015; Saxenian, 2002; Varma, 2024). Israeli entrepreneurs benefit from robust innovation networks based in Israel but still face hesitation from U.S.-based investors unfamiliar with their technological frameworks (Gold, 2018; Saxenian, 2006). Korean American women encounter even greater obstacles, as their experiences are shaped by intersecting exclusions that restrict access to investment and leadership networks (Chen & Lee, 2024). As of 2020, women-led startups received only 2.3% of VC funding in the U.S., highlighting the structural imbalances in the entrepreneurial finance system (Bittner & Lau, 2021). These patterns point to the need for a reimagined funding infrastructure that reflects the diversity of entrepreneurial pathways within Silicon Valley.

Breaking the silicon ceiling: strategies of resilient immigrant entrepreneurs

In response to persistent structural barriers, immigrant entrepreneurs develop adaptive strategies that mobilise transnational and community-based resources to establish competitive ventures. Indian entrepreneurs frequently rely on co-ethnic mentorship networks that facilitate knowledge exchange, practical training and peer-based access to investment opportunities not typically available through formal VC channels (Basu & Virick, 2015; Saxenian, 2002; Varma, 2011). Israeli founders, supported by integrated professional and academic networks, benefit from Israel's alignment of state-sponsored innovation and private capital, which enables them to develop proof-of-concept technologies before entering U.S. markets (Gold, 2018; Saxenian, 2006). Korean American female entrepreneurs turn to community-rooted financial practices such as rotating savings and credit associations (ROSCAs) and informal cooperative models, building resilience and preserving ownership autonomy amidst exclusion from institutional finance (Chen & Lee, 2024; Lee & Lee, 2020). These collective strategies exemplify embedded entrepreneurial agency, allowing founders to circumvent formal constraints by cultivating parallel infrastructures for support and growth.

Another layer of resilience is found in the ways immigrant entrepreneurs harness transnational networks to secure technical expertise, labour flexibility and access to alternative markets. Indian founders increasingly collaborate with India's expanding technology sector, outsourcing development tasks to cost-effective teams while retaining managerial and intellectual property control in the U.S. (Saxenian, 2006; Varma, 2011). Israeli entrepreneurs similarly embed transnational capabilities into their ventures by leveraging Israel's cybersecurity and artificial intelligence (AI) expertise, often cultivated through elite military training to attract transnational investment and form strategic partnerships (Gold, 2018; Saxenian, 2000). Korean American female entrepreneurs utilise their bicultural fluency to design products and services that resonate with trans-Pacific consumer trends, particularly between the U.S. and South Korea (Chen & Lee, 2024). These globally integrated strategies enable immigrant founders to transform cultural and national affiliations into forms of entrepreneurial capital, thereby establishing sustainable positions in highly competitive sectors.

Collective advocacy and institutional engagement have also emerged as critical strategies through which immigrant entrepreneurs challenge exclusionary systems and reshape access to opportunity. Indian entrepreneurs increasingly use professional organisations and public-facing platforms to advocate for policy reforms, including founder visas and more inclusive capital frameworks, leveraging their growing influence in the technology sector to shape policy debates (Chodavadia et al., 2024; Varma, 2024; Wadhwa et al., 2007). Israeli entrepreneurs contribute to the U.S. innovation ecosystem by exporting technologies that address both commercial and national priorities, thereby fostering institutional legitimacy and long-term strategic partnerships (Gold, 2018; Saxenian, 2006). Korean American female entrepreneurs have emerged as visible advocates for gender and racial equity in startup funding, contributing to research, public dialogue and industry reforms that aim to dismantle systemic exclusion (Chen & Lee, 2024; Lee & Lee, 2020). Through these collective efforts, immigrant entrepreneurs not only improve their individual prospects but also catalyse broader transformation within Silicon Valley's entrepreneurial infrastructure, challenging exclusionary norms and expanding institutional access.

New York City's economy: immigrant diversity and enterprise in a global financial capital

New York City's status as a global economic and cultural centre is strongly shaped by the contributions of immigrant entrepreneurs across a wide range of industries. These actors play a central role in maintaining the city's economic vitality, often establishing businesses that serve both co-ethnic and cross-cultural markets while reflecting broader dynamics of global migration and urban change (Morawska, 2004; You & Zhou, 2019). Their entrepreneurial activities are embedded in transnational ties, community-based infrastructures and bicultural knowledge, and they contribute not only to economic growth but also to the city's cultural and civic life (Chen, 2021; Kim, 2001). Immigrant entrepreneurship has become a key driver of innovation and resilience within New York's fast-evolving urban economy. This study examines the experiences of Chinese, Korean, Bangladeshi and African female immigrant entrepreneurs, focusing on their roles in shaping local markets, sustaining community economies and contributing to the city's identity as an inclusive and globally competitive entrepreneurial ecosystem.

The concrete maze of New York City: barriers to success for immigrant entrepreneurs

Navigating the entrepreneurial landscape in New York City presents systemic challenges that often constrain immigrant entrepreneurs' ability to launch and sustain successful ventures. Access to capital remains a central obstacle, with stringent financial criteria such as high credit scores, documented income and substantial collateral frequently excluding immigrant founders from traditional funding avenues (Savazzi et al., 2020; Waldinger, 1989). African female entrepreneurs working in personal care and fashion industries often depend on informal savings groups and community-based lending systems. While these provide crucial early support, they typically lack the scale and sustainability required for long-term growth (Oloke & Halkias, 2020). Bangladeshi entrepreneurs face similar limitations, where restricted financial access undermines their capacity to innovate, scale or compete effectively (Rahman et al., 2021). Korean entrepreneurs encounter institutional reluctance to fund culturally specific enterprises that do not align with conventional financial norms or market expectations (Kim, 2020; Yoo, 2014). Chinese entrepreneurs often rely on personal savings and informal lending due to limited credit access, which inhibits business expansion and long-term viability (You & Zhou, 2019). In the absence of scalable financial support, many immigrant ventures remain small and vulnerable to broader systemic barriers, particularly those imposed by regulatory frameworks.

Regulatory structures further entrench financial exclusion, intensifying marginalisation for immigrant entrepreneurs across sectors. African female founders in healthcare and technology face prohibitive licensing fees, bureaucratic delays and cumbersome approval processes that stifle competitiveness (Davidson et al., 2010). Chinese entrepreneurs contend with heightened scrutiny concerning labour regulations and zoning compliance, increasing operational costs and limiting growth (Kim & Chandrasekhar, 2024; You & Zhou, 2019). Korean entrepreneurs in manufacturing and retail struggle to meet exacting product safety and labelling requirements, which obstruct access to broader markets (Kim, 2020). Bangladeshi founders frequently operate with minimal institutional support in navigating complex legal environments, rendering them especially vulnerable to penalties and closures (Rahman et al., 2021). Although framed as neutral governance mechanisms, such regulatory systems often encode institutional biases that favour established, native-born enterprises. Dheer (2018) highlights how limited access to legal resources and institutional advocacy leaves immigrant entrepreneurs poorly equipped to meet regulatory expectations. As a result, these frameworks reproduce structural inequities, stratify opportunity and deepen the socio-economic marginalisation of immigrant communities.

Language and cultural barriers add a further layer of disadvantage by shaping how immigrant entrepreneurs interact with markets, networks and institutions. Access to mentorship and professional development programmes is often limited for African female and Bangladeshi entrepreneurs, restricting their ability to build market knowledge and acquire strategic resources (Oloke & Halkias, 2020; Rahman et al., 2021). Korean entrepreneurs, while embedded in strong co-ethnic networks, may struggle to engage wider consumer audiences unfamiliar with their cultural products or branding narratives (Kim, 2020). Chinese entrepreneurs face similar constraints, where language and cultural perceptions can hamper communication with clients and broader professional communities (You & Zhou, 2019). Although ethnic networks provide vital early-stage support, they may also constrain broader integration by anchoring businesses within niche market spaces (Yoo, 2014). These cultural and linguistic gaps frequently result in misrecognition, miscommunication and exclusion from key entrepreneurial ecosystems (Brinkerhoff, 2016). Such challenges are not simply individual deficits, but manifestations of a system that privileges dominant cultural norms and institutional familiarity. Consequently, immigrant entrepreneurs must navigate intersecting forms of disadvantage while striving to maintain cultural identity and achieve economic sustainability in a structurally unequal environment.

Breaking through the concrete maze: strategies for immigrant entrepreneurial success in New York City

In response to systemic barriers, immigrant entrepreneurs in New York City, particularly those from African, Bangladeshi, Chinese and Korean backgrounds, have developed innovative strategies to achieve business success. One critical approach involves leveraging transnational networks to access resources, talent and market opportunities. African female entrepreneurs in personal care and fashion industries draw on these networks to source affordable materials, blending traditional aesthetics with contemporary trends to attract both niche and mainstream consumers (Oloke & Halkias, 2020). Bangladeshi entrepreneurs engage international partners to access market intelligence on emerging trends and shifting consumer behaviours, enabling them to refine their business models (Rahman et al., 2021). Chinese entrepreneurs in e-commerce rely on global supply chains and digital platforms to streamline operations, reduce costs and extend their market reach in an increasingly digitised economy (You & Zhou, 2019). Korean entrepreneurs use transnational ties to import unique products and specialised equipment, allowing them to offer distinct goods and services tailored to diverse consumer preferences (Kim, 2020). By fostering international collaborations and optimising global resources, these immigrant entrepreneurs not only overcome localised constraints but also contribute meaningfully to urban economic dynamism.

Alongside global linkages, local community-based collaboration within ethnic enclaves serves as a cornerstone of entrepreneurial resilience, offering essential support for adaptation and continuity. Chinese entrepreneurs, for instance, drew upon co-ethnic labour and resources during the COVID-19 pandemic to accelerate digital transformation, adopting e-commerce platforms and contactless payment systems to sustain business operations and foster post-pandemic resilience (Kim & Chandrasekhar, 2024). Bangladeshi entrepreneurs rely on close-knit community networks for mentorship, shared resources and informal credit systems that support business establishment and scaling (Rahman et al., 2021). Korean entrepreneurs benefit from joint marketing efforts and peer-to-peer knowledge sharing, fostering collective innovation and improving market access (Yoo, 2014). African female entrepreneurs collaborate on shared retail ventures and bulk purchasing schemes, reducing operational costs and enhancing their market leverage (Davidson et al., 2010; Oloke & Halkias, 2020). These communal strategies not only help immigrant communities navigate systemic challenges but also reinforce the social and economic infrastructure of immigrant enclaves. However, while ethnic networks provide essential early-stage support, they are not, in themselves, sufficient for long-term scalability or integration into broader markets.

To move beyond niche sectors and scale their ventures, immigrant entrepreneurs increasingly adopt cultural branding and mentorship as strategic pathways to mainstream economic participation. African female entrepreneurs integrate cultural heritage with contemporary aesthetics to develop products that appeal to diverse consumer bases (Oloke & Halkias, 2020). Bangladeshi entrepreneurs participate in mentorship programmes and adaptive learning initiatives that enable them to access transnational networks, navigate complex regulatory systems and secure alternative funding (Rahman et al., 2021). Chinese entrepreneurs employ cultural branding to position their products as both distinctive and accessible, reaching a wide audience that spans ethnic boundaries (You & Zhou, 2019). Korean entrepreneurs draw upon bicultural fluency to operate effectively across both U.S. and South Korean markets, combining authenticity with innovation to maintain a competitive edge (Yoo, 2014). This dual-market strategy is supported by the global expansion of Korean banking, which provides tailored financial infrastructure that reinforces entrepreneurial success in the U.S. (Nopper, 2009). Through continuous adaptation, strategic positioning and global connectivity, immigrant entrepreneurs both respond to systemic inequities and reinforce New York City's status as a global centre of diversity and enterprise.

Canada

Toronto's mosaic economy: immigrant entrepreneurs shaping a global hub of diversity and innovation

Immigrant entrepreneurs are integral to Toronto's economic and cultural landscape, contributing to the transformation of communities across the city's diverse neighbourhoods. Their businesses play a vital role in supporting economic growth, cultural plurality and neighbourhood renewal, particularly in sectors such as food services, retail and e-commerce (George et al., 2024; Hackworth & Rekers, 2005; Machado et al., 2021). These enterprises are embedded in transnational networks, social infrastructures and context-based practices that reflect the broader dynamics of mobility and urban change (Chand & Tung, 2019; Kariv et al., 2009). Immigrant entrepreneurship is increasingly visible in areas undergoing demographic or economic transition, where it contributes to local vitality and community resilience (Zhuang, 2021). This study focuses on the experiences of Chinese, Bangladeshi and Brazilian female immigrant entrepreneurs, exploring their roles within Toronto's evolving entrepreneurial landscape.

Behind Toronto's open doors: the barriers for immigrant entrepreneurs

Despite their substantial contributions to the local economy, immigrant entrepreneurs in Toronto continue to face persistent financial barriers that constrain their ability to scale and sustain their businesses (Wang, 1999; Zhuang & Chen, 2017). Canadian financial institutions often impose rigid credit requirements that disadvantage newcomers who lack conventional credit histories or sufficient collateral. Chinese entrepreneurs in suburban areas frequently encounter difficulties in securing formal loans to upgrade operations or diversify product lines, leaving them vulnerable to competition from larger firms (Hackworth & Rekers, 2005; Zhuang, 2021). Bangladeshi entrepreneurs, many of whom run family-operated ventures, rely on informal community-based lending systems that offer essential early-stage financing but limit scalability and future planning (Rahman, 2018). Brazilian female entrepreneurs, particularly those in service-oriented sectors, face the dual challenge of gender bias and financial exclusion, often struggling to access formal credit and institutional support (Machado et al., 2021, 2023). While initiatives such as those offered by the BDC provide grants and loans targeting immigrant entrepreneurs (BDC, n.d.), outreach and accessibility remain limited. These financial and gendered constraints reinforce systemic inequalities, restricting immigrant entrepreneurs' competitiveness within Toronto's broader entrepreneurial ecosystem.

In addition to financial exclusion, immigrant entrepreneurs must navigate complex regulatory systems and spatial pressures that inhibit business development. Licensing, compliance and zoning requirements are often particularly onerous for small enterprises rooted in cultural practices or informal economies. Chinese entrepreneurs report difficulties with restrictive zoning regulations in suburban commercial zones, resulting in higher overhead costs and heightened scrutiny (Zhuang, 2021). Bangladeshi business owners, especially in grocery and textile retail, encounter opaque permitting processes and inconsistent enforcement, which disrupt operational continuity (Rahman, 2018). Brazilian female entrepreneurs, particularly in the service sector, face administrative burdens, linguistic barriers and high regulatory expectations when dealing with municipal authorities (Machado et al., 2021). These challenges are compounded by the effects of gentrification in neighbourhoods such as Scarborough and North York, where rising rents and redevelopment displace long-established, community-rooted businesses (Wang & Lo, 2000; Zhuang & Chen, 2017). As immigrant entrepreneurs lose access to stable commercial spaces and local clientele, they face increased precarity. In this context, regulatory complexity and spatial marginalisation intersect to constrain the continuity and sustainability of immigrant-led enterprises.

Cultural and linguistic barriers further inhibit immigrant entrepreneurs' ability to engage with mainstream markets and business networks. Chinese entrepreneurs are often perceived as catering exclusively to co-ethnic consumers, limiting their visibility and access to broader customer bases (Zhuang, 2015, 2021). Bangladeshi entrepreneurs may lack marketing capacity or English-language proficiency, restricting their ability to reach audiences beyond ethnic enclaves (Rahman, 2018). Brazilian female entrepreneurs frequently encounter cultural stereotypes and gendered assumptions that undermine their perceived professionalism, especially when operating in service-based industries (Machado et al., 2021, 2023). These constraints are compounded by limited access to formal mentorship programmes and professional networks, which are essential for navigating Toronto's competitive business environment. While organisations such as the MaRS Discovery District offer targeted incubation, mentorship and development services, uptake varies significantly across geographic, cultural and linguistic lines. Entrepreneurs from Bangladeshi, Chinese and Brazilian backgrounds have accessed these supports to expand their networks and diversify their clientele (Machado et al., 2021; Rahman, 2018; Zhuang, 2021), yet persistent disparities in access continue to reinforce inequalities in visibility, resources and growth.

Unlocking the potential of Toronto's open doors: overcoming barriers through adaptability and innovation

In response to structural barriers, immigrant entrepreneurs in Toronto draw upon transnational networks, cultural capital and global supply chains to navigate structural exclusion. Bangladeshi entrepreneurs frequently source products from South Asia, addressing cultural market gaps while building cost-efficient retail models (Rahman, 2018). Chinese entrepreneurs, particularly those from second-generation backgrounds, leverage global trade connections to import niche goods and integrate digital platforms into their operations (Zhuang, 2021). Brazilian female entrepreneurs in service sectors such as beauty and fashion maintain transnational ties by importing speciality products and adapting global trends to appeal to local consumer tastes (Machado et al., 2021, 2023). These strategies enable immigrant entrepreneurs to differentiate their offerings and expand beyond ethnically defined markets. They also exemplify embedded transnationalism, wherein local businesses operate within broader global economic and cultural flows. By blending traditional practices with contemporary technologies and international sourcing, immigrant entrepreneurs contribute to the transformation of Toronto's retail and service sectors, demonstrating resilience through innovation and redefining urban entrepreneurship in a multicultural context.

Community-based collaboration remains a cornerstone of immigrant entrepreneurial success, particularly in response to institutional and financial exclusion. Chinese entrepreneurs in suburban retail areas frequently engage in cooperative strategies such as pooled purchasing, informal mentorship and resource sharing to reduce operational costs and enhance business resilience (Golob & Giles, 2017; Zhuang & Chen, 2017). Bangladeshi entrepreneurs draw on kinship labour, informal knowledge networks and religious community spaces to navigate logistical and marketing challenges (Rahman, 2018). Brazilian female entrepreneurs establish diasporic support systems, particularly in the beauty and food industries, where they share clients, offer informal training and co-organise cultural events to increase visibility (Machado et al., 2021). These collaborative strategies proved particularly vital during the COVID-19 pandemic, when immigrant-owned businesses rapidly shifted to digital platforms and adapted health protocols through mutual support (Zhuang, 2021). Such forms of solidarity not only foster business continuity but also sustain cultural presence, transforming immigrant enclaves into spaces of innovation and mutual care. Through grassroots collaboration, immigrant entrepreneurs construct alternative infrastructures that address institutional shortcomings and promote socio-economic resilience.

Digital entrepreneurship and cultural branding have also emerged as critical tools for overcoming market exclusion and broadening outreach. Brazilian female entrepreneurs in beauty and fashion increasingly utilise social media and e-commerce to promote their services and reach audiences beyond their ethnic communities (Machado et al., 2021). Bangladeshi entrepreneurs incorporate digital tools into transnational operations, using messaging apps and online platforms to coordinate imports, manage logistics and market products to both local and diasporic consumers (Rahman, 2018). Chinese entrepreneurs, especially among the second generation, deploy multilingual branding and digital storytelling to challenge cultural stereotypes and reposition their businesses within the mainstream market (Zhuang, 2021). These strategies enable immigrant entrepreneurs to present cultural identity as a strength rather than a constraint. Through bilingual communication, narrative marketing and product diversification, they reshape how immigrant businesses are perceived, pushing back against exclusionary logics and contributing to a more inclusive vision of entrepreneurship within Toronto's evolving urban economy.

Vancouver's pacific nexus: immigrant entrepreneurs driving economic transformation in a global gateway city

Vancouver's position as Canada's Pacific gateway has produced a distinctive environment for immigrant entrepreneurship, shaped by transnational flows, regional migration and dense diasporic networks (Walton-Roberts & Hiebert, 1997; Wong & Ng, 1998). The city's geographic proximity to Asia, coupled with its historical role as a settlement hub, has supported the emergence of entrepreneurial ecosystems that are both globally connected and locally grounded. Immigrant entrepreneurship is a defining feature of Vancouver's urban economy, reflected in the formation of businesses that span multiple sectors and neighbourhoods. These enterprises operate within a broader context of mobility, demographic diversity and urban transformation, contributing to the city's economic vitality and cultural pluralism (Golob & Giles, 2017; Hiebert, 2002; Teixeira & Salinas, 2024). This study draws on existing literature to examine the experiences of Mexican, Chinese and Indian immigrant entrepreneurs, focusing on their roles in shaping Vancouver's evolving multicultural economy.

The fractured pathways of Vancouver: barriers to immigrant entrepreneurship

Despite Vancouver's reputation as a hub of multicultural economic activity, immigrant entrepreneurs face systemic regulatory barriers that limit their ability to contribute fully to the city's growth and innovation. Complex licensing procedures in sectors such as retail and food services pose significant obstacles, particularly for newcomers unfamiliar with Canadian bureaucratic systems (CFIB, 2025; Hiebert, 2002; Mayuto et al., 2023). Mexican entrepreneurs often encounter unclear regulatory frameworks, language barriers during permit applications and a lack of culturally appropriate support services, which hinder formalisation and business development (Teixeira & Salinas, 2024). Overlapping municipal, provincial and federal regulations inflate compliance costs and delay operational milestones, disproportionately affecting small-scale enterprises (Li et al., 2016; Wang & Hii, 2019). Zoning restrictions further limit access to affordable commercial spaces, restricting the expansion of Chinese transnational ventures (Ray et al., 1997; Wong & Ng, 2002). Indian entrepreneurs in construction also face regulatory inefficiencies, particularly around informal labour practices and the need for formal accreditation to scale operations (Walton-Roberts & Hiebert, 1997). These systemic inefficiencies constrain entrepreneurial activity, undermining innovation, economic diversification and inclusive growth within Vancouver's business ecosystem.

Financial exclusion compounds these regulatory challenges. Immigrant entrepreneurs are frequently denied access to mainstream financing due to strict eligibility criteria that favour established businesses with extensive credit histories and collateral (BDC, 2024; Leung et al., 2018). Mexican entrepreneurs often rely on personal savings or informal lending from family networks, as they typically lack the documentation or institutional literacy required to obtain traditional loans (Teixeira & Salinas, 2024). Chinese entrepreneurs operating small businesses face comparable barriers and frequently turn to family-based lending and informal financial systems (Li et al., 2016). Indian entrepreneurs in construction similarly depend on pooled resources from co-ethnic communities to finance equipment and labour (Walton-Roberts & Hiebert, 1997). Some entrepreneurs also make use of ROSCAs to access short-term capital, though most research on these systems centres on cities like Toronto (Hossein, 2017; Leung et al., 2018). Evidence suggests similar informal lending mechanisms exist within Vancouver's immigrant communities. While these are effective in early stages, they rarely provide the capital needed for long-term growth or innovation (Green et al., 2023; Love, 2024). These financial limitations are further exacerbated by Vancouver's high commercial rents, which restrict investment in marketing, staffing and resilience planning (Hutchison & Lin, 2021), leaving many immigrant businesses undercapitalised and vulnerable.

Cultural biases and restricted access to professional networks further marginalise immigrant entrepreneurs in Vancouver. Despite the city's strong narrative of multiculturalism, stereotypes persist that confine immigrant-owned businesses to ethnically segmented markets, limiting their visibility and expansion potential (Hiebert, 2002). Mexican entrepreneurs, particularly recent arrivals, are often constrained by limited English proficiency, lack of awareness of support services and minimal access to formal mentorship (Salinas & Teixeira, 2020; Teixeira & Salinas, 2024). These barriers reduce their capacity to scale and diversify. Chinese and Indian entrepreneurs face similar constraints, including unfamiliarity with Canadian business norms and limited engagement with broader networks (Walton-Roberts & Hiebert, 1997; Wong & Ng, 2002). As a result, many remain reliant on co-ethnic networks for operational support. While these networks are essential for early-stage stability, they may restrict broader market integration (Wang & Hii, 2019). Furthermore, structural biases in public funding programmes often favour capital-intensive ventures and wealthier investors, sidelining small immigrant-led enterprises (Li, 1997; Li et al., 2016). These intersecting exclusions highlight the persistent barriers immigrant entrepreneurs face in a city that positions itself as inclusive yet frequently falls short of providing equitable access to opportunity.

Pathways to success in Vancouver: strategies for overcoming barriers in immigrant entrepreneurship

Immigrant entrepreneurs in Vancouver adopt diverse strategies to navigate the city's fragmented and often restrictive regulatory environment. Mexican entrepreneurs rely on informal community networks to exchange practical knowledge about licensing systems and zoning regulations. These peer-based systems operate as culturally grounded support structures, helping entrepreneurs interpret institutional procedures and build confidence in engaging with municipal authorities (Salinas & Teixeira, 2022; Teixeira & Salinas, 2024). Chinese entrepreneurs leverage transnational business ties and flexible supply chains linked to East Asia, which enable them to circumvent local zoning barriers and regulatory inefficiencies by drawing on international suppliers, investment capital and transnational market continuity (Wong & Ng, 2002; Ray et al., 1997). Indian entrepreneurs in the construction sector adapt through apprenticeship-based training models embedded in co-ethnic networks. These informal systems promote skill development and trust-building, enabling access to contracts and labour opportunities without relying on formal certification (Walton-Roberts & Hiebert, 1997). Collectively, these strategies reflect the mobilisation of embedded knowledge, social capital and translocal resources to sustain entrepreneurial activity within a complex institutional context.

To address financial exclusion and spatial constraints, immigrant entrepreneurs in Vancouver turn to community-rooted economic models and digital technologies that offer flexibility and autonomy. Mexican entrepreneurs frequently utilise family-based lending and informal savings systems as alternatives to formal credit institutions, enabling quick and low-barrier access to startup capital while reinforcing community reciprocity and shared risk-taking (Salinas & Teixeira, 2022; Teixeira & Salinas, 2024). Chinese entrepreneurs participate in ROSCAs, which facilitate pooled investment and maintain autonomy from mainstream finance by operating within trust-based business circles (Wong & Ng, 2002; Li et al., 2016). Indian entrepreneurs, particularly those requiring capital for equipment or labour, adopt resource pooling and cost-sharing models within co-ethnic networks, enhancing efficiency and reducing dependence on external funding (Walton-Roberts & Hiebert, 1997). Spatially, many Mexican entrepreneurs use e-commerce and social media platforms to bypass high-rent commercial zones, expanding their reach while avoiding geographic exclusion (Teixeira & Salinas, 2024). These strategies reveal how immigrant entrepreneurs employ hybrid economic practices and digital tools to remain viable within constrained urban environments.

In addition, deeply embedded community networks function as vital platforms for entrepreneurial resilience, resource exchange and market expansion. Mexican entrepreneurs draw on familial and social ties for staffing, informal training and financial support, fostering cultural familiarity and sustaining businesses during periods of uncertainty (Salinas & Teixeira, 2022; Teixeira & Salinas, 2024). Chinese entrepreneurs engage with trade associations and family guilds that offer mentoring, pooled infrastructure and institutional backing, contributing to long-term business stability and collective adaptability (Wong & Ng, 2002). Indian entrepreneurs in construction and related services use subcontracting chains and cooperative labour arrangements to distribute workload and financial risk while scaling operations through trusted relationships (Walton-Roberts & Hiebert, 1997). Increasingly, immigrant entrepreneurs also challenge ethnic market segmentation by employing inclusive branding and digital outreach to attract diverse consumers, resisting confinement to co-ethnic clientele (Hiebert, 2002). These practices show how immigrant community networks serve not only as safety nets but as strategic assets for growth, diversification and redefinition of entrepreneurial norms within Vancouver's multicultural economy.

Comparative synthesis: immigrant entrepreneurship in the U.S. and Canada

Immigrant entrepreneurship in the U.S. and Canada unfolds within distinct institutional frameworks yet converges around shared structural barriers. These include financial exclusion, regulatory complexity and fragmented support systems, experienced unevenly across urban contexts and identity positions. In both countries, immigrant entrepreneurs mobilise transnational capital, community-based networks and cultural identity to navigate exclusion and engage with segmented markets. In the U.S., visa precarity and institutional fragmentation constrain entrepreneurial access and continuity. In Canada, while more structured support mechanisms such as the Start-Up Visa are available, their accessibility varies across regions and demographic groups. The comparative dimensions summarised in Table 4.1 provide a foundation for context-sensitive policy development by highlighting both national divergences and convergent barriers.

Strategic policy interventions for North America

Immigrant entrepreneurship in North America is shaped by divergent national policy regimes and uneven access to opportunity across urban landscapes. As summarised in Table 4.1, while Canada offers more coherent and targeted support for immigrant entrepreneurs, both countries present persistent barriers, including restricted financial access, regulatory complexity and cultural exclusion. These challenges manifest unevenly across cities and identity groups, shaping entrepreneurial trajectories in differentiated ways.

TABLE 4.1 Key comparative dimensions of immigrant entrepreneurship in the U.S. and Canada

Category	*U.S.*	*Canada*
Immigration policy framework	Limited entrepreneurial pathways. Absence of a dedicated Start-Up Visa. High dependence on employer-sponsored visas like H-1B restricts founder mobility and delays entrepreneurial transition.	Structured support through the Start-Up Visa and coordinated federal programmes. Policy coherence enables more direct entry and participation in entrepreneurial activity.
Institutional ecosystem	Fragmented and uneven support infrastructure. Racialised and gendered groups often excluded from formal networks, particularly in tech and finance sectors.	Stronger institutional partnerships (e.g., BDC and MaRS) and newcomer-targeted programmes, though access remains uneven by geography, language and sector.
Financial access and inclusion	Structural exclusion from VC persists; gender and racial biases are widespread. Informal finance (e.g., co-ethnic investor networks) fills gaps but limits scalability.	Community-based models (e.g., ROSCAs) provide early-stage financing. Federal lending exists but is often inaccessible due to credit constraints and language barriers.
Regulatory environment	Inconsistent and bureaucratic systems (e.g., licensing and zoning) vary by city. Entrepreneurs in Silicon Valley and NYC face enforcement disparities and long delays.	More consistent municipal–provincial alignment but restrictive zoning and gentrification in cities like Toronto and Vancouver displace immigrant-led enterprises.
Community and ethnic networks	Dense enclaves (e.g., Flushing and Little Bangladesh) offer resilience and informal support but can reinforce market segmentation.	Embedded ethnic economies support cooperative practices (e.g., shared retail and kinship labour), helping entrepreneurs navigate exclusionary institutions.
Transnational strategies	Entrepreneurs leverage global talent, capital and branding to overcome domestic exclusion (e.g., outsourcing and dual-market targeting in tech sectors).	Founders integrate diaspora supply chains and digital tools to reach transnational markets and adapt products to diverse consumer segments.
Cultural identity and market positioning	Identity mobilised to resist exclusion and navigate dominant norms, particularly among women and racialised founders (e.g., Korean American and African women).	Cultural branding, bilingual marketing and cross-ethnic collaboration enable identity to become a strategic advantage (e.g., among Brazilian, Chinese, and Bangladeshi founders).

In response, immigrant entrepreneurs draw on transnational linkages, embedded community networks and cultural knowledge to navigate institutional barriers and expand their access to markets, resources and mobility. These practices reflect the interplay between agency and structure, as entrepreneurs mobilise informal capital, social expertise and relational resources to contest exclusion (Kloosterman, 2010). Identity operates not as a static attribute but as a dynamic and relational resource shaped by race, gender, class and legal status (Fernández-Kelly &

Konczal, 2005; Zhou, 2004). Understanding entrepreneurship through these intersecting dimensions clarifies how innovation emerges in response to uneven development. This framing provides the foundation for the following policy interventions, which aim to support inclusive and context-responsive entrepreneurial ecosystems across North America.

Reforming immigration pathways to unlock entrepreneurial potential

Immigration policy serves as both a gatekeeper and an enabler of entrepreneurial opportunity. Yet significant asymmetries persist across North American cities. In Silicon Valley, the absence of a dedicated startup visa limits access for immigrant founders, even within one of the world's most dynamic innovation ecosystems (Chodavadia et al., 2024; Saxenian, 2000). This is particularly restrictive for highly skilled immigrants on H-1B visas, whose status is tied to employer sponsorship, thereby constraining their ability to establish independent ventures (Varma, 2020). New York City faces similar limitations, particularly for immigrant entrepreneurs in non-technology sectors such as food services and retail (Rahman et al., 2021). In contrast, Toronto and Vancouver benefit from Canada's Start-Up Visa programme, although access remains uneven, especially for low-income entrepreneurs and those outside high-growth sectors (Teixeira & Salinas, 2024; Zhuang, 2021).

To reduce these disparities, local and federal governments should co-design immigration pathways that are both regionally adaptive and inclusive across sectors. Canada's Start-Up Visa model offers a promising foundation but should be expanded to include a broader range of industries and demographic groups. Priority should be given to visa programmes that are accessible to entrepreneurs regardless of income level, education or sector. A clear target for reform would be a 25% increase in non-technology sector visa applications and greater demographic diversity among applicants within five years. Framing immigration policy as an instrument of inclusive economic development would help align entrepreneurial opportunity with broader equity goals.

Expanding access to capital through financial innovation

Persistent inequities in financial systems continue to limit the scalability of immigrant-led enterprises. In Silicon Valley, VC circulates through exclusive, socially embedded networks that often marginalise immigrant founders (Kerr & Kerr, 2019). In New York, entrepreneurs from Bangladeshi and African backgrounds face restrictive credit requirements that divert them to informal lending systems with limited capacity for growth (Oloke & Halkias, 2020; Rahman et al., 2021). In Toronto and Vancouver, although institutions such as the BDC offer formal financing, these resources remain out of reach for many small immigrant businesses due to credit, documentation and linguistic barriers (Machado et al., 2021; Salinas & Teixeira, 2024).

To address these gaps, municipalities and financial technology providers should co-develop digital lending platforms that are culturally responsive and tailored to the needs of undercapitalised entrepreneurs. Financial institutions can pilot microfinance programmes that integrate formal mechanisms with community-based lending practices, balancing affordability with potential for scale. These solutions should be embedded within broader financial ecosystems through partnerships between public agencies and private actors. Policy effectiveness can be assessed by a 20% increase in immigrant-led businesses accessing formal capital and improved sectoral diversity in loan distribution. Financial inclusion must encompass not only access, but equitable participation and measurable outcomes across the entrepreneurial lifecycle.

Simplifying regulatory processes to reduce bureaucratic barriers

Regulatory complexity remains a persistent and often underestimated constraint on immigrant entrepreneurship. In cities such as Silicon Valley and New York, zoning restrictions and licensing procedures contribute to delays and elevated entry costs, particularly in sectors like food services and personal care (Rahman et al., 2021; Saxenian, 2000). In Toronto and Vancouver, overlapping municipal, provincial and federal requirements create procedural inefficiencies that disproportionately affect entrepreneurs with limited legal and administrative support (Li et al., 2016; Zhuang, 2021).

Governments at all levels must prioritise the development of unified, user-friendly regulatory systems. Municipalities should invest in multilingual digital platforms that consolidate business registration, permitting and compliance procedures. These systems should be co-designed with immigrant entrepreneurs to ensure practical accessibility. At the provincial and federal levels, harmonising registration and licensing requirements is essential to reduce administrative burden. Policy success can be measured by a 30% reduction in processing times and an increase in successful business registrations within the first year of operation. Streamlining regulation is not merely an efficiency measure; it is a structural investment in equitable economic inclusion.

Building inclusive mentorship and knowledge networks

Mentorship and professional networks are essential to business development, yet access remains uneven across North American cities. In Silicon Valley, Indian entrepreneurs benefit from established mentorship infrastructures that connect them with VC and industry expertise (Basu & Virick, 2015). In contrast, immigrant entrepreneurs in New York often lack access to formal mentorship, resulting in professional isolation and limited business growth (Oloke & Halkias, 2020). In Toronto and Vancouver, informal networks within communities such as the Chinese and Bangladeshi offer crucial support but remain largely disconnected from mainstream entrepreneurial ecosystems (Rahman, 2018; Wong & Ng, 2002).

To bridge these gaps, governments should establish inclusive mentorship hubs that link ethnic networks with mainstream professional ecosystems. These initiatives should prioritise underrepresented sectors such as retail, childcare and construction, where formal support is often lacking. Digital platforms can further expand access by facilitating cross-regional mentorship and peer-to-peer learning. Public funding and private sponsorship should be mobilised to build and sustain these networks. A key benchmark includes a 25% increase in mentorship participation by immigrant entrepreneurs and a measurable rise in business scaling over five years. Inclusive mentorship is not only a source of expertise but a mechanism for advancing equity, visibility and long-term economic integration.

Challenging cultural bias and expanding market access

Cultural bias continues to limit the visibility and growth of immigrant-owned businesses by confining them to ethnically segmented consumer bases. In Silicon Valley, female immigrant entrepreneurs face intersecting exclusions based on gender and ethnicity, which restrict access to VC and hinder integration into mainstream markets (Kerr & Mandorff, 2023; Lee & Lee, 2020). In New York, Korean and African entrepreneurs often encounter consumer stereotyping that obscures the value of their products and services despite clear innovation (Kim, 2020; Oloke & Halkias, 2020; Yoo, 2014). In Toronto and Vancouver, entrepreneurs have leveraged cultural branding to reach wider audiences, yet institutional support for these efforts remains limited (Wong & Ng, 2002; Zhuang, 2021).

Policymakers should develop public campaigns that promote cultural awareness and counter consumer bias through education and storytelling. Targeted subsidies for marketing initiatives, in partnership with local business associations, can enhance the visibility of immigrant-owned brands. Mainstream firms should be incentivised to engage in co-branding and joint distribution with immigrant entrepreneurs, creating shared market pathways. Policy outcomes can be measured through a 20% increase in businesses expanding beyond ethnic niche markets and improved digital engagement across diverse consumer demographics. Expanding market access is not only a matter of business development but a step towards equitable visibility, cultural recognition and inclusive economic participation.

Investing in long-term infrastructure for sustainable growth

The long-term sustainability of immigrant entrepreneurship depends on targeted investments in infrastructure that support innovation, global integration and intergenerational business continuity. In Silicon Valley, second-generation immigrant entrepreneurs increasingly draw on global networks and digital technologies to build high-growth ventures (Chodavadia et al., 2024; Saxenian, 2000). Toronto benefits from a diverse entrepreneurial base but requires greater investment in physical and institutional infrastructure to enable business scaling (George et al., 2024). Vancouver's Pacific Rim position offers strategic trade advantages, yet high real estate costs and regulatory inefficiencies continue to constrain expansion (Hutchison & Lin, 2021). In New York, the breadth of immigrant-led industries demands infrastructure that connects local enterprises to global supply chains while also addressing entrenched local barriers (Rahman et al., 2021).

Governments should prioritise the development of innovation hubs, incubators and accelerators designed to support immigrant entrepreneurs across a range of sectors, not solely technology. These initiatives should be accompanied by investment in digital infrastructure to facilitate international trade, transnational networking and platform-based market access. Public-private partnerships and global exchange platforms can further extend the reach and resilience of immigrant ventures. Policy effectiveness can be assessed through increased participation in global supply chains and a 20% rise in international market access within three years. Infrastructure must be understood not only as physical or digital assets but as the foundation for equitable, long-term economic inclusion.

Conclusion

This chapter has demonstrated that immigrant entrepreneurs in Silicon Valley, New York City, Toronto and Vancouver navigate exclusion not as passive subjects but as strategic agents who mobilise transnational networks, community-based resources and identity-informed practices. Through the RMEF, the analysis traced patterns of institutional engagement, identity negotiation and strategic adaptation across contrasting urban and policy environments. The reconceptualised framework repositions identity as a dynamic and relational resource shaped by race, gender, class and migration status, offering a more nuanced understanding of entrepreneurial opportunity and constraint. The findings challenge universalistic policy prescriptions and underscore the need for context-sensitive, equity-oriented interventions that recognise differentiated entrepreneurial experiences. By clarifying how immigrant entrepreneurship is both structured by systemic inequalities and actively reshaped through entrepreneurial agency, this chapter advances theoretical understanding and calls for future empirical testing, adaptation and refinement of the reconceptualised framework across diverse urban contexts.

Reference

Aliaga-Isla, R., & Rialp, A. (2013). Systematic review of immigrant entrepreneurship literature: Previous findings and ways forward. *Entrepreneurship & Regional Development, 25*(9–10), 819–844. https://doi.org/10.1080/08985626.2013.845694

American Immigration Council. (2024). *New American Fortune 500 in 2024*. https://www.americanimmigrationcouncil.org/research/new-american-fortune-500-2024

Azoulay, P., Jones, B. F., Kim, J. D., & Miranda, J. (2022). Immigration and entrepreneurship in the United States. *American Economic Review: Insights, 4*(1), 71–88. https://doi.org/10.1257/aeri.20200588

Basu, A., & Virick, M. (2015). Silicon Valley's Indian diaspora: Networking and entrepreneurial success. *South Asian Journal of Global Business Research, 4*(2), 190–208. https://doi.org/10.1108/SAJGBR-04-2014-0021

Bittner, A., & Lau, B. (2021). *Women-led startups received just 2.3% of VC funding in 2020*. Harvard Business Review. https://hbr.org/2021/02/women-led-startups-received-just-2-3-of-vc-funding-in-2020

Brinkerhoff, J. M. (2016). *Institutional reform and diaspora entrepreneurs: The in-between advantage*. Oxford University Press.

Business Development Bank of Canada. (2024). *Immigrant entrepreneurship taking centre stage in Canada*. https://www.bdc.ca/en/articles-tools/blog/immigrant-entrepreneurship-taking-centre-stage-canada

Business Development Bank of Canada. (n.d.). *Newcomer entrepreneur: Owning a business as a new immigrant to Canada*. https://www.bdc.ca/en/i-am/newcomer-entrepreneur

Canadian Federation of Independent Business. (2025). *Newcomer entrepreneurs face unique challenges in Canada*. Retail Insider. https://retail-insider.com/retail-insider/2025/02/newcomer-entrepreneurs-face-unique-challenges-in-canada-cfib/

Chand, M., & Tung, R. L. (2019). Skilled immigration to fill talent gaps: A comparison of the immigration policies of the United States, Canada, and Australia. *Journal of International Business Policy, 2*, 333–355. https://doi.org/10.1057/s42214-019-00039-4

Chen, X. (2021). Immigrant-owned small businesses' participation in diaspora philanthropy: A case study during the COVID-19 outbreak. *New England Journal of Entrepreneurship, 24*(2), 105–121. https://doi.org/10.1108/NEJE-08-2020-0033

Chen, Z. F., & Lee, J. Y. (2024). Relationship cultivation and social capital: Female transnational entrepreneurs' relationship-based communication on social media. In S. R. Dillard & M. L. Kienzler (Eds.), *Start-up and entrepreneurial communication* (pp. 59–82). Routledge.

Chodavadia, S. A., Kerr, S. P., Kerr, W. R., & Maiden, L. J. (2024). Immigrant entrepreneurship: New estimates and a research agenda. *NBER Working Paper No. 32400*. National Bureau of Economic Research. https://doi.org/10.3386/w32400

Dabić, M., Vlačić, B., Paul, J., Dana, L. P., Sahasranamam, S., & Glinka, B. (2020). Immigrant entrepreneurship: A review and research agenda. *Journal of Business Research, 113*, 25–38. https://doi.org/10.1016/j.jbusres.2020.03.013

Davidson, M. J., Fielden, S. L., & Omar, A. (2010). Black, Asian and minority ethnic female business owners: Discrimination and social support. *International Journal of Entrepreneurial Behaviour & Research, 16*(1), 58–80. https://doi.org/10.1108/13552551011020072

Desiderio, M. V. (2014). *Policies to support immigrant entrepreneurship*. Migration Policy Institute and Transatlantic Council on Migration. https://www.migrationpolicy.org/sites/default/files/publications/TCM_Cities_Entrepreneurship-FINALWEB.pdf

Dheer, R. J. S. (2018). Entrepreneurship by immigrants: A review of existing literature and directions for future research. *International Entrepreneurship and Management Journal, 14*(3), 555–614. https://doi.org/10.1007/s11365-018-0506-7

Fernández-Kelly, P., & Konczal, L. (2005). "Murdering the alphabet": Identity and entrepreneurship among second-generation Cubans, West Indians, and Central Americans. *Ethnic and Racial Studies, 28*(6), 1153–1181. https://doi.org/10.1080/0141987050022451 3

George, U., Escobar Olivo, V., & McDermott, T. (2024). Understanding immigrant entrepreneurship activities in the Greater Toronto Area. In M. Elmi, W. Cukier, Z. Hassannezhad Chavoushi, & G. Y. Mo (Eds.), *Immigrant entrepreneurship* (pp. xx–xx). Palgrave Macmillan. https://doi.org/10.1007/978-3-031-69642-8_6

Gold, S. J. (2018). Israeli infotech migrants in Silicon Valley. *RSF: The Russell Sage Foundation Journal of the Social Sciences, 4*(1), 130–148. https://doi.org/10.7758/RSF.2018.4.1.08

Golob, M. I., & Giles, A. R. (2017). Immigrant entrepreneurship in Canada: Sites for cultural preservation, inclusion, and community development. *Journal of Multicultural Discourses, 12*(1), 27–41. https://doi.org/10.1080/17447143.2016.1260135

Green, D. A., Liu, H., Ostrovsky, Y., & Picot, G. (2023). *Are immigrants particularly entrepreneurial? Policy lessons from a selective immigration system* (No. 2304). Vancouver School of Economics, University of British Columbia. https://economics.ubc.ca/wp-content/uploads/sites/38/2023/10/immigrant-entrepreneurial-entry-hk2.pdf

Hackworth, J., & Rekers, J. (2005). Ethnic packaging and gentrification: The case of four neighbourhoods in Toronto. *Urban Affairs Review, 41*(2), 211–236. https://doi.org/10.1177/1078087405280859

Hiebert, D. (2002). The spatial limits to entrepreneurship: Immigrant entrepreneurs in Canada. *Tijdschrift voor economische en sociale geografie, 93*(2), 173–190. https://doi.org/10.1111/1467-9663.00193

Hossein, C. S. (2017). Fringe banking in Canada: A study of rotating savings and credit associations (ROSCAs) in Toronto's inner suburbs. *Canadian Journal of Nonprofit and Social Economy Research, 8*(1), 29–49. https://anserj.ca/index.php/cjnser/article/view/234

Hutchison, C., & Lin, L.-W. (2021). The growth of Vancouver as an innovation hub: Challenges and opportunities. *UBC Law Review*, 54(3), 693.

Kariv, D., Menzies, T. V., Brenner, G. A., & Filion, L. J. (2009). Transnational networking and business performance: Ethnic entrepreneurs in Canada. *Entrepreneurship and regional development, 21*(3), 239–264. https://doi.org/10.1080/08985620802261641

Kerr, S. P., & Kerr, W. R. (2019). Immigrant networking and collaboration: Survey evidence from CIC. In K. Ganguli, S. Kahn, & M. MacGarvie (Eds.), *The roles of immigrants and foreign students in U.S. science, innovation, and entrepreneurship* (Working Paper No. 25509). National Bureau of Economic Research. https://doi.org/10.3386/w25509

Kerr, S. P., & Kerr, W. R. (2021). Immigration policy levers for US innovation and start-ups. In A. B. Jaffe & B. F. Jones (Eds.), *Innovation and public policy* (pp. 85–116). University of Chicago Press.

Kerr, W. R., & Mandorff, M. (2023). Social networks, ethnicity, and entrepreneurship. *Journal of Human Resources*, 58(1), 183–220. https://doi.org/10.3368/jhr.58.3.0719-10306R2

Kim, D. Y. (2001). *Immigrant entrepreneurship and intergenerational mobility among second-generation Korean Americans in New York*. City University of New York.

Kim, J. (2020). Transnational entrepreneurship in Manhattan's Koreatown. In *Koreatowns: Exploring the economics, politics, and identities of Korean spatial formation* (pp. 41–61). Lexington Books. https://doi.org/10.5040/9781666997910.ch-003

Kim, S., & Chandrasekhar, D. (2024). Harnessing social capital for post-COVID-19 resilience: A study of Asian businesses in New York City. *Journal of Planning Education and Research*. https://doi.org/10.1177/0739456X241276127

Kloosterman, R. C. (2010). Matching opportunities with resources: A framework for analysing (migrant) entrepreneurship from a mixed embeddedness perspective. *Entrepreneurship and Regional Development, 22*(1), 25–45. https://doi.org/10.1080/08985620903220488

Kloosterman, R. C, Van Der Leun, J., & Rath, J. (1999). Mixed embeddedness:(In) formal economic activities and immigrant businesses in the Netherlands. *International Journal of Urban and Regional Research, 23*(2), 252–266. https://doi.org/10.1111/1468-2427.00194

Lee, J. Y., & Lee, J. Y. (2020). Female transnational entrepreneurs (FTEs): A case study of Korean American Female immigrant entrepreneurs in Silicon Valley. *Journal of Entrepreneurship and Innovation in Emerging Economies, 6*(1), 67–83. https://doi.org/10.1177/2393957519881925

Lee, S. R., & Glennon, B. (2023). The effect of immigration policy on founding location choice: Evidence from Canada's start-up visa program (No. w31634). *National Bureau of Economic Research*. https://doi.org/10.3386/w31634

Leung, D., Ostrovsky, Y., & Picot, G. (2018). *The financing of immigrant-owned firms in Canada* (Analytical Studies Branch Research Paper Series, No. 404, Catalogue No. 11F0019M). Statistics Canada. https://www150.statcan.gc.ca/n1/pub/11f0019m/11f0019m2018404-eng.htm

Li, E. X., Li, P. S., & Zong, L. (2016). Profile of small businesses among Chinese in Vancouver. *Canadian Ethnic Studies, 48*(2), 53–70. https://doi.org/10.1353/ces.2016.0013

Li, P. S. (1997). Asian capital and Canadian business: The recruitment and control of investment capital and business immigrants to Canada. In W. W. Isajiw (Ed.), *Multiculturalism in North America and Europe: Comparative perspectives on interethnic relations and social incorporation* (pp. 363–379). Canadian Scholars' Press.

Light, I., & Dana, L. P. (2013). Boundaries of social capital in entrepreneurship. *Entrepreneurship Theory and Practice, 37*(3), 603–624. https://doi.org/10.1111/etap.12016

Love, K. (2024). *ROSCAs are an overlooked but vital part of the co-operative sector*. Canadian Worker Co-op Federation. https://canadianworker.coop/roscas-are-an-overlooked-but-vital-part-of-the-co-operative-sector/

Machado, M. M., Cruz, E. P., & de Queiroz Falcão, R. P. (2023). Immigrant entrepreneurship of Brazilian women in Toronto, Canada. *Internext – Revista Eletrônica de Negócios Internacionais, 18*(2), 113–129. https://doi.org/10.18568/internext.v18i2.727

Machado, M. M., Falcão, R. P. Q., Cruz, E. P., & Hossein, C. S. (2021). The Canadian experience from the perspective of Brazilian entrepreneurship in Toronto. *Iberoamerican Journal of Entrepreneurship and Small Business, 10*(3), Article e1963. https://doi.org/10.14211/regepe.e1963

Mayuto, R., Su, Z., & Mohiuddin, M. (2023). Antecedents of immigrants' entrepreneurial intention formation process: An empirical study of immigrant entrepreneurs in Canada. *Frontiers in Psychology*, 14, Article 1153142. https://doi.org/10.3389/fpsyg.2023.1153142

Morawska, E. (2004). Immigrant transnational entrepreneurs in New York: Three varieties and their correlates. *International Journal of Entrepreneurial Behaviour & Research, 10*(5), 325–348. https://doi.org/10.1108/13552550410554311

Nee, V., & Drouhot, L. G. (2020). Immigration, opportunity, and assimilation in a technology economy. *Theoretical Sociology, 49*(6), 965–990. https://doi.org/10.1007/s11186-020-09414-0

Nopper, T. K. (2009). The globalisation of Korean banking and Korean entrepreneurship in the United States. *Race, Gender & Class, 16*(3/4), 248–270. https://www.jstor.org/stable/41674687

Oloke, T., & Halkias, D. (2020). Nigerian female immigrant entrepreneurs within the service industry in New York City, USA: An integrative literature review. *SSRN*. https://doi.org/10.2139/ssrn.3529631

Rahman, M. M. (2018). Development of Bangladeshi entrepreneurship in Canada. *Asian and Pacific Migration Journal, 27*(4), 404–430. https://doi.org/10.1177/0117196818810096

Rahman, M. M., Alshawi, A. A. H., & Hasan, M. (2021). Entrepreneurship in ethnic enterprises: The making of new immigrant businesses in New York. *Sustainability, 13*(20), 11183. https://doi.org/10.3390/su132011183

Ray, B. K., Halseth, G., & Johnson, B. (1997). The changing 'face' of the suburbs: Issues of ethnicity and residential change in suburban Vancouver. *International Journal of Urban and Regional Research, 21*(1), 75–99. https://doi.org/10.1111/1468-2427.00059

Romero, M., & Valdez, Z. (2016). Introduction to the special issue: Intersectionality and entrepreneurship. *Ethnic and Racial Studies, 39*(9), 1553–1565. https://doi.org/10.1080/01419870.2016.1171374

Salinas, A. L., & Teixeira, C. (2022). Settlement and housing experiences of recent Mexican immigrants in Vancouver suburbs. *GeoJournal, 87*(2), 377–402. https://doi.org/10.1007/s10708-020-10257-6

Savazzi, V., Solano, G., & Xhani, A. (2020). *Financial inclusion of migrant entrepreneurs: Barriers, challenges and support measures*. Migration Policy Group.

Saxenian, A. (2000). *Silicon Valley's new immigrant entrepreneurs* (Working Paper No. 15). The Centre for Comparative Immigration Studies, University of California, San Diego. https://escholarship.org/uc/item/88x6505q

Saxenian, A. (2002). Silicon Valley's new immigrant high-growth entrepreneurs. *Economic Development Quarterly, 16*(1), 20–31. https://doi.org/10.1177/0891242402016001003

Saxenian, A. (2006). *The new Argonauts: Regional advantage in a global economy*. Harvard University Press.

Saxenian, A., & Edulbehram, J. (1998). Immigrant entrepreneurs in Silicon Valley. *Berkeley Planning Journal, 12*(1). https://doi.org/10.5070/BP312113042

Teixeira, C., & Salinas, A. L. (2024). Mexican entrepreneurs in the Greater Vancouver Area (GVA), Canada. In *Immigrant Entrepreneurship: Challenges and Opportunities* (pp. 289–322). Springer Nature Switzerland.

Tremper, N. (2024). *Immigrants started nearly 1 in 5 new businesses in 2023*. Gusto. https://gusto.com/company-news/2024-immigrant-entrepreneur-report

U.S. Citizenship and Immigration Services. (2024). *International entrepreneur rule*. U.S. Department of Homeland Security. https://www.uscis.gov/working-in-the-united-states/international-entrepreneur-rule

Varma, R. (2011). Transnational migration and entrepreneurialism: Indians in the U.S. technology sector. *Perspectives on Global Development and Technology, 10*(3–4), 270–287.

Varma, R. (2020). To be or not to be on H-1B: Engineers from India in the United States. *Perspectives on Global Development and Technology, 19*(3), 281–302.

Varma, R. (2022). Tech coolies: Indian scientists and engineers entering U.S. on H-1B visa. In L. Saucedo & R. Rodriguez (Eds.), *Race, gender and contemporary international labour migration regimes: 21st century coolies?* (pp. 89–108). Edward Elgar Publishing.

Varma, R. (2024). Transnational innovators: Indian immigrants in shaping entrepreneurship in the U.S. tech sector. In M. Elmi, W. Cukier, Z. Hassannezhad Chavoushi, & G. Y. Mo (Eds.), *Immigrant entrepreneurship* (pp. 413–435). Palgrave Macmillan. https://doi.org/10.1007/978-3-031-69642-8_17

Wadhwa, V., Saxenian, A. L., Rissing, B. A., & Gereffi, G. (2007). *America's new immigrant entrepreneurs: Part I* (Duke Science, Technology & Innovation Paper No. 23). SSRN. https://doi.org/10.2139/ssrn.990152

Waldinger, R. (1989). Structural opportunity or ethnic advantage? Immigrant business development in New York. *International Migration Review, 23*(1), 48–72. https://doi.org/10.1177/019791838902300103

Walton-Roberts, M., & Hiebert, D. (1997). Immigration, entrepreneurship, and the family: Indo-Canadian enterprise in the construction industry of Greater Vancouver. *Canadian Journal of Regional Science, 20*(1), 119–140.

Wang, S. (1999). Chinese commercial activity in the Toronto CMA: New development patterns and impacts. *The Canadian Geographer/Le Géographe Canadien, 43*(1), 19–35. https://doi.org/10.1111/j.1541-0064.1999.tb01358.x

Wang, S., & Lo, L. (2000). Economic impacts of immigrants in the Toronto CMA: A tax-benefit analysis. *International Migration & Integration, 1*(3), 273–303. https://doi.org/10.1007/s12134-000-1015-3

Wang, S., & Hii, R. (2019). *Influence of immigration policies on supply of ethnic business entrepreneurs in Canada*. Ryerson Centre for Immigration and Settlement.

Wong, L. L., & Ng, M. (1998). Chinese immigrant entrepreneurs in Vancouver: A case study of ethnic business development. *Canadian Ethnic Studies, 30*(1), 64–85. https://link.gale.com/apps/doc/A81220969/AONE?u=anon~ece3e91e&sid=googleScholar&xid=c8e01819

Wong, L. L., & Ng, M. (2002). The emergence of small transnational enterprise in Vancouver: The case of Chinese entrepreneur immigrants. *International Journal of Urban and Regional Research, 26*(3), 508–530. https://doi.org/10.1111/1468-2427.00396

Yoo, J. K. (2014). *Korean entrepreneurs: Networks and ethnic resources*. Routledge.

You, T. L., & Zhou, M. (2019). Simultaneous embeddedness in immigrant entrepreneurship: Global forces behind Chinese-owned nail salons in New York City. *American Behavioural Scientist, 63*(2), 166–184. https://doi.org/10.1177/0002764218793684

Zhou, M. (2004). Revisiting ethnic entrepreneurship: Convergencies, controversies, and conceptual advancements. *International Migration Review, 38*(3), 1040–1074. https://doi.org/10.1111/j.1747-7379.2004.tb00228.x

Zhuang, Z. C. (2015). Construction and reconstruction of ethnicity in retail landscapes: Case studies in the Toronto area. *Journal of Urban Design, 20*(5), 677–697. https://doi.org/10.1080/13574809.2015.1071652

Zhuang, Z. C. (2021). The impact of immigrant entrepreneurship on city building: Learning from Toronto. In C. Y. Liu (Ed.), *Immigrant entrepreneurship in cities* (pp. 185–206). The Urban Book Series. Springer. https://doi.org/10.1007/978-3-030-50363-5_9

Zhuang, Z. C., & Chen, A. X. (2017). The role of ethnic retailing in retrofitting suburbia: Case studies from Toronto, Canada. *Journal of Urbanism: International Research on Place-Making and Urban Sustainability, 10*(3), 275–295. https://doi.org/10.1080/17549175.2016.1254671

5

IMMIGRANT ENTREPRENEURSHIP IN WESTERN EUROPE

Embedded agency, cultural capital and urban transformation

Introduction

Immigrant entrepreneurship plays a critical role in shaping the economic, cultural and social dynamics of urban centres across Western Europe. In both the United Kingdom (UK) and Germany, immigrant entrepreneurs contribute significantly to employment, innovation and the diversification of urban economies, particularly in sectors such as retail, hospitality, logistics and knowledge-based industries (Basu & Altinay, 2002; Ram et al., 2021; Rashid & Cepeda-García, 2021).These ventures often emerge in response to structural exclusions, including restricted access to formal employment, limited financing options and discriminatory regulatory regimes (Jones et al., 2014; Rath & Swagerman, 2016). At the same time, they fulfil important social functions by offering culturally embedded services, building solidarity networks and fostering collective belonging (Bagwell, 2015; Polychronopoulos & Nguyen-Duc, 2024). However, their potential is shaped and often constrained by uneven institutional support and stratified opportunity structures.

Despite increasing policy and scholarly interest, existing research on immigrant entrepreneurship in Western Europe remains conceptually limited. The mixed embeddedness framework (MEF) (Kloosterman et al., 1999) continues to be widely applied, highlighting how institutional and market contexts shape entrepreneurial outcomes. However, its use often underplays the significance of identity, gender and intersectionality in structuring access to opportunity and legitimacy (Essers & Benschop, 2009; Poggesi & Mari, 2024). Financial and regulatory systems are not neutral; they reflect broader power relations that systematically disadvantage refugees, women and racialised minorities (Basit, 2017; Carter et al., 2015; Degler & Liebig, 2017). More recent scholarship calls for frameworks that better capture the dynamic role of identity and the positionality of immigrant entrepreneurs within layered national and urban systems (Anthias, 2013; Ram et al., 2021; Rashid & Cepeda-García, 2021).

This chapter responds to these limitations by applying a reconceptualised mixed embeddedness framework (RMEF) introduced in Chapter 2. The framework extends the original by integrating institutional theory and placing entrepreneurial identity, shaped through intersectionality, at the centre of a context-sensitive analysis of immigrant entrepreneurship in Western Europe.

DOI: 10.4324/9781003605072-7

It draws on secondary data from studies of immigrant entrepreneurship in urban contexts in the UK and Germany to demonstrate the framework's analytical value. The analysis examines how entrepreneurs mobilise informal finance, activate transnational ties and adopt identity-based strategies to access resources, navigate exclusion and create opportunities. It explores how racialised and gendered identities intersect with institutional structures to shape entrepreneurial practices within environments marked by regulatory complexity, cultural stratification and spatial inequality (Bruni et al., 2004; Essers & Benschop, 2007; Rath & Swagerman, 2016). In doing so, the chapter shows how the reconceptualised framework can be used to trace patterns of identity negotiation, institutional engagement and transnational strategy across structurally constrained entrepreneurial fields.

The analysis draws on case studies from four cities: London and Birmingham in the UK, and Berlin and Hamburg in Germany. These cities were selected for their contrasting migration histories, economic geographies and governance frameworks. London's super-diverse and globalised economy supports a wide range of immigrant-led enterprises (Jones et al., 2015; Nathan & Lee, 2013). Birmingham reflects long-standing entrepreneurial traditions among South Asian and African-Caribbean communities, which have contributed to local regeneration and mobility (Hall et al., 2015; Ram et al., 2002). Berlin's entrepreneurial landscape is marked by regulatory rigidity and symbolic exclusion, despite vibrant ethnic economies (Schmiz, 2017). Hamburg's port economy, underpinned by transnational trade, offers insight into the role of diasporic capital in navigating institutional barriers (Räuchle & Schmiz, 2019; Schüller & Schüler-Zhou, 2013). These cases provide a robust empirical basis for analysing how structure, identity and agency intersect across national contexts.

The chapter proceeds as follows. It begins with an analysis of immigrant entrepreneurship in the UK, focusing on London and Birmingham, before turning to Germany with case studies from Berlin and Hamburg. This is followed by a thematic synthesis identifying commonalities and divergences across the two national contexts. The next section develops a set of policy recommendations related to informal finance, intercultural mentorship and gender-responsive enterprise support. The chapter concludes by reflecting on the theoretical and practical contributions of the RMEF and outlining future research directions on immigrant entrepreneurship in Western Europe.

The United Kingdom

London's hybrid economy: immigrant entrepreneurs transforming urban capitalism

London, as a global and multicultural city, provides a fertile context for immigrant entrepreneurship shaped by diverse social networks, cultural resources and institutional complexity (Jones et al., 2015; Nathan & Lee, 2013). Entrepreneurs operate across formal and informal domains, often combining cultural heritage with regulatory awareness and market adaptability (Basu & Altinay, 2002; Kloosterman et al., 1999). Their ventures reflect complex forms of embeddedness, blurring boundaries between ethnic and mainstream economies and challenging fixed notions of EI (Ram et al., 2017; Sepulveda et al., 2008). Immigrant entrepreneurs in London are not only responding to local institutional and economic conditions but also contributing to the city's evolving entrepreneurial landscape (Bagwell, 2015; Osaghae et al., 2021). This section introduces key dynamics that shape immigrant entrepreneurship in London, with a focus on how African (Nigerian), South Asian (Bangladeshi and Pakistani) and East and Southeast Asian (Chinese and Vietnamese) entrepreneurs navigate and reshape the urban economy.

Navigating the urban maze: structural barriers facing immigrant entrepreneurs in London

Immigrant entrepreneurs in London operate within a stratified institutional landscape that constrains business formation and growth. Regulatory inconsistencies, opaque licensing procedures and complex tax obligations disproportionately affect those unfamiliar with the UK's administrative systems (Basu & Altinay, 2002; Jones et al., 2014, 2022). Although London is often portrayed as an entrepreneurial hub, fragmented governance weakens access to support and renders inclusion rhetoric ineffective (Hack-Polay et al., 2020; Sepulveda et al., 2008, 2011). These challenges have intensified post-Brexit, amid growing uncertainty around immigration, regulation and local economic policy (Migration Observatory, 2020; Virdee & McGeever, 2017). Nigerian entrepreneurs often lack access to culturally appropriate legal and advisory services, reducing institutional trust and compliance capacity (Nwankwo, 2005; Ojo, 2021; Ojo et al., 2013). South Asian entrepreneurs, particularly Bangladeshi and Pakistani, face language barriers, bureaucratic unfamiliarity and limited local authority engagement (Basu & Goswami, 1999; Mavrommatis, 2015; McPherson, 2017). Chinese and Vietnamese entrepreneurs encounter borough-level inconsistencies in enforcement, especially in highly regulated sectors like food services (Bagwell, 2015; Kitching et al., 2009; Zhang, 2015).

Institutional constraints are compounded by financial exclusion, which limits access to credit and reinforces racial and gender disparities in business ownership (Carter et al., 2015; Levie, 2007; Levie & Smallbone, 2006). Nigerian entrepreneurs face disproportionately high credit denial rates due to limited collateral, informal credit histories and racialised perceptions of financial risk (Nwankwo, 2005; Ojo, 2021; Ojo et al., 2013). South Asian entrepreneurs often rely on community-based savings and informal lending to bypass mainstream financial gatekeeping. Pakistani and Bangladeshi women face further exclusion shaped by patriarchal norms and institutional bias, limiting their access to credit (Basit, 2017; George & Dhaliwal, 2025; Halkias et al., 2016). Chinese and Vietnamese entrepreneurs frequently operate outside formal banking systems, drawing on ethnic-specific networks often overlooked by mainstream lenders (Bagwell, 2015; Kitching et al., 2009; Zhang, 2015). These practices reflect deep structural biases in London's financial infrastructure, where creditworthiness is filtered through race, gender and migration status.

Socio-cultural exclusion further restricts legitimacy and market mobility. While some entrepreneurs adopt strategic responses to marginalisation (Basu, 2011; Sepulveda et al., 2011), many remain constrained by hierarchies and stereotyping. Nigerian entrepreneurs report racial discrimination and imposed identities that limit access to wider markets (Nwankwo, 2005; Ojo, 2021). Pakistani and Bangladeshi women often face tensions between cultural expectations of respectability and the public visibility required for business growth (Basit, 2017; George & Dhaliwal, 2025; Halkias et al., 2016). Chinese and Vietnamese entrepreneurs face misrecognition, ethnic stereotyping and limited product visibility (Bagwell, 2015; Kitching et al., 2009; Zhang, 2015). Ethnic economies provide initial support and resilience but may also reinforce segmentation and limit broader market integration (Jones et al., 2014; Kloosterman et al., 1999). Entrepreneurial identities are continuously shaped in response to these exclusions, particularly within a post-Brexit landscape marked by increasing fragmentation (Hack-Polay et al., 2020; Migration Observatory, 2020). These dynamics underscore how entrepreneurial activity is shaped by the interaction of institutional barriers, social hierarchies and identity-based positioning.

Forging hybrid pathways: adaptive strategies of immigrant entrepreneurs in London's urban economy

Immigrant entrepreneurs in London respond to a fragmented and exclusionary institutional environment by mobilising community-based and transnational strategies to navigate regulatory opacity and administrative inconsistency (Edwards et al., 2018). Nigerian entrepreneurs draw on informal advisory networks and transnational ties to compensate for limited access to culturally appropriate institutional support. Peer-led knowledge exchange within ethnic networks enables interpretation of complex licensing systems and reduces reliance on official guidance (Hack-Polay et al., 2020; Ojo, 2021; Ojo et al., 2013). South Asian entrepreneurs from Bangladeshi and Pakistani backgrounds similarly engage intergenerational networks that offer mentorship and institutional orientation, particularly for new entrants facing linguistic barriers and limited engagement from local authorities (Basu & Goswami, 1999; Mavrommatis, 2015; McPherson, 2017). Chinese and Vietnamese entrepreneurs address borough-level inconsistencies in enforcement through operational flexibility, adapting to local regulatory expectations while maintaining cohesion within ethnic networks (Bagwell, 2015; Kitching et al., 2009; Zhang, 2015).

In response to systemic financial exclusion and racialised perceptions of creditworthiness, immigrant entrepreneurs adopt culturally embedded financing practices that reshape access to capital. Nigerian entrepreneurs rely on rotating savings models such as *ajo*, building financial resilience through collective trust in the absence of institutional credit access (Ojo et al., 2013). South Asian entrepreneurs draw on community-based savings schemes to support new ventures, with women from Pakistani and Bangladeshi communities often establishing home-based businesses that align with cultural norms while enabling economic autonomy (Basit, 2017; George & Dhaliwal, 2025; Halkias et al., 2016). East and Southeast Asian entrepreneurs operate within intra-ethnic financial systems that function alongside mainstream credit institutions, providing capital and trust-based support largely unrecognised by formal lenders (Bagwell, 2015; Kitching et al., 2009; Zhang, 2015). These financial strategies reflect adaptive responses to structural exclusion and enable business development despite systemic barriers (Edwards et al., 2018).

Socio-cultural barriers are addressed through strategic efforts to build legitimacy and expand market presence. Nigerian entrepreneurs contest racialised stereotypes by asserting visibility across both ethnic and mainstream markets, using entrepreneurship as a platform for identity and resistance (Hack-Polay et al., 2020; Nwankwo, 2005). South Asian women, particularly from Pakistani and Bangladeshi communities, navigate gendered expectations by forming cooperative models that support public participation while maintaining cultural legitimacy (Basit, 2017; George & Dhaliwal, 2025; Halkias et al., 2016). Chinese and Vietnamese entrepreneurs counter consumer misrecognition through targeted branding and digital tools that broaden their audience and increase product visibility beyond ethnic niches (Bagwell, 2015; Kitching et al., 2009; Zhang, 2015). These practices reflect how immigrant entrepreneurs blend cultural resources with market adaptation to overcome exclusion, build legitimacy and contribute to London's evolving entrepreneurial economy.

Birmingham's entrepreneurial landscape: immigrant agency and the remaking of a post-industrial city

Birmingham's transformation from an industrial centre to a post-industrial city has been shaped by economic restructuring, racialised labour markets and uneven urban investment. In this context, immigrant entrepreneurs have become central to local economic life, contributing to commercial vitality and reshaping the city's spatial and cultural landscape, particularly in areas marked by socioeconomic disadvantage (Ram et al., 2012, 2017). Their entrepreneurial activity has helped sustain neighbourhood economies, foster community networks and support urban regeneration, as seen in districts such as Rookery Road and the Balti Quarter (Hall et al., 2015, 2017; Jones et al., 2004; Ram et al., 2002). Despite limited institutional recognition, immigrant entrepreneurs continue to influence how opportunity, identity and economic space are negotiated in Birmingham's fragmented urban economy. This section introduces the role of South Asian (Pakistani, Bangladeshi and Indian) and African-Caribbean (Somali and Jamaican) entrepreneurs in shaping the city's evolving post-industrial landscape.

Navigating post-industrial constraints: structural barriers facing immigrant entrepreneurs in Birmingham

Birmingham's post-industrial transition has produced a fragmented regulatory and financial environment that presents persistent challenges for immigrant entrepreneurs. South Asian business owners, particularly those of Pakistani and Bangladeshi origin, frequently encounter opaque licensing systems and inconsistent enforcement, especially in sectors such as catering and retail, where scrutiny is high and institutional support minimal (Jones et al., 2004; Ram et al., 2002). Somali and Jamaican entrepreneurs face similar barriers, exacerbated by institutional suspicion and racialised assumptions of informality, which introduce additional administrative friction and hinder access to formal support mechanisms (Jones et al., 2010; Ram et al., 2008). Access to finance remains a core obstacle. Across all groups, entrepreneurs report exclusion from mainstream lending due to limited collateral, thin credit histories and discriminatory lending practices. Many rely on informal savings circles and community-based lending, which provide initial capital but limit long-term expansion (Carter et al., 2015; Smallbone et al., 2003). South Asian businesses in the Balti Quarter have struggled to attract investment for innovation, while Somali entrepreneurs in Lozells and Jamaican-owned businesses in Handsworth often remain confined to low-capital ventures with limited opportunities for growth (Hall et al., 2017; Jones et al., 2015; Ram et al., 2002).

Beyond regulatory and financial barriers, immigrant entrepreneurs contend with entrenched socio-cultural exclusions that shape both business sectors and market access. South Asian entrepreneurs, especially those from Bangladeshi and Indian backgrounds, are often steered into sectors perceived as culturally appropriate, such as restaurants and clothing retail, restricting entry into higher-value or emerging markets (Jones et al., 2004; Ram et al., 2002). Somali and Jamaican entrepreneurs similarly face racialised perceptions that categorise their businesses as marginal or informal, limiting legitimacy and access to broader networks (Jones et al., 2010; Ram et al., 2008). Gendered norms further constrain entrepreneurial participation. South Asian women frequently face expectations around visibility and autonomy that restrict public-facing business activities, compounded by limited access to credit (Jones et al., 2015; Ram et al., 2002). Jamaican and Somali women often establish home-based enterprises as a pragmatic response, but these ventures typically lack formal recognition and support structures (Hall et al., 2017; Jones et al., 2015). Across all groups, cultural stereotyping and gendered expectations reinforce segmented entrepreneurial pathways and cumulative disadvantage that policy and finance alone cannot resolve.

The spatial concentration of immigrant enterprises in Birmingham reflects deeper patterns of disinvestment and uneven development. Neighbourhoods such as Lozells, Rookery Road and Handsworth, where African-Caribbean and South Asian businesses are concentrated, remain underserved in terms of infrastructure, business support and public investment (Hall et al., 2015, 2017). These conditions increase operating costs and logistical challenges, including rising rents and unreliable services, which disproportionately affect small and micro-enterprises. Entrepreneurs in the Balti Quarter report declining footfall, deteriorating premises and a lack of coordinated regeneration initiatives, weakening previously thriving commercial clusters (Ram et al., 2002). Somali and Jamaican entrepreneurs in similarly neglected areas face exclusion from citywide economic planning and minimal engagement from municipal authorities (Jones et al., 2015; Ram et al., 2012). These conditions are not incidental but reflect planning decisions that systematically marginalise immigrant businesses (Jones et al., 2022; McEwan et al., 2005). Without targeted investment and inclusive regeneration strategies, immigrant entrepreneurs will remain confined to peripheral spaces that constrain business development, reduce visibility and limit access to broader economic opportunities.

Reconstructing opportunity: adaptive strategies of immigrant entrepreneurs in Birmingham's post-industrial economy

Immigrant entrepreneurs in Birmingham respond to financial exclusion and regulatory complexity through embedded financial practices and informal infrastructures that support business continuity under structural barriers. South Asian entrepreneurs, particularly those of Pakistani and Bangladeshi origin, rely on community-based lending networks, rotating savings and credit associations (ROSCAs) and extended family contributions to secure startup capital, especially in sectors such as restaurants and retail where formal finance is limited (Jones et al., 2004; Ram et al., 2002). Somali entrepreneurs draw on transnational networks, including remittances, informal Islamic finance and diaspora-based trust systems, to fund commercial activity while avoiding institutions viewed as exclusionary (Jones et al., 2010; Ram et al., 2008). Jamaican entrepreneurs, similarly, excluded from mainstream lending due to racialised perceptions of risk, access capital through informal savings groups and reciprocal community support systems (Jones et al., 2015; Ram et al., 2012). While these mechanisms often lack scalability, they reflect deliberate strategies for maintaining financial autonomy and economic agency in the absence of institutional support (Carter et al., 2015; Smallbone et al., 2003).

In addressing socio-cultural and gendered exclusions, immigrant entrepreneurs use identity as a strategic resource to access opportunity, redefine legitimacy and expand market reach. South Asian entrepreneurs, particularly from Indian and Bangladeshi backgrounds, respond to saturated ethnic markets by adapting product offerings, incorporating contemporary trends and rebranding for wider appeal (Ram et al., 2002). Somali entrepreneurs engage in both co-ethnic and cross-cultural markets by leveraging religious affiliation, language skills and community standing to build trust and customer loyalty (Jones et al., 2010; Ram et al., 2008). Jamaican entrepreneurs integrate cultural expression into businesses across food, fashion and music, creating inclusive brand identities that challenge stereotypes and appeal to diverse consumers (Jones et al., 2015; Ram et al., 2017). South Asian and African-Caribbean women frequently convert domestic spaces into production hubs, balancing caregiving with income generation in the absence of affordable workspaces (Hall et al., 2017). Collective and family-run models often emerge where institutional support is limited, particularly in catering, clothing and childcare (Jones et al., 2015). These strategies reflect not only adaptation but the transformation of identity-based constraints into resources for locally grounded enterprise development.

Spatial strategies also play a central role in the adaptation of immigrant entrepreneurs operating in Birmingham's marginalised areas. In neighbourhoods such as Lozells and Rookery Road, Somali and Jamaican entrepreneurs repurpose neglected commercial spaces to build local economies that provide culturally specific goods and services while generating employment (Hall et al., 2015, 2017). South Asian entrepreneurs in the Balti Quarter rework long-established business identities through digital marketing, updated interiors and menu innovation to maintain cultural relevance and attract new consumer segments (Ram et al., 2002). These practices challenge exclusionary urban planning by embedding enterprise within disinvested spaces and asserting the presence of immigrant businesses in neighbourhood development. In many cases, entrepreneurs also serve as intermediaries between their communities and local authorities, advocating for improved services and infrastructure in areas often overlooked by municipal agendas (Jones et al., 2015; Ram et al., 2012). These actions underscore the political dimension of entrepreneurship, where business ownership becomes a means of claiming space, negotiating urban belonging and shaping Birmingham's post-industrial future.

Germany

Berlin's multicultural economy: immigrant entrepreneurs and the politics of belonging

Berlin's development as a multicultural metropolis has been shaped in part by the entrepreneurial activity of immigrants, who contribute to the city's economic dynamism and urban diversity. Immigrant-owned businesses are increasingly visible across sectors and neighbourhoods, playing a key role in sustaining local economies and introducing new forms of cultural and commercial expression (Rashid & Cepeda-García, 2021; Schmiz & Räuchle, 2020). These enterprises emerge within complex urban conditions shaped by Berlin's migration histories, economic transitions and planning regimes. They are embedded in community networks, transnational ties and socio-cultural infrastructures that reflect broader patterns of global mobility and local transformation (Schmiz, 2011, 2017; Terstriep et al., 2022). This analysis focuses on Vietnamese, Afro-Brazilian and Syrian (refugee) entrepreneurs, whose experiences highlight the varied pathways through which immigrant entrepreneurship unfolds in Berlin's evolving urban economy.

Contours of constraint: structural barriers facing immigrant entrepreneurs in Berlin

Immigrant entrepreneurs in Berlin face intersecting structural barriers shaped by exclusionary planning practices, limited institutional support and racialised recognition regimes. Vietnamese-owned commercial hubs such as the Dong Xuan Centre illustrate tensions between entrepreneurial activity and municipal oversight, where efforts to impose reductive ethnic branding risk oversimplifying complex business ecosystems (Schmiz, 2017; Schmiz & Kitzmann, 2017). These interventions often obscure community heterogeneity and constrain entrepreneurial expression. Syrian entrepreneurs, many of whom arrived through forced migration, encounter additional restrictions linked to legal precarity and integration frameworks that prioritise assimilation over autonomy (Embiricos, 2020; Terstriep et al., 2022). For Afro-Brazilian entrepreneurs, particularly women working in under-recognised sectors such as beauty and care, intersections of race, gender and spatial inequality further compound exclusion, limiting their visibility in both policy and planning (Lidola, 2014). Together, these cases point to an urban development model that remains poorly aligned with the spatial and institutional needs of Berlin's immigrant entrepreneurial communities.

Financial exclusion further restricts immigrant entrepreneurs' capacity to establish and expand their businesses. Vietnamese entrepreneurs, despite their long-standing presence, often depend on intra-community lending due to limited access to formal banking systems, which are contingent on documentation and credit history (Schmiz, 2011). Syrian entrepreneurs face similar constraints, with temporary residence status and limited credit history excluding them from institutional lending and state-funded startup programmes (Terstriep et al., 2022). These barriers hinder business growth and reinforce financial precarity, particularly among recently arrived groups. Afro-Brazilian entrepreneurs encounter financial gatekeeping shaped by racialised views of informality, which discourage investment and limit access to mainstream credit channels (Lidola, 2014). Existing financial support systems frequently adopt standardised approaches that overlook differentiated needs arising from migration histories, gendered labour roles and racialised positioning (Schmiz & Räuchle, 2020).

Cultural and social biases further reinforce exclusion and shape how immigrant entrepreneurs are perceived and supported. Afro-Brazilian women often navigate exoticised representations that draw consumer attention but confine business identities to narrow cultural frames, limiting their legitimacy in mainstream economic spaces (Lidola, 2014). Vietnamese entrepreneurs, despite decades of economic contribution, remain largely excluded from public narratives of innovation, with their businesses treated as static ethnic enterprises rather than dynamic actors in Berlin's urban economy (Schmiz, 2017; Schmiz & Kitzmann, 2017). Syrian entrepreneurs contend with humanitarian discourses that emphasise dependency over autonomy, undermining perceptions of their entrepreneurial capacity (Embiricos, 2020; Terstriep et al., 2022). These forms of symbolic marginalisation affect not only public perception but also access to networks, capital and policy resources. By reinforcing cultural hierarchies, they limit immigrant entrepreneurs' ability to claim visibility, assert institutional presence and participate in shaping Berlin's entrepreneurial landscape on equitable terms.

Acts of navigation: immigrant entrepreneurial strategies and claims to belonging in Berlin

In response to systemic exclusion, immigrant entrepreneurs in Berlin develop strategies that assert agency, reclaim space and contest marginalisation. Vietnamese entrepreneurs at the Dong Xuan Centre resist institutional misrepresentation by cultivating a commercial hub that reflects cultural specificity and cross-ethnic exchange, challenging municipal efforts to impose simplified narratives onto migrant economies (Schmiz, 2017; Schmiz & Räuchle, 2020). Afro-Brazilian female entrepreneurs deploy cultural branding and embodied labour to transform visibility into entrepreneurial capital, particularly within Berlin's fragmented beauty and wellness sector (Lidola, 2014). These actions reframe racialised and gendered identities as sources of innovation and economic strength. Syrian entrepreneurs, operating under conditions of legal precarity, draw on refugee support networks and community-based initiatives to establish ventures that reflect resilience and cultural meaning (Terstriep et al., 2022). Across these groups, entrepreneurship becomes a means of navigating spatial and institutional barriers, enabling immigrant actors to reshape belonging and challenge the bureaucratic flattening of identity.

To counter financial exclusion, immigrant entrepreneurs adopt alternative strategies rooted in informal systems, community solutions and digital innovation. Vietnamese entrepreneurs often participate in rotating savings groups and peer-based credit arrangements that provide flexible financing outside conventional institutions, reinforcing community trust and supporting business growth (Schmiz, 2011). Syrian entrepreneurs access capital through diaspora networks, religious charities and non-profit incubators designed for refugee-led startups (Terstriep et al., 2022). Though often limited in scope, these mechanisms enable initial enterprise formation in the absence of institutional credit. Afro-Brazilian entrepreneurs increasingly use social media to market services, attract clients and build reputational capital, particularly in sectors where formal registration remains inaccessible (Lidola, 2014). These digital strategies offer autonomy while reducing reliance on structurally biased systems. Taken together, these practices transform financial marginality into opportunity, challenging dominant assumptions about business formality and inclusion.

Immigrant entrepreneurs also counter social exclusion through symbolic practices, public engagement and collective advocacy that assert claims to visibility and belonging. Afro-Brazilian entrepreneurs participate in public events such as the Carnival of Cultures, where entrepreneurial activity becomes a stage for expressing cultural identity and challenging stereotypical representations (Lidola, 2014). Vietnamese entrepreneurs also engage in similar public forums, where economic presence intersects with cultural visibility to contest institutional marginalisation and promote community recognition (Schmiz & Kitzmann, 2017; Schmiz & Räuchle, 2020). Syrian entrepreneurs increasingly use narrative-based branding, online storytelling and collaborative media projects to reframe public perceptions, positioning themselves as active contributors rather than passive recipients of aid (Terstriep et al., 2022). Across these communities, solidarity networks facilitate mutual support, knowledge exchange and coordinated advocacy, offering a collective response to exclusionary governance structures. These practices highlight how immigrant entrepreneurship operates not only as an economic strategy but also as a means of performing urban citizenship and asserting cultural legitimacy.

Hamburg as a port of possibility: immigrant entrepreneurs and the remaking of urban belonging

Hamburg's emergence as a global port city has been shaped not only by its logistics infrastructure but also by the economic contributions of immigrant entrepreneurs. These actors play a key role in sustaining the city's commercial vitality and expanding its multicultural urban fabric, particularly in neighbourhoods shaped by mobility and demographic change (Tolciu, 2011; Wahlbeck, 2018). Immigrant entrepreneurship in Hamburg is situated at the intersection of transnational mobility and local urban development, supported by diasporic networks, informal economies and community infrastructures (Schüller & Schüler-Zhou, 2017; Tolciu, 2011). These enterprises reflect broader transformations in how economic participation, cultural presence and institutional access are negotiated in globalising cities. This study examines the experiences of Chinese, Turkish and Syrian (refugee) entrepreneurs, selected for their demographic relevance and contrasting migration trajectories, to explore how immigrant-led ventures engage with Hamburg's evolving urban and institutional landscape.

Navigating against the current: structural barriers of immigrant entrepreneurs in Hamburg

Immigrant entrepreneurs in Hamburg face a complex set of structural barriers shaped by intersecting institutional, cultural and market exclusions. Chinese entrepreneurs, while embedded in transnational commercial circuits, often struggle to integrate into local economic systems due to linguistic challenges, bureaucratic complexity and reliance on tightly knit diaspora networks (Schüller & Schüler-Zhou, 2017; Schüler-Zhou & Schüller, 2013). These networks enable initial market access but can also isolate entrepreneurs from broader commercial infrastructures and policy support (Leung, 2003). Turkish entrepreneurs, despite their long-standing presence, frequently encounter limitations tied to overreliance on co-ethnic markets. While ethnic social capital provides stability, it may restrict sectoral mobility and access to institutional networks (Tolciu, 2011). Syrian entrepreneurs, many with refugee status, contend with more acute barriers, including precarious legal conditions, the non-recognition of qualifications and limited entry into formal support systems (Hartmann & Schilling, 2019). The disconnect from both official frameworks and established migrant infrastructures places these entrepreneurs at a structural disadvantage, constraining both economic participation and integration into the urban fabric (Wang, 2013).

Financial exclusion reinforces these structural inequalities and restricts entrepreneurial capacity across all three groups. Chinese entrepreneurs frequently rely on intra-community lending networks due to barriers in accessing formal credit, including documentation requirements, language fluency and limited collateral histories (Schüller & Schüler-Zhou, 2017). This reliance on informal capital constrains business development and limits the ability to respond to evolving regulatory demands. Turkish entrepreneurs, despite widespread economic presence, continue to face structural discrimination in financial institutions, where migrant-led ventures are often categorised as high-risk or informal. This perception confines many to operate within narrow financial margins that inhibit innovation and expansion (Tolciu, 2011). For Syrian refugee entrepreneurs, legal insecurity and lack of assets block access to both public and private funding mechanisms, severely restricting enterprise formation and scalability (Hartmann & Schilling, 2019). These financial barriers contribute to informalisation, reduce entrepreneurial visibility and deepen disengagement from Hamburg's institutional economy.

Cultural and symbolic exclusions further shape the entrepreneurial trajectories of immigrant communities, undermining their social legitimacy and institutional recognition. Chinese entrepreneurs are often subject to stereotypes of cultural insularity or opportunism, which frame their economic activity as isolated from the broader economy and restrict opportunities for diversification and support (Leung, 2002, 2003). Turkish entrepreneurs face long-standing associations with informality and low-skilled labour, even as many diversify into professionalised, second-generation business models across varied sectors (Wahlbeck, 2018). These reductive narratives marginalise entrepreneurial achievements and hinder engagement with policy actors. Syrian refugee entrepreneurs are often viewed through a humanitarian lens that emphasises vulnerability over agency, reducing public recognition of their contributions and limiting access to partnerships or professional networks (Hartmann & Schilling, 2019). These cultural framings interact with material constraints, shaping how immigrant entrepreneurs are perceived, supported and positioned within Hamburg's evolving urban economy. Together, they restrict not only access to resources but also the capacity to claim visibility, legitimacy and belonging.

Charting new courses: immigrant entrepreneurial strategies and pathways to belonging in Hamburg

In response to structural and cultural exclusion, immigrant entrepreneurs in Hamburg adopt adaptive strategies that integrate transnational resources with local market practices. Chinese entrepreneurs combine diaspora knowledge with locally oriented approaches by forming bilingual teams, engaging German-speaking clients and building ties with local firms (Schüler-Zhou &

Schüller, 2013; Schüller & Schüler-Zhou, 2017). These actions reduce dependence on co-ethnic networks and increase visibility within the broader economy (Leung, 2003). Turkish entrepreneurs similarly blend traditional business models with market-responsive adaptation. Turkish-run establishments in gastronomy and retail now incorporate German consumer trends and digital outreach, expanding their reach beyond familiar communities (Tolciu, 2011). Syrian refugee entrepreneurs, working under conditions of legal and institutional precarity, establish micro-enterprises in sectors such as food and personal services by relying on religious communities and intercultural initiatives for support (Hartmann & Schilling, 2019). These strategies demonstrate how immigrant entrepreneurship evolves in response to local barriers, using hybrid practices to generate legitimacy, mobility and economic agency.

Community-based strategies also play a central role in sustaining and scaling immigrant enterprises. Chinese entrepreneurs frequently engage in ROSCAs and peer-based lending schemes that provide flexible capital outside formal institutions (Schüller & Schüler-Zhou, 2017). These mechanisms support ventures ineligible for institutional credit while reinforcing financial resilience within diaspora networks. Turkish entrepreneurs cultivate intergenerational business models by involving younger family members and facilitating entry into new sectors through informal mentorship and shared resources (Tolciu, 2011). This ensures continuity while enabling adaptation. Syrian entrepreneurs collaborate through non-governmental organisations (NGOs), language cafés and intercultural workshops, where they exchange knowledge, build networks and access early-stage support (Hartmann & Schilling, 2019). These informal infrastructures enable access to capital, expertise and clientele, circumventing structural exclusion. Collectively, these community-rooted strategies sustain entrepreneurial agency and foster embedded, trust-based alternatives to mainstream economic systems.

Beyond economic survival, immigrant entrepreneurs in Hamburg deploy symbolic and spatial strategies to assert presence and challenge exclusion. Turkish entrepreneurs participate in cultural festivals, street markets and neighbourhood revitalisation initiatives, using commerce to counter reductive ethnic framings and increase civic visibility (Wahlbeck, 2018). Chinese entrepreneurs build symbolic legitimacy through commercial anchoring in neighbourhoods marked by sectoral specialisation, where businesses serve as nodes of transnational identity and local economic participation (Leung, 2002, 2003). These enclaves function as culturally resonant spaces that enable negotiated forms of integration. Syrian entrepreneurs increasingly engage in narrative-based branding, media storytelling and public collaborations to resist humanitarian framings and reassert agency (Hartmann & Schilling, 2019). Across these groups, symbolic strategies expand the role of immigrant entrepreneurs beyond the economic sphere, positioning them as actors engaged in cultural negotiation and spatial transformation. Entrepreneurship thus becomes a mode of civic participation and belonging in a city shaped by super-diversity and evolving forms of embeddedness (Ram et al., 2013; Vertovec, 2007).

Comparative synthesis: immigrant entrepreneurship in the UK and Germany

Immigrant entrepreneurship in the UK and Germany unfolds within distinct institutional systems but is shaped by common structural exclusions. Entrepreneurs across both contexts contend with racialised financial exclusion, regulatory complexity and limited institutional responsiveness. National policy frameworks and municipal governance mediate access to resources, producing differentiated yet similarly segmented entrepreneurial pathways. In both cases, entrepreneurs respond by mobilising transnational capital, community networks and cultural identity to sustain enterprise and navigate exclusion. As shown in Table 5.1, these dynamics vary across local and national contexts but converge in reinforcing informality and restricting upward mobility.

Strategic policy interventions for Western Europe

Effective support for immigrant entrepreneurship in Western Europe requires more than comparative analysis. While institutional contexts differ, Table 5.1 highlights recurring constraints shaped by migration regimes, regulatory systems and socio-cultural hierarchies. These overlapping barriers, including financial exclusion, administrative opacity and symbolic misrecognition, limit access to opportunity and reinforce segmented entrepreneurial trajectories.

The MEF (Kloosterman et al., 1999) provides a valuable lens on how institutional structures shape entrepreneurial outcomes but gives limited attention to identity. As Anthias (2013) and Essers & Benschop (2009) argue, identity is not fixed but shaped by social positioning and power relations. Immigrant entrepreneurs mobilise cultural capital, diasporic infrastructures and locally embedded networks to navigate exclusion and construct alternative pathways. These dynamics reveal the limits of generic policy approaches and underscore the need for equity-oriented and context-sensitive interventions. The following section outlines five targeted proposals to build more inclusive and responsive entrepreneurial ecosystems across Western Europe.

TABLE 5.1 Key comparative dimensions of immigrant entrepreneurship in the UK and Germany

Category	*UK*	*Germany*
Immigration policy framework	Post-Brexit uncertainty; fragmented governance; limited municipal coordination.	Asylum-linked restrictions; delayed legal integration; disjointed federal-local implementation.
Institutional ecosystem	Inconsistent local governance; limited migrant-specific programming; weak municipal engagement.	Rigid planning regimes; narrow definitions of enterprise; low institutional flexibility.
Financial access and inclusion	Racialised lending practices; exclusion from formal finance; reliance on ROSCAs and informal community capital.	Documentation barriers; exclusion from state schemes; informal lending and diaspora capital.
Regulatory environment	Borough-level inconsistency; licensing opacity; unpredictable enforcement.	Centralised planning systems; limited procedural flexibility; restricted access to licensing and zoning approvals.
Community & ethnic networks	Dense co-ethnic networks enable startup but constrain scalability and visibility.	Diaspora networks support access but remain marginal in institutional terms.
Transnational strategies	Diasporic capital and hybrid ventures link ethnic markets with digital platforms.	Informal remittances, branding and transnational trade underpin entrepreneurial strategies.
Cultural identity and market positioning	Identity mobilised to access hybrid sectors (e.g., digital, fashion and care).	Identity mobilised through public branding, cultural participation and informal economies to assert visibility.

Harmonising regulatory frameworks to strengthen institutional accessibility

Fragmented and inconsistent regulatory systems impose significant burdens on immigrant entrepreneurs across Western European cities. In London, borough-level licensing variations delay business operations for Chinese and Vietnamese entrepreneurs in the food and retail sectors (Bagwell, 2015; Kitching et al., 2009). In Berlin, municipal branding of Vietnamese commercial spaces reinforces reductive ethnic narratives, undermining business legitimacy and spatial integration (Schmiz & Kitzmann, 2017). In Birmingham, South Asian and African-Caribbean entrepreneurs operate within opaque regulatory environments, with limited access to procedural guidance or institutional support (Jones et al., 2015; Ram et al., 2008). These conditions disproportionately affect those unfamiliar with legal systems or lacking access to regulatory translation and culturally appropriate advisory services. Without structural reform, they entrench spatial segmentation and weaken institutional trust.

To address these challenges, national and municipal governments should implement multilingual, user-centred digital platforms that consolidate business registration, licensing and compliance. These systems should be co-designed with immigrant entrepreneurs to ensure transparency, accessibility and usability, and must include sector-specific legal updates in real time. In cities like Hamburg, bilateral regulatory coordination with diaspora chambers can ease entry barriers for immigrant-led and transnational ventures. Municipalities should track progress through measurable targets, including a 30% reduction in registration and licensing times and a corresponding rise in immigrant business formation within three years. Regulatory simplification is essential not only to reduce administrative burden but also to foster inclusive participation and entrepreneurial mobility across diverse urban economies.

Expanding equitable access to finance through inclusive lending ecosystems

Access to finance remains a central barrier for immigrant entrepreneurs in Western Europe, particularly for those operating outside formal networks or with precarious legal status. In London, South Asian and African entrepreneurs report racialised lending decisions and limited access to institutional credit, prompting reliance on rotating savings associations (Basit, 2017; Ojo, 2021; Ojo et al., 2013). In Berlin, Afro-Brazilian and Syrian entrepreneurs face compounded constraints, including documentation barriers, exclusion from public schemes and discriminatory risk profiling (Lidola, 2014; Terstriep et al., 2022). In Hamburg, Turkish and Chinese entrepreneurs often depend on intra-ethnic credit systems that support early-stage activity but limit long-term scalability and institutional engagement (Schüller & Schüler-Zhou, 2017; Tolciu, 2011). These exclusions are embedded in financial infrastructures that privilege collateral, formal credit histories and normative financial behaviour.

To address these disparities, governments should establish inclusive microfinance initiatives co-developed with community organisations and financial technology providers. These programmes should incorporate digital tools such as blockchain-enabled peer lending and artificial intelligence-based credit scoring that can account for informal financial practices, including savings group participation and peer guarantees. Culturally tailored financial education and digital wallets can further support trust-building and expand access. Policy effectiveness should be measured through a 25% increase in immigrant access to formal credit and broader participation in non-ethnic sectors within five years. By recognising and integrating alternative financial behaviours, these interventions can expand the foundations of financial inclusion and support more sustainable entrepreneurial growth.

Strengthening social capital through cross-cultural mentorship and networking infrastructure

Immigrant entrepreneurs frequently rely on co-ethnic networks for business knowledge, regulatory navigation and resource mobilisation. However, these networks often remain disconnected from formal support structures and wider economic ecosystems. In Birmingham, Somali and South Asian entrepreneurs operate within robust community infrastructures but have limited access to cross-sector mentorship and city-level development initiatives (Hall et al., 2017; Ram et al., 2012). In Berlin, Vietnamese entrepreneurs at the Dong Xuan Centre sustain transnational commercial activity yet remain marginal in public narratives of entrepreneurship and innovation (Schmiz, 2017). These patterns reflect not a lack of initiative but structural barriers that limit integration into diverse professional networks capable of supporting growth and visibility.

Policymakers should invest in inclusive mentorship hubs that connect ethnic and mainstream business communities. These hubs should provide sector-specific coaching, regulatory guidance and funding access, co-developed with community-based organisations and delivered through both in-person and virtual platforms. Transnational mentorship programmes, particularly among diasporas operating in multiple European cities, can foster transnational collaboration and scaling. Progress should be assessed by tracking a 20% increase in immigrant participation in structured mentorship programmes and growth in collaborative ventures across ethnic and mainstream sectors. Social capital must be understood not only as an informal resource but as an institutional asset necessary for equitable participation in entrepreneurial ecosystems.

Advancing gender-inclusive policies for entrepreneurial empowerment

Gender-based exclusion remains a structural barrier within immigrant entrepreneurship across Western Europe. In Birmingham, South Asian female entrepreneurs often establish home-based businesses to align with community expectations yet face limited access to institutional finance and business support (Basit, 2017; Hall et al., 2017). In Berlin, Afro-Brazilian women encounter compounded marginalisation across race and gender, frequently operating in undervalued or exoticised sectors such as personal care (Lidola, 2014). In Hamburg, Syrian refugee women navigate legal insecurity, social isolation and exclusion from mainstream entrepreneurial support systems (Hartmann & Schilling, 2019). These constraints reflect institutional frameworks that narrowly define entrepreneurial legitimacy and fail to accommodate caregiving responsibilities, migration histories, or cultural norms.

Policy responses should include the creation of female-led incubators that offer culturally responsive mentorship, childcare support and targeted training in sectors such as digital services, care economies and sustainable enterprise. Support structures should also integrate mobile-accessible business planning tools, peer-led financial literacy and planning programmes and flexible workspaces designed to accommodate domestic responsibilities. Partnerships with migrant women's advocacy organisations can ensure that interventions are designed with intersectional awareness and embedded in long-term institutional systems. Governments should aim to increase immigrant women's business registrations by 25% and expand sectoral diversity within five years. Supporting immigrant women as entrepreneurs requires frameworks that recognise social reproduction, transnational mobility and cultural embeddedness as central to business strategy.

Embedding digital and technological infrastructure to foster innovation

Digital infrastructure has become a central component of immigrant entrepreneurial strategy, particularly among second-generation entrepreneurs and those excluded from formal markets. In London, digital platforms facilitate cross-market branding and direct-to-consumer sales for South Asian and East Asian entrepreneurs (Pruthi & Tasavori, 2022). In Berlin, Syrian and Afro-Brazilian entrepreneurs use social media and online storytelling to gain visibility and legitimacy in the absence of formal retail space (Hartmann & Schilling, 2019; Lidola, 2014). Despite this potential, access to digital tools and training remains uneven. In Birmingham, gaps in digital literacy and underinvestment in immigrant-concentrated neighbourhoods continue to limit technology adoption and business scalability (Hall et al., 2017).

Municipal governments should prioritise the development of digital entrepreneurship accelerators that provide accessible training in e-commerce, logistics and data-driven business operations. Programmes should be designed for mobile-first use and offered in multiple languages to accommodate diverse user needs. Partnerships with universities and technology firms can support mentorship, innovation grants and the adaptation of digital tools, including blockchain applications and automated supply-chain systems. Digital upskilling should be framed as a condition of equitable market access rather than a competitive edge. Policy outcomes should include a 30% increase in immigrant-led digital business launches and demonstrable improvement in online market reach across ethnic and mainstream sectors within three years. These interventions provide the digital foundation needed for inclusive entrepreneurial innovation and sustainable growth.

Conclusion

This chapter has demonstrated how immigrant entrepreneurship in Western Europe is shaped by intersecting forms of institutional, financial and symbolic exclusion and how these barriers are navigated through identity-based strategies, transnational capital and community-embedded practices. Drawing on documented case studies from London, Birmingham, Berlin and Hamburg, it applied the RMEF as a core analytical lens. Rather than offering generalisable claims, the chapter used the framework to trace patterns of resource mobilisation, identity negotiation and institutional engagement across diverse urban contexts. The analysis highlights how immigrant entrepreneurship operates not as a linear pathway to integration but as a negotiated and contested process embedded within broader regimes of race, gender, class and migration status. Future research should apply and empirically test the framework across migration contexts, institutional settings and identity formations. In doing so, immigrant entrepreneurship can be more fully understood as both a site of economic participation and a form of political agency that reshapes belonging and drives urban transformation.

References

Anthias, F. (2013). Intersectional what? Social divisions, intersectionality and levels of analysis. *Ethnicities, 13*(1), 3–19. https://doi.org/10.1177/1468796812463547

Bagwell, S. (2015). Transnational entrepreneurship amongst Vietnamese communities in London. *Journal of Ethnic and Migration Studies, 41*(2), 329–349. https://doi.org/10.1080/1369183X.2014.907739

Basit, A. (2017). Ethnography of female diaspora networks: The emerging case of Pakistani Female immigrant entrepreneurs in London. *Journal of Entrepreneurship and Innovation in Emerging Economies, 3*(1), 1–15. https://doi.org/10.1177/2393957516684467

Basu, A. (2011). From "break out" to "breakthrough": Successful market strategies of immigrant entrepreneurs in the UK. *International Journal of Entrepreneurship, 14,* 59.

Basu, A., & Altinay, E. (2002). The interaction between culture and entrepreneurship in London's immigrant businesses. *International Small Business Journal, 20*(4), 371–393. https://doi.org/10.1177/0266242602204001

Basu, A., & Goswami, A. (1999). Determinants of South Asian entrepreneurial growth in Britain: A multivariate analysis. *Small Business Economics, 13*(1), 57–70. https://doi.org/10.1023/A:1008025628570

Bruni, A., Gherardi, S., & Poggio, B. (2004). Doing gender, doing entrepreneurship: An ethnographic account of intertwined practices. *Gender, Work & Organisation, 11*(4), 406–429. https://doi.org/10.1111/j.1468-0432.2004.00240.x

Carter, S., Mwaura, S., Ram, M., Trehan, K., & Jones, T. (2015). Barriers to ethnic minority and female's enterprise: Existing evidence, policy tensions and unsettled questions. *International Small Business Journal, 33*(1), 49–69. https://doi.org/10.1177/0266242614556823

Degler, E., & Liebig, T. (2017). *Finding their way: Labour market integration of refugees in Germany.* OECD. https://www.oecd.org/migration

Embiricos, A. (2020). From refugee to entrepreneur? Challenges to refugee self-reliance in Berlin, Germany. *Journal of Refugee Studies, 33*(1), 245–267. https://doi.org/10.1093/jrs/fez073

Edwards, P., Ram, M., Jones, T., & Doldor, S. (2018). New migrant businesses and their workers: Developing, but not transforming, the ethnic economy. In J. Agius Vallejo & S. L. Canizales (Eds.), *Intersectionality and ethnic entrepreneurship* (pp. 35–65). Routledge. https://doi.org/10.4324/9781315164373-3

Essers, C., & Benschop, Y. (2007). Enterprising identities: Female immigrant entrepreneurs of Moroccan or Turkish origin in the Netherlands. *Organisation Studies, 28*(1), 49–69. https://doi.org/10.1177/0170840606068256

Essers, C., & Benschop, Y. (2009). Muslim business female doing boundary work: The negotiation of Islam, gender and ethnicity within entrepreneurial contexts. *Human Relations, 62*(3), 403–423. https://doi.org/10.1177/0018726708101042

George, R., & Dhaliwal, S. (2025). *Navigating uncertainty: Challenges faced by Bangladeshi female entrepreneurs in East London, UK. The Journal of Entrepreneurship, 33*(4), 839–861. https://doi.org/10.1177/09713557241309481

Hack-Polay, D., Igwe, P. A., & Madichie, N. O. (2020). The role of institutional and family embeddedness in the failure of Sub-Saharan African migrant family businesses. The *International Journal of Entrepreneurship and Innovation, 21*(4), 237–249. https://doi.org/10.1177/1465750320909732

Halkias, D., Arifeen, S., & Mourad, L. (2016). United Kingdom: The rise of South Asian female entrepreneurship. In D. Halkias & M. Hassannezhad Chavoushi (Eds.), *Female immigrant entrepreneurs* (pp. 135–148). Taylor & Francis.

Hall, S., King, J., & Finlay, R. (2015). *City street data profile on ethnicity, economy and migration: Rookery Road, Birmingham.* ESRC Report.

Hall, S., King, J., & Finlay, R. (2017). *Migrant infrastructure: Transaction economies in Birmingham and Leicester, UK. Urban Studies, 54*(6), 1311–1327. https://doi.org/10.1177/0042098016634586

Hartmann, C., & Schilling, K. (2019). Cham Saar: The first Syrian-German cheese manufacturer. In S. Heilbrunn, J. Freiling, & A. Harima (Eds.), *Refugee entrepreneurship* (pp. 51–70). Palgrave Macmillan. https://doi.org/10.1007/978-3-319-92534-9_3

Jones, T., Ram, M., & Edwards, P. (2004). Illegal immigrants and the informal economy: Worker and employer experiences in the Asian underground economy. *International Journal of Economic Development, 6*(2), 98–120.

Jones, T., Ram, M., Edwards, P., Kiselinchev, A., & Muchenje, L. (2014). *Mixed embeddedness and new migrant enterprise in the UK. Entrepreneurship & Regional Development, 26*(5–6), 500–520. https://doi.org/10.1080/08985626.2014.950697

Jones, T., Ram, M., Li, Y., Edwards, P., & Villares, M. (2015). *Super-diverse Britain and new migrant enterprises.* Institute for Research into Super Diversity (IRiS) Working Paper Series, WP8.

Jones, T., Ram, M., & Theodorakopoulos, N. (2010). Transnationalism as a force for ethnic minority enterprise? The case of Somalis in Leicester. *International Journal of Urban and Regional Research, 34*(3), 565–585. https://doi.org/10.1111/j.1468-2427.2010.00913.x

Jones, T., Roberts, R., & Ram, M. (2022). Much ado about very little: The dubious connection between ethnic minority business policy and ethnic minority entrepreneurship. *International Migration, 61*(2), 9–26. https://doi.org/10.1111/imig.12959

Kitching, J., Smallbone, D., & Athayde, R. (2009). Ethnic diasporas and business competitiveness: Minority-owned enterprises in London. *Journal of Ethnic and Migration Studies, 35*(4), 689–705. https://doi.org/10.1080/13691830902765368

Kloosterman, R. C, Van Der Leun, J., & Rath, J. (1999). Mixed embeddedness:(in) formal economic activities and immigrant businesses in the Netherlands. *International Journal of Urban and Regional Research, 23*(2), 252–266. https://doi.org/10.1111/1468-2427.00194

Leung, M. W. (2003). Beyond Chinese, beyond food: Unpacking the regulated Chinese restaurant business in Germany. *Entrepreneurship & Regional Development, 15*(2), 103–118. https://doi.org/10.1080/0898562032000075140

Leung, M. W. H. (2002). From four-course Peking duck to take-away Singapore rice: An inquiry into the dynamics of the ethnic Chinese catering business in Germany. *International Journal of Entrepreneurial Behaviour & Research, 8*(1/2), 134–147. https://doi.org/10.1108/13552550210423769

Levie, J. (2007). Immigration, in-migration, ethnicity and entrepreneurship in the United Kingdom. *Small Business Economics, 28*(2–3), 143–169. https://doi.org/10.1007/s11187-006-9013-2

Levie, J., & Smallbone, D. (2006). Immigration, ethnicity and entrepreneurial behaviour. In M. Minniti, A. Zacharakis, S. Spinelli Jr., M. P. Rice, & T. G. Habbershon (Eds.), *Entrepreneurship* (pp. 157–180). Praeger.

Lidola, M. (2014). Negotiating integration in Berlin's waxing studios: Brazilian migrants' gendered appropriation of urban consumer spaces and "ethnic" entrepreneurship. *Journal of Contemporary History, 49*(1), 228–251. https://doi.org/10.1177/0022009413505664

Mavrommatis, G. (2015). South Asian tales: Ethnic entrepreneurship and narratives of spatialized transnational identities emerging in an East London (UK), inner-city area. *Diaspora Studies, 8*(2), 89–103. https://doi.org/10.1080/09739572.2015.1029710

McEwan, C., Pollard, J., & Henry, N. (2005). The 'global' in the city economy: Multicultural economic development in Birmingham. *International Journal of Urban and Regional Research, 29*(4), 916–933. https://doi.org/10.1111/j.1468-2427.2005.00628.x

McPherson, M. C. (2017). Identity and difference: Re-thinking UK South Asian entrepreneurship. *Journal of Enterprising Communities: People and Places in the Global Economy, 11*(5), 564–589. https://doi.org/10.1108/JEC-04-2016-0012

Migration Observatory. (2020). *Integration in the UK and the post-Brexit immigration system*. University of Oxford. https://migrationobservatory.ox.ac.uk/resources/commentaries/integration-in-the-uk-and-the-post-brexit-immigration-system/

Nathan, M., & Lee, N. (2013). *Cultural diversity, innovation, and entrepreneurship: Firm-level evidence from London. Economic Geography, 89*(4), 367–394. https://doi.org/10.1111/ecge.12016

Nwankwo, S. (2005). *Characterisation of Black African entrepreneurship in the UK: A pilot study. Journal of Small Business and Enterprise Development, 12*(1), 120–136. https://doi.org/10.1108/14626000510579680

Ojo, S. (2021). *Black African perceptions of entrepreneurial outcomes in the UK. Society and Business Review, 16*(2), 278–305. https://doi.org/10.1108/SBR-06-2020-0087

Ojo, S., Nwankwo, S., & Gbadamosi, A. (2013). African diaspora entrepreneurs: Navigating entrepreneurial spaces in 'home' and 'host' countries. *The International Journal of Entrepreneurship and Innovation, 14*(4), 289–299. https://doi.org/10.5367/ijei.2013.0126

Osaghae, O. G., & Cooney, T. M. (2019). Exploring the relationship between immigrant enclave theory and transnational diaspora entrepreneurial opportunity formation. *Journal of Ethnic and Migration Studies, 46*(10), 2086–2105. https://doi.org/10.1080/1369183X.2018.1560001

Polychronopoulos, D., & Nguyen-Duc, A. (2024). *Migrant entrepreneurship support in Europe: A PRISMA systematic literature review. F1000Research, 12,* 1300.

Poggesi, S., & Mari, M. (2024). Immigrant female immigrant entrepreneurship research: Mapping the field. *Journal of Management History, Advance online publication.* https://doi.org/10.1108/JMH-09-2023-0099

Pruthi, S., & Tasavori, M. (2022). Staying in or stepping out? Growth strategies of second-generation immigrant entrepreneurs. *International Business Review, 31*(5), Article 101997. https://doi.org/10.1016/j.ibusrev.2022.101997

Ram, M., & Deakins, D. (1996). African-Caribbeans in business. *Journal of Ethnic and Migration Studies, 22*(1), 67–84. https://doi.org/10.1080/1369183X.1996.9976522

Ram, M., Jones, T., Abbas, T., & Sanghera, B. (2002). Ethnic minority enterprise in its urban context: South Asian restaurants in Birmingham. *International Journal of Urban and Regional Research, 26*(1), 24–40. https://doi.org/10.1111/1468-2427.00361

Ram, M., Jones, T., Doldor, S., Villares-Varela, M., & Li, H. (2021). What happens to refugee-origin entrepreneurs? Combining mixed embeddedness and strategy perspectives in a longitudinal study. *Ethnic and Racial Studies, 45*(16), 1–27. https://doi.org/10.1080/01419870.2021.1991970

Ram, M., Jones, T., & Edwards, P. (2013). Engaging with super-diversity: New migrant businesses and the research-policy nexus. *International Small Business Journal, 31*(4), 337–356. https://doi.org/10.1177/0266242611429979

Ram, M., Jones, T., & Villares-Varela, M. (2017). Migrant entrepreneurship: Reflections on research and practice. *International Small Business Journal, 35*(1), 3–18.

Ram, M., Theodorakopoulos, N., & Jones, T. (2008). Forms of capital, mixed embeddedness and Somali enterprise. *Work, employment and society, 22*(3), 427–446. https://doi.org/10.1177/0950017008093479

Ram, M., Trehan, K., Rouse, J., Woldesenbet, K., & Jones, T. (2012). Ethnic minority business support in the West Midlands: Challenges and developments. *Environment and Planning C: Government and Policy, 30*(3), 504–519. https://doi.org/10.1068/c11167b

Rashid, L., & Cepeda-García, S. (2021). *Self-categorising and othering in migrant integration: The case of entrepreneurs in Berlin. Sustainability, 13*(4), Article 2145. https://doi.org/10.3390/su13042145

Rath, J., & Swagerman, A. (2016). Promoting ethnic entrepreneurship in European cities: Sometimes ambitious, mostly absent, rarely addressing structural features. *International Migration, 54*(1), 152–166. https://doi.org/10.1111/imig.12215

Räuchle, C., & Schmiz, A. (2019). Migrant economies: Opportunity structures and potential in different city types. *Ethnic and Racial Studies, 42*(10), 1766–1787. https://doi.org/10.1080/01419870.2018.1506143

Schmiz, A. (2011). *Transnationalität als Ressource? Netzwerke vietnamesischer Migrantinnen und Migranten zwischen Berlin und Vietnam*. transcript Verlag.

Schmiz, A. (2017). Staging a 'Chinatown' in Berlin: The role of city branding in the urban governance of ethnic diversity. *European Urban and Regional Studies, 24*(3), 290–303. https://doi.org/10.1177/0969776416637208

Schmiz, A., & Kitzmann, R. (2017). Negotiating an Asiatown in Berlin: Ethnic diversity in urban planning. *Cities, 70*, 1–10. https://doi.org/10.1016/j.cities.2017.06.001

Schmiz, A., & Räuchle, C. (2020). Migrantische Ökonomie als Teil der lokalen Ökonomie. In S. Henn, M. Behling, & S. Schäfer (Eds.), *Lokale Ökonomie – Konzepte, Quartierskontexte und Interventionen* (pp. 1–17). Springer. https://doi.org/10.1007/978-3-662-57780-6_5

Schüler-Zhou, Y., & Schüller, M. (2013). An empirical study of Chinese subsidiaries' decision-making autonomy in Germany. *Asian Business & Management, 12*(4), 321–350. https://doi.org/10.1057/abm.2013.1

Schüller, M., Schüler-Zhou, Y., & Zhou, (2017). Chinese investment strategies and migration: Does diaspora matter? A case study on Germany. In M. Sanfilippo & A. Weinar (Eds.), *Chinese migration and economic relations with Europe* (pp. 140–170). Routledge.

Sepulveda, R. L., Syrett, S., & Lyon, F. (2008). *New ethnic minority business communities in Britain: Challenges of diversity and informality for the UK business and policy frameworks* (Working Paper No. 1). Social Policy Research Centre, Middlesex University.

Sepulveda, R. L., Syrett, S., & Lyon, F. (2011). Population superdiversity and new migrant enterprise: The case of London. *Entrepreneurship & Regional Development, 23*(7–8), 469–497. https://doi.org/10.1080/08985620903420211

Smallbone, D., Ram, M., Deakins, D., & Baldock, R. (2003). Access to finance by ethnic minority businesses in the UK. *International Small Business Journal, 21*(3), 291–314. https://doi.org/10.1177/02662426030213003

Terstriep, J., David, A., Ruthemeier, A., & Elo, M. (2022). *The role of local embeddedness of transnational migrant start-ups in the COVID-19 crises: Examples from the Berlin start-up ecosystem* (No. 22/05). IAT Discussion Paper. https://doi.org/10.53190/dp/202205

Tolciu, A. (2011). Migrant entrepreneurs and social capital: A revised perspective. *International Journal of Entrepreneurial Behaviour & Research, 17*(4), 409–427. https://doi.org/10.1108/13552551111139647

Vertovec, S. (2007). Super-diversity and its implications. *Ethnic and Racial Studies, 30*(6), 1024–1054. https://doi.org/10.1080/01419870701599465

Virdee, S., & McGeever, B. (2017). Racism, crisis, Brexit. *Ethnic and Racial Studies, 41*(10), 1802–1819. https://doi.org/10.1080/01419870.2017.1361544

Wahlbeck, Ö. R. (2018). Combining mixed embeddedness and transnationalism: The utilization of social resources among Turkish migrant entrepreneurs. *Sociologica: International Journal for Sociological Debate, 12*(2), 73–86. https://doi.org/10.6092/issn.1971-8853/8623

Wang, Q. (2013). Constructing a multilevel spatial approach in ethnic entrepreneurship studies. *International Journal of Entrepreneurial Behaviour & Research, 19*(1), 97–113. https://doi.org/10.1108/13552551311299279

Zhang, J. (2015). A preliminary study of barriers to bank financing of ethnic Chinese entrepreneurs in the UK. *Open Journal of Social Sciences, 3*, 105–110. https://doi.org/10.4236/jss.2015.37018

6

IMMIGRANT ENTREPRENEURSHIP IN OCEANIA

Intersectionality, translocal agency and institutional navigation

Introduction

Immigrant entrepreneurship plays a central role in shaping the economic, social and cultural fabric of urban environments across Oceania. In both Australia and New Zealand, migrant entrepreneurs contribute to economic diversification, employment creation and intercultural exchange across sectors including retail, hospitality, logistics, services and innovation-driven industries (Collins, 2003; Krivokapic-Skoko et al., 2023; Spoonley et al., 2014). These businesses often emerge in response to systemic barriers such as segmented labour markets, racialised and gendered exclusion and restricted access to formal financial services (Duan et al., 2021; Rametse et al., 2018). In addressing these barriers, entrepreneurs mobilise cultural heritage, diasporic networks and transnational capital to develop hybrid models that span formal and informal economies (Cain & Spoonley, 2013; Collins et al., 2020). Their ventures not only support local economic activity but also contribute to community resilience in contexts shaped by displacement, inequality or limited institutional support, often in collaboration with non-governmental organisations (NGOs) (Choi, 2022; Collins & Kunz, 2009; Song, 2013).

Despite their economic contributions, migrant entrepreneurs frequently operate within institutionally complex and socially contested settings. Regulatory systems in both countries tend to favour established actors, leaving immigrants to navigate unfamiliar legal frameworks, limited support infrastructure and exclusionary licensing procedures (Choi, 2022; Rametse et al., 2018). These barriers are further shaped by broader socio-political conditions, including settler-colonial legacies, shifting immigration regimes and contested narratives of multiculturalism (Burnley, 1999; Collins, 2021). While both countries express policy commitments to inclusion, access to resources, legitimacy and support services remains uneven, particularly for racialised communities, women and refugees. These constraints are not only institutional but spatial, reinforced by patterns of segregation, uneven service delivery and urban inequalities that restrict visibility and entrepreneurial mobility (Guadagno et al., 2017; Spoonley et al., 2014).

Although the literature on immigrant entrepreneurship in Oceania is growing, significant conceptual and methodological gaps persist. Existing studies often focus on specific groups or localised cases, limiting comparative insights and intersectional analysis (Verheijen et al., 2014;

DOI: 10.4324/9781003605072-8

Xu et al., 2019). While the mixed embeddedness framework (MEF) (Kloosterman et al., 1999; Kloosterman & Rath, 2001) has informed global scholarship on migrant entrepreneurship, its application in Oceania has been limited and insufficiently responsive to regional factors such as legal precarity, informal economies and postcolonial governance. Moreover, the roles of identity and intersectionality are inconsistently addressed, constraining efforts to understand how entrepreneurs negotiate exclusion, perform legitimacy and position themselves within unequal institutional environments (Essers & Benschop, 2009; Pio & Dana, 2014; Wang & Warn, 2018). Without sustained attention to embedded social and political dynamics, prevailing frameworks that risk analytical oversimplification.

This chapter applies the reconceptualised mixed embeddedness framework (RMEF) introduced in Chapter 2 to demonstrate its analytical value by using secondary case study material on immigrant entrepreneurship in urban contexts shaped by settler-colonial legacies and post-disaster reconstruction. Integrating institutional theory and placing entrepreneurial identity, shaped through intersectionality, alongside translocal agency, at the centre of the analysis, the framework is used to show how immigrant entrepreneurs in Australia and New Zealand respond to opportunity structures characterised by regulatory complexity, spatial inequality and symbolic exclusion (Collins, 2003; Pio & Dana, 2014; Rametse et al., 2018). It highlights how identity is not only shaped by institutional contexts but is also strategically mobilised to access markets, construct legitimacy and adapt to structural barriers. Through this approach, the chapter illustrates how immigrant entrepreneurs draw on cultural capital, symbolic strategies and translocal networks to sustain their ventures. Rather than treating entrepreneurial outcomes as structurally determined, the framework emphasises the role of agency and adaptation in shaping entrepreneurial pathways.

The chapter focuses on four urban case studies: Sydney and Melbourne in Australia and Auckland and Christchurch in New Zealand. These cities are selected for their demographic diversity, contrasting governance frameworks and varied migration trajectories, which make them valuable sites for examining immigrant entrepreneurship under different institutional and spatial conditions. Sydney and Melbourne, as Australia's largest cities, offer dynamic markets and cultural diversity but also present regulatory fragmentation and uneven access to enterprise support (Burnley, 1999; Choi, 2022; Collins, 2021). Auckland, shaped by Pacific and Asian migration, supports ethnic niche markets and transnational entrepreneurial forms (Spoonley et al., 2014). Christchurch, as a post-disaster city, presents a distinct context where immigrant entrepreneurs have played a central role in economic recovery and social integration (Christchurch City Council [CCC], 2017; Guadagno et al., 2017; Pio & Dana, 2014).

The chapter begins with an analysis of immigrant entrepreneurship in the Australian cities of Sydney and Melbourne, followed by Auckland and Christchurch in New Zealand. It then identifies key patterns and contextual variations across the two national contexts. The next section considers policy challenges, with attention to informality, intersectional exclusion and the need for spatially responsive support mechanisms. The chapter concludes by evaluating the contribution of the RMEF and outlining directions for future research.

Australia

Sydney's multicultural nexus: how immigrant entrepreneurs drive innovation and urban growth

Sydney is one of Australia's most globally connected cities and a central hub for immigration, shaped by longstanding migration from East Asia, South Asia and the Middle East (Ley &

Murphy, 2001; Forrest & Johnston, 2001). Immigrant entrepreneurs contribute significantly to the city's economy, generating employment, revitalising neighbourhoods and introducing new forms of cultural and commercial expression (Collins, 2021; Wang & Warn, 2019). These businesses are active across a range of sectors, including food services, personal care, retail and logistics, reflecting the city's complex and diverse entrepreneurial ecology (Xu et al., 2019; Choi, 2022). Sydney's institutional environment, marked by multilayered regulatory systems and spatial inequalities, shapes how immigrant entrepreneurs engage with local markets and navigate urban space (Forrest & Dunn, 2006; Markus et al., 2009). These dynamics intersect with broader questions of multiculturalism, inclusion and access to opportunity in Australia's evolving urban landscape (Shin & Collins, 2012; Rametse et al., 2018). This analysis draws on the experiences of Chinese, Korean and Hazara Afghan (refugee) entrepreneurs, selected for their varied migration histories and their embeddedness within Sydney's diverse economic and social fabric.

Urban fault lines: structural and cultural barriers confronting Sydney's immigrant entrepreneurs

Access to finance remains a critical barrier for immigrant entrepreneurs in Sydney, shaping their capacity to establish, sustain and grow businesses. Hazara Afghan refugees face compounded exclusion due to insecure migration status and limited credit histories, which often restrict them to informal lending practices such as rotating savings and credit associations (ROSCAs). While these systems provide vital startup capital, they lack the scale and security needed for business expansion (Collins, 2017; Rametse et al., 2018). Korean entrepreneurs tend to bypass mainstream financial institutions due to language barriers, perceived cultural misalignment or distrust, instead relying on family and community-based loans. These informal arrangements, though accessible, can limit strategic investment and heighten vulnerability during economic shocks (Shin & Collins, 2012). Chinese entrepreneurs, despite strong transnational ties, also report challenges accessing local credit when seeking to formalise operations or diversify beyond ethnic market enclaves (Wang & Warn, 2018, 2019; Xu et al., 2019). Together, these cases reveal how financial exclusion reinforces economic segmentation, leaving many immigrant-led ventures undercapitalised and exposed to disruption within Sydney's competitive urban economy.

Regulatory systems in Sydney present layered barriers for immigrant entrepreneurs, particularly in navigating licensing, taxation and compliance regimes that demand institutional fluency and legal literacy. Chinese entrepreneurs often face administrative delays and customs-related restrictions when managing transnational supply chains, limiting their ability to scale and align with national standards (Wang & Warn, 2018; Xu et al., 2019). Korean entrepreneurs, especially in hospitality, report labour shortages due to restrictive immigration policies that constrain access to culturally specific staff, increasing costs and reducing operational flexibility (Shin & Collins, 2012). For Hazara Afghan refugees, limited familiarity with commercial regulations and registration procedures contributes to overrepresentation in informal micro-enterprises and reliance on non-contractual arrangements (Collins, 2017). Across all three groups, these challenges underscore how bureaucratic systems disproportionately affect those without established institutional knowledge or support. In the absence of targeted advisory mechanisms, regulatory frameworks act as exclusionary filters, limiting market entry and reinforcing structural marginalisation (Rametse et al., 2018).

Beyond financial and institutional barriers, immigrant entrepreneurs in Sydney face cultural bias and racialised perceptions that influence legitimacy, customer reach and institutional recognition. Hazara Afghan refugees are often viewed through dominant narratives of vulnerability and dependence, which undermine public trust and reduce access to investment and support (Collins, 2017). Korean and Chinese entrepreneurs, particularly those operating in ethnic precincts such as Strathfield and Chinatown, report limited cross-cultural appeal due to assumptions that their businesses primarily serve co-ethnic communities (Choi, 2022; Collins & Kunz, 2009). These spatial associations can restrict brand expansion and institutional engagement. Racialised framings also shape how public and private actors evaluate entrepreneurial legitimacy, limiting access to formal procurement schemes and support programmes (Patrickson & Hallo, 2021; Xu et al., 2019). These dynamics reveal how identity, migration status and urban geography intersect to mediate entrepreneurial opportunity. As Anthias (2013) emphasises, legitimacy is not neutral but shaped by power-laden imaginaries that determine whose identities are recognised within institutional and commercial spaces.

Building from the margins: adaptive strategies and entrepreneurial resilience among immigrant entrepreneurs in Sydney

In response to systemic barriers, immigrant entrepreneurs in Sydney have developed adaptive strategies grounded in ethnic, diasporic and community-based networks. Hazara Afghan refugees rely on close-knit support systems that facilitate trust-based lending, resource sharing and informal labour exchanges, enabling microenterprise development despite limited access to formal capital (Collins, 2017). Korean entrepreneurs mobilise ethnic ties to secure supply chains, access funding and recruit culturally aligned staff, often drawing on transnational linkages with South Korea to sustain operations and maintain market distinctiveness (Shin & Collins, 2012). Chinese entrepreneurs leverage regional networks to source goods, navigate regulatory environments and expand market reach, using bilingual communication and transnational business practices to maintain flexibility (Wang & Warn, 2019; Xu et al., 2019). These embedded practices enable entrepreneurs to bypass formal institutional barriers by drawing on alternative forms of social and economic capital. Network-based strategies also support collaboration with community organisations and NGOs, strengthening resilience and collective capacity within Sydney's segmented entrepreneurial landscape.

Immigrant entrepreneurs in Sydney also engage in forms of innovation that fuse cultural identity with market responsiveness, developing hybrid models to overcome exclusion and reposition their businesses. Chinese entrepreneurs utilise e-commerce platforms, digital marketing and multilingual branding to attract broader audiences and move beyond enclave-based markets (Wang & Warn, 2019). Korean restaurateurs reframe traditional cuisine through contemporary presentation, streamlined service models and strong online presence, expanding their appeal while preserving cultural authenticity (Choi, 2022). Hazara Afghan entrepreneurs embed cultural narratives into their services, offering community-oriented spaces that support refugee integration and convey histories of displacement (Collins, 2017). These strategies are not only adaptive but constitute deliberate identity work that contests marginalisation and constructs legitimacy in segmented market environments (Hyndman-Rizk & De Klerk, 2019; Patrickson & Hallo, 2021). As Bruni et al. (2004) argue, entrepreneurship is a culturally situated and performative process. In this context, immigrant entrepreneurs actively reshape dominant economic scripts to assert visibility and value within Sydney's racialised urban economy.

Institutional partnerships and community collaborations provide immigrant entrepreneurs in Sydney with critical avenues to formalise operations, expand market reach and enhance legitimacy. Hazara Afghan entrepreneurs benefit from targeted support through refugee micro-enterprise programmes, which offer training, small loans and mentorship to ease the transition from informal to semi-formal activity (Collins, 2017; Rametse et al., 2018). Korean entrepreneurs engage in city-led multicultural initiatives, including local food festivals and council-run business expos, which facilitate visibility and access to diverse consumer groups (Shin & Collins, 2012). Chinese entrepreneurs increasingly collaborate with regulatory agencies and trade associations to improve compliance, engage in policy forums and position their businesses within Sydney's broader economic planning frameworks (Xu et al., 2019). These strategic engagements signal a shift from enclave-based entrepreneurship towards greater institutional embeddedness. They also highlight the role of immigrant entrepreneurs as active contributors to inclusive economic development, co-producing urban futures through negotiation, adaptation and institutional alignment.

Melbourne's entrepreneurial innovation: immigrant contributions to economic growth and cultural diversity

Melbourne is one of Australia's most diverse and economically dynamic cities, shaped by sustained immigration and a longstanding multicultural policy framework (Collins, 2003; Forrest & Johnston, 2001). Immigrant entrepreneurship plays a vital role in the city's urban economy, contributing to employment, innovation and the development of community infrastructure across sectors ranging from retail and food services to logistics and digital enterprise (Soydas & Aleti, 2015; Zhang et al., 2021). These ventures are embedded in neighbourhoods marked by distinct cultural geographies and are integral to the everyday economic life of the city (Forrest et al., 2017). Within this landscape, immigrant entrepreneurs navigate complex regulatory systems and institutional structures that influence access to resources and market participation (Collins & Low, 2010). Their activities are also situated within broader debates around cultural recognition, legitimacy and economic inclusion in Australia's urban policy discourse (Collins, 2003). This analysis focuses on Chinese and Turkish entrepreneurs in Melbourne, selected for their demographic significance and for the contrasting ways they engage with institutional systems, co-ethnic networks and transnational economic linkages.

Systemic barriers to immigrant enterprise: navigating institutional and social exclusion in Melbourne

Financial exclusion remains a core structural barrier constraining immigrant entrepreneurship in Melbourne, particularly for Chinese and Turkish entrepreneurs. For many Chinese entrepreneurs, especially those operating within precincts like Box Hill or Chinatown, formal lending is difficult to access due to limited credit histories, risk-averse lending practices and unfamiliarity with mainstream financial systems. As a result, they often rely on co-ethnic networks, ROSCAs or personal savings, which restrict scalability and increase vulnerability in times of economic uncertainty (Selvarajah & Masli, 2011). Similarly, Turkish entrepreneurs frequently depend on familial loans and community support to fund their initial ventures. While this enables low-barrier market entry, it limits growth potential and can lead to cycles of undercapitalisation (Soydas & Aleti, 2015). These patterns reflect how systemic financial structures in Melbourne often fail to accommodate the embedded realities of immigrant entrepreneurs, reinforcing informal practices that operate outside the scope of institutional credit systems (Burnley, 2001; Collins & Low, 2010).

Regulatory complexity presents another major barrier for immigrant entrepreneurs in Melbourne, particularly in terms of zoning laws, licensing processes and operational compliance. Chinese entrepreneurs, especially those involved in import-export or food sectors, encounter logistical delays and administrative hurdles related to customs procedures, health inspections and fluctuating tariffs, often without culturally appropriate support (Selvarajah & Masli, 2011). Turkish entrepreneurs, while more concentrated in service-based industries like retail and hospitality, face similar constraints when attempting to formalise or scale their businesses. Compliance with health and safety standards, labour laws and taxation procedures often requires institutional literacy that many first-generation entrepreneurs lack, creating friction between informal business knowledge and formal regulatory expectations (Soydas & Aleti, 2015). Without targeted resources or intermediary support structures, regulatory frameworks in Melbourne function as exclusionary mechanisms that intensify entrepreneurial precarity (Collins, 2003).

Cultural and racialised perceptions further marginalise immigrant entrepreneurs by shaping how legitimacy, trust and consumer value are distributed across the marketplace. Chinese businesses, particularly those operating in concentrated ethnic zones, are frequently perceived as catering solely to co-ethnic markets, limiting their broader market reach and perpetuating exclusion from mainstream economic circuits (Selvarajah & Masli, 2011). Turkish entrepreneurs encounter similar cultural stereotyping, especially when their businesses are associated with traditional services or perceived to be family-run, which can deter non-ethnic consumers and limit external investment opportunities (Soydas & Aleti, 2015). These symbolic barriers intersect with structural exclusion, reinforcing segmented participation in Melbourne's economy and narrowing pathways to formal legitimacy. The ethnicisation of urban space and divergent attitudes towards multiculturalism continue to shape how immigrant entrepreneurs are perceived in public and institutional discourse (Forrest & Dunn, 2011).

Adaptive entrepreneurial practices: resilience and identity work in Melbourne's immigrant economy

In response to systemic barriers, Chinese and Turkish entrepreneurs in Melbourne have developed embedded strategies of resilience grounded in ethnic, familial and community-based networks. Chinese entrepreneurs regularly mobilise *guanxi*, or interpersonal trust-based connections, to secure informal loans, navigate bureaucratic hurdles and source culturally competent labour, allowing for greater flexibility and resource sharing within their communities (Selvarajah & Masli, 2011). Turkish entrepreneurs similarly rely on close-knit family and ethnic ties to form business partnerships, share knowledge and maintain financial circulation within the community (Soydas & Aleti, 2015). These networks operate as informal institutions that help mitigate formal exclusions while reinforcing cultural coherence. Such strategies align with broader regional patterns in Oceania, where immigrant entrepreneurs frequently depend on embedded social capital to circumvent institutional gatekeeping (Cain & Spoonley, 2013; Collins & Low, 2010).

Adaptation through innovation and identity reconfiguration has also become central to entrepreneurial success. Chinese entrepreneurs have embraced digital transformation, utilising e-commerce platforms, mobile payment systems and bilingual marketing campaigns to reach younger and more diverse consumer bases beyond the bounds of traditional precincts like Chinatown (Selvarajah & Masli, 2011). These practices enable them to maintain cultural specificity while expanding their visibility within broader markets. Turkish entrepreneurs, particularly those from the second generation, have diversified into sectors such as Information Technology (IT), education and design, integrating professional training and modern aesthetics to rebrand their businesses as dynamic and mainstream-facing (Soydas & Aleti, 2015). This generational shift illustrates a move from survivalist entrepreneurship towards opportunity-driven models that emphasise adaptability, professionalism and cross-cultural fluency (Hyndman-Rizk & De Klerk, 2019). These strategies reflect deliberate forms of identity work that not only address exclusion but also recast immigrant entrepreneurs as agents of innovation and transformation.

Collaboration with local institutions and participation in city-wide initiatives has further enabled Chinese and Turkish entrepreneurs to increase resilience and enhance visibility. Chinese entrepreneurs engage with multicultural business expos and local council programmes that promote inclusive economic participation, helping them expand beyond ethnic markets and engage in city-wide branding (Selvarajah & Masli, 2011). Turkish entrepreneurs have benefitted from community training programmes and workshops focused on regulatory compliance, marketing and financial planning, helping them formalise operations and build long-term sustainability (Soydas & Aleti, 2015). These interventions play a critical role in bridging the gap between community knowledge and institutional expectations, offering a foundation for more inclusive participation. More broadly, they illustrate how immigrant entrepreneurs actively contribute to urban economic development not only as market participants but as cultural and civic stakeholders (Collins et al., 2020). Through this co-production of Melbourne's entrepreneurial fabric, Chinese and Turkish entrepreneurs demonstrate how resilience, innovation and identity work converge in the making of a plural urban economy.

New Zealand

Auckland's Pacific identity: immigrant entrepreneurs steering a multicultural economy

Auckland is New Zealand's most culturally diverse city and a central node in the Pacific economy, shaped by sustained immigration from Asia, Africa and the Pacific Islands (Cain & Spoonley, 2013). Immigrant entrepreneurs are a visible part of the city's commercial landscape, contributing to employment generation, neighbourhood revitalisation and the expansion of small and medium-sized enterprises across a range of sectors (Spoonley et al., 2014). These businesses are concentrated in areas such as Dominion Road and Meadowlands, where economic activity is closely linked to patterns of ethnic settlement and cultural expression (Song, 2013). As a city marked by spatial inequality and uneven institutional support, Auckland presents both opportunities and constraints for migrant enterprise. This analysis examines the experiences of Chinese, African and Korean entrepreneurs, selected for their demographic significance and the distinct ways they engage with the city's regulatory systems, commercial infrastructure and urban geography.

Navigating structural and cultural barriers: the experiences of immigrant entrepreneurs in Auckland

Immigrant entrepreneurs in Auckland face persistent financial barriers that limit business development and formalisation. Chinese entrepreneurs frequently depend on family-based lending and ROSCAs, reflecting restricted access to institutional credit and a reliance on trust-based financial systems within co-ethnic networks (Cain & Spoonley, 2013). Korean entrepreneurs follow similar patterns, securing startup capital through informal networks that offer initial flexibility but constrain scalability and integration into formal financial structures (Choi, 2022; Nel & Abdullah, 2016). African entrepreneurs, particularly those from smaller diaspora communities, often encounter difficulties with credit access due to limited financial histories and unfamiliarity with local banking institutions, leading to a reliance on personal savings or community-based lending schemes (Omisakin et al., 2015). Chinese female entrepreneurs are especially affected, as their ventures are often concentrated in undervalued sectors such as childcare or domestic retail, where institutional visibility and access to business support remain limited (Verheijen et al., 2014). These financial barriers reflect broader structural dynamics that marginalise informal capital practices and limit immigrant entrepreneurs' access to growth-oriented support systems.

Institutional regulations in Auckland pose significant challenges for immigrant entrepreneurs by introducing administrative demands that often do not accommodate diverse business models or cultural practices. Korean restaurateurs report difficulties complying with food safety standards, labour laws and zoning requirements that are not designed for enterprises operating with specific cultural formats or staffing needs (Nel & Abdullah, 2016; Song, 2013). These challenges are compounded by limited access to culturally aligned migrant labour, constrained by immigration policies that restrict sector-specific recruitment (Choi, 2022). Chinese entrepreneurs also face regulatory friction, particularly in navigating customs, taxation and import procedures that delay shipments and disrupt supply chains (Cain & Spoonley, 2013). African entrepreneurs often struggle to interpret complex compliance requirements, especially when these diverge from business norms in their countries of origin. This can result in inadvertent non-compliance and exposure to fines or operational shutdowns (Omisakin et al., 2015). Chinese female entrepreneurs encounter additional constraints when combining caregiving roles with entrepreneurial work, as administrative procedures rarely account for hybrid livelihood arrangements or flexible enterprise structures (Verheijen et al., 2014). These patterns underscore how regulatory systems, while formally uniform, reproduce structural exclusions when access to institutional knowledge and navigation tools is unevenly distributed.

Cultural perceptions and spatial marginalisation play a significant role in shaping the entrepreneurial trajectories of immigrant business owners in Auckland. Korean and Chinese entrepreneurs operating in commercial precincts such as Dominion Road and Meadowlands are frequently perceived as serving exclusively co-ethnic communities, which constrains their ability to attract broader clientele and limits opportunities for brand diversification (Song, 2013; Spoonley et al., 2014). Korean businesses often struggle to shift public perceptions, even when adopting pan-Asian product lines or modern retail aesthetics aimed at mainstream consumers (Nel & Abdullah, 2016). Similarly, Chinese entrepreneurs encounter difficulties transcending assumptions of cultural insularity, particularly in business environments that reinforce spatial and symbolic separation (Cain & Spoonley, 2013). African entrepreneurs face racialised stereotypes that affect customer trust and deter engagement from outside their communities, reinforcing market segmentation and restricting opportunities for business expansion (Omisakin et al., 2015). Chinese female entrepreneurs contend with gendered assumptions that frame their enterprises as extensions of domestic or caregiving roles rather than formal economic activity, limiting both visibility and access to institutional recognition (Verheijen et al., 2014). These forms of symbolic exclusion contribute to uneven access to legitimacy, capital and support infrastructure, reinforcing structural inequality in Auckland's urban economy.

Resilience and strategic adaptation: immigrant entrepreneurial practices in Auckland

Immigrant entrepreneurs in Auckland respond to structural exclusion through adaptive strategies rooted in community-based networks and cultural practices. Chinese entrepreneurs rely on *guanxi* ties to access informal credit, maintain supply chains and manage relationships across linguistic and institutional barriers, often integrating platforms such as WeChat and AliExpress into daily operations (Cain & Spoonley, 2013). Korean entrepreneurs similarly mobilise co-ethnic networks to secure financing, source culturally aligned staff and maintain supplier relationships that support operational continuity and trust (Choi, 2022; Nel & Abdullah, 2016). African entrepreneurs draw on strong communal ties to build informal support systems that facilitate knowledge exchange, resource sharing and collective problem-solving, helping them navigate unfamiliar regulatory and financial environments (Omisakin et al., 2015). Chinese female entrepreneurs use these networks to balance entrepreneurial activity with caregiving responsibilities, often through shared labour and community-based enterprises that align with social expectations (Verheijen et al., 2014). These embedded strategies enable immigrant entrepreneurs to bypass formal barriers, sustain their businesses and cultivate resilience in a fragmented and competitive urban economy.

Immigrant entrepreneurs in Auckland respond to market exclusion by adapting their products, services and brand identities to engage wider audiences beyond co-ethnic communities. Korean restaurateurs blend traditional cuisine with contemporary presentation and streamlined service models to appeal to diverse consumer segments, often leveraging the global visibility of Korean popular culture to enhance market positioning (Nel & Abdullah, 2016; Song, 2013). Chinese entrepreneurs adopt bilingual signage, social media outreach and cross-cultural branding strategies to move beyond ethnic enclaves and attract broader customer bases (Cain & Spoonley, 2013). African entrepreneurs diversify their offerings and develop inclusive marketing approaches to counter cultural stereotyping and broaden their appeal across Auckland's varied demographic landscape (Omisakin et al., 2015). Chinese female entrepreneurs combine entrepreneurial activity with community-oriented services such as cultural education and caregiving, creating hybrid business models that reflect both economic and social values (Verheijen et al., 2014). These practices reflect the dynamics of what Vertovec (2007) terms *super-diversity*, where migration trajectories, identity markers and urban locality interact to shape entrepreneurial agency and adaptive innovation in pluralistic urban markets.

Institutional and community collaborations have become key avenues through which immigrant entrepreneurs in Auckland expand market access, formalise operations and build entrepreneurial legitimacy. Korean entrepreneurs engage with local councils, food expos and multicultural festivals, using these platforms to reach broader audiences and reposition their businesses beyond ethnic precincts (Nel & Abdullah, 2016). Chinese entrepreneurs benefit from multilingual training programmes and targeted regulatory support, which enhance their capacity to navigate licensing systems and transition into formal economic sectors (Cain & Spoonley, 2013). African entrepreneurs participate in business associations and community-led initiatives that offer mentorship, peer support and advocacy, strengthening their organisational resilience and visibility (Omisakin et al., 2015). For Chinese female entrepreneurs, culturally responsive training and informal mentorship networks support the integration of business activities with caregiving responsibilities, reinforcing social embeddedness and economic agency (Verheijen et al., 2014). These collaborative practices illustrate how immigrant entrepreneurs engage with and reshape institutional landscapes, co-producing more inclusive and responsive urban economies in Auckland.

Christchurch's post-disaster economy: immigrant entrepreneurs driving local and global integration

Christchurch has undergone substantial economic and urban transformation since the 2011 earthquake, with immigrant entrepreneurs contributing significantly to the city's recovery and renewal. As Christchurch rebuilds its commercial infrastructure and redefines its urban identity, immigrant-owned businesses have become increasingly visible across a range of sectors, including food services, construction and retail (Canterbury Development Corporation [CDC], 2016; CCC, 2017). These enterprises form part of a broader pattern of migration-driven entrepreneurship in New Zealand, reflecting shifts in settlement, labour market participation and local economic development (Collins, 2013; Ranabahu et al., 2024). In Christchurch, immigrant entrepreneurship intersects with post-disaster reconstruction and evolving demographic trends, offering insights into how migrant-led ventures contribute to economic revitalisation and social cohesion in a changing city (de Vries et al., 2021). This analysis examines the experiences of Indian and Afghan refugee entrepreneurs, selected for their demographic presence and the ways they engage with Christchurch's urban and economic landscape in the context of recovery.

Navigating uneven ground: barriers facing immigrant entrepreneurs in post-disaster Christchurch

Immigrant entrepreneurs in Christchurch encounter significant financial barriers that hinder business viability and growth. Afghan refugees are often excluded from formal financial systems due to insufficient credit history, lack of collateral and unfamiliarity with New Zealand's banking norms (Najib, 2015). Indian entrepreneurs similarly depend on personal savings or informal networks, which may enable initial survival but limit long-term expansion (Pio & Dana, 2014). Following the 2011 earthquake, recovery funding and institutional support largely bypassed small migrant-run enterprises, deepening their economic marginalisation (CCC, 2017; Canterbury Mayoral Forum, 2016). These experiences align with broader trends in refugee entrepreneurship, where financial exclusion stems from institutional systems that overlook informal capital mobilisation and culturally embedded financial practices (Ranabahu et al., 2024). As a result, many immigrant entrepreneurs remain confined to low-margin sectors with limited pathways to upward mobility or formal market integration.

Institutional and regulatory barriers further constrain immigrant entrepreneurship in Christchurch's evolving economic landscape. Indian entrepreneurs, particularly in hospitality, must navigate complex licensing, zoning and health compliance regimes that are resource-intensive and often inaccessible due to linguistic and cultural mismatches (Pio & Dana, 2014). Afghan refugees face greater difficulty due to limited institutional literacy and minimal access to legal or regulatory guidance, reducing their ability to formalise and grow their ventures (Najib, 2015). Post-disaster tightening of regulatory frameworks increased expectations without providing immigrant-specific support, further disadvantaging marginalised groups (CCC, 2017). These issues reflect a wider pattern across New Zealand, where refugee entrepreneurs struggle to reconcile local regulatory systems with their lived experiences and informal business models (de Vries et al., 2021; Ranabahu et al., 2024). Without targeted assistance, institutional systems continue to reinforce exclusion, acting as structural filters that disproportionately limit immigrant participation in Christchurch's formal economy (CDC, 2016; Canterbury Mayoral Forum, 2016).

Cultural and spatial exclusion create additional barriers that hinder immigrant entrepreneurs' legitimacy and market reach. Indian entrepreneurs often face assumptions that their services are only relevant to co-ethnic consumers, which narrows their opportunities to engage mainstream clientele and secure investment (Pio & Dana, 2014). Afghan refugees experience more pronounced bias due to their migration status and religious identity, which can diminish trust in consumer-facing sectors such as retail and services (Najib, 2015). The post-earthquake redevelopment in Christchurch focused largely on central business areas, while many immigrant-owned businesses were in suburban or underserved zones (CCC, 2017). This spatial disparity reduced visibility and customer access, compounding existing cultural marginalisation. Broader studies suggest that refugee entrepreneurs across New Zealand often remain invisible within urban development agendas, reinforcing symbolic boundaries between immigrant ventures and the economic mainstream (Ranabahu et al., 2024). These intersecting forms of exclusion limit not just economic opportunity but also access to recognition and legitimacy.

Building forward: strategic adaptation and entrepreneurial resilience in Christchurch's immigrant economy

In Christchurch's post-disaster environment, immigrant entrepreneurs have drawn on embedded community and transnational networks to sustain their ventures. Indian entrepreneurs often rely on longstanding connections with suppliers in India and the wider South Asian region, allowing them to access specialised goods, maintain authenticity and respond flexibly to shifting consumer demand (Pio & Dana, 2014). For Afghan refugee entrepreneurs, success often depends on tightly knit community structures that facilitate knowledge-sharing, mutual support and informal lending mechanisms (Najib, 2015). These networks offer stability in contexts where formal financial and institutional support, including from NGOs, remains inaccessible. Studies of refugee entrepreneurship in New Zealand affirm that such support systems serve as crucial substitutes for formal assistance, especially in navigating uncertainty and limited resources (de Vries et al., 2021; Ranabahu et al., 2024). In Christchurch, this embeddedness has played a vital role in ensuring business continuity amid both post-earthquake disruption and longer-term institutional marginalisation (CCC, 2017).

Adaptation and innovation are central to the strategies immigrant entrepreneurs use to navigate market segmentation and cultural barriers. Indian restaurateurs frequently adjust traditional menus to suit local preferences by reducing spice levels or introducing fusion dishes that retain cultural identity while expanding consumer appeal (Pio & Dana, 2014). Similarly, Afghan entrepreneurs introduce culturally significant goods such as halal food, sweets and artisanal crafts that serve both ethnic communities and the broader Christchurch population (Najib, 2015). These entrepreneurs also develop bilingual signage, accessible customer service and branding that bridges cultural divides. Broader research on refugee-owned enterprises shows that such adaptive practices reflect proactive identity negotiation and are key to gaining consumer trust and institutional legitimacy (Ranabahu et al., 2024). In the aftermath of Christchurch's earthquake, immigrant entrepreneurs responded to new spatial and social needs by offering essential services in underserved areas, positioning themselves as community anchors in a time of urban restructuring (CCC, 2017).

Collaborations with local organisations and civic institutions have enhanced the capacity of immigrant entrepreneurs to integrate and scale. Indian entrepreneurs benefit from city-led initiatives such as multicultural expos, regulatory workshops and small business support programmes that expand market access and improve legal literacy (Pio & Dana, 2014). Afghan refugee entrepreneurs engage with employment and resettlement organisations that provide tailored training in compliance, marketing and financial planning, helping them move towards formalisation (Najib, 2015). These partnerships help bridge gaps between community-based knowledge and mainstream economic expectations. Research on refugee entrepreneurship highlights how culturally responsive interventions significantly enhance economic inclusion and resilience (de Vries et al., 2021; Ranabahu et al., 2024). In Christchurch, participation in community events and business networks has allowed immigrant entrepreneurs to enhance their visibility and build public trust. These engagements not only promote entrepreneurial success but also support a more inclusive model of urban development that recognises migrant contributions to local recovery and growth.

Comparative synthesis: immigrant entrepreneurship in Australia and New Zealand

Immigrant entrepreneurship in Australia and New Zealand unfolds within distinct institutional and policy frameworks shaped by national priorities and local governance. Entrepreneurs in both countries face barriers related to finance, regulation and cultural recognition, shaped by legal status, spatial inequality and the availability of social capital. These conditions influence how businesses are initiated, sustained and scaled. While specific experiences vary across groups and locations, shared structural patterns are evident. Table 6.1 outlines key dimensions of immigrant entrepreneurship that inform the strategic analysis and policy recommendations in the following section.

Strategic policy interventions for Oceania

Recognising the shared structural barriers outlined in Table 6.1 provides a foundation for designing more inclusive and context-sensitive forms of entrepreneurial support across the region. Although immigrant entrepreneurship in Australia and New Zealand is shaped by different institutional configurations, it is consistently constrained by limited access to finance, regulatory opacity and symbolic exclusion. These challenges intersect with race, gender, migration status and geography, producing uneven access to opportunity and institutional support across urban contexts.

In response to these constraints, immigrant entrepreneurs develop hybrid models that draw on embedded community networks, informal financial systems such as ROSCAs, NGO support and transnational linkages. These strategies reflect the dynamic interplay between structure and agency that is central to the mixed embeddedness framework (Kloosterman et al., 1999), while extending it by foregrounding identity as a relational and strategic mechanism for navigating exclusion and constructing legitimacy (Bruni et al., 2004; Wang & Warn, 2019). To promote more inclusive and resilient entrepreneurial ecosystems, the next section outlines five targeted policy interventions that reflect the complexity and diversity of immigrant enterprise across Oceania.

TABLE 6.1 Key comparative dimensions of immigrant entrepreneurship in Australia and New Zealand

Category	*Australia*	*New Zealand*
Immigration policy framework	Points-based system with pathways for skilled migrants; limited support for refugee entrepreneurs; fragmented municipal engagement.	Streamlined visa categories; limited post-settlement support for refugees; entrepreneurship by refugee communities often informal and under-recognised.
Institutional ecosystem	Multicultural policies at state level; uneven support at municipal level; limited coordination between community initiatives and formal programmes.	Local government support varies; stronger NGO presence; limited integration of immigrant needs into mainstream economic development strategies.
Financial access and inclusion	Structural exclusion from mainstream finance; reliance on ROSCAs, family loans, and ethnic lending networks; refugee entrepreneurs face pronounced credit barriers.	Informal finance central for early-stage ventures; bank requirements often exclusionary; refugee and female entrepreneurs face compounded financial exclusion.
Regulatory environment	Complex compliance systems; high bureaucratic thresholds; licensing and zoning vary by state; limited access to culturally tailored guidance.	Compliance systems perceived as opaque; refugee entrepreneurs lack institutional literacy and guidance; limited support for informal-to-formal transition.
Community and ethnic networks	Strong co-ethnic support structures; dense diasporic ties facilitate startup and resilience; limited bridging capital restricts broader integration.	Community networks central to business formation; often substitute for formal mentorship and training; limited crossover into mainstream ecosystems.
Transnational strategies	Entrepreneurs leverage transnational trade, digital tools, and diaspora capital; hybrid ventures serve ethnic and mainstream markets.	Heavy reliance on diaspora linkages, remittances, and niche trade; identity used to establish cross-cultural and Pacific-facing brands.
Cultural identity and market positioning	Identity expressed through culturally embedded goods, bilingual branding, and hybrid innovation; refugee entrepreneurs embed social value in market strategies.	Entrepreneurs use identity for community recognition and legitimacy; refugee status, gender, and spatial marginalisation shape branding and consumer engagement.

Reforming regulatory access through decentralised, multilingual service hubs

Immigrant entrepreneurs across Oceania face regulatory barriers shaped by bureaucratic complexity, language exclusion and limited institutional guidance. In Australia, Hazara Afghan, Turkish and Chinese business owners report challenges with navigating licensing and zoning systems due to a lack of translated materials and culturally responsive support (Rametse et al., 2018; Selvarajah & Masli, 2011; Soydas & Aleti, 2015). In New Zealand, Korean and Chinese entrepreneurs encounter fragmented compliance regimes, while refugee-background entrepreneurs in post-disaster Christchurch remain disconnected from formal registration processes (Cain & Spoonley, 2013; Najib, 2015; Pio & Dana, 2014). These conditions restrict formalisation and disproportionately affect those unfamiliar with dominant legal systems.

To address these gaps, municipal governments should establish decentralised, multilingual service hubs in immigrant-dense commercial areas. These hubs should offer legal navigation, compliance support and mobile outreach, co-designed with community associations and integrated into local licensing frameworks. In Christchurch, this model should respond to longstanding institutional disconnection through mobile delivery. A 40% increase in first-time formal business registrations within three years should serve as a benchmark for policy success. Embedding regulatory access into local governance infrastructure is critical for building inclusive urban entrepreneurship.

Expanding inclusive finance through cultural intermediation and financial technology innovation

Access to finance remains a major barrier for immigrant entrepreneurs in Oceania, especially where formal credit systems overlook culturally embedded financial practices. In Australia, South Asian, Hazara Afghan, Chinese and Turkish entrepreneurs frequently rely on informal networks such as ROSCAs and family lending due to limited credit histories and systemic discrimination (Collins, 2017; Rametse et al., 2018; Soydas & Aleti, 2015). In New Zealand, Korean, Chinese and African business owners report similar challenges, with mainstream lenders failing to acknowledge strong repayment records within informal systems (Cain & Spoonley, 2013; Nel & Abdullah, 2016; Omisakin et al., 2015). These patterns are particularly acute among refugee entrepreneurs, who are often excluded from state-backed schemes and depend on unregulated peer finance.

Governments should establish inclusive microfinance programmes that incorporate blockchain-enabled peer lending and artificial intelligence-supported credit scoring to validate informal credit behaviours. These initiatives should include multilingual digital wallets and financial literacy support, co-delivered by fintech firms and community organisations. Policy success should be measured by a 30% increase in approved loan applications from immigrant entrepreneurs over five years. Recognising embedded financial practices as legitimate is essential to expanding formal economic participation and building resilient entrepreneurial ecosystems.

Institutionalising mentorship through intercultural networks and diaspora mobility

Access to structured mentorship remains fragmented across Oceania, particularly for immigrant entrepreneurs operating outside mainstream business ecosystems. In Australia, Korean, Chinese and Turkish entrepreneurs often report limited awareness of, or exclusion from, municipal initiatives linked to innovation and procurement (Choi, 2022; Soydas & Aleti, 2015; Wang & Warn, 2018). In New Zealand, African and Korean entrepreneurs are embedded in strong co-ethnic networks but remain disconnected from broader cross-sectoral platforms (Nel & Abdullah, 2016; Omisakin et al., 2015). In Christchurch, mentorship gaps are especially pronounced, with Afghan refugee entrepreneurs relying solely on informal peer support in the absence of structured programmes (Najib, 2015).

Governments across Oceania should establish intercultural mentorship platforms that offer sector-specific coaching, multilingual training and cross-city linkages among key cities such as Sydney, Melbourne, Auckland and Christchurch. These initiatives should be co-designed with diaspora business associations, NGOs and municipal development agencies and delivered through flexible digital and in-person formats that reflect diverse entrepreneurial realities. A 25% increase in structured mentorship participation over three years should be adopted as a performance benchmark. Strengthening mentorship infrastructure is essential for addressing network segmentation and enabling inclusive, growth-oriented entrepreneurship across Oceania.

Gender-responsive incubation for inclusive entrepreneurial ecosystems

Across Australia and New Zealand, female immigrants and refugees face intersecting structural and cultural barriers in accessing entrepreneurial support, particularly in sectors undervalued by formal institutions. In Australia, Afghan women in Sydney and Turkish women in Melbourne often operate home-based or care-related micro-enterprises but face linguistic exclusion, caregiving responsibilities and a lack of flexible training and finance options (Collins, 2017; Soydas & Aleti, 2015). In New Zealand, Chinese women in Auckland and Afghan refugees in Christchurch lead ventures in cultural retail and domestic services but remain marginalised by policy frameworks that overlook informal labour and gendered constraints (Najib, 2015; Verheijen et al., 2014).

Governments should establish gender-responsive incubation programmes that include onsite childcare, flexible training schedules and tailored support in sectors such as care, micro-franchising and digital services. These programmes must be co-designed with women's migrant organisations and NGOs and embedded in broader settlement and economic strategies. A 30% increase in female immigrant business registrations over five years should serve as a benchmark of success. Gender inclusion must be treated as a foundational feature of entrepreneurial ecosystems across Oceania, not a peripheral concern.

Investing in digital inclusion as a platform for entrepreneurial growth

Digital exclusion continues to hinder immigrant entrepreneurs across Australia and New Zealand, limiting their ability to access online markets, adopt new technologies and compete in innovation-driven sectors. In Australia, Chinese entrepreneurs in Melbourne and migrant communities in Sydney increasingly engage with e-commerce and multilingual branding but face gaps in logistics training, digital strategy and infrastructure, particularly in immigrant-dense neighbourhoods (Collins, 2021; Selvarajah & Masli, 2011). In New Zealand, Korean and Chinese entrepreneurs in Auckland leverage platform-based sales but struggle with broadband access and payment integration, while Afghan refugees in Christchurch face acute digital illiteracy and limited connectivity that inhibit online business development (Choi, 2022; Najib, 2015; Song, 2013).

Local governments should invest in digital accelerators that provide mobile-first, multilingual training in e-commerce, logistics and digital branding. These programmes should include subsidised broadband, digital tools and innovation grants targeting underserved immigrant groups. Partnerships with universities and tech firms can enhance delivery and mentorship. A 35% increase in digital business launches within three years should serve as the benchmark of success. Digital inclusion must be embedded in economic development strategies to ensure equitable participation in emerging entrepreneurial sectors across Oceania.

Conclusion

This chapter has demonstrated that immigrant entrepreneurs across Oceania navigate structural barriers through embedded community networks, transnational linkages and strategic identity practices, contributing significantly to urban resilience, economic diversification and cultural innovation. Through the application of the RMEF, the analysis highlighted how race, gender, migration status and spatial inequality interact to shape entrepreneurial opportunities and outcomes. Comparative insights from Sydney, Melbourne, Auckland and Christchurch show that, despite persistent exclusion, immigrant entrepreneurs exercise agency by innovating, adapting and constructing hybrid business models that span formal and informal economies. These findings point to the need for targeted policy interventions aimed at enhancing financial inclusion, regulatory accessibility, digital participation, intercultural mentorship and gender-responsive entrepreneurial support. Future research should focus on empirically applying and refining the reconceptualised framework across diverse urban and migration contexts to deepen theoretical understanding and support more inclusive policy development. Strengthening these analytical approaches is essential for advancing equitable economic futures across Oceania.

References

Anthias, F. (2013). Intersectional what? Social divisions, intersectionality and levels of analysis. *Ethnicities, 13*(1), 3–19. https://doi.org/10.1177/1468796812463547

Bruni, A., Gherardi, S., & Poggio, B. (2004). Doing gender, doing entrepreneurship: An ethnographic account of intertwined practices. *Gender, Work & Organization, 11*(4), 406–429. https://doi.org/10.1111/j.1468-0432.2004.00240.x

Burnley, I. H. (1999). Levels of immigrant residential concentration in Sydney and their relationship with disadvantage. *Urban Studies, 36*, 1295–1315. https://doi.org/10.1080/0042098993006

Burnley, I. H. (2001). *The impact of immigration on Australia: A demographic approach*. Oxford University Press.

Cain, T., & Spoonley, P. (2013). *Making it work: The mixed embeddedness of immigrant entrepreneurs in New Zealand*. Institute for the Study of Labor (Discussion Paper Series 7332). https://doi.org/10.2139/ssrn.2250331

Canterbury Development Corporation. (2016). *Christchurch and Canterbury quarterly economic report*, March 2016. https://www.cdc.org.nz/wp-content/uploads/2016/06/Q1-2016-Economic-Update.pdf

Canterbury Mayoral Forum. (2016). *CREDS Economic Indicators Report: June 2016*. https://canterburymayors.org.nz/wp-content/uploads/2016/09/CREDS-economic-indicators_Jun-16.pdf

Choi, T. (2022). Ethnic enclaves in immigrant entrepreneurship: Korean immigrant entrepreneurship in Australia. *Journal of the International Council for Small Business, 3*(3), 214–227. https://doi.org/10.1080/26437015.2021.1976081

Christchurch City Council. (2017). *Christchurch Multicultural Strategy Te Rautaki Mātāwaka Rau*. Christchurch City Council. https://www.ccc.govt.nz/assets/Documents/The-Council/Plans-Strategies-Policies-Bylaws/Strategies/Multicultural-Strategy.pdf

Collins, J. (2003). Cultural diversity and entrepreneurship: Policy responses to immigrant entrepreneurs in Australia. *Entrepreneurship & Regional Development, 15*(2), 137–149. https://doi.org/10.1080/0898562032000075168

Collins, J. (2013). Multiculturalism and Immigrant Integration in Australia. *Canadian Ethnic Studies, 45*(3), 133–149. https://doi.org/10.1353/ces.2013.0037

Collins, J. (2017). *From refugee to entrepreneur in Sydney in less than three years*. UTS Business School.

Collins, J. (2021). Immigrant entrepreneurship in Sydney: Australia's leading global city. In C. Y. Liu (Ed.), *Immigrant entrepreneurship in cities* (pp. 47–65). The Urban Book Series. Springer. https://doi.org/10.1007/978-3-030-50363-5_3

Collins, J., Krivokapic-Skoko, B., Jordan, K., Babacan, H., & Gopalkrishnan, N. (2020). *Cosmopolitan place making in Australia: Immigrant minorities and the built environment in cities, regional and rural areas*. Springer Nature.

Collins, J., & Kunz, P. (2009). Ethnicity and public space in the city: Ethnic precincts in Sydney. *Cosmopolitan Civil Societies: An Interdisciplinary Journal, 1*(1), 39–70. https://search.informit.org/doi/10.3316/informit.135845751478999

Collins, J., & Low, A. (2010). Asian female immigrant entrepreneurs in small and medium-sized businesses in Australia. *Entrepreneurship and Regional Development, 22*(1), 97–111. https://doi.org/10.1080/08985620903220553

de Vries, H. P., Ranabahu, N., & Basharati, Z. (2021). From taking flight to putting down roots: A narrative perspective of the entrepreneurial journey of a refugee. In T. M. Cooney (Ed.), *The Palgrave handbook of minority entrepreneurship* (pp. 409–431). Palgrave Macmillan. https://doi.org/10.1007/978-3-030-66603-3_17

Duan, C., Sandhu, K., & Kotey, B. (2021). Understanding immigrant entrepreneurship: A home-country entrepreneurial ecosystem perspective. *New England Journal of Entrepreneurship, 24*(1), 2–20. https://doi.org/10.1108/NEJE-05-2020-0013

Essers, C., & Benschop, Y. (2009). Muslim businesswomen doing boundary work: The negotiation of of Islam, gender and ethnicity within entrepreneurial contexts. *Human Relations, 62*(3), 403–423. https://doi.org/10.1177/0018726708101042

Forrest, J., & Johnston, R. (2001). The geography of the new ethnicity: Ethnic residential segregation in metropolitan Sydney 1996. *Tijdschrift voor Economische en Sociale Geografie, 92*(1), 42–59. https://doi.org/10.1111/1467-9663.00138

Forrest, J., & Dunn, K. (2006). Racism and intolerance in eastern Australia: A geographic perspective. *Australian Geographer, 37*(2), 167–186. https://doi.org/10.1080/00049180600711082

Forrest, J., & Dunn, K. (2011). Attitudes to diversity: New perspectives on the ethnic geography of Brisbane, Australia. *Australian Geographer, 42*(4), 435–453. https://doi.org/10.1080/00049182.2012.619957

Forrest, J., Johnston, R., Siciliano, F., Manley, D., & Jones, K. (2017). Are Australia's suburbs swamped by Asians and Muslims? Countering political claims with data. *Australian Geographer, 48*(4), 457–472. https://doi.org/10.1080/00049182.2017.1329383

Guadagno, L., Fuhrer, M., & Twigg, J. (2017). *Migrants in disaster risk reduction: Practices for inclusion*. Council of Europe.

Hyndman-Rizk, N., & de Klerk, S. (2019). Culture as opportunity: Skilled migration and entrepreneurship in Australia. In V. Ratten, P. Jones, V. Braga, & C. S. Marques (Eds.), *Sustainable entrepreneurship* (pp. 33–45). Contributions to Management Science. Springer. https://doi.org/10.1007/978-3-030-12342-0_3

Kloosterman, R. C., & Rath, J. (2001). Immigrant entrepreneurs in advanced economies: Mixed embeddedness further explored. *Journal of Ethnic and Migration Studies, 27*(2), 189–201. https://doi.org/10.1080/13691830020041561

Kloosterman, R. C., van der Leun, J., & Rath, J. (1999). Mixed embeddedness: (In)formal economic activities and immigrant businesses in the Netherlands. *International Journal of Urban and Regional Research, 23*(2), 252–266. https://doi.org/10.1111/1468-2427.00194

Krivokapic-Skoko, B., Watson, K., & Collins, J. (2023). Being global and being regional: Refugee entrepreneurship in regional Australia. In N. Kerrigan & P. de Lima (Eds.), *The rural-migration nexus* (pp. 103–118). Rethinking Rural. Palgrave Macmillan. https://doi.org/10.1007/978-3-031-18042-2_7

Ley, D., & Murphy, P. (2001). Immigration in gateway cities: Sydney and Vancouver in comparative perspective. *Progress in Planning, 55*(3), 119–194. https://doi.org/10.1016/S0305-9006(00)00025-8

Markus, A. B., Jupp, J., & McDonald, P. (2009). *Australia's Immigration Revolution*. Allen & Unwin.

Najib, H. (2015). *Accounting for the business start-up experiences of Afghan refugees in Christchurch, New Zealand* [Master's thesis, University of Canterbury]. University of Canterbury Research Repository. https://hdl.handle.net/10092/10336

Nel, P., & Abdullah, M. (2016). Immigrant entrepreneurs and their perceived success in small retail businesses: Preliminary New Zealand findings. In *Proceedings of Annual South Africa Business Research Conference* (pp. 11–12).

Omisakin, O. M., Nakhid, C., Littrell, R., & Verbitsky, J. (2015). Exploring the migrant experience in small business activities in Auckland: A case study of African migrants. *Journal of Business Administration Research, 4*(2), 9–19. https://doi.org/10.5430/jbar.v4n2p9

Patrickson, M., & Hallo, L. (2021). Female immigrant entrepreneurship: The experience of Chinese migrants to Australia. *Administrative Sciences, 11*(4), 145. https://doi.org/10.3390/admsci11040145

Pio, E., & Dana, L. P. (2014). An empirical study of Indian entrepreneurs in Christchurch, New Zealand. *International Journal of Entrepreneurship and Small Business, 22*(1), 17–35. https://doi.org/10.1504/IJESB.2014.062128

Ranabahu, N., de Vries, H. P., & Basharati, Z. (2024). Entrepreneurial identity and business success: Former refugee women's navigation of (in)visibility paradoxes. *Journal of Management & Organization*, 1–16. https://doi.org/10.1017/jmo.2024.43

Rametse, N., Moremong-Nganunu, T., Ding, M. J., & Arenius, P. (2018). Entrepreneurial motivations and capabilities of migrant entrepreneurs in Australia. *International Migration, 56*(4), 217–234. https://doi.org/10.1111/imig.12452

Selvarajah, C., & Masli, E. K. (2011). Ethnic entrepreneurial business cluster development: Chinatowns in Melbourne. *Journal of Asia Business Studies, 5*(1), 42–60. https://doi.org/10.1108/15587891111100796

Shin, J., & Collins, J. (2012). *Korean immigrant entrepreneurs in the Sydney restaurant industry* (Technical Report). UTS Cosmopolitan Civil Societies Research Centre. https://hdl.handle.net/10453/19943

Song, C. (2013). Ethnic entrepreneurship of Korean New Zealanders: Restaurant business as self-employment practice. *New Zealand Journal of Asian Studies, 15*(2), 94–109.

Soydas, Y., & Aleti, T. (2015). Immigrant and second-generation Turkish entrepreneurs in Melbourne Australia: A qualitative investigation of entrepreneurial motivations. *International Journal of Entrepreneurial Behaviour & Research, 21*(2), 154–174. https://doi.org/10.1108/IJEBR-11-2013-0185

Spoonley, P., Meares, C., Peace, R., & Cain, T. (2014). The changing immigrant cartography of Auckland, New Zealand: An Asian ethnic precinct. *MMG Working Paper* (14-05). https://hdl.handle.net/11858/00-001M-0000-0024-1FAE-1

Verheijen, V. W., Nguyen, H., & Chin, B. (2014). The making of ethnic migrant Female immigrant entrepreneurs in New Zealand. *International Journal of Entrepreneurship and Small Business, 23*(3), 296–312. https://doi.org/10.1504/IJESB.2014.065517

Vertovec, S. (2007). Super-diversity and its implications. *Ethnic and Racial Studies, 30*(6), 1024–1054. https://doi.org/10.1080/01419870701599465

Wang, Y., & Warn, J. (2019). Break-out strategies of Chinese immigrant entrepreneurs in Australia. *International Journal of Entrepreneurial Behaviour & Research, 25*(2), 217–242. https://doi.org/10.1108/IJEBR-03-2017-0108

Wang, Y., & Warn, J. (2018). Chinese immigrant entrepreneurship: Embeddedness and the interaction of resources with the wider social and economic context. *International Small Business Journal, 36*(2), 131–148. https://doi.org/10.1177/0266242617726364

Xu, K., Drennan, J., & Mathews, S. (2019). Immigrant entrepreneurs and their cross-cultural capabilities: A study of Chinese immigrant entrepreneurs in Australia. *Journal of International Entrepreneurship, 17*(4), 520–557. https://doi.org/10.1007/s10843-019-00261-4

Zhang, T., Seet, P. S., Redmond, J., Sharafizad, J., & Tan, W. L. (2021). Chinese immigrant entrepreneurs. In *World Encyclopedia of Entrepreneurship* (pp. 1–21). Edward Elgar Publishing. https://doi.org/10.4337/9781839104145.00008

7

IMMIGRANT ENTREPRENEURSHIP IN THE MIDDLE EAST

Navigating institutional fragmentation, legal precarity and adaptive strategies

Introduction

Immigrant entrepreneurship is an increasingly prominent feature of urban economies across the Middle East. In cities shaped by transnational mobility, rapid development and shifting economic priorities, migrant business activity spans sectors such as retail, hospitality, logistics, construction and digital services (Barak-Bianco & Raijman, 2015; Elmassah et al., 2022; Malit & Oliver, 2013). For many migrants, enterprise creation is not solely driven by opportunity but emerges in response to exclusion from formal labour markets and the structural barriers imposed by migration regimes. While some governments have introduced targeted reforms to attract skilled labour and foreign investment, the dominant model remains one of temporary migration, which restricts access to permanent residency, legal protections and business infrastructure (Abdul Reda et al., 2023; International Labour Organisation [ILO], 2017; Thiollet & Assaf, 2021). Migrant entrepreneurs operating under these conditions often encounter financial exclusion, administrative opacity and spatial inequality. In response, they draw on communal networks, diasporic linkages and informal practices to establish and sustain economic activity (Pelican, 2014; Wang, 2019).

Although scholarly interest in immigrant entrepreneurship in the region has grown, the academic literature remains conceptually narrow and inattentive to the structural inequalities that shape minority enterprise. Much existing research draws on theoretical frameworks developed in Western contexts, which typically assume stable migration status, welfare access and institutionalised integration (Nazareno et al., 2019). These assumptions diverge significantly from the precarious conditions under which many entrepreneurs operate in the Middle East (Elmassah et al., 2022; Thiollet, 2011). While the mixed embeddedness framework (MEF) offers valuable tools for analysing opportunity structures (Kloosterman, 2010; Kloosterman & Rath, 2018), it has been underutilised in the region and insufficiently addresses informality, legal precarity and spatial exclusion (Barak-Bianco & Raijman, 2015; Said & Vyas, 2025; Thiollet, 2011). Furthermore, identity is often treated descriptively rather than analytically, with limited attention to how regulatory systems and social hierarchies shape entrepreneurial subjectivities (Abu-Asbah & Heilbrunn, 2011; Erogul & McCrohan, 2008; Said & Vyas, 2025). Although

DOI: 10.4324/9781003605072-9

recent studies have begun to address the intersections of gender, legal status and geography, the lack of cross-national comparisons continues to constrain the development of context-sensitive analytical frameworks.

This chapter applies the reconceptualised mixed embeddedness framework (RMEF) introduced in Chapter 2 to demonstrate its analytical value in examining how immigrant entrepreneurs navigate institutional fragmentation, legal precarity and constrained opportunity structures in the Middle East. Integrating institutional theory, translocal agency and entrepreneurial identity (EI) shaped through intersectionality, the RMEF responds to earlier frameworks' neglect of regulatory precarity and spatial marginalisation. The United Arab Emirates (UAE) and Israel have been selected for their regional importance, distinct institutional architectures and contrasting migration governance models. Both serve as major economic hubs characterised by high transnational mobility and entrepreneurial activity (Malit & Oliver, 2013; Said & Vyas, 2025; Thiollet & Assaf, 2021), yet their policy regimes create divergent conditions for immigrant entrepreneurs. In the UAE, the sponsorship-based migration system produces legal insecurity and dependence, compelling entrepreneurs to rely on informal networks and communal strategies (Abdul Reda et al., 2023; Elmassah et al., 2022; Hamdan, 2019). In contrast, Israel's stratified citizenship system results in differentiated access to resources among Arab citizens, migrant workers and asylum seekers (Barak-Bianco & Raijman, 2015; Said & Vyas, 2025; Schnell & Sofer, 2002). These cases reveal how institutional environments shape entrepreneurial strategies and opportunity access across fragmented institutional landscapes.

To explore these dynamics, the chapter synthesises documented case studies and existing research across three urban contexts: Dubai in the UAE and Tel Aviv and the Triangle region in Israel. These sites were selected for their economic relevance, demographic diversity and contrasting institutional structures. Dubai, shaped by temporary labour migration and regulatory complexity, highlights how gendered exclusion and institutional opacity constrain entrepreneurial activity (Mahdavi, 2011; Vora, 2013; Yasin, 2022). Tel Aviv, despite its global reputation for technological innovation, restricts immigrant and minority participation through administrative and legal barriers (Barak-Bianco & Raijman, 2015; Senor & Singer, 2011). The Triangle region, comprising Arab-majority towns in northern Israel, reflects the long-term effects of spatial marginalisation and systemic underinvestment on minority business development (Said & Vyas, 2025; Schnell & Sofer, 2002).

The chapter is structured as follows. It begins with an analysis of immigrant entrepreneurship in the UAE, focusing on Dubai, followed by the Israeli context, examining Tel Aviv and the Triangle region. A comparative synthesis highlights key differences and commonalities across the two countries. This is followed by a policy discussion aimed at enhancing institutional support. The chapter concludes with reflections on broader implications and directions for future research.

The United Arab Emirates

Dubai's cosmopolitan nexus: immigrant entrepreneurs driving economic dynamism

Dubai's emergence as a hyper-globalised city has been shaped by its strategic positioning within transnational flows of capital, labour and culture (Acuto, 2010; Kanna, 2011). Central to this evolution are immigrant entrepreneurs, who have helped shape Dubai's reputation as a global economic hub by operating within a system of state-driven entrepreneurship and selective openness to global influences (Mahdavi, 2020), immigrant enterprise both harnesses and navigates the opportunities and frictions embedded in Dubai's development model. Although the city promotes an image of openness and economic inclusion, access to entrepreneurial success remains deeply structured by regulatory frameworks, social hierarchies and informal practices (Elmassah et al., 2022; Yasin, 2022). This analysis examines the entrepreneurial trajectories of Chinese, South Asian and African immigrants, whose varied forms of embeddedness within Dubai's sociocultural and economic landscape illuminate the complex intersections of opportunity, exclusion and agency in the city's evolving global identity.

Beneath the glare: barriers facing immigrant entrepreneurs in Dubai

Beneath Dubai's polished image as a global city of opportunity lies a stratified entrepreneurial environment that systematically disadvantages immigrant business owners. While official discourse promotes economic diversification and openness, underlying structures of control and differentiation persist through nationality-based hierarchies and restrictive legal mechanisms (Acuto, 2010; Kanna, 2011). South Asian entrepreneurs, many operating in small-scale retail and service sectors, are frequently constrained by exploitative sponsorship systems and precarious visa conditions that limit autonomy and heighten legal and financial vulnerability (Vora, 2013; Yasin, 2022). African entrepreneurs, particularly those from sub-Saharan countries, encounter barriers rooted in racialised suspicion and institutionalised marginalisation, impeding access to business licensing and subjecting them to intensified regulatory scrutiny (Malit & Oliver, 2013; Pelican, 2014). Chinese entrepreneurs, despite a growing presence in wholesale and trade sectors, face challenges related to language, legal literacy and navigating administrative procedures without established local intermediaries (Wang, 2019). These barriers are not isolated technical difficulties but are embedded within broader power structures that shape who is permitted to participate in Dubai's entrepreneurial economy and under what conditions.

Institutional opacity and the uneven enforcement of regulations further entrench exclusionary dynamics across Dubai's entrepreneurial landscape. Regulatory procedures are often characterised by discretionary decision-making, informal gatekeeping and inconsistent policy implementation, creating uncertainty for entrepreneurs who lack exclusive access to insider networks or Emirati intermediaries (Alsarhan et al., 2024). Chinese entrepreneurs frequently experience difficulties securing commercial space due to ambiguous zoning regulations and the shifting priorities of urban development plans that fail to account for the needs of migrant business owners (Wang, 2019). African entrepreneurs report being subject to informal restrictions and inconsistent inspection regimes that disproportionately affect their ability to maintain legal operations (Malit & Oliver, 2013; Pelican, 2014). For South Asian entrepreneurs, particularly those engaged in informal or home-based enterprises, enforcement crackdowns, often framed as urban regulation, disproportionately target migrant-run ventures while reinforcing a narrative of illegality and impermanence (Yasin, 2022). These practices reflect more than regulatory inefficiencies; they reveal a broader institutional logic in which entrepreneurial legitimacy is unequally distributed and frequently contingent upon socio-political proximity rather than compliance or innovation.

Beyond legal and regulatory exclusion, immigrant entrepreneurs face persistent barriers to physical infrastructure, financial services and social inclusion that significantly constrain their entrepreneurial potential. Access to affordable commercial property is shaped by racialised and class-based geographies that marginalise African and South Asian entrepreneurs into peripheral or lower-tier retail spaces, limiting visibility and market integration (Pelican, 2014; Yasin, 2022). Chinese entrepreneurs, often clustered in ethno-commercial zones, face restrictions that confine their operations within narrowly defined sectors and limit opportunities for expansion (Wang, 2019). Financial institutions, while well-established in the formal economy, frequently exclude immigrant entrepreneurs through stringent documentation requirements, nationality-based risk assessments and a lack of tailored financial products, particularly for those without Emirati sponsorship or long-term residency (Elmassah et al., 2022). These structural exclusions are compounded by social stigma and informal discrimination in consumer markets and professional networks, where assumptions about competence, legality and legitimacy continue to shape economic interactions (Pelican, 2014; Yasin, 2022). Taken together, these barriers reveal a deeply unequal urban economy in which immigrant entrepreneurship is permitted but not equally supported, embedded within a broader regime of selective inclusion that sustains Dubai's global ambitions while reproducing systemic exclusions.

Forging paths in Dubai: adaptive strategies of immigrant entrepreneurs

In response to restrictive legal conditions and regulatory precarity, immigrant entrepreneurs in Dubai adopt embedded, community-driven strategies that enable business continuity in the absence of formal institutional support. Chinese entrepreneurs, often navigating linguistic barriers and administrative complexity, draw on co-ethnic networks that provide translation services, legal navigation and culturally informed market advice tailored to Dubai's commercial environment (Wang, 2019). South Asian entrepreneurs, who face constraints tied to the sponsorship system and informal economic positioning, rely on dense ethnic business communities that facilitate resource pooling, rotating credit systems and informal labour exchange to support daily operations and risk-sharing (Yasin, 2022). African entrepreneurs, often excluded from prime commercial areas and subject to regulatory suspicion, mobilise diasporic solidarity and flexible business models that allow them to operate in mobile or informal markets across urban peripheries (Malit & Oliver, 2013; Pelican, 2014). These strategies reflect deeply embedded forms of resilience grounded in social capital, demonstrating how immigrant entrepreneurs forge continuity through trust, reciprocity and shared migratory experience in an otherwise exclusionary environment.

Immigrant entrepreneurs also adopt calculated strategies to navigate regulatory ambiguity and discretionary enforcement by calibrating their visibility and legal compliance. South Asian entrepreneurs frequently engage in informal partnerships with Emirati sponsors or register businesses under the names of relatives and trusted associates to navigate restrictions on ownership and licensing (Yasin, 2022). Chinese business owners similarly make use of proxy ownership arrangements and joint ventures that allow them to meet regulatory requirements while retaining de facto control over business decisions (Wang, 2019). African entrepreneurs, particularly those operating in sectors subject to heightened oversight, often rely on digital platforms and mobile operations that reduce exposure to formal inspection while maintaining customer access and operational flexibility (Malit & Oliver, 2013; Pelican, 2014). These strategies are not simply reactive but reflect sophisticated responses to structural uncertainty, as immigrant entrepreneurs actively manage the risks of overexposure in a system where legality and legitimacy are inconsistently applied and often negotiated through informal means.

Beyond survival and compliance, immigrant entrepreneurs engage in strategic identity work to align their ventures with Dubai's aspirational narratives of cosmopolitanism and innovation.

Chinese entrepreneurs diversify beyond ethno-specific goods, participate in regional trade fairs and rebrand their enterprises to appeal to a broader consumer base, signalling adaptability and global business sensibilities (Wang, 2019). South Asian entrepreneurs adopt professional branding, enhance their digital presence and pursue certifications or training programmes to position themselves as modern and competitive contributors to the local economy (Yasin, 2022). African entrepreneurs, often operating on the margins of formal recognition, strategically focus their business models on community development, cultural entrepreneurship and enhancing social visibility to build legitimacy and differentiate themselves within competitive markets (Malit & Oliver, 2013; Pelican, 2014). These practices reflect more than branding or market adaptation; they are forms of entrepreneurial agency through which immigrant business owners assert their relevance, negotiate belonging and reshape perceptions in an urban environment where opportunity remains selectively granted.

Dubai's gendered enterprise terrain: female immigrant entrepreneurs navigating structural and legal exclusion

Within Dubai's evolving economy, female immigrant entrepreneurs represent an important but often overlooked dimension of entrepreneurial activity. Motivated by a combination of opportunity and necessity, their ventures reflect aspirations for financial independence, personal fulfilment and responses to constrained access to formal employment (Hughes, 2003; Vardhan et al., 2020; Yaseen, 2013). Although Dubai positions itself as a progressive hub for women's entrepreneurship through initiatives such as the Dubai Business Women Council (DBWC), immigrant women's experiences are shaped by intersecting dynamics of gender, migration status and socio-economic position (Erogul & McCrohan, 2008; Vardhan, 2020). EI, as theorised by Bruni et al. (2004) and Anthias (2001), emerges as a negotiated space where structural conditions, cultural expectations and individual agency interact. This analysis focuses on South Asian (Indian and Pakistani), African (Cameroonian) and Arab (Egyptian and Lebanese) female immigrant entrepreneurs, selected for their strong presence in Dubai's migrant economy and the distinct gendered dynamics documented in existing research.

Sandstorms of structural exclusion: barriers facing female immigrant entrepreneurs in Dubai

Despite Dubai's promotion of female empowerment, structural exclusions and entrenched gender norms continue to constrain the entrepreneurial activities of female immigrants, often placing traditional roles in conflict with the demands of business ownership. Indian and Pakistani female entrepreneurs frequently face pressure to prioritise caregiving and domestic responsibilities, limiting their time and autonomy for business activity (Yaseen, 2013). Cameroonian female entrepreneurs encounter compounded exclusion based on race and gender, facing marginalisation from mainstream business networks and heightened regulatory scrutiny (Pelican, 2014). Egyptian and Lebanese female entrepreneurs often operate within conservative family structures that restrict decision-making authority and discourage entrepreneurial risk-taking (Erogul & McCrohan, 2008). Across these groups, Dubai's kafala sponsorship system reinforces legal and economic dependency by tying residency to employers, thereby limiting mobility, rights and business autonomy (Abdul Reda et al., 2023). For those on family visas, residency may also be tied to male relatives, further restricting entrepreneurial engagement (Erogul & McCrohan,

2008; Pelican, 2014). Although Dubai has established formal initiatives to support female entrepreneurship, such as mentorship platforms and business councils, these programmes often fail to reach immigrant communities due to language barriers, limited outreach and restrictive eligibility criteria (Vardhan, 2020).

Access to finance remains one of the most persistent structural barriers limiting the capacity of female immigrant entrepreneurs to scale their businesses. Indian and Pakistani female entrepreneurs often face institutional bias and lack the formal collateral or banking histories required to access credit, leaving them reliant on microfinance schemes that are insufficient for business expansion (Yaseen, 2013). Cameroonian female entrepreneurs are similarly excluded from formal financing due to racialised risk perceptions and documentation barriers, restricting their engagement with established financial institutions (Pelican, 2014). Egyptian and Lebanese female entrepreneurs, particularly those operating in male-dominated sectors, often encounter subtle forms of investor discrimination that diminish their access to growth capital and mentorship (Erogul & McCrohan, 2008). Broader financial systems in Dubai tend to favour established businesses led by male nationals, reinforcing gendered and citizenship-based disparities (Goby & Erogul, 2011). While support mechanisms such as the DBWC and private accelerator programmes exist, many immigrant female entrepreneurs remain unaware of these resources or are excluded by informal gatekeeping and citizenship requirements (Vardhan et al., 2020). These financial barriers force many into low-capital ventures with limited growth potential.

The concentration of female immigrant entrepreneurs in low-growth sectors further illustrates the institutional and socio-economic barriers that shape their trajectories. Indian and Pakistani female entrepreneurs are often limited to culturally sanctioned domains such as tailoring, catering and informal tutoring, which are seen as extensions of domestic roles and therefore more socially acceptable (Yaseen, 2013). Cameroonian female entrepreneurs frequently operate in spatially marginalised locations or through mobile setups in informal markets, where visibility is low and access to regulatory protections is limited (Pelican, 2014). Egyptian and Lebanese female entrepreneurs are often directed into feminised service sectors such as wellness, fashion or early childhood education, which are perceived as appropriate but offer limited opportunities for innovation or scalability (Erogul & McCrohan, 2008). Across these groups, restricted access to Science, Technology, Engineering and Mathematics (STEM) education, digital training and venture capital (VC) entrenches exclusion from high-growth industries such as technology and finance (Vardhan et al., 2020). These patterns reflect systemic barriers, not individual choice and continue to limit both personal advancement and Dubai's broader economic diversification goals.

Navigating shifting sands: adaptive strategies of female immigrant entrepreneurs in Dubai

In response to these structural barriers, female immigrant entrepreneurs in Dubai mobilise adaptive strategies that rely on community networks, cultural knowledge and entrepreneurial ingenuity. Indian and Pakistani entrepreneurs often rely on tightly knit ethnic communities for resource pooling, informal lending and labour exchange, providing support where institutional assistance is absent (Yaseen, 2013). Cameroonian female entrepreneurs engage in diasporic solidarity networks that provide mutual aid, rotating savings and credit associations (ROSCAs) and peer mentorship, creating a collective safety net for navigating regulatory and financial barriers (Pelican, 2014). Egyptian and Lebanese entrepreneurs utilise extended family and diaspora-based professional connections to access referrals, clients and legal advice, sustaining business operations under restrictive conditions (Erogul & McCrohan, 2008). These network-based strategies reflect a form of embedded agency through which female entrepreneurs mitigate exclusion and maintain enterprise viability despite their marginalised position in Dubai's economic landscape (Hughes, 2003; Vardhan et al., 2020).

Cultural identity serves as a strategic resource, enabling female immigrant entrepreneurs to build niche enterprises that align cultural familiarity with consumer demand. Indian and Pakistani entrepreneurs leverage traditional food, fashion and wellness practices to serve both co-ethnic and diverse clienteles, creating differentiation within saturated markets (Vardhan et al., 2020; Yaseen, 2013). Cameroonian entrepreneurs offer Afrocentric beauty services, cultural cuisine and care-based ventures that foster community cohesion while addressing unmet consumer needs (Pelican, 2014). Egyptian and Lebanese entrepreneurs draw on shared linguistic, religious and cultural capital to develop offerings in education, event planning and consultancy, navigating Dubai's multicultural yet stratified social landscape (Erogul & McCrohan, 2008). These identity-anchored strategies demonstrate the agency and creativity of female entrepreneurs, who simultaneously preserve cultural heritage and respond to market expectations (Essers & Benschop, 2009; Vardhan et al., 2020). By embedding their businesses within culturally resonant narratives, they sustain livelihoods, reinforce community ties and enhance the visibility and legitimacy of their EIs.

The adoption of digital technology has emerged as a transformative strategy through which female immigrant entrepreneurs navigate exclusion and build competitive resilience. Indian and Pakistani entrepreneurs use social media and e-commerce platforms to operate home-based businesses, increasing market reach and operational efficiency while maintaining flexibility (Haan, 2004; Yaseen, 2013). Cameroonian entrepreneurs leverage mobile technology and informal online marketplaces to sustain entrepreneurial activity across marginalised zones, using digital tools to overcome limitations in visibility and access (Pelican, 2014). Egyptian and Lebanese entrepreneurs enhance their professional image and outreach by integrating online branding, virtual services and remote consultancy, particularly in education and design sectors (Erogul & McCrohan, 2008). This technological shift reduces reliance on formal infrastructure, which remains financially and logistically inaccessible to many (Vardhan et al., 2020). These digital adaptations represent not only a response to structural exclusion but also a proactive embrace of innovation, positioning female immigrant entrepreneurs as contributors to Dubai's evolving knowledge economy and as active agents of transformation within constrained environments.

Israel

Tel Aviv's entrepreneurial mosaic: immigrant innovation amid systemic exclusion

Tel Aviv's dynamic urban economy, often described as the heart of Israel's *Startup Nation*, offers a compelling site for analysing immigrant entrepreneurship within a landscape shaped by innovation, exclusion and resilience (Senor & Singer, 2011). While the city is globally recognised for its vibrant startup ecosystem, its entrepreneurial opportunities remain unevenly distributed, particularly for immigrant groups facing legal precarity, racialised discrimination and spatial segregation (Barak-Bianco & Raijman, 2015; Paz, 2011). Immigrant entrepreneurs frequently navigate the intersection of necessity and opportunity, contributing to the city's cultural vibrancy and economic sustainability (Anteby-Yemini, 2017; Said & Vyas, 2025). This analysis examines the entrepreneurial experiences of African asylum seekers (Eritrean and Sudanese) and Arab citizens of Israel, two groups whose demographic presence in Tel Aviv's marginalised urban zones and distinct encounters with legal, spatial and identity-based constraints, offer critical insights into the dynamics of immigrant enterprise in conditions of systemic exclusion.

Navigating structural labyrinths: barriers facing immigrant entrepreneurs in Tel Aviv

Legal and regulatory exclusion constitutes a foundational barrier for immigrant entrepreneurs in Tel Aviv, shaping their access to economic participation and institutional legitimacy. African asylum seekers, primarily from Eritrea and Sudan, are systematically denied formal refugee status and are classified as *infiltrators* under Israeli policy. This designation precludes their access to legal employment, municipal support or residency rights, thereby relegating them to the informal economy where they must operate under conditions of legal precarity (Barak-Bianco & Raijman, 2015). Many navigate this exclusion through proxy ownership arrangements in which Israeli citizens are listed as the legal owners. This exposes the actual entrepreneurs to exploitation and legal disputes (Paz, 2011). In contrast, Arab entrepreneurs, while formally recognised as Israeli citizens, experience structural marginalisation through spatial exclusion. Their businesses are frequently located in under-resourced neighbourhoods such as Jaffa, where inadequate infrastructure and limited access to urban development support restrict their integration into Tel Aviv's mainstream entrepreneurial ecosystem (Said & Vyas, 2025; Schnell & Sofer, 2002). In both cases, the regulatory environment reproduces a tiered system of access to entrepreneurship that reinforces patterns of inequality embedded within urban governance.

Financial exclusion further constrains the entrepreneurial potential of both groups by limiting their ability to secure capital, invest in infrastructure and expand operations. For African asylum seekers, the lack of formal legal status disqualifies them from banking services, credit lines and government-backed financing. Commercial banks routinely deny loan applications, citing undocumented status and lack of collateral as disqualifying factors. This forces entrepreneurs to rely on community-based savings systems or informal lenders with few protections (Anteby-Yemini, 2017; Barak-Bianco & Raijman, 2015). Arab entrepreneurs face parallel challenges despite their citizenship. They are often perceived as commercially high risk due to systemic discrimination and geographic isolation from Tel Aviv's financial centres, resulting in limited access to investment and growth capital (Said & Vyas, 2025). The financial burden of starting a business in Tel Aviv, including lease deposits, licensing fees and infrastructure setup, can exceed 165,000 NIS or approximately 45,000 USD. This is a prohibitive cost for those excluded from institutional lending (Barak-Bianco & Raijman, 2015). These financial constraints push both groups into low-capital, necessity-driven sectors that reinforce a cycle of economic precarity and limit their capacity for upward mobility.

Social exclusion compounds legal and financial barriers by shaping the legitimacy, visibility and consumer reach of immigrant entrepreneurs. African-owned businesses are often confined to segregated districts such as Neve Sha'anan, where racialised perceptions and xenophobia restrict their engagement with broader urban markets. These entrepreneurs are frequently subjected to harassment and hostility, with the 2012 anti-immigrant riots exemplifying the depth of societal antagonism they face (Human Rights Watch, 2012; Sabar & Posner, 2013). Such incidents not only threaten the physical security of business owners but also damage the public image and consumer trust necessary for market diversification. Arab entrepreneurs encounter a parallel form of exclusion rooted in socio-political marginalisation. Although integrated into the legal framework, they face persistent discrimination in hiring networks, media representation and institutional procurement, which limits their opportunities for business scaling and brand legitimacy (Said & Vyas, 2025). In both contexts, immigrant entrepreneurs are structurally positioned at the margins of Tel Aviv's entrepreneurial ecosystem, where institutional bias and public perception constrain their ability to grow beyond enclave-based markets.

Weaving resilience: adaptive strategies of immigrant entrepreneurs in Tel Aviv

In response to structural exclusion, immigrant entrepreneurs in Tel Aviv have developed resourceful and culturally grounded strategies that enable them to sustain their businesses and assert agency within an unequal urban landscape. African asylum seekers have transformed small businesses, particularly restaurants, cafés and community retail outlets in Neve Sha'anan, into cultural and economic spaces that foster social cohesion among displaced populations (Anteby-Yemini, 2017; Sabar & Posner, 2013). These establishments act as informal community centres, offering culturally familiar goods and services while creating a sense of belonging in the absence of state recognition. Arab entrepreneurs similarly pursue strategic forms of identity mobilisation that are often guided by values such as self-direction and universalism. These values empower them to transcend ethnic boundaries and enter more diverse, growth-oriented sectors including education, technology and media (Said & Vyas, 2025; Sofer & Schnell, 2017). By embedding entrepreneurial practice within frameworks of cultural resilience and civic engagement, both groups navigate exclusion not only as a constraint but also as a terrain of creative possibility and identity affirmation.

Community networks serve as alternative infrastructures of support, enabling immigrant entrepreneurs to mobilise financial and social capital in the absence of institutional inclusion. Among African asylum seekers, informal financial mechanisms such as rotating credit associations and savings clubs offer vital startup funds that circumvent formal banking restrictions (Barak-Bianco & Raijman, 2015). These networks also facilitate proxy arrangements that enable undocumented individuals to operate businesses under the legal cover of trusted intermediaries, thereby navigating restrictive licensing regimes (Paz, 2011). Arab entrepreneurs, while increasingly accessing formal support systems, continue to benefit from culturally tailored initiatives such as entrepreneurship hubs, mentorship programmes and business incubators. Recent efforts led by public-private partnerships have begun targeting Arab communities with funding, training and digital infrastructure aimed at increasing their participation in Israel's innovation economy (Jewish News Syndicate, 2022). These community-based resources act not only as coping mechanisms but also as drivers of resilience that allow entrepreneurs to establish sustainable ventures within structurally exclusionary environments.

Digital innovation has become a transformative tool through which immigrant entrepreneurs expand market access, gain visibility and challenge spatial and social segregation. African entrepreneurs increasingly utilise platforms such as Facebook and Instagram to advertise their services, engage with customers and distribute products beyond the geographic constraints of Neve Sha'anan (Barak-Bianco & Raijman, 2015). Social media provides low-cost avenues for outreach and reputation building, allowing entrepreneurs to bypass traditional marketing channels and connect with niche audiences. Arab entrepreneurs have similarly leveraged digital technologies to enter high-growth sectors including software development, biotechnology and e-commerce. Supported by selective government initiatives that aim to diversify Israel's high-tech landscape, Arab-owned startups are gaining a foothold in national and international markets (Said & Vyas, 2025; Sofer & Schnell, 2017). In both cases, digital platforms serve as vehicles for reconfiguring entrepreneurial geographies. These tools enable marginalised groups to reshape Tel Aviv's economic fabric while resisting the limitations imposed by legal status, racialised spatiality and systemic discrimination.

The Triangle region of Israel: a nexus of female immigrant entrepreneurship

Immigrant entrepreneurship in the Triangle region of Israel reflects a complex response to regional underdevelopment, geopolitical instability and sociocultural exclusion. The areas collectively referred to as *HaMeshulash* are predominantly Arab and have historically experienced spatial and economic marginalisation within Israel's national development framework (Schnell & Sofer, 2003). Prolonged institutional neglect and restricted access to broader markets have shaped the local entrepreneurial landscape (Snider et al., 2024), where minority-owned businesses have become critical drivers of economic activity and community resilience (Abu-Asbah & Heilbrunn, 2011). In recent years, Arab female entrepreneurs have assumed increasingly prominent roles, balancing cultural traditions with economic aspirations in ways that reflect evolving forms of agency and innovation. This analysis focuses specifically on Arab female entrepreneurs in the Triangle region, selected for their significance in illuminating how gendered and cultural identities intersect with regional economic development under conditions of systemic exclusion.

Challenges in the Triangle region of Israel: overcoming barriers in female immigrant entrepreneurship

Arab female entrepreneurs in Israel's Triangle face a spectrum of cultural, economic and institutional challenges that complicate their pursuit of economic independence and growth (Abu-Asbah & Heilbrunn, 2011; Heilbrunn & Abu-Asbah, 2011). In many Arab communities in Israel, cultural norms prioritise female roles as caregivers and homemakers, limiting their ability to fully engage in entrepreneurial activities. These expectations create time and resource constraints that reinforce their dependence on local, community-based businesses (Abu-Asbah & Heilbrunn, 2011). Additionally, restricted mobility exacerbated by limited public transportation in many Arab towns further isolates Arab female entrepreneurs from external markets and broader economic opportunities (Keinan et al, 2007; Schnell & Sofer, 2002). The cultural stigma surrounding female participation in public economic activities also curtails engagement in wider networks, which are essential for business success. Societal perceptions of immigrant groups as threats further exacerbate barriers to social and economic inclusion (Snider et al., 2024). This combination of cultural expectations and logistical barriers significantly restricts Arab female entrepreneurs' capacity to scale their ventures (Abu-Asbah & Heilbrunn, 2011; Schnell et al., 1999).

Economic exclusion further compounds these challenges. Financial access is particularly constrained for Arab female entrepreneurs, who frequently encounter barriers in securing loans due to systemic neglect of Arab localities and limited infrastructure development (Heilbrunn et al., 2014; Heilbrunn & Palgi, 2015). This exclusion often forces reliance on informal funding mechanisms, which are limited in scope and inadequate for business growth. Financial literacy gaps, combined with an over-reliance on kinship-based networks, restrict opportunities for economic independence and expansion by limiting access to broader financial systems and professional connections (Abu-Asbah & Heilbrunn, 2011; Schnell & Sofer, 2002). Many Arab female entrepreneurs also lack financial literacy, which inhibits their ability to navigate complex financial systems or develop robust business plans (Abu-Asbah & Heilbrunn, 2011). Additionally, over-embeddedness in kinship and community-based systems has been identified as a factor limiting expansion into broader inter-ethnic economic networks (Schnell & Sofer, 2003). Studies highlight that such financial and social constraints are especially acute for Arab female entrepreneurs operating in peripheral areas, where resources are scarcer (Keinan et al, 2007; Schnell & Sofer, 2002).

Institutional barriers exacerbate the struggles of Arab female entrepreneurs. The Israel-Palestine conflict disrupts business activity and trade, creating economic instability that limits resources for marginalised groups (Bhowmick, 2024). Additionally, the spatial segregation of Arab communities restricts access to industrial zones and urban hubs, leaving Arab female entrepreneurs reliant on small, localised markets (Schnell & Sofer, 2002; Sofer & Schnell, 2017). Labour market discrimination compounds this issue, as Arab female entrepreneurs are often relegated to low-income, informal roles. For example, a study reveals that Palestinian Israeli females are overrepresented in low-paying sectors such as caregiving and cleaning services, highlighting systemic barriers to accessing higher-income opportunities (Heilbrunn et al., 2014). The lack of affordable childcare infrastructure disproportionately affects entrepreneurial mothers, who bear the dual responsibility of managing both family and business. Without affordable childcare or reliable public transportation, Arab female entrepreneurs' ability to balance professional and domestic responsibilities is significantly curtailed (Abu-Asbah & Heilbrunn, 2011; Keinan et al, 2007). This lack of institutional support reinforces disparities, limiting many to small-scale, survival-focused enterprises (Heilbrunn et al., 2014; Heilbrunn & Abu-Asbah, 2011).

Navigating success in the Triangle region of Israel: resilient strategies for female immigrant entrepreneurs

Despite systemic challenges, Arab female entrepreneurs in Israel's Triangle region demonstrate remarkable resilience by leveraging community networks to navigate economic and social barriers. These networks provide crucial financial resources through informal lending circles and cooperative groups, offering an alternative to traditional banking systems that often exclude them. Beyond financial support, they serve as platforms for mentorship and knowledge-sharing, enabling Arab female entrepreneurs to develop strategies grounded in collective experience and mutual trust (Heilbrunn & Abu-Asbah, 2011). In Baqa al-Gharbiyye, for example, cooperative initiatives have facilitated access to funding and strengthened small-scale enterprises in sectors such as food production and traditional crafts (Abu-Asbah & Heilbrunn, 2011). Exclusionary attitudes shaped by societal perceptions of threat create additional barriers, influencing Arab female entrepreneurs' ability to access economic opportunities (Snider et al., 2024). The emphasis on collective success mitigates isolation and enhances economic participation, reinforcing agency in an otherwise restrictive socio-economic landscape (Keinan et al, 2007; Schnell et al., 1999).

Leveraging cultural heritage represents another cornerstone of entrepreneurial strategy. Many Arab female entrepreneurs build businesses rooted in traditional crafts, culinary skills and other culturally significant practices. By aligning their ventures with community needs and values, they create niche markets that help them stand out in competitive spaces. This approach not only ensures economic sustainability but also preserves and promotes cultural identity. For instance, businesses offering traditional products or services often attract both local consumers and external markets, enhancing their growth potential (Abu-Asbah & Heilbrunn, 2011; Heilbrunn et al., 2014). Cultural preservation through these ventures strengthens Arab female entrepreneurs' roles as custodians of their communities' identity. These culturally grounded enterprises build trust within communities, differentiate offerings in saturated markets and open unique opportunities that support resilience in the face of structural exclusion (Heilbrunn et al., 2014). As shown by Essers & Benschop (2007), female entrepreneurs from minority or migrant backgrounds frequently engage in *boundary work* that fuses religious, gendered and EIs to negotiate legitimacy and market access, particularly in contexts of sociocultural barrier. In this way, identity becomes not only a source of differentiation but a strategic asset that enables agency within restrictive economic systems.

The adoption of technology has become a transformative strategy for overcoming structural barriers. E-commerce platforms and social media tools allow Arab female entrepreneurs to reach wider markets without the need for physical mobility, which is often limited in their communities (Schnell & Sofer, 2002). These digital platforms support cost-effective marketing and facilitate connections with customers, suppliers and collaborators. By integrating transnational resources such as expertise or materials sourced through diaspora ties, Arab female entrepreneurs have established ventures that operate across local and global markets (Abu-Asbah & Heilbrunn, 2011). Technology empowers them to bypass traditional gatekeepers in the entrepreneurial ecosystem and maintain direct relationships with market actors, a critical step for sustainable scaling (Keinan et al., 2007). Through these adaptive strategies, Arab female entrepreneurs in Israel's Triangle not only sustain their businesses but also reshape the boundaries of participation in socially and spatially constrained economic systems.

Comparative synthesis: immigrant entrepreneurship in the United Arab Emirate and Israel

Immigrant entrepreneurship in the UAE and Israel unfolds within sharply contrasting political, legal and institutional contexts. Despite these differences, entrepreneurs in both settings encounter systemic barriers that shape how ventures emerge and evolve. Legal status, access to finance and institutional support vary widely, influencing business formation and survival. Entrepreneurial practices reflect adaptations to these structural barriers, shaped by national and local dynamics. Table 7.1 outlines key dimensions of immigrant entrepreneurship across both countries, providing the foundation for a more detailed strategic analysis and policy discussion in the following section.

Strategic policy interventions for the Middle East

Immigrant entrepreneurship is central to urban and peripheral economies in the Middle East, where migration-driven diversity meets institutional fragmentation. Table 7.1 highlights how restrictive migration regimes, institutional fragmentation and constrained access to formal finance shape immigrant entrepreneurship in the UAE and Israel. These structural conditions intersect with race, gender, legal status and geography to produce segmented entrepreneurial

TABLE 7.1 Key comparative dimensions of immigrant entrepreneurship in the United Arab Emirates and Israel

Category	*United Arab Emirates*	*Israel*
Immigration policy framework	Temporary migration regime with limited rights and no path to citizenship; entrepreneurship tied to sponsorship systems.	Stratified citizenship and asylum frameworks; some groups lack legal status while others face systemic marginalisation.
Institutional ecosystem	Limited formal support; access often mediated by elite networks; weak coordination between municipal and third-sector actors.	Institutional support uneven; NGOs play a critical role; immigrant entrepreneurship remains peripheral to mainstream policy agendas.
Financial access and inclusion	Access to finance constrained by nationality and legal status; entrepreneurs rely on informal systems such as ROSCAs and community pooling.	Formal banking often inaccessible; informal lending and proxy arrangements are essential for business survival.
Regulatory environment	Opaque and inconsistently applied regulations; heightened scrutiny of migrant-owned ventures.	Regulatory barriers tied to legal status and spatial exclusion; formalisation is difficult without legal recognition.
Community and social networks	Dense social networks substitute for institutional support; trust-based practices sustain enterprise.	Embedded networks provide access to capital, labour and legitimacy; essential in navigating exclusion.
Transnational strategies	Transnational trade, diaspora capital and hybrid branding used to bypass institutional constraints.	Informal transnational ties and digital tools expand reach and enable flexible, low-barrier market entry.
Cultural identity and market positioning	Cultural identity leveraged for consumer trust and legitimacy; gender norms shape business models and sector entry.	Identity mobilised in branding and positioning; used to build niche markets and establish visibility.

outcomes. In response, immigrant entrepreneurs mobilise cultural identity, transnational ties and embedded networks to sustain enterprise and negotiate visibility.

While the MEF (Kloosterman, 2010) provides a valuable foundation for analysing institutional barriers, it must be extended to account for identity as a strategic and relational force shaped by social hierarchies and exclusion (Anthias, 2001; Bruni et al., 2004). Building on this analysis, five targeted interventions are proposed to foster inclusive and context-responsive entrepreneurial ecosystems across the region.

Reform legal and regulatory frameworks to foster inclusive entrepreneurship

Immigrant entrepreneurs across the Middle East often operate under legal regimes that restrict autonomy, limit protections and reinforce dependency. In cities like Tel Aviv and Dubai, these legal barriers disproportionately affect groups such as African asylum seekers and South Asian entrepreneurs. In Israel, migrants without formal refugee status are denied work permits and business registration, forcing them into unprotected informal markets (Barak-Bianco & Raijman, 2015; Paz, 2011). In the UAE, the kafala system mandates citizen sponsorship for non-national entrepreneurs, curtailing business control and increasing vulnerability to exploitation (Abdul Reda et al., 2023). Regulatory enforcement remains inconsistent and discretionary, exacerbating uncertainty and limiting transparency (Pelican, 2014). These frameworks do not simply obstruct access; they reproduce stratified entrepreneurial environments controlled by legal and political gatekeepers. Similar dynamics are evident across GCC countries, where migrant status often determines the scope of entrepreneurial agency (ILO, 2017; Kagan & Chloewinski, 2022; Thiollet, 2011).

Governments across the Middle East must reform legal frameworks to prioritise entrepreneurial autonomy for immigrant communities. In the GCC, this includes abolishing sponsor-based licensing requirements and enabling non-citizens to independently own and operate businesses. In Israel, asylum seekers should be granted recognised legal status and access to work permits for lawful business activity. Municipal and national authorities should create multilingual regulatory platforms to streamline licensing and expand legal guidance for immigrant entrepreneurs. These reforms must be guided by principles of equity and inclusion, with success measured by a 30% increase in legally registered immigrant-owned businesses and a reduction in sponsorship-related dependency within five years.

Establish comprehensive entrepreneurial support ecosystems

Across the Middle East, immigrant entrepreneurs often lack access to the institutional support necessary to scale and sustain their ventures. This is particularly evident among female entrepreneurs and undocumented individuals who face structural isolation and policy fragmentation. In Israel's Triangle towns and parts of the Gulf, entrepreneurial support systems remain centralised and exclusionary. While initiatives such as Israel's MATI Centre provide some assistance, limited outreach, eligibility barriers and spatial inequality prevent these models from reaching the most marginalised (Abu-Asbah & Heilbrunn, 2011; Keinan et al., 2007). Access to finance, mentorship, training and digital infrastructure often remains fragmented or concentrated in urban cores. Without inclusive support ecosystems, immigrant ventures remain trapped in informal, low-growth sectors with limited opportunities for upward mobility (Heilbrunn & Palgi, 2015; Roomi & Parrot, 2008).

Governments should establish entrepreneurial hubs that consolidate access to mentorship, funding, training and digital resources. These hubs must be in underserved areas and digitally accessible to entrepreneurs with mobility constraints. Existing models, such as Dubai's DBWC and Israel's MATI framework, should be expanded and adapted to serve broader migrant communities. Regional coordination with public and private stakeholders is essential to promote inclusion across sectors such as technology, logistics and renewable energy. Measurable outcomes should include a 25% increase in immigrant ventures receiving institutional support and successfully entering scalable industries within five years.

Leverage community and cultural networks to promote economic resilience

Community-based networks offer critical infrastructure for immigrant entrepreneurs across the Middle East, particularly where formal systems exclude or marginalise. These networks are vital for South Asian, African and Arab immigrant communities, who rely on peer support and culturally embedded strategies. In Dubai, South Asian entrepreneurs engage in rotating savings associations and community-based lending to overcome financial barriers (Yasin, 2022). In Tel Aviv, African entrepreneurs operate within solidarity economies that foster peer mentorship and shared risk (Pelican, 2014). These practices reflect broader regional patterns where cultural businesses provide both economic livelihood and collective social value. Despite their significance, such networks remain largely invisible in formal policy frameworks and economic development strategies (Wang, 2019).

Governments must integrate community-based and culturally anchored enterprises into national entrepreneurship strategies. This includes providing targeted funding, legal recognition and business development support for cooperative models and cultural businesses. Municipalities should promote visibility through multicultural trade fairs, cultural entrepreneurship platforms and grants that preserve cultural heritage. Programmes modelled on Dubai's cultural sector initiatives and Israel's community enterprise zones should be adapted and scaled regionally. These efforts should target a 20% increase in immigrant-led cultural ventures reaching broader markets and diversifying their consumer base within three years.

Drive technological integration to expand market access

Across the Middle East, digital innovation has emerged as a transformative strategy for immigrant entrepreneurs navigating legal, spatial and infrastructural barriers. In Dubai, Cameroonian entrepreneurs use mobile platforms to maintain flexibility and reduce reliance on formal retail channels (Pelican, 2014). In Israel's Triangle region, Arab female entrepreneurs leverage digital commerce to expand market reach and mitigate geographic isolation (Schnell & Sofer, 2002; Vardhan et al., 2020). Digital tools offer mobility-constrained entrepreneurs alternative entry points into entrepreneurial ecosystems. However, persistent digital divides, including infrastructure gaps, low digital literacy and minimal institutional support, continue to restrict growth potential (Heilbrunn et al., 2014; Keinan et al., 2007).

Governments must invest in digital entrepreneurship hubs that offer training, infrastructure and digital financial literacy programmes tailored to immigrant communities. National digital initiatives such as the UAE's eGovernment services and Israel's Digital Israel Initiative provide models for regional adaptation. Policymakers should prioritise mobile-first solutions to address the needs of entrepreneurs operating in peri-urban and informal settings. Expanding internet access, subsidising digital tools and developing accessible online marketplaces must become central policy goals. These interventions should aim for a 20% increase in immigrant-led digital enterprises and greater participation in transnational e-commerce within three years.

Empower female immigrant entrepreneurs through gender-sensitive infrastructure and legal reform

Female immigrant entrepreneurs across the Middle East face compounded structural barriers shaped by gender norms, legal restrictions and institutional neglect. In Dubai, South Asian women on family or dependent visas remain tied to male sponsors under the kafala system, limiting mobility and restricting economic autonomy (Erogul & McCrohan, 2008; Pelican, 2014). In Israel's Triangle region, Arab female entrepreneurs contend with mobility constraints, inadequate childcare and limited access to capital, collectively hindering their participation in entrepreneurship (Vardhan, 2020). Across the region, exclusion from mentorship, public support and formal networks persists. Despite official narratives of empowerment, female immigrant entrepreneurs remain underrepresented in high-growth sectors and are disproportionately concentrated in low-capital, home-based enterprises (Pelican, 2014; Yaseen, 2013).

Governments must adopt gender-sensitive reforms to enhance female entrepreneurs' legal, spatial and economic agency. These include abolishing sponsor-dependent licensing, investing in affordable childcare and transport and expanding access to formal finance. Initiatives like the DBWC and MATI's female entrepreneurship programmes should be adapted to serve non-citizen women across the region. Licensing schemes for home-based and mobile businesses can further reduce entry barriers. These reforms should aim for a 25% increase in immigrant female-led businesses in non-traditional sectors and measurable engagement in cross-sector mentorship programmes within five years.

Conclusion

This chapter has demonstrated that immigrant entrepreneurship in the Middle East constitutes a strategic response to exclusionary migration systems, legal precarity and fragmented institutional environments. Through a secondary analysis of documented case studies from Dubai, Tel Aviv and the Triangle region, it has shown how immigrant entrepreneurs mobilise EI shaped through intersectionality, translocal agency and embedded community networks to sustain economic activity under conditions of structural marginalisation. Applying the RMEF, the chapter has highlighted how entrepreneurial strategies emerge from the interplay between institutional structures, social hierarchies and cross-border resource mobilisation. Rather than treating entrepreneurship as a linear pathway to integration, the RMEF reveals it as a negotiated process shaped by differentiated opportunity structures. Although policy discourses increasingly valorise entrepreneurship, institutional reforms across the region remain partial, reinforcing gendered, racialised and legal exclusions. Building inclusive entrepreneurial ecosystems will require not only regulatory reforms but also deeper institutional transformations towards equity, accessibility and recognition. Future research should empirically apply and refine the RMEF through primary fieldwork across under-studied Middle Eastern cities, where migration, informality and spatial exclusion intersect in complex and distinctive ways.

References

Abdul Reda, A., Fraser, N. A., & Khattab, A. (2023). Does social mobility matter? The Kafala System and Anti-Immigrant Sentiment. *Political Studies Review, 21*(4), 801–824. https://doi.org/10.1177/14789299221130901

Abu-Asbah, K., & Heilbrunn, S. (2011). Patterns of entrepreneurship of Arab women in Israel. *Journal of Enterprising Communities: People and Places in the Global Economy, 5*(3), 184–198. https://doi.org/10.1108/17506201111156661

Acuto, M. (2010). High-rise Dubai: Urban entrepreneurialism and the technology of symbolic power. *Cities, 27*(4), 272–284. https://doi.org/10.1016/j.cities.2010.01.003

Alsarhan, F., Horak, S., & Darwish, T. K. (2024). Relational gatekeeper behaviour of HR managers in the Middle East: The role of informal networks. *The International Journal of Human Resource Management, 35*(16), 2635–2673. https://doi.org/10.1080/09585192.2024.2359517

Anteby-Yemini, L. (2017). African asylum-seekers in Israel: Illegalization, incorporation and race relations. *Hagira, 7*, 7–20.

Anthias, F. (2001). New hybridities, old concepts: The limits of 'culture'. *Ethnic and Racial Studies, 24*(4), 619–641. https://doi.org/10.1080/01419870120049815

Barak-Bianco, A., & Raijman, R. (2015). Asylum seeker entrepreneurs in Israel. *Economic Sociology: The European Electronic Newsletter, 16*(2), 4–13. https://hdl.handle.net/10419/156049

Bhowmick, R. (2024). Impact of Israel–Palestine conflict on the economy and businesses of the region. *SSRN Electronic Journal*. https://doi.org/10.2139/ssrn.4759320

Bruni, A., Gherardi, S., & Poggio, B. (2004). Doing gender, doing entrepreneurship: An ethnographic account of intertwined practices. *Gender, Work & Organisation, 11*(4), 406–429. https://doi.org/10.1111/j.1468-0432.2004.00240.x

Elmassah, S., James, R., & Bacheer, S. M. (2022). Ethnic entrepreneurial success factors: Evidence from the United Arab Emirates. *Heliyon, 8*(6), e09732. https://doi.org/10.1016/j.heliyon.2022.e09732

Erogul, M. S., & McCrohan, D. (2008). Preliminary investigation of Emirati women entrepreneurs in the UAE. *African Journal of Business Management, 2*(10), 177.

Essers, C., & Benschop, Y. (2007). Enterprising identities: Female entrepreneurs of Moroccan or Turkish origin in the Netherlands. *Organisation Studies, 28*(1), 49–69. https://doi.org/10.1177/0170840607068256

Essers, C., & Benschop, Y. (2009). Muslim businesswomen doing boundary work: The negotiation of Islam, gender and ethnicity within entrepreneurial contexts. *Human Relations, 62*(3), 403–423. https://doi.org/10.1177/0018726708101042

Goby, V. P., & Erogul, M. S. (2011). Female entrepreneurship in the United Arab Emirates: Legislative encouragements and cultural constraints. *Women's Studies International Forum, 34*(4), 329–334. https://doi.org/10.1016/j.wsif.2011.04.006

Haan, H. C. (2004). Small enterprises: Women entrepreneurs in the UAE. CLMRI.

Hamdan, A. M. M. (2019). Entrepreneurship and economic growth: An Emirati perspective. *The Journal of Developing Areas, 53*(1), 65–78. https://www.jstor.org/stable/26501887

Heilbrunn, S., & Abu-Asbah, K. M. (2011). Disadvantaged and embedded: Arab women entrepreneurs in Israel. *International Journal of Business and Social Science, 2*(11), 26–36.

Heilbrunn, S., Abu-Asbah, K., & Nasra, M. A. (2014). Difficulties facing women entrepreneurs in Israel: A social stratification approach. *International Journal of Gender and Entrepreneurship, 6*(2), 142–162. https://doi.org/10.1108/IJGE-02-2013-0007

Heilbrunn, S., & Palgi, M. (2015). Women entrepreneurs in the rural periphery of Israel: Comparing Israeli Palestinians and Israeli Jews. In P. McKiernan & D. Purg (Eds.), *Women's voices in management: Identifying innovative and responsible solutions* (pp. 216–235). Palgrave Macmillan UK.

Human Rights Watch. (2012). Measure denies asylum seekers protections of refugee convention. https://www.hrw.org/news/2012/06/10/israel-amend-anti-infiltration-law

Hughes, K. D. (2003). Pushed or pulled? Women's entry into self-employment and small business ownership. *Gender, Work & Organization, 10*(4), 433–454. https://doi.org/10.1111/1468-0432.00205

International Labour Organisation. (2017). *Employer-migrant worker relationships in the Middle East: Exploring scope for internal labour market mobility and fair migration.* https://www.ilo.org/wcmsp5/groups/public/---arabstates/---ro-beirut/documents/publication/wcms_552697.pdf

Jewish News Syndicate. (2022). *Israel Innovation Authority, government commit NIS 225 million to Arabs in high-tech.* https://www.jns.org/israel-innovation-authority-govt-commit-nis-225-million-to-arabs-in-high-tech/

Kagan, S., & Cholewinski, R. (2022). *Reforming the sponsorship system in the Gulf Cooperation Council countries: Opportunities and challenges as a result of COVID-19 and the fiscal crisis.* Gulf Research Centre. https://gulfmigration.grc.net/media/pubs/exno/Kagan%20%26%20Cholewinski%20-%20EN%20No.1%20-%202022.pdf

Kanna, A. (2011). *Dubai, the city as corporation.* University of Minnesota Press.

Keinan, T., Bar, D., & Alahmad, T. (2007). *Mobility among Arab women in Israel.* Kayan Feminist Organisation. https://www.transportation.org.il/sites/default/files/pirsum/mobility05final_0.pdf

Kloosterman, R. C. (2010). Matching opportunities with resources: A framework for analysing (migrant) entrepreneurship from a mixed embeddedness perspective. *Entrepreneurship and Regional Development, 22*(1), 25–45. https://doi.org/10.1080/08985620903220488

Kloosterman, R. C., & Rath, J. (2018). Mixed embeddedness revisited: A conclusion to the symposium. *Sociologica, 12*(2), 103–114.

Mahdavi, P. (2011). *Gridlock: Labor, migration, and human trafficking in Dubai.* Stanford University Press.

Malit, F. T., & Oliver, T. (2013). Labor migration and deskilling in the United Arab Emirates: Impacts on Cameroonian labour migrants. Cornell University, ILR School. https://ecommons.cornell.edu/items/29cf5521-41f4-4e06-a639-f9c2042340ec

Nazareno, J., Zhou, M., & You, T. (2019). Global dynamics of immigrant entrepreneurship: Changing trends, ethnonational variations, and reconceptualisations. *International Journal of Entrepreneurial Behaviour & Research, 25*(5), 780–800. https://doi.org/10.1108/IJEBR-03-2018-0141

Paz, Y. (2011). *Ordered disorder: African asylum seekers in Israel and discursive challenges to an emerging refugee regime*. United Nations High Commissioner for Refugees. https://www.unhcr.org/sites/default/files/legacy-pdf/4d7a26ba9.pdf

Pelican, M. (2014). Urban lifeworlds of Cameroonian migrants in Dubai. *Urban Anthropology and Studies of Cultural Systems and World Economic Development, 43*(1/2/3), 255–309. https://www.jstor.org/stable/24643112

Roomi, M. A., & Parrott, G. (2008). Barriers to development and progression of women entrepreneurs in Pakistan. *The Journal of Entrepreneurship, 17*(1), 59–72. https://doi.org/10.1177/097135570701700105

Sabar, G., & Posner, R. (2013). Remembering the past and constructing the future over a communal plate: Restaurants established by African asylum seekers in Tel Aviv. *Food, Culture & Society, 16*(2), 197–222. https://doi.org/10.2752/175174413X13589681351692

Said, I. S., & Vyas, V. (2025). Intersectionality of place and race: Entrepreneurial performance of Arab citizens of Israel. *International Journal of Entrepreneurial Behaviour & Research, 31*(1), 53–79. https://doi.org/10.1108/IJEBR-07-2022-0615

Schnell, I., Benenson, I., & Sofer, M. (1999). The spatial pattern of Arab industrial markets in Israel. *Annals of the Association of American Geographers, 89*(2), 311–336. https://doi.org/10.1111/1467-8306.00147

Schnell, I., & Sofer, M. (2003). Embedding entrepreneurship in social structure: Israeli-Arab entrepreneurship. *International Journal of Urban and Regional Research, 27*(2), 300–318. https://doi.org/10.1111/1468-2427.00449

Schnell, I., & Sofer, M. (2002). Unbalanced embeddedness of ethnic entrepreneurship: The Israeli Arab case. *International Journal of Entrepreneurial Behaviour & Research, 8*(1/2), 54–68. https://doi.org/10.1108/13552550210423714

Senor, D., & Singer, S. (2011). *Start-up nation: The story of Israel's economic miracle*. McClelland & Stewart.

Snider, K. L., Hefetz, A., & Canetti, D. (2024). Terrorized by immigration? Threat perceptions and policy preferences. *Terrorism and Political Violence, 36*(4), 552–566. https://doi.org/10.1080/09546553.2023.2180287

Sofer, M., & Schnell, I. (2017). Over-and under-embeddedness: Failures in developing mixed embeddedness among Israeli Arab entrepreneurs. In S. Leonard & M. Taylor (Eds.), *Embedded enterprise and social capital* (pp. 225–247). Routledge.

Thiollet, H. (2011). Migration as diplomacy: Labor migrants, refugees, and Arab regional politics in the oil-rich countries. *International Labor and Working-Class History, 79*(1), 103–121. https://doi.org/10.1017/S0147547910000293

Thiollet, H., & Assaf, L. (2021). Migrant cosmopolitanism in Emirati and Saudi cities: Practices and belonging in exclusionary contexts. In C. Lejeune, D. Pagès-El Karoui, C. Schmoll, & H. Thiollet (Eds.), *Migration, urbanity and cosmopolitanism in a globalised world* (pp. 151–165). Springer. https://doi.org/10.1007/978-3-030-67365-9_12

Vardhan, J., Bohra, S., Abdullah, A., Thennarasu, K., & Jagannathan, S. K. (2020). Push or pull motivation? A study of migrant women entrepreneurs in UAE. *International Journal of Family Business and Regional Development, 1*(1), 8–24. https://doi.org/10.1504/IJFBRD.2020.111443

Vora, N. (2013). *Impossible citizens: Dubai's Indian diaspora*. Duke University Press.

Wang, Y. (2019). Making Chinese spaces in Dubai: A spatial consideration of Chinese transnational communities in the Arab Gulf states. *Journal of Arabian Studies, 9*(2), 269–287. https://doi.org/10.1080/21534764.2019.1762313

Yaseen, Z. K. (2013). Women entrepreneurs: Challenges and opportunities in the Arab world, UAE case. *Business & Entrepreneurship Journal, 2*(1), 43–48. https://www.scienpress.com/Upload/BEJ/Vol%202_1_4.pdf

Yasin, N. (2022). Cold grass or hot sands? A comparative study of immigrant Punjabi–Pakistani entrepreneurs in London and Dubai. *Strategic Change, 31*(4), 387–396. https://doi.org/10.1002/jsc.2511

8

IMMIGRANT ENTREPRENEURSHIP IN LATIN AMERICA

Transnational adaptation, informal practices and institutional fragmentation

Introduction

Latin America is undergoing profound socio-economic and institutional transformations that are reshaping its urban economies. Within this evolving landscape, immigrants have emerged as significant economic actors, contributing to employment generation, market diversification, social mobility, innovation and more inclusive forms of urban development (Lesser, 2013; Martínez Rivera, 2024; Mendoza, 2018). While immigrant entrepreneurship has been widely examined in North American and European contexts (Aliaga-Isla & Rialp, 2013; Light, 2005; Nazareno et al., 2019), its dynamics in Latin America remain underexplored. This gap is particularly urgent given the region's distinctive patterns of informality, institutional fragmentation and regulatory volatility, which shape how immigrant entrepreneurs engage with urban economies.

Much of the foundational literature on immigrant entrepreneurship has emerged from Global North contexts characterised by relatively stable institutional environments, structured access to finance and coherent policy frameworks (Kloosterman & Rath, 2001; Malerba & Ferreira, 2020). One of the most influential conceptual contributions, the mixed embeddedness framework (MEF), emphasises the interplay between opportunity structures, institutional settings and social networks in shaping entrepreneurial outcomes (Kloosterman et al., 1999). However, this framework remains largely underapplied in Latin America, where pervasive informality, financial exclusion and fragmented governance challenge many of its core assumptions (Baeninger et al., 2017; Lugosi & Allis, 2019). These differences call for grounded, context-sensitive approaches that reflect the patterns of exclusion and precarity structuring entrepreneurship in the region (Aliaga-Isla & Rialp, 2013; Lugosi & Allis, 2019). While MEF has been foundational in advancing a multidimensional view of migrant entrepreneurship, its limited uptake in Latin American research has contributed to a theoretical gap that this chapter seeks to address. Comparative analyses of urban immigrant entrepreneurship across Latin American cities also remain scarce, despite significant intra-regional variation in institutional arrangements and migration regimes (Baeninger et al., 2018; Itzigsohn, 2000; Mendoza, 2020).

Latin America presents a distinct socio-institutional landscape where immigrant entrepreneurs frequently operate across formal and informal domains. Inconsistent state support compels

DOI: 10.4324/9781003605072-10

many to rely on transnational networks, community-based knowledge and alternative financial practices to sustain their ventures (Guarnizo, 2003; Nascimento, 2018). These dynamics are particularly evident in urban contexts shaped by colonial inequality, uneven development and institutional instability, which structure how legitimacy, recognition and belonging are negotiated (Faist, 2000; Itzigsohn, 2000). In the absence of stable opportunity structures, entrepreneurs mobilise cross-border resources, diasporic infrastructures and transnational capital (Drori et al., 2009; Montiel, 2023). Beyond structural responses, identity emerges as a strategic element of entrepreneurial practice. Immigrant entrepreneurs actively build social credibility through culturally embedded practices, local engagement and visibility strategies (Bruni et al., 2004; Essers & Benschop, 2007). These actions are shaped by intersecting hierarchies of gender, race, legal status and class, which condition access to opportunity and shape entrepreneurial trajectories (Anthias, 2013; Fernández-Kelly & Konczal, 2005; Romero & Valdez, 2016). The reconceptualised MEF (RMEF) introduced in Chapter 2 offers a multidimensional lens for tracing patterns of identity negotiation, institutional engagement and transnational strategy across diverse entrepreneurial contexts.

To demonstrate the analytical value of RMEF, this chapter offers a comparative analysis of immigrant entrepreneurship in Brazil and Mexico based on a synthesis of existing scholarly research. These countries, characterised by significant immigrant populations and differing migration trajectories, provide valuable insights into the regional dynamics of immigrant entrepreneurship (Baeninger et al., 2018; Itzigsohn, 2000; Martínez Rivera, 2024). The analysis examines four urban centres: São Paulo and Rio de Janeiro in Brazil and Mexico City and Guadalajara in Mexico, each offering distinct contexts for studying the integration of immigrant business communities within complex urban environments. In São Paulo, immigrant entrepreneurs operate in garment manufacturing, food services and retail, often concentrated within ethnic commercial corridors that facilitate informal finance, cultural exchange and niche market access (Araújo et al., 2006; Choi, 2022; El-Hachem Kirby, 2015). In Rio de Janeiro, decentralised governance and socio-spatial inequality have shaped an entrepreneurial landscape supported by kinship networks, rotating savings groups and local trading practices (Baeninger et al., 2017; da Cunha et al., 2014; De Queiroz Falcão et al., 2020). In Mexico City, immigrant entrepreneurs mobilise transnational capital, diasporic institutions and hybrid governance arrangements within a fragmented regulatory environment (Martínez Rivera, 2024; Villalever & López-Calvo, 2020). Guadalajara, although less extensively documented, is emerging as a hub where immigrant entrepreneurs engage in digital commerce, cultural production and community-based partnerships (Artasu & Niglio, 2019; Cerutti, 1999; Mendoza, 2020).

The chapter is structured as follows. It begins with a detailed analysis of immigrant entrepreneurship in Brazil (São Paulo and Rio de Janeiro) and Mexico (Mexico City and Guadalajara). A comparative synthesis then identifies key parallels and distinctions between the two national contexts. This is followed by a policy discussion proposing ways to improve institutional responsiveness and support immigrant entrepreneurship. The chapter concludes with reflections on broader implications and directions for future research.

Brazil

São Paulo's multicultural dynamo: immigrant entrepreneurs and the making of Brazil's economic powerhouse

São Paulo, as Brazil's principal economic centre and a major multicultural metropolis, offers a dynamic environment for immigrant entrepreneurship shaped by layered migration trajectories, diverse social networks and persistent socio-economic inequalities (Araújo et al., 2006; De Ferrari et al., 2024; Lugosi & Allis, 2019). Immigrant entrepreneurs participate across formal and informal economic sectors, drawing on cultural resources, co-ethnic ties and transnational networks to establish and sustain diverse forms of business activity (Choi, 2022; Cruz et al., 2020; Le Blanc, 2016). Their ventures are situated within a segmented and evolving urban economy, reflecting varied forms of economic and social embeddedness that connect local, national and transnational spheres (Aliaga-Isla & Rialp, 2013; Karam, 2008; Malerba & Ferreira, 2020). Rather than occupying a peripheral role, immigrant entrepreneurs have historically contributed to São Paulo's industrial expansion, commercial diversification and urban development through their entrepreneurial initiatives and sociocultural participation (Araújo et al., 2006; Dionisio, 2024; Lugosi & Allis, 2019). This analysis examines key immigrant groups in São Paulo by focusing on Korean, Lebanese and Afro-Brazilian female entrepreneurs, chosen for their distinct migration trajectories and differentiated roles in the city's industrial, commercial and cultural sectors.

Structural exclusion and cultural segmentation: structural barriers facing immigrant entrepreneurs in São Paulo

Immigrant entrepreneurs in São Paulo operate within a regulatory system marked by complex procedures, opaque licensing structures and uneven enforcement. Korean garment producers in Bom Retiro face substantial administrative delays linked to customs, import documentation and legal formalisation requirements, which hinder business registration and operational scalability (Choi, 2022). Lebanese entrepreneurs, although historically integrated into São Paulo's commercial sphere, were excluded from early industrial incentive schemes and often relied on familial investment and informal networks to expand their ventures (El-Hachem Kirby, 2015; Truzzi, 1992). Afro-Brazilian female entrepreneurs encounter additional institutional barriers, including discriminatory licensing processes and exclusion from commercial zoning protections, reflecting racial and gender hierarchies embedded in bureaucratic systems (Dionisio, 2024; Murphy, 2024). These barriers frequently push immigrant entrepreneurs into informality, where they operate without legal protections or visibility. The institutional complexity of São Paulo's urban economy exacerbates this precarity, particularly for racialised and gendered entrepreneurs navigating formal systems structured around elite norms (Araújo et al., 2006; De Ferrari et al., 2024; Lugosi & Allis, 2019). Across these cases, exclusion from the regulatory mainstream is not incidental but structurally embedded, reproducing unequal access to opportunity and limiting pathways to formal entrepreneurial growth.

Financial exclusion remains a defining barrier for immigrant entrepreneurs, who must navigate limited access to formal credit and discriminatory lending practices. Korean entrepreneurs, despite cohesive ethnic networks, are frequently denied loans due to inadequate collateral or legal residency documentation, relying instead on rotating savings groups within their community to sustain operations (Choi, 2022). Lebanese entrepreneurs, even with established commercial legitimacy, face institutional scepticism towards immigrant-led enterprises and continue to depend on transnational family-based capital to fund expansion and mitigate risk (El-Hachem Kirby, 2015; Truzzi, 1992). Afro-Brazilian female entrepreneurs confront compounded financial exclusion due to intersecting racial and gendered biases within Brazil's banking sector, which routinely denies them access to credit based on assumptions about their reliability and capacity (Dionisio, 2024). In response, many turn to microfinance programmes and community-based lending associations that offer limited support but often restrict business scalability (Murphy, 2024). These financial strategies, though adaptive, reflect broader systemic failures that disproportionately affect entrepreneurs outside Brazil's white, male, middle-class business paradigm.

Financial marginalisation is thus a structural condition shaped not only by income inequality but by embedded hierarchies that determine who can access capital and under what terms (De Ferrari et al., 2024; Lugosi & Allis, 2019).

Cultural segmentation and symbolic exclusion further shape the entrepreneurial landscape, reinforcing stratified access to consumer markets and legitimacy. Korean entrepreneurs in Bom Retiro benefit from strong co-ethnic solidarity but often remain confined to ethnic retail enclaves, where linguistic isolation and cultural stereotyping limit access to broader consumer bases (Choi, 2022; Galetti, 1995). Lebanese entrepreneurs, despite their commercial visibility, have historically been excluded from elite Brazilian business networks and have had to construct parallel economic systems based on family investment and ethnic cooperation (El-Hachem Kirby, 2015; Truzzi, 1992). Afro-Brazilian female entrepreneurs in the beauty and fashion sectors are routinely marginalised by Eurocentric aesthetic norms that restrict Afrocentric products from entering mainstream distribution channels, reducing both market exposure and product legitimacy (Dionisio, 2024; Murphy, 2024). These patterns of exclusion are sustained by cultural hierarchies that render nonwhite and immigrant-led ventures as niche, preventing their full integration into São Paulo's economic mainstream. Rather than temporary barriers, cultural segmentation is deeply embedded in the urban market and contributes to persistent disparities in visibility, credibility and commercial growth (Araújo et al., 2006; De Ferrari et al., 2024).

Strategic adaptation and entrepreneurial resistance: how immigrant entrepreneurs thrive in São Paulo's business landscape

Despite structural exclusion, immigrant entrepreneurs have developed strategic approaches to navigate barriers and build resilient ventures. Korean garment manufacturers in Bom Retiro have adopted *just in time production* and *modinha*, a form of small batch, trend driven clothing that enables quick market response while minimising surplus and overheads (Choi, 2022; Kontic, 2001; Lesser, 2013). These innovations reduce dependency on formal credit and allow efficient inventory turnover. Lebanese entrepreneurs have diversified beyond traditional commerce into real estate, logistics and wholesale sectors, enabling capital reinvestment and multi sector resilience in the face of institutional neglect (El-Hachem Kirby, 2015; Truzzi, 1992). Afro-Brazilian female entrepreneurs engage in dignity work and redefine entrepreneurial success as a collective, culturally rooted pursuit. Their enterprises often combine economic activity with social transformation, challenging dominant norms and expanding the scope of what constitutes entrepreneurial legitimacy (Dionisio, 2024; Murphy, 2024). These practices reflect not only entrepreneurial resilience but also strategic cultural resistance. In São Paulo's stratified economic ecosystem, immigrant entrepreneurs actively reshape business models, reject passive assimilation and create new forms of economic belonging that reframe exclusion as a catalyst for innovation (Lugosi & Allis, 2019).

In the absence of reliable access to formal credit, immigrant entrepreneurs across ethnic groups have built community-based systems for saving and lending money. Korean entrepreneurs leverage ROSCAs and community-based savings cooperatives that ensure liquidity and reinvestment without navigating exclusionary bank systems (Choi, 2022). Lebanese entrepreneurs sustain intergenerational wealth flows through diasporic financial networks that provide startup and expansion capital independently of Brazilian formal institutions (El-Hachem Kirby, 2015; Truzzi, 1992). Afro-Brazilian female entrepreneurs rely on microcredit, collective savings clubs and grassroots financial innovation to circumvent discriminatory loan structures and build financial autonomy (Dionisio, 2024; Murphy, 2024). These practices are not merely survival tactics but strategic adaptations that foster entrepreneurial independence and preserve community-based economic sovereignty. They also reveal how financial exclusion prompts structural creativity, generating new forms of economic organisation that are embedded in cultural identities and collective priorities. Rather than defaulting to formal institutions, these entrepreneurs actively construct parallel financial ecosystems that are more inclusive, trust based and culturally aligned with their lived experiences (Araújo et al., 2006).

Digital transformation has expanded entrepreneurial possibilities, offering new tools to counter spatial, symbolic and market-based exclusion. Korean entrepreneurs have integrated digital platforms into their business operations, using e-commerce, logistics applications and social media to reach broader consumer markets and reduce dependence on localised retail infrastructure (Choi, 2022). Afro-Brazilian female entrepreneurs have harnessed digital tools to assert racial identity and market Afrocentric aesthetics through influencer collaborations, targeted branding and online sales strategies that circumvent mainstream retail exclusion (Dionisio, 2024; Murphy, 2024). While direct evidence remains limited, Lebanese entrepreneurs' established diversification into real estate and commercial networks (El-Hachem Kirby, 2015; Truzzi, 1992) suggests an emerging engagement with digital tools for asset coordination and client outreach. These strategies demonstrate how immigrant entrepreneurs extend their market reach and reshape consumer narratives while building economic resilience outside formal systems. More broadly, São Paulo's immigrant entrepreneurs have long developed alternative forms of value creation that reflect cultural resistance and adaptive agency within restrictive urban environments (De Ferrari et al., 2024; Lugosi & Allis, 2019). As digital tools become increasingly accessible, they hold transformative potential for scaling, asserting identity and challenging exclusion in the city's evolving marketplace.

Rio de Janeiro's entrepreneurial mosaic: the role of immigrant business communities

Rio de Janeiro, one of Brazil's most iconic and complex urban economies, has long attracted immigrants whose entrepreneurial activities contribute to the city's commercial dynamism and spatial restructuring (da Cunha et al., 2014; Scherer & Grisci, 2022). Situated within a broader context of deep social inequalities, informal economic practices and fragmented governance, immigrant entrepreneurs engage across diverse sectors, mobilising cultural resources, community ties and transnational networks to develop and sustain business ventures. These activities are embedded within Rio's heterogeneous urban fabric, connecting local, national and transnational economic circuits and contributing to the city's ongoing commercial transformation (Aliaga-Isla & Rialp, 2013; Malerba & Ferreira, 2020). While the scholarly literature has predominantly concentrated on immigrant entrepreneurship in São Paulo (Araújo et al., 2006; Cruz et al., 2020), recent studies have begun to highlight the distinct dynamics unfolding in Rio de Janeiro's urban context. This analysis examines immigrant entrepreneurship in Rio de Janeiro through the experiences of Syrian and Chinese entrepreneurs, selected to illustrate contrasting migration trajectories and economic engagements across emergent and established commercial spaces.

Institutional and market barriers in Rio de Janeiro: structural challenges facing immigrant entrepreneurs

Immigrant entrepreneurs in Rio de Janeiro face a fragmented institutional environment where bureaucratic inefficiencies and inconsistent enforcement hinder the formalisation of small businesses. For Syrian refugees, this often begins with precarious immigration status, leading to lengthy administrative processes when seeking legal documentation, business registration and tax identification. These delays force many to operate informally, particularly in the food and retail sectors, exposing them to legal penalties and limiting access to essential business services (de Queiroz Falcão et al., 2020). Chinese entrepreneurs, though more established in Rio's commercial economy, also face regulatory hurdles such as inconsistent customs procedures, high import taxes and opaque trade policies (da Cunha et al., 2014). These structural conditions complicate inventory turnover, increase transaction costs and discourage expansion beyond localised networks. In both cases, entrepreneurs must navigate unstable policy environments with limited institutional support. These challenges reflect Rio's broader governance issues, where immigrant business communities operate within uneven regulatory terrains that disproportionately impact newcomers and small-scale operators, reinforcing their marginal status in the urban economy (Baeninger et al., 2017).

Limited access to formal financial systems presents an enduring barrier that shapes the scale and sustainability of immigrant ventures in Rio. Syrian entrepreneurs, especially recent arrivals, often lack the legal status, collateral and documentation required by financial institutions. Excluded from formal credit markets, many rely on informal lending circles and mutual aid systems within the community, which provide short-term capital but limit long-term investment capacity (de Queiroz Falcão et al., 2020). Chinese entrepreneurs, despite their longstanding commercial presence, face barriers to accessing public credit and state-sponsored incentives due to institutional bias and the informal nature of their operations. To compensate, many turn to transnational remittances and rotating credit associations, sustaining their businesses through collective financial strategies (da Cunha et al., 2014). While these mechanisms enhance community resilience, they restrict broader integration into Rio's formal financial ecosystem. Both groups remain subject to patterns of financial exclusion that perpetuate self-reliance and constrain upward mobility, demonstrating how institutional barriers continue to shape entrepreneurial trajectories and reinforce structural inequities across ethnic lines.

Even when legal and financial challenges are partially overcome, cultural bias and market segmentation limit immigrant entrepreneurs' access to broader commercial opportunities. Syrian-owned businesses, especially in food and hospitality, often face discriminatory perceptions that prevent them from securing space in central retail zones or reaching mainstream Brazilian consumers (de Queiroz Falcão et al., 2020). These perceptions result in spatial clustering and reinforce dependency on niche markets within immigrant enclaves. Chinese entrepreneurs, despite their economic strength in electronics and retail trade, are frequently subject to scepticism around product authenticity and service quality, which weakens trust with local business partners and consumers (da Cunha et al., 2014). These cultural dynamics affect branding, customer retention and supply chain partnerships. Broader research on immigrant businesses in Brazil indicates that these exclusions are embedded in historical patterns of economic stratification and racialised consumer behaviour (Lesser, 2013). Consequently, immigrant entrepreneurs are often confined to segmented markets shaped more by ethnicity than merit or innovation. These barriers deepen their marginalisation within the urban economy and limit the visibility and legitimacy of their ventures within Rio's dominant commercial networks.

Resilient pathways: how immigrant entrepreneurs navigate and transform Rio de Janeiro's economy

Despite systemic exclusion, immigrant entrepreneurs in Rio de Janeiro have adopted adaptive strategies that allow them to sustain and expand their businesses in the face of institutional adversity. Syrian refugees, particularly in the food sector, have turned to digital platforms such as delivery apps and social media marketing to bypass bureaucratic delays and engage directly with local consumers (de Queiroz Falcão et al., 2020). These tools enable visibility and reach while minimising dependence on formal commercial infrastructure. At the same time, co-ethnic networks offer mentorship, labour sharing and pooled resources, facilitating business development in the absence of external support. Chinese entrepreneurs, who also face regulatory exclusion, have leveraged digital commerce and logistics systems to distribute goods efficiently while maintaining autonomy from state-dependent mechanisms (da Cunha et al., 2014). These strategies reflect broader patterns among immigrant communities across Brazil, where community-rooted resilience mechanisms compensate for structural exclusion (Valdés, 2024). These digital and relational adaptations not only support immediate business viability but also reflect how immigrant entrepreneurs reshape access and opportunity under systemic barriers, using identity, networks and technology to carve space within Rio's informal and formal economies.

For both groups, financial sustainability depends heavily on alternative financing models developed in response to exclusion from mainstream credit systems. Syrian entrepreneurs frequently rely on mutual credit groups, informal savings arrangements and co-ethnic capital to launch or maintain small enterprises, particularly food stalls and micro-shops (de Queiroz Falcão et al., 2020). These grassroots systems enable basic operational liquidity while fostering trust and collaboration within their communities. Chinese entrepreneurs draw on transnational capital flows and family-based lending institutions, which sustain business expansion without requiring engagement with state-backed credit programmes (da Cunha et al., 2014). These practices exemplify how immigrant entrepreneurs develop parallel financial infrastructures that ensure operational resilience and community interdependence (Light, 2005). However, these same systems can constrain business growth, limit credit history formation and reduce eligibility for public or private investment. The persistence of these financial adaptations reflects the dual function of ethnic networks as both survival mechanisms and structural barriers, reinforcing the self-contained nature of immigrant economies in Rio's competitive urban marketplace.

Although immigrant entrepreneurs in Rio have demonstrated innovation and adaptability, their continued dependence on informal networks and segmented markets underscores the enduring nature of structural exclusion. Syrian-owned businesses remain largely excluded from institutional channels due to legal ambiguity, while cultural barriers continue to restrict their expansion into mainstream commercial spaces (de Queiroz Falcão et al., 2020). Chinese entrepreneurs, despite digital expansion and capital resilience, struggle with branding limitations and consumer mistrust that hinder broader retail integration (da Cunha et al., 2014). These experiences illustrate how immigrant entrepreneurship is not simply a response to opportunity, but a negotiated process involving shifting regulatory frameworks, reputational politics and differentiated access to capital and visibility (Lesser, 2013). Business development becomes a continuous act of repositioning, requiring entrepreneurs to manage identity, community affiliation and institutional navigation simultaneously. Despite their strategic agency, immigrant entrepreneurs remain situated at the margins of Rio's urban economy, where legitimacy and growth are unevenly distributed and constantly renegotiated within exclusionary systems.

Mexico

Mexico City's Chinese entrepreneurs: economic barriers, strategic adaptation and urban market integration

Mexico City has long been a major destination for immigrant entrepreneurs, whose business activities contribute to the city's commercial diversification, informal economies and spatial restructuring (Martínez Rivera & Dussel Peters, 2016; Villalever & Rubio, 2019). Operating within a fragmented institutional landscape shaped by bureaucratic complexity, uneven regulatory enforcement and spatial inequalities, immigrant entrepreneurs engage across formal and informal sectors, drawing on cultural resources, community networks and transnational linkages to establish and sustain economic ventures (Cinco Basurto, 2015). Their activities are embedded within the city's evolving market infrastructure, connecting local commercial circuits with broader transnational flows and contributing to urban economic transformation (Martínez Rivera, 2024). Although Mexico City hosts a wide range of immigrant groups, systematic academic research on immigrant entrepreneurship remains limited, particularly within English-language scholarship (Martínez Rivera & Dussel Peters, 2016; Villalever & Rubio, 2019). This analysis examines the experiences of Chinese entrepreneurs in Mexico City, selected for their longstanding commercial presence, economic visibility and evolving role within the city's urban market networks.

Navigating historical constraints: systemic barriers facing Chinese entrepreneurs in Mexico City

Chinese entrepreneurship in Mexico City has historically developed under conditions of structural exclusion, ethnic marginalisation and legal precarity. Initial waves of Chinese migrants arrived during the late 19th and early 20th centuries, engaging in laundries, retail and food services, often concentrated in segregated urban zones (Cinco Basurto, 2015). These entrepreneurs encountered significant hostility, including anti-Chinese campaigns and restrictive immigration laws, which limited their access to formal employment and commercial property (Martínez Rivera, 2024). In response, Chinese communities established informal economic circuits supported by kinship networks, enabling them to build self-reliant businesses despite legal and social exclusion. While these adaptations allowed for continuity, they also reinforced spatial and institutional separation from the city's mainstream economy, making it difficult for Chinese businesses to scale beyond ethnic enclaves such as Barrio Chino and Viaducto Piedad (Cinco Basurto, 2015).

Bureaucratic complexity in Mexico City continues to affect Chinese entrepreneurs, especially first-generation business owners with limited formal training in administrative systems. Regulatory processes such as business registration, import licensing and tax compliance are lengthy and opaque, increasing operational costs and legal uncertainty (Martínez Rivera, 2024). Chinese retailers and wholesalers operating in Viaducto Piedad often circumvent these processes by working through informal channels, including unregistered business models, verbal leasing agreements and undocumented workers (Villalever & López-Calvo, 2020). While these methods enable market participation, they expose entrepreneurs to unpredictable enforcement and limit access to state protections such as credit programmes or commercial insurance. This duality reinforces their marginal position within the city's economic hierarchy and constrains efforts to expand into more formalised or regulated commercial sectors (Martínez Rivera & Dussel Peters, 2016).

Limited access to credit and investment capital further exacerbates the structural vulnerability of Chinese businesses in Mexico City. Financial institutions often require formal business status, long-term residency and verifiable tax records, all of which are barriers for entrepreneurs operating within informal or semi-formal structures (Martínez Rivera & Dussel Peters, 2016). As a result, many Chinese entrepreneurs rely on community-based lending systems, including family loans and rotating credit pools, to finance inventory, rent and expansion (Martínez Rivera, 2024). These networks provide vital liquidity but limit long-term investment, scalability and eligibility for public-sector support. Moreover, reliance on ethnic financial ecosystems reinforces a cycle of economic isolation, making it more difficult for Chinese entrepreneurs to access broader credit markets or forge partnerships outside the community (Villalever & Rubio, 2019). This persistent exclusion illustrates how formal financial barriers compound bureaucratic and social marginalisation in shaping the contours of immigrant entrepreneurship in Mexico City.

Strategic responses and market shifts: adaptive practices among Chinese entrepreneurs in Mexico City

Despite enduring structural challenges, Chinese entrepreneurs in Mexico City have developed a range of adaptive strategies to navigate exclusion and sustain economic viability. One major strategy is generational diversification. First-generation entrepreneurs typically maintain traditional business models in retail and food services, drawing on co-ethnic labour and transnational supply networks. In contrast, second-generation are increasingly entering higher-growth sectors such as hospitality, education and technology, aided by bilingualism and deeper integration into local institutions (Cinco Basurto, 2015). This generational shift allows Chinese-owned businesses to reposition themselves within more diverse market segments while preserving the communal support structures that have historically underpinned their survival (Martínez Rivera, 2024). Such adaptations demonstrate an evolving balance between continuity and innovation, enabling new forms of economic participation beyond enclave-based commerce.

Technological innovation has emerged as another key lever of adaptation. Chinese entrepreneurs are leveraging digital platforms, including e-commerce websites, online payment systems and social media marketing to expand customer reach and streamline operations (Villalever & Rubio, 2019). These tools offer a pathway around physical space constraints and regulatory red tape by enabling remote transactions and digital inventory management. Moreover, digital infrastructure helps mitigate some forms of discrimination by allowing businesses to reach clients directly, bypassing intermediaries who may harbour biases or restrict access to commercial space (Villalever & López-Calvo, 2020). These digital strategies have allowed Chinese-owned businesses to diversify their consumer base, modernise their branding and enhance their competitiveness within Mexico City's increasingly digitised retail economy (Eng Menéndez, 2021).

Transnational linkages and market diversification also play a central role in the strategic evolution of Chinese entrepreneurship. Business owners have expanded trade relationships with suppliers in China and the United States, using these ties to develop agile, transnational supply chains that allow them to remain responsive to shifting consumer demand (Martínez Rivera & Dussel Peters, 2016). Simultaneously, Chinese entrepreneurs have introduced new business models such as upscale dining, boutique hotels and digital wholesale platforms that cater to broader urban demographics. These adaptations signal a deliberate move beyond the survivalist mode of immigrant entrepreneurship, positioning Chinese-owned firms as innovators and market leaders in Mexico City's competitive urban economy (Martínez Rivera, 2024). The integration of local and global strategies reflects how Chinese entrepreneurs reshape ethnic economic structures to engage with the broader urban market while continuing to navigate structural exclusion through community-based resilience.

Guadalajara's economic landscape: challenges, strategies and market integration among Southern European Entrepreneurs

Guadalajara, one of Mexico's most dynamic economic hubs, has become an important site for immigrant entrepreneurship, shaped by its position as the country's second-largest metropolitan area and an emerging centre for innovation and market diversification (Mendoza, 2020). Immigrant entrepreneurs engage across sectors such as design, hospitality, technology and artisanal production, mobilising cultural resources, business expertise and transnational networks to establish and sustain ventures within the city's evolving economic landscape (Artasu & Niglio, 2019; Mendoza, 2020). Their activities are embedded in Guadalajara's heterogeneous market structures, connecting local opportunities with broader diasporic and transnational economic circuits (Cerutti, 1999; Mendoza, 2018). Despite Guadalajara's increasing relevance, systematic academic research on immigrant entrepreneurship in the city remains limited, particularly in English-language scholarship. This analysis examines Southern European entrepreneurs, specifically Italians and Spaniards, whose business activities illuminate the connections between migration processes, entrepreneurial practices and the evolving urban economy of Guadalajara.

Structural barriers facing Southern European entrepreneurs in Guadalajara: bureaucracy, finance and market access

Southern European entrepreneurs in Guadalajara encounter a range of institutional barriers that complicate business formation and growth. Bureaucratic inefficiencies, such as delayed business registration, visa requirements and complex tax systems, create significant obstacles, especially for newly arrived entrepreneurs (Mendoza, 2020). Although the Mexican regulatory framework is less restrictive than in parts of Europe, inconsistent enforcement and shifting administrative processes generate uncertainty and increase compliance costs. Italian and Spanish entrepreneurs, unfamiliar with Mexico's legal environment, often require local consultants to navigate documentation requirements, adding financial burdens and delaying market entry. Forming partnerships with Mexican businesses has become one strategy to reduce administrative barriers and gain access to institutional channels more efficiently (Mendoza, 2018).

Financial exclusion presents another layer of difficulty. Many Southern European entrepreneurs struggle to secure loans or access credit lines due to limited local financial histories or residency status (Mendoza, 2020). Banks and credit institutions frequently prioritise established local firms, excluding foreign entrepreneurs from mainstream financial tools. To compensate, entrepreneurs rely on personal savings, remittances from family abroad or private investments sourced through transnational networks (Ambrosini, 2012). This dependence on informal financial sources limits scalability and deters long-term investment. Moreover, fluctuations in the exchange rate between the euro and Mexican peso introduce additional instability in pricing, procurement and profit margins, affecting both planning and operations (Mendoza, 2018).

Market access further constrains entrepreneurial growth. While Italian and Spanish entrepreneurs enjoy strong brand recognition in sectors like food, fashion and design, their products are often perceived as high-end or exclusive, limiting mass market appeal (Mendoza, 2020). Competition from local firms with more affordable offerings poses a challenge, requiring adjustments to pricing, marketing and product design. Entrepreneurs must also navigate cultural differences in consumer preferences and business negotiations, which influence market penetration. Efforts to adapt include hybridising products, localising branding and engaging in industry fairs and collaborations. However, language barriers and limited institutional support continue to restrict full integration into Guadalajara's broader commercial ecosystem (Artasu & Niglio, 2019).

Adaptive strategies among Southern European entrepreneurs in Guadalajara: navigating bureaucracy, finance and market barriers

Southern European entrepreneurs in Guadalajara have developed a variety of strategies to address structural barriers. Transnational ties have proven instrumental in ensuring business continuity and quality. Entrepreneurs maintain relationships with European suppliers and investors, which allows for consistent product standards and access to specialised materials (Cerutti, 1999; Faist, 2000). These transnational networks also offer informal mentorship, business intelligence and financial backing, enabling Southern European entrepreneurs to operate in specialised niches such as boutique hospitality, artisanal products and architectural design (Artasu & Niglio, 2019; Mendoza, 2020). In some cases, European business alliances in Guadalajara have emerged, creating platforms for knowledge sharing, resource pooling and market collaboration (Mendoza, 2018).

Joint ventures with Mexican partners are another key adaptive mechanism. These collaborations improve credibility, ease bureaucratic compliance and provide market access through established local networks (Mendoza, 2020). By sharing responsibilities, Italian and Spanish entrepreneurs reduce entry risks and deepen their understanding of local consumer behaviour. Accessing government-sponsored entrepreneurship programmes, though limited, has also been a strategic avenue for some, helping them obtain grants, subsidies or participation in formal business forums (Cerutti, 1999; Mendoza, 2020). Such programmes, when accessible, enhance legitimacy and visibility while offering a gateway to policy resources that are otherwise difficult for immigrant entrepreneurs to access independently.

Digital entrepreneurship has become a defining feature of the recent business strategies deployed by Southern European entrepreneurs. Online platforms enable direct-to-consumer models, reducing reliance on brick-and-mortar stores and allowing entrepreneurs to test new products at low cost (Ambrosini, 2012; Mendoza, 2020). Social media and digital advertising facilitate brand building and allow entrepreneurs to reach niche audiences across Mexico. Integration of e-commerce logistics has further optimised supply chains, enhancing delivery times and customer satisfaction. Some entrepreneurs use data analytics to track consumer trends and customise their offerings accordingly. As digital tools become more central to Mexico's commercial landscape, leveraging them has allowed Southern European entrepreneurs to strengthen resilience, improve agility and maintain competitiveness in Guadalajara's evolving economic environment (Artasu & Niglio, 2019; Mendoza, 2018, 2020).

Comparative synthesis: immigrant entrepreneurship in Brazil and Mexico

Distinct institutional environments in Brazil and Mexico give rise to similarly fragmented entrepreneurial ecosystems. In cities such as São Paulo, Rio de Janeiro, Mexico City and Guadalajara, immigrant entrepreneurs face overlapping barriers related to legal status, regulatory burdens, financial exclusion and cultural segmentation. These barriers intersect with race, gender and migration history to structure differentiated access to resources and market participation. In response, entrepreneurs mobilise community networks, transnational capital and identity-based strategies to sustain their ventures. Table 8.1 outlines key dimensions that shape immigrant entrepreneurship across both contexts.

Strategic policy interventions for Latin America

Immigrant entrepreneurship in Latin America is shaped by fragmented institutions, legal ambiguity, limited financial access and burdensome regulatory frameworks. Table 8.1 highlights how these barriers intersect with race, gender, class and migration status to structure entrepreneurial opportunities in Brazil and Mexico. Entrepreneurs respond by leveraging informal capital, transnational linkages and embedded networks to sustain their businesses and navigate

TABLE 8.1 Key comparative dimensions of immigrant entrepreneurship in Brazil and Mexico

Category	*Brazil*	*Mexico*
Immigration policy framework	Formal pathways for immigrant entrepreneurship are limited; visa restrictions and legal precarity constrain long-term business participation.	Policy frameworks are inconsistent; informalisation is widespread due to limited entrepreneurial pathways and irregular enforcement of legal provisions.
Institutional ecosystem	Support structures are fragmented across municipal and third-sector initiatives; coordination is limited and access remains uneven.	Institutional support is weak and unevenly distributed; Non-Governmental Organisations (NGOs) and diaspora-led efforts fill gaps but lack systemic integration.
Financial access and inclusion	Immigrant entrepreneurs face exclusion from formal credit markets; many rely on microfinance, informal lending and community-based financial systems.	Access to finance is constrained by documentation and credit history requirements; informal mechanisms are essential, particularly in early stages.
Regulatory environment	Bureaucratic opacity and high compliance costs discourage formalisation; regulatory systems are difficult to navigate and inconsistently applied.	Administrative processes are complex and unevenly enforced; many entrepreneurs operate informally to avoid prohibitive costs and delays.
Community and social networks	Entrepreneurial activity is often supported by co-ethnic and local networks that provide labour, knowledge and startup resources in lieu of formal support.	Community networks offer critical resources for business formation and survival, though connections to mainstream ecosystems remain limited.
Transnational strategies	Entrepreneurs mobilise transnational supply chains, remittances and digital tools to expand markets and mitigate institutional constraints.	Transnational ties enable inventory flow, consumer outreach and market diversification through digital platforms and diaspora connections.
Cultural identity and market positioning	Identity is strategically employed in branding, product differentiation and consumer engagement, particularly in response to exclusionary norms.	Cultural identity is mobilised to build trust, access niche markets and enhance visibility through hybrid branding and multilingual marketing.

exclusion. These dynamics illustrate the interaction between agency and structural barriers outlined in the MEF (Kloosterman & Rath, 2001). Identity also functions as a relational and strategic resource, shaped by intersecting hierarchies of legitimacy and belonging (Anthias, 2013; Fernández-Kelly & Konczal, 2005). Building more inclusive and context-responsive ecosystems requires targeted interventions that directly address these structural conditions. The following section outlines five such measures grounded in the lived experiences of immigrant entrepreneurs across Latin America.

Reform legal and regulatory frameworks to enhance business formalisation

Immigrant entrepreneurs in Latin American cities routinely face bureaucratic inefficiencies, opaque licensing systems and unstable immigration regimes that restrict access to the formal economy. These barriers manifest across diverse contexts: Korean garment manufacturers in São Paulo encounter administrative opacity in customs and registration processes (Choi, 2022); Chinese entrepreneurs in Mexico City face prolonged delays in securing business permits and tax identification, often relying on informal leases to operate (Martínez Rivera, 2024; Villalever & López-Calvo, 2020); Southern European entrepreneurs in Guadalajara struggle with complex registration and visa requirements unfamiliar to their legal backgrounds (Mendoza, 2020); and in Rio de Janeiro, redundant and inconsistently enforced procedures push immigrant entrepreneurs into informality despite long-term market engagement (de Queiroz Falcão et al., 2020). These systemic legal obstacles embed exclusion along lines of ethnicity, gender and migration status, undermining efforts towards formal market integration.

Governments must simplify registration procedures through digitised platforms, clarify legal requirements and implement transparent visa and residency pathways tailored to immigrant entrepreneurs. Following Chile's *Tu Empresa en un Día* model, which streamlined business registration through digital platforms (Organisation for Economic Co-operation and Development [OECD], 2019), countries should adopt multilingual e-government systems to enable real-time registration and documentation updates. Legal aid services, developed in partnership with universities and NGOs, could assist entrepreneurs in precarious immigration situations. Municipal authorities should implement standardised permit frameworks to promote regulatory consistency across districts. These reforms should be evaluated through a 30% increase in formally registered immigrant-owned businesses and a measurable reduction in informality over five years.

Expand financial access through inclusive credit infrastructure

Formal financial institutions in Latin America often deny loans to immigrant entrepreneurs due to insufficient documentation, limited credit histories, lack of collateral or institutional bias. As a result, Afro-Brazilian female entrepreneurs in São Paulo rely on community savings circles with restricted resources (Dionisio, 2024; Murphy, 2024), while Chinese and Syrian entrepreneurs in Mexico City and Rio de Janeiro depend on rotating credit associations and family remittances to finance their businesses (de Queiroz Falcão et al., 2020; Martínez Rivera, 2024). In Guadalajara, Southern European entrepreneurs similarly turn to personal savings and transnational remittances due to exclusion from mainstream financial products (Mendoza, 2020). These patterns of financial exclusion systematically constrain scalability, reinvestment and long-term business growth across urban contexts.

To counter these barriers, governments should expand immigrant-inclusive financial tools through public banking initiatives, fintech partnerships and community-based guarantee schemes. Colombia's Bancóldex provides a strong regional model by combining microfinance access with targeted institutional support (Bancóldex, 2023). Policymakers should implement revenue-based lending and non-collateralised loan products that accommodate irregular income streams, particularly for female and refugee entrepreneurs. Fintech platforms supported by multilingual financial literacy programmes can broaden participation and enhance creditworthiness. These efforts should aim to achieve a 25% increase in immigrant access to formal credit and a measurable reduction in dependence on informal lending within five years.

Strengthen entrepreneurial support ecosystems

Despite their contributions to local economies, immigrant entrepreneurs in Latin America often lack structured access to mentorship, business training and institutional support. Informal guidance through co-ethnic networks in São Paulo and Rio de Janeiro helps with basic labour and market entry but remains insufficient for navigating complex regulations or scaling into high-growth sectors (Araújo et al., 2006; de Queiroz Falcão et al., 2020). In Guadalajara, Italian and Spanish entrepreneurs partner with local firms to overcome administrative hurdles, reflecting the absence of immigrant-focused institutional mechanisms (Mendoza, 2020). In Mexico City, immigrant-owned businesses rely heavily on community-based knowledge systems but remain disconnected from formal entrepreneurship programmes (Martínez Rivera & Dussel Peters, 2016). These structural gaps are particularly acute for female and racialised entrepreneurs, who remain excluded from elite networks and public support initiatives (Murphy, 2024).

To bridge this divide, governments should establish immigrant-focused business incubators and accelerators offering access to capital, mentorship and targeted training. These hubs should be located in both urban centres and peripheral areas and staffed by culturally competent advisors with relevant language skills. Public-private partnerships with universities and chambers of commerce can support sector-specific programmes in areas such as food safety, e-commerce and sustainable energy. Government subsidies should fund certification and skills training that align with the operational realities of immigrant-led enterprises. These initiatives should aim for a 20% increase in immigrant businesses accessing formal support services and scaling into growth sectors within five years.

Leverage transnational and cultural networks for market expansion

Transnational and diasporic networks provide critical economic resources for immigrant entrepreneurs in Latin America yet remain largely underutilised by formal policy frameworks. Lebanese entrepreneurs in São Paulo draw on kinship-based remittances and wholesale networks to expand into logistics and real estate (El-Hachem Kirby, 2015), while Chinese entrepreneurs in Mexico City sustain agile distribution channels through transnational supply chains (Martínez Rivera, 2024). In Rio de Janeiro, informal trade relationships within immigrant communities help sustain small-scale operations but receive little institutional support (de Queiroz Falcão et al., 2020). Spanish and Italian entrepreneurs in Guadalajara leverage diaspora connections to import artisanal goods and establish boutique hospitality ventures, although bureaucratic inefficiencies constrain broader market access (Mendoza, 2020). Despite these diverse strategies, formal engagement with transnational networks remains limited, restricting immigrant entrepreneurs' capacity to scale and diversify.

Governments should formalise engagement with diaspora networks by establishing export assistance programmes offering financial incentives, multilingual documentation and streamlined tariffs for immigrant-run enterprises. Programmes such as Peru's trade facilitation initiatives and Argentina's immigrant commerce hubs provide relevant models for promoting transnational trade and formal economic participation (Inter-American Development Bank, n.d.; Migration Policy Institute, 2020). Trade-focused business councils, such as a Latin America–Asia Business Forum, can foster partnerships through consular channels and industry associations. These initiatives should also incorporate compliance training and digital trade platform integration to ensure sustained growth. The goal is to increase immigrant participation in transnational trade by 20% within three years.

Promote digital integration to overcome spatial and market segmentation

Digital entrepreneurship allows immigrant entrepreneurs in Latin America to bypass spatial exclusion and limited visibility in local markets, yet access to digital tools remains uneven.

Afro-Brazilian female entrepreneurs in São Paulo use social media to expand beyond ethnic consumer bases and challenge Eurocentric beauty norms (Dionisio, 2024), while Syrian and Chinese entrepreneurs in Rio de Janeiro and Mexico City leverage mobile delivery apps and e-commerce platforms to serve dispersed clients and reduce operational costs (de Queiroz Falcão et al., 2020; Martínez Rivera, 2024). In Guadalajara, immigrant entrepreneurs in food, design and hospitality sectors increasingly rely on digital branding and logistics to overcome competitive barriers in local retail markets (Artasu & Niglio, 2019; Mendoza, 2020). However, persistent gaps in infrastructure, training and language accessibility constrain the full benefits of digital entrepreneurship and reinforce existing inequalities.

To address these disparities, governments should launch comprehensive digital inclusion initiatives that combine subsidised internet access, cloud-based logistics support and multilingual digital skills training. Business incubators should integrate e-commerce development, social media marketing and partnerships with fintech and logistics providers. Programmes such as Start-Up Chile and Mexico's expanding network of tech incubators offer scalable models for supporting immigrant entrepreneurs through equity-free funding, mentorship and institutional backing (OECD, 2024; Start-Up Chile, n.d.). These measures should aim to increase the number of immigrant-led digital enterprises by 20% and improve online business revenues within three years.

Conclusion

This chapter demonstrates that immigrant entrepreneurship plays a vital yet structurally constrained role in shaping Latin America's urban economies. Through a comparative analysis of São Paulo, Rio de Janeiro, Mexico City and Guadalajara, it illustrates how immigrant entrepreneurs respond to financial exclusion, bureaucratic complexity and cultural marginalisation by leveraging community-based practices, transnational networks and strategic identity work. Building on the MEF, this chapter has applied the RMEF to analyse immigrant entrepreneurship in these complex urban contexts. The findings reveal that immigrant entrepreneurs exercise significant agency in navigating fragmented and volatile institutional environments, while also exposing the structural barriers that limit their opportunities. These insights emphasise the urgent need for inclusive legal, financial and regulatory reforms that recognise immigrant entrepreneurs as essential contributors to urban innovation and economic resilience. Rather than treating exclusion as inevitable, policy interventions must directly confront systemic inequalities. Future research should empirically test and refine the RMEF across diverse Latin American cities to strengthen theoretical frameworks and guide more context-sensitive policy development.

References

Aliaga-Isla, R., & Rialp, A. (2013). Systematic review of immigrant entrepreneurship literature: Previous findings and ways forward. *Entrepreneurship and Regional Development, 25*(9–10), 819–844. https://doi.org/10.1080/08985626.2013.845694

Ambrosini, M. (2012). Migrants' entrepreneurship in transnational social fields: Research in the Italian context. *International Review of Sociology, 22*(2), 273–292. https://doi.org/10.1080/03906701.2012.696970

Anthias, F. (2013). Intersectional what? Social divisions, intersectionality and levels of analysis. *Ethnicities, 13*(1), 3–19. https://doi.org/10.1177/1468796812463547

Araújo, R. de C., Paiva, O. da C., & Rodriguez, C. L. (2006). Immigrants and entrepreneurs in São Paulo, Brazil: Economic development in the Brazilian 'melting pot'. In C. S. Galbraith & C. H. Stiles (Eds.),

Developmental entrepreneurship: Adversity, risk, and isolation (Vol. 5, pp. 297–322). Emerald Group Publishing. https://doi.org/10.1016/S1074-7877(06)05016-1

Artasu, M. C., & Niglio, O. (2019). *Italianos en México: Arquitectos, ingenieros, artistas entre los siglos XIX y XX.* Aracne Editrice.

Baeninger, R., Peres, R., Fernandes, D., da Silva, S. A., de Oliveira Assis, G., Maria da Consolação, G. C., & Cotinguiba, M. P. (2017). *Imigração haitiana no Brasil.* Paco Editorial.

Baeninger, R., Silva, S. R., Domeniconi, J., & Fernandes, D. (2018). *Migrações Sul-Sul* (2nd ed.). NEPO/Unicamp.

Bancóldex. (2023). *About Bancóldex.* Bancóldex. https://www.bancoldex.com/en/about-bancoldex

Bruni, A., Gherardi, S., & Poggio, B. (2004). Doing gender, doing entrepreneurship: An ethnographic account of intertwined practices. *Gender, Work & Organisation, 11*(4), 406–429. https://doi.org/10.1111/j.1468-0432.2004.00240.x

Cerutti, M. (1999). Empresarios españoles en el Norte de México (1850–1912). *Revista de Historia Económica / Journal of Iberian and Latin American Economic History, 17*(S1), 143–189. https://doi.org/10.1017/S0212610900002299

Choi, W. (2022). Ethnic resources reviving: The case of the Korean ethnic economy in Bom Retiro, São Paulo. *Korea Journal, 62*(4), 78–102. https://doi.org/10.25024/kj.2022.62.4.78

Cinco Basurto, M. (2015). Espacios de la Sinidad [Sinological spaces]. In *La Ciudad Transnacional Comparada: Modos de Vida, Gubernamentalidad y Desposesión* (pp. 151–173). UAM & Juan Pablos.

Cruz, E. P., Falcão, R. P. Q., & Mancebo, R. C. (2020). Market orientation and strategic decisions on immigrant and ethnic small firms. *Journal of International Entrepreneurship, 18*(2), 227–255. https://doi.org/10.1007/s10843-019-00263-2

da Cunha, N. V., de Mello, P. P. T., & Amar, P. (2014). Rio de Janeiro's global bazaar: Syrian, Lebanese, and Chinese merchants in the Saaral. In *The Middle East and Brazil: Perspectives on the new global south* (p. 228). Indiana University Press.

De Ferrari, R. H., Ocepek, A., Travis, R., & Armony, A. C. (2024). Migration and urban development in São Paulo. In A. C. Armony & R. H. De Ferrari (Eds.), *Urbanization and migration in three continents* (pp. 71–91). Routledge.

de Queiroz Falcão, R. P., Cruz, E. P., Piccoli, D. A. C., & Mancebo, R. C. (2020). Self-employment of Syrian refugees: Unveiling social networks and human capital of food stall owners in Rio de Janeiro. *Revista da Micro e Pequena Empresa, 14*(2), 100–124.

Dionisio, M. (2024). Analysing the transformational role of Black women entrepreneurs in the Brazilian beauty sector. *Social Enterprise Journal, 20*(5), 750–765. https://doi.org/10.1108/SEJ-12-2023-0154

Drori, I., Honig, B., & Wright, M. (2009). Transnational entrepreneurship: An emergent field of study. *Entrepreneurship Theory and Practice, 33*(5), 1001–1022. https://doi.org/10.1111/j.1540-6520.2009.00332.x

El-Hachem Kirby, E. (2015). *Lebanese entrepreneurship: An agency for integration and upward social mobility in São Paulo, Brazil* (Research Paper Series No. 1/2015). Lebanese Emigration Research Center, Notre Dame University–Louaizé. https://www.ndu.edu.lb/lerc/researchpaperseries/Lebanese%20Entrepreneurs-El%20Hachem-LERC-RPS-March%202015.pdf

Eng Menéndez, Y. G. (2021). De los barrios chinos en Latinoamérica y el Caribe. *Rumbos TS, 16*(24), 151–166. https://doi.org/10.51188/rrts.num24.468

Essers, C., & Benschop, Y. (2007). Enterprising identities: Female immigrant entrepreneurs of Moroccan or Turkish origin in the Netherlands. *Organisation Studies, 28*(1), 49–69. https://doi.org/10.1177/0170840606068256

Faist, T. (2000). *The volume and dynamics of international migration and transnational social spaces.* Oxford University Press. https://doi.org/10.1093/acprof:oso/9780198293910.001.0001

Fernández-Kelly, P., & Konczal, L. (2005). "Murdering the alphabet": Identity and entrepreneurship among second-generation Cubans, West Indians, and Central Americans. *Ethnic and Racial Studies, 28*(6), 1153–1181. https://doi.org/10.1080/01419870500224513

Galetti, R. (1995). Migrantes estrangeiros no centro de São Paulo: Coreanos e bolivianos. In *Emigração e imigração internacionais no Brasil contemporâneo* (pp. 133–143). SP FUNAP.

Guarnizo, L. E. (2003). The economics of transnational living. *International Migration Review, 37*(3), 666–699. https://doi.org/10.1111/j.1747-7379.2003.tb00154.x

Inter-American Development Bank. (n.d.). *Support the reform agenda to improve Peruvian trade facilitation services*. https://www.iadb.org/en/project/PE-T1548

Itzigsohn, J. (2000). Immigration and the boundaries of citizenship: The institutions of immigrants' political transnationalism. *International Migration Review, 34*(4), 1126–1154. https://doi.org/10.1177/019791830003400403

Karam, J. T. (2008). *Another arabesque: Syrian-Lebanese ethnicity in neoliberal Brazil.* Temple University Press.

Kloosterman, R. C., & Rath, J. (2001). Immigrant entrepreneurs in advanced economies: Mixed embeddedness further explored. *Journal of Ethnic and Migration Studies, 27*(2), 189–201. https://doi.org/10.1080/13691830020041561

Kloosterman, R. C., Van Der Leun, J., & Rath, J. (1999). Mixed embeddedness:(In) formal economic activities and immigrant businesses in the Netherlands. *International Journal of Urban and Regional Research, 23*(2), 252–266.

Kontic, B. (2001). *Aprendizado e metrópole: A reestruturação produtiva da indústria do vestuário em São Paulo* (Master's thesis, Universidade de São Paulo).

Le Blanc, S. (2016). *Immigrant entrepreneurs in the city: Collaboration, competition, and survival in São Paulo.* University of Delaware.

Lesser, J. (2013). *Immigration, ethnicity, and national identity in Brazil, 1808 to the present.* Cambridge University Press.

Light, I. (2005). The ethnic economy. In N. J. Smelser & R. Swedberg (Eds.), *The Handbook of Economic Sociology* (pp. 650–677). Princeton University Press. https://doi.org/10.1515/9781400835584.650

Lugosi, P., & Allis, T. (2019). Migrant entrepreneurship, value-creation practices, and urban transformation in São Paulo, Brazil. *Revista Brasileira de Pesquisa em Turismo, 13*, 141–163.

Malerba, R. C., & Ferreira, J. J. (2020). Immigrant entrepreneurship and strategy: A systematic literature review. *Journal of Small Business & Entrepreneurship*, Advance online publication. https://doi.org/10.1080/08276331.2020.1804714 https://doi.org/10.1080/08276331.2020.1804714

Martínez Rivera, S. E. (2024). Constructing Chinese spaces in Mexico City: The case of the Viaducto Piedad neighbourhood. *Journal of Current Chinese Affairs, 53*(1), 111–129. https://doi.org/10.1177/18681026241242488

Martínez Rivera, S. E., & Dussel Peters, E. (2016). La diáspora china en México: Asociaciones chinas en el Distrito Federal, Mexicali y Tapachula. *Migración y Desarrollo, 14*(26), 111–143.

Mendoza, C. (2018). Southern Europe skilled migration into Mexico: The impact of the economic crisis. *Regional Studies, 54*(4), 495–504. https://doi.org/10.1080/00343404.2018.1447101

Mendoza, C. (2020). Mexico, a country for immigrant business: Small-scale entrepreneurs and self-employed workers from Southern Europe. *Revue Européenne des Migrations Internationales, 2*(3), 305–327.

Migration Policy Institute. (2020). *Argentina: A new era of migration and migration policy*. https://www.migrationpolicy.org/article/argentina-new-era-migration-and-migration-policy

Montiel, O. (2023). Dark side of Institutional Entrepreneurship in Latin America: Vistas from reflexivity. *Instituto de Ciencias Sociales y Administración.*

Murphy, D. M. (2024). "Quem pode ser a dona?": Afro-Brazilian women entrepreneurs and gendered racism. *Gender, Work & Organisation, 31*(4), 1149–1165. https://doi.org/10.1111/gwao.13090

Nascimento, E. Q. (2018). *Afroempreendedorismo como estratégia de inclusão socioeconômica.* In *Anais do Seminário de Ciências Sociais PGCS-UFES* (Vol. 3). UFES. https://periodicos.ufes.br/scs/article/view/21718.

Nazareno, J., Zhou, M., & You, T. (2019). Global dynamics of immigrant entrepreneurship: Changing trends, ethnonational variations, and reconceptualisations. *International Journal of Entrepreneurial Behaviour & Research, 25*(5), 780–800. https://doi.org/10.1108/IJEBR-03-2018-0141

OECD. (2019). *Latin America and the Caribbean 2019: Policies for competitive SMEs in the Pacific alliance and participating South American countries*. OECD Publishing. https://www.oecd.org/en/publications/2019/04/latin-america-and-the-caribbean-2019_e41bc8eb.html

OECD. (2024). *SME policy index: Latin America and the Caribbean 2024*. Organisation for Economic Co-operation and Development. https://www.oecd.org/en/publications/2024/07/sme-policy-index-latin-america-and-the-caribbean-2024_d0ab1c40.html

Romero, M., & Valdez, Z. (2016). Introduction to the special issue: Intersectionality and entrepreneurship. *Ethnic and Racial Studies, 39*(9), 1553–1565. https://doi.org/10.1080/01419870.2016.1171374

Scherer, L. A., & Grisci, C. L. I. (2022). The migrant and refugee entrepreneur (of the self): Vernacular modes of immaterial labor as (re) invention of the self in the destination country. *BBR. Brazilian Business Review, 19*(2), 189–207. https://doi.org/10.15728/bbr.2021.19.2.5

Start-Up Chile. (n.d.). *What is start-up Chile?* https://startupchile.org/en/

Truzzi, O. (1992). *De mascates a doutores: Sírios e libaneses em São Paulo* (Vol. 2). Idesp Editora Sumaré.

Valdés, R. (2024). A comparative analysis of ethnic networks and internationalisation of Latin American agri-SMEs: The case of Argentina, Brazil, and Chile. *Agriculture, 14*(11), 1918. https://doi.org/10.3390/agriculture14111918

Villalever, X. A., & López-Calvo, I. (2020). *The migration of Chinese women to Mexico City.* Springer International Publishing.

Villalever, X. A., & Rubio, F. (2019). New patterns of Chinese migration to the Americas: Mexico City and Lima. In A. Feldmann, X. Bada, & S. Schütze (Eds.), *New migration patterns in the Americas*. Palgrave Macmillan. https://doi.org/10.1007/978-3-319-89384-6_10

9

IMMIGRANT ENTREPRENEURSHIP IN SUB-SAHARAN AFRICA

Navigating informality, exclusion and transnational opportunity structures

Introduction

Immigrant entrepreneurship is an increasingly visible feature of Sub-Saharan Africa's urban and regional economies, contributing to employment generation, industrial diversification and transnational trade networks. Immigrant entrepreneurs operate across formal and informal domains, often serving as intermediaries between local markets and transnational supply chains. Their activities frequently take place in environments marked by limited institutional support, bureaucratic uncertainty and exclusion from conventional financial systems (Adebayo, 2010; Fatoki, 2014; World Bank, 2019). Despite these constraints, immigrant-owned enterprises demonstrate considerable strategic adaptability, particularly in sectors such as retail, logistics, construction and small-scale manufacturing (Dubinsky, 2022; Fubah & Moos, 2022). In addition to strengthening local market dynamics, they contribute to regional integration through diaspora-led commerce and informal transnational exchange (Fofack, 2018; Nkongolo-Bakenda & Chrysostome, 2013). However, their growing economic presence can also provoke tensions around legitimacy, belonging and market competition, especially in contexts influenced by protectionist policies and xenophobic sentiment (Crush & Tawodzera, 2024; Griffin-EL & Olabisi, 2018). Although policy interest in immigrant entrepreneurship is rising, scholarly analysis remains uneven and often lacks cross-national comparative depth.

Academic studies of immigrant entrepreneurship in Sub-Saharan Africa continue to rely mainly on theoretical frameworks developed in Western European and North American contexts. One of the most influential, the mixed embeddedness framework (MEF), conceptualises entrepreneurship as shaped by both institutional environments and opportunity structures (Kloosterman et al., 1999). While the MEF has been valuable for analysing structured institutional settings, it has rarely been applied in Sub-Saharan African contexts, reflecting a broader underrepresentation of Global South experiences in immigrant entrepreneurship research (Nazareno et al., 2019). Its limited use highlights a theoretical gap: the MEF does not fully capture the fragmented, informal and often unpredictable environments in which many African entrepreneurs operate. Furthermore, although the MEF focuses on structural factors, other scholars have shown the importance of identity, intersectionality and power relations in

DOI: 10.4324/9781003605072-11

shaping entrepreneurial strategies (Anthias, 2013; Essers & Benschop, 2007). These issues are particularly important in Sub-Saharan Africa, where legal status, gender, race and nationality play a major role in determining access to resources and markets. While these factors are discussed in several case-specific studies (Crush, 2022; Tengeh, 2013), they are rarely incorporated into broader theoretical frameworks, limiting their relevance for comparative analysis.

This chapter applies the reconceptualised multidimensional embeddedness framework (RMEF) developed in Chapter 2 to show its analytical value for studying immigrant entrepreneurship in Sub-Saharan African cities. Instead of analysing primary data, the chapter uses secondary case studies to demonstrate how the RMEF helps explain the interaction between structural conditions, individual strategies and social networks. The RMEF focuses on the importance of identity, informal practices and translocal connections in shaping entrepreneurial activities. It offers a way to understand how immigrant entrepreneurs overcome exclusion, mobilise resources and build legitimacy in unstable institutional environments. In many Sub-Saharan African cities, informal systems are central to economic life, and business success depends on entrepreneurs' ability to adapt to policy changes, gain social recognition and maintain access to trust-based networks of finance and knowledge (Crush & Ramachandran, 2014; Fubah & Moos, 2022). Through culturally embedded practices, diasporic ties and adaptive strategies, immigrant entrepreneurs not only maintain their ventures but also influence local market structures (Guzman & Kacperczyk, 2019; Peberdy, 2016). By linking institutional pressures, identity-driven actions and informal networks, the RMEF provides a clearer and more accurate framework for understanding entrepreneurial practices in these settings.

To illustrate these dynamics in different regional and institutional contexts, the chapter draws on secondary case studies from four Sub-Saharan African countries: Nigeria and Ghana in West Africa and South Africa and Zimbabwe in Southern Africa. These countries were selected because of their distinct migration patterns and contrasting institutional environments. In West Africa, Nigeria and Ghana host longstanding immigrant business communities, including Chinese and Lebanese traders, who operate within dense informal markets shaped by rapid urbanisation, inconsistent policies and infrastructure gaps (Akyeampong, 2006; Falola, 1990; Liu, 2022). In Southern Africa, South Africa presents a highly politicised economic setting where immigrant entrepreneurs face administrative exclusion, legal insecurity and repeated xenophobic attacks (Crush, 2022; Fubah & Moos, 2022; Misago & Landau, 2022). Zimbabwe, by contrast, represents a post-crisis economy where the collapse of formal systems has expanded informal entrepreneurship. In this setting, immigrant traders play major roles in transnational supply chains, survivalist markets and informal financial systems (Gukurume, 2020; Mushonga & Makwara, 2023). These documented cases provide a strong foundation for analysing how immigrant entrepreneurs respond to structural challenges, establish legitimacy and adjust their strategies in response to changing political and economic conditions.

The chapter is organised as follows. It begins with an examination of immigrant entrepreneurship in West Africa, focusing on Nigeria and Ghana, followed by Southern Africa, with case studies of South Africa and Zimbabwe. A synthesis section highlights key patterns and regional distinctions across these contexts. This is followed by a section on strategic policy interventions to support immigrant entrepreneurship, before the chapter concludes with a reflection on broader implications and directions for future research.

West Africa

Nigeria's transnational business evolution: the role of immigrant entrepreneurs

Nigeria, Africa's largest economy, has long been a destination for immigrant entrepreneurs whose business activities have contributed to the country's commercial expansion and integration into global trade circuits (Adepoju, 2005; Akinyoade et al., 2017). Over successive waves of migration, immigrant entrepreneurs have shaped diverse sectors including retail, construction, technology and manufacturing, often introducing new goods, services and business models (Mickiewicz & Olarewaju, 2020). Their ventures are embedded within Nigeria's evolving institutional and market environments, linking local commerce to broader regional and transnational economic networks (Meagher, 2010; Raimi & Aslani, 2019). While immigrant entrepreneurship remains a longstanding feature of Nigeria's economic landscape, systematic academic analysis of its sectoral diversity and long-term impacts is still developing. This analysis examines Lebanese and Chinese entrepreneurs, noted for their sustained commercial presence, alongside South Asian female entrepreneurs from India and Pakistan, whose economic activities illuminate the intersection of gender, migration and entrepreneurship.

Market frictions and institutional barriers: challenges facing immigrant entrepreneurs in Nigeria

Nigeria's unstable regulatory environment presents persistent challenges for immigrant entrepreneurs. Frequent policy shifts, ambiguous frameworks and bureaucratic inefficiencies complicate long-term planning, particularly for foreign investors unfamiliar with local governance. Entrepreneurs face sudden changes in customs procedures, inconsistent import duties and delays in securing operational permits (Adegbite & Adesina, 2021; Ovie-D'Leone & Esuga, 2024). These barriers are especially acute for Chinese entrepreneurs reliant on high-volume imports and intricate supply chains (Liu, 2019; Zhou et al., 2023). Lebanese entrepreneurs in real estate and manufacturing contend with overlapping regulations on land, construction and licensing, often inconsistently applied across jurisdictions (Mickiewicz & Olarewaju, 2020). South Asian female entrepreneurs, particularly in retail and food sectors, face gendered barriers including restricted financial access and male-dominated regulatory institutions (Nwajiuba et al., 2016). Without regulatory transparency, many immigrant entrepreneurs resort to informal negotiations with officials, reinforcing a fragmented business environment that hinders consistency and predictability (Gadzala, 2015).

Beyond regulatory hurdles, immigrant entrepreneurs contend with deeply embedded social and political perceptions that influence their legitimacy in Nigerian markets. A common narrative among segments of the local population portrays immigrant entrepreneurs as extractive, occupying economic spaces perceived as belonging to indigenous Nigerians (de Sardan, 2006; Xiao, 2015). This perception is pronounced towards Lebanese business families, who are often viewed as exclusive due to longstanding networks and perceived monopolisation of retail and property sectors (Agbim, 2018; Oladejo, 2021). Chinese entrepreneurs face similar scrutiny, with public complaints focused on aggressive pricing and saturation of local markets with imported goods, leading to regulatory pushback and strained relations with Nigerian traders (Chen, 2021; Xiao, 2018; Zhou et al., 2023). South Asian female entrepreneurs also experience legitimacy challenges, often being sidelined within male-dominated community networks and facing scepticism from local competitors in informal market spaces (Nwajiuba et al., 2016). These social narratives contribute to discriminatory enforcement, reduced access to collaborative networks and a tense business climate that reinforces the marginalisation of immigrant-led enterprises (Aluko & Adetola, 2021; Raimi & Aslani, 2019).

Nigeria's underdeveloped infrastructure and macroeconomic instability present additional challenges for immigrant entrepreneurs. The unreliable electricity grid compels businesses to rely on alternative power sources, increasing operational costs for manufacturers and retailers across all groups (Misztal, 2002; Oladele & Bamkole, 2024). Lebanese and Chinese entrepreneurs, whose businesses often require consistent energy and logistical coordination, are especially affected by these inefficiencies. Transport delays resulting from congested ports and poor road conditions disrupt supply chains for Chinese firms and constrain Lebanese operations that depend on regional distribution (Liu, 2019). South Asian female entrepreneurs, many of whom operate small-scale food and textile enterprises, struggle with inconsistent supply delivery and heightened costs of local transportation, limiting profitability and expansion potential (Nwajiuba et al., 2016). Across all groups, rising inflation and currency depreciation exacerbate these pressures by destabilising pricing structures and undermining financial planning (Dandago & Ango, 2015). These conditions affect not only short-term survival but also long-term investment strategies and entrepreneurial confidence.

Strategic hustle and embedded innovation: adaptive pathways of immigrant entrepreneurs in Nigeria

Despite systemic barriers, immigrant entrepreneurs in Nigeria have developed adaptive strategies to sustain and expand their ventures. Strong business networks serve as a central mechanism of resilience. Lebanese entrepreneurs often rely on intergenerational family enterprises that offer pooled capital, risk mitigation and strategic knowledge transfer (Agbim, 2018; Mambula, 2010; Okafor, 2022). Chinese entrepreneurs utilise cooperative associations and transnational networks to access bulk imports, streamline logistics and maintain supply chain flexibility (Chen, 2021; Xiao, 2018; Zhou et al., 2023). South Asian female entrepreneurs draw support from informal rotating savings schemes and community-based financial networks that facilitate business entry despite exclusion from formal credit markets (Nwajiuba et al., 2016). While these networks increase operational stability, they can also entrench economic insularity. To overcome these limitations, some immigrant entrepreneurs engage in partnerships with Nigerian stakeholders, enhancing legitimacy and creating opportunities for broader market integration (Adebayo, 2010; Olaniyan, 2017).

Community engagement and visibility have emerged as additional strategies to build social legitimacy and reduce local hostility. Lebanese entrepreneurs increasingly fund local infrastructure, education and social programmes to demonstrate civic contribution and reposition themselves as stakeholders in Nigeria's development (Adebayo, 2010; Olaniyan, 2017). Chinese entrepreneurs have pursued membership in local trade associations and participated in community forums to counter narratives of exclusion and improve regulatory compliance (Xiao, 2015; Xiao & Liu, 2021). South Asian female entrepreneurs engage in neighbourhood-level initiatives, including food distribution and informal mentorship, to foster community ties and build reputational capital within competitive informal markets (Nwajiuba et al., 2016). These acts of strategic visibility have yielded mixed results. In some contexts, they have strengthened collaborative ties, while in others they are viewed with suspicion, highlighting the ongoing need for trust-building in contested commercial environments (Aluko & Adetola, 2021; Raimi & Aslani, 2019).

Technology adoption and business diversification also play a crucial role in enabling immigrant entrepreneurs to navigate Nigeria's volatile market conditions. Chinese entrepreneurs employ digital logistics systems to manage inventory and ensure timely delivery, maintaining competitive advantage in high-volume retail (Liu, 2019). Lebanese entrepreneurs, particularly in real estate and retail, use mobile banking and digital accounting platforms to improve transaction efficiency and enhance customer interaction (Agbim, 2018; Mambula, 2010). South Asian female entrepreneurs have increasingly embraced mobile payment systems and social media marketing to promote products, engage customers and reduce dependency on informal cash transactions (Nwajiuba et al., 2016). These digital adaptations not only reduce exposure to infrastructural bottlenecks but also enable immigrant entrepreneurs to operate more flexibly across formal and informal market spaces. Collectively, these strategies illustrate how immigrant entrepreneurs convert structural barriers into opportunities for innovation, resilience and economic agency within Nigeria's evolving commercial landscape.

Ghana's economic dynamics: immigrant entrepreneurs and market transformation

Ghana's relatively stable political environment and consistent economic growth have positioned the country as a regional hub for entrepreneurial activity. In recent decades, immigrant entrepreneurs have played a significant role in Ghana's market transformation, contributing to the expansion of trade, infrastructure development and urban real estate (Akyeampong, 2004; Ayertey et al., 2024). These entrepreneurs operate across both formal and informal sectors, introducing new capital, supply chains and business models that have reshaped competitive dynamics in key industries. Their ventures are embedded within Ghana's evolving regulatory and commercial systems, linking local economic activities with broader regional and transnational networks (Dankwah & Valenta, 2019; Malki, 2013). Although immigrant-led businesses have become important drivers of sectoral diversification and employment generation, systematic academic engagement with the diversity of their entrepreneurial practices remains limited. This analysis examines Lebanese and Chinese entrepreneurs, whose distinct migration histories and economic trajectories offer insights into the ongoing transformation of Ghana's urban and regional economies.

Navigating economic hurdles: barriers facing immigrant entrepreneurs in Ghana

Ghana's investment climate, while broadly favourable to foreign capital, presents institutional challenges that constrain immigrant entrepreneurship. Policy inconsistency, licensing ambiguity and bureaucratic inefficiencies remain persistent obstacles to long-term planning and sustainable business development (Marfo, 2012; Yendaw, 2022). The Ghana Investment Promotion Centre (GIPC) Act restricts non-citizens from participating in certain economic sectors, notably small-scale retail, to protect local enterprises (GIPC, 2013). These restrictions have posed challenges for Chinese entrepreneurs, many of whom operate in informal or semi-formal trade networks and have faced regulatory enforcement, shop closures and negative media scrutiny when perceived to be in violation of sectoral guidelines (Dankwah & Amoah, 2018). Lebanese entrepreneurs, though more institutionally embedded, encounter challenges related to land acquisition and expansion in sectors affected by evolving investment regulations and non-citizen land ownership laws (Dubinsky, 2022; Malki, 2013). These overlapping legal barriers produce significant uncertainty, raise transaction costs and limit immigrant entrepreneurs' ability to secure long-term footholds in Ghana's rapidly transforming economy (Yendaw, 2022).

Social and political dynamics further complicate immigrant entrepreneurs' ability to establish legitimacy and market presence. Lebanese business families, some with a century-long presence in Ghana, are frequently perceived as exclusive and dominant in high-value sectors such as construction, finance and logistics (Akyeampong, 2004; Dubinsky, 2022). Their perceived insulation from broader local business communities has led to narratives of economic monopolisation and exclusion, prompting calls for increased indigenous participation and heightened regulatory scrutiny, particularly during election cycles or policy reforms (Malki, 2013). Chinese entrepreneurs face a different, though equally salient, challenge. Their expanding presence in urban retail markets has drawn criticism from Ghanaian trade associations for allegedly underpricing goods and violating local business norms (Dankwah & Valenta, 2019; Marfaing & Thiel, 2011). Public discourse frequently frames Chinese commercial activity as exploitative and destabilising, reinforcing negative stereotypes that influence regulatory enforcement and shape community relations (Ayertey et al., 2024; Marfaing & Thiel, 2013). These narratives undermine the social embeddedness of immigrant entrepreneurs and hinder collaborative efforts with indigenous businesses and institutions.

Infrastructural limitations and economic volatility present further barriers that immigrant entrepreneurs must navigate. Ghana's inadequate road systems, unreliable electricity supply and port congestion all increase operating costs and disrupt supply chains, particularly for trade-dependent ventures (Marfo, 2012; Yendaw, 2022). Lebanese enterprises, especially those in construction and industrial services, often invest heavily in alternative logistics and energy infrastructure to ensure operational continuity (Malki, 2013). These self-provisioning strategies, while effective, significantly increase fixed costs and reduce profit margins. Chinese entrepreneurs, who typically operate in fast-moving consumer goods sectors, have responded by vertically integrating their supply chains and using private distribution channels to reduce dependency on inefficient public systems (Lam, 2015). These efforts improve inventory control and delivery efficiency but require considerable capital. Additionally, ongoing depreciation of the Ghanaian cedi and inflationary pressures undermine financial stability and complicate pricing strategies for both groups, particularly those with international trade exposure (Ayertey et al., 2024). These structural challenges demand continuous strategic adjustment and reduce the capacity of immigrant businesses to scale sustainably.

Strategic adaptation and market engagement: immigrant entrepreneurial responses in Ghana

In response to these institutional and structural challenges, immigrant entrepreneurs in Ghana have drawn on transnational networks to mobilise resources, reduce risk and maintain competitiveness. Lebanese entrepreneurs frequently leverage diaspora relationships and longstanding family networks across West Africa and the Middle East to access informal credit, pooled capital and business expertise (Akyeampong, 2006; Malki, 2013). These networks offer flexibility in financial planning and reduce reliance on Ghana's formal banking systems, which are often inaccessible or costly for immigrant businesses (Marfo, 2012; Yendaw, 2022). Chinese entrepreneurs similarly benefit from direct supply chain linkages with Chinese manufacturers and exporters, allowing them to import goods at competitive prices and minimise middlemen in procurement (Lam, 2015; Marfaing & Thiel, 2011). These transnational relationships help navigate Ghana's customs procedures and mitigate logistical delays, offering strategic insulation from domestic economic fluctuations. Transnational embeddedness thus provides immigrant entrepreneurs with operational continuity and adaptive capacity in the face of regulatory uncertainty and infrastructural shortcomings.

Efforts to foster legitimacy and reduce social tensions have become a second major pillar of immigrant entrepreneurial adaptation. Lebanese businesses, often perceived as insular, have increasingly invested in local community development initiatives, including education, healthcare and infrastructure projects, to demonstrate commitment to Ghana's long-term development (Akyeampong, 2004; Malki, 2013). These corporate social responsibility efforts have helped reframe public narratives by positioning Lebanese firms as contributors rather than extractive outsiders. Chinese entrepreneurs, while operating within a shorter historical window, have begun to adopt locally grounded strategies by partnering with Ghanaian businesses, increasing local hiring and joining municipal trade associations to meet regulatory requirements and improve their social standing (Ayertey et al., 2024; Dankwah & Amoah, 2018). These efforts have helped to ease tensions and reduce community pushback, particularly in markets where competition with local traders is most intense. Although challenges remain, these forms of engagement reflect a growing awareness that social legitimacy is fundamental to long-term market integration and political resilience.

Technology adoption has also played a transformative role in enabling immigrant entrepreneurs to adapt to Ghana's evolving business landscape. Lebanese-owned firms have integrated mobile payment systems, digital accounting platforms and e-commerce solutions to enhance operational efficiency and broaden market access (Marfo, 2012; Yendaw, 2022). These digital tools allow for greater financial transparency, reduce reliance on cash and improve client interactions in sectors such as real estate and professional services. Chinese entrepreneurs, often working in high-volume retail and supply chains, have leveraged digital logistics software to streamline inventory management, track shipments and reduce transaction friction across borders (Lam, 2015; Marfaing & Thiel, 2013). Both groups have also embraced financial technology (fintech) and mobile money platforms to navigate currency volatility and facilitate faster, more secure payments across national and regional markets (Yendaw, 2022). These technological innovations not only address infrastructural gaps but also enhance entrepreneurial agility, positioning immigrant-owned enterprises as leaders in Ghana's emerging digital economy. Together, these strategies underscore the multidimensional adaptability of immigrant entrepreneurs and their integral role in Ghana's broader economic transformation.

Southern Africa

South Africa's economic paradox: immigrant entrepreneurship between inequality and innovation

South Africa, as a major regional economic powerhouse, has long attracted immigrant entrepreneurs whose ventures have significantly shaped its commercial and service sectors. Active across both formal and informal economies, these entrepreneurs contribute to employment generation, service delivery and innovation, particularly in underserved spaces such as townships, rural settlements and inner-city areas (Fubah & Moos, 2022; Griffin-EL & Olabisi, 2018; Ngota et al., 2019). Their activities are embedded within South Africa's evolving urban and economic structures, linking local market opportunities with broader regional trade and service networks. Although immigrant entrepreneurship has become increasingly visible in the post-apartheid economy, systematic academic engagement with its complexity and sectoral diversity remains limited (Gordon, 2020; Khosa & Kalitanyi, 2015). This analysis examines African immigrant entrepreneurs from Zimbabwe, Nigeria and Somalia, alongside Asian entrepreneurs from China and Pakistan, focusing on their varied economic trajectories and contributions to South Africa's urban transformation.

Institutional maze: structural barriers hindering immigrant entrepreneurs in South Africa

Immigrant entrepreneurs in South Africa navigate a deeply exclusionary institutional-environment shaped by restrictive immigration laws, bureaucratic inconsistencies and limited access to formal economic channels. The Immigration Act 13 of 2002, as amended in 2014, requires immigrant-owned businesses to meet stringent capital and employment quotas, disproportionately disadvantaging African immigrant entrepreneurs from Zimbabwe, Nigeria and Somalia who often lack access to large startup capital or formal banking services (Crush & Tawodzera, 2024; Tengeh, 2013). Without legal documentation, many operate informally and face frequent police harassment, extortion and arbitrary closures that undermine business continuity (Charman & Piper, 2012; Fatoki & Patswawairi, 2012). Chinese and Pakistani entrepreneurs, despite stronger transnational ties and initial capital, face challenges in navigating high import duties, customs delays and shifting trade regulations that constrain profitability (Fatoki, 2014; Fubah & Moos, 2022). Across all groups, exclusion from formal registration denies entrepreneurs access to banking, insurance and business support services, reinforcing structural marginalisation (Peberdy & Rogerson, 2000). These barriers create a segmented economy in which immigrant entrepreneurs are forced to operate within institutional voids, exposing them to systemic vulnerabilities that impede sustainable enterprise development.

While formal institutional hurdles restrict business formation, immigrant entrepreneurs also encounter embedded social and political exclusions. For Somali, Nigerian and Zimbabwean entrepreneurs, hostility from local enforcement agents and municipal authorities compounds their precarious legal status, often resulting in displacement and dispossession (Khosa & Kalitanyi, 2016; Misago & Landau, 2022). Their exclusion from formal tendering systems and urban zoning policies further entrenches spatial and economic marginality. Chinese and Pakistani entrepreneurs, by contrast, face heightened scrutiny from customs officials and local competitors, who accuse them of monopolistic pricing and non-compliance with trade regulations (Fubah & Moos, 2022; Landau, 2018). While some benefit from informal agreements with municipal stakeholders, inconsistent enforcement fosters corruption and erodes trust in institutional systems (Charman & Piper, 2012). Intra-ethnic business networks often provide short-term protections but deepen isolation from the mainstream economy (Khosa & Kalitanyi, 2015). The resulting fragmentation of entrepreneurial ecosystems undermines efforts towards inclusive growth and perpetuates patterns of socio-economic exclusion. These challenges reflect how systemic institutional failures are compounded by social inequalities, creating layered barriers that immigrant entrepreneurs must continuously navigate.

Xenophobia constitutes one of the most severe barriers to immigrant entrepreneurship in South Africa, particularly affecting African immigrants who often operate in highly visible, vulnerable sectors. Somali and Nigerian shopkeepers have endured recurring waves of violence, notably during the 2008, 2015 and 2019 xenophobic riots, which destroyed livelihoods and intensified economic insecurity (Gordon, 2020; Misago & Landau, 2022). Although business clustering and community-led security have emerged as protective mechanisms, these adaptations cannot resolve entrenched social hostilities. Chinese and Pakistani entrepreneurs, while less frequent targets of physical violence, are commonly portrayed as economic threats by local business associations, reinforcing perceptions of unfair competition and foreign economic dominance (Fubah & Moos, 2022; Landau, 2018). These narratives, often amplified through political discourse, justify restrictive policies and discriminatory enforcement practices. Language barriers, cultural disconnects and limited civic participation further prevent meaningful social integration across all groups (Crush & Ramachandran, 2010). The persistent gap between legal exclusion and social hostility reveals how immigrant entrepreneurship is shaped not only by structural barriers but by deep-rooted narratives of belonging, competition and exclusion within South Africa's socio-economic fabric.

Entrepreneurial ingenuity: adaptive strategies of immigrant entrepreneurs in South Africa

In response to layered institutional and social barriers, immigrant entrepreneurs across South Africa have developed adaptive strategies rooted in resilience, collective action and innovation. African immigrant entrepreneurs, especially from Somalia, Nigeria and Zimbabwe, draw heavily on co-ethnic networks for access to startup capital, inventory and market entry (Charman & Piper, 2012; Griffin-EL & Olabisi, 2018). Informal rotating savings schemes and group lending models enable financial inclusion despite exclusion from formal banking (Khosa & Kalitanyi, 2016; Tengeh & Nkem, 2017). Nigerian and Somali entrepreneurs also use WhatsApp-based supply chains and mobile payment systems to bypass transactional friction and reduce vulnerability to theft or informal taxation (Crush & Tawodzera, 2024). Chinese and Pakistani entrepreneurs similarly rely on tightly knit diaspora networks for bulk purchasing and shared warehousing, reducing operating costs and insulating against regulatory disruptions (Fatoki, 2014; Fubah & Moos, 2022). These networks provide both operational support and a cultural buffer, though they may limit broader market integration. Still, such resourcefulness illustrates how immigrant entrepreneurs mobilise identity, trust and technology to respond to persistent exclusions and sustain competitive micro-enterprises in uncertain environments.

Alongside financial cooperation, many immigrant entrepreneurs adapt their businesses to local markets to gain legitimacy and navigate social challenges. Somali and Nigerian entrepreneurs have developed relationships with local leaders and civic organisations to secure protection and promote inclusion, often employing local staff and participating in township-level development initiatives (Khosa & Kalitanyi, 2016; Misago & Landau, 2022). These efforts, while sometimes constrained by mistrust, help counter xenophobic narratives and demonstrate local embeddedness. Chinese and Pakistani entrepreneurs have increasingly pursued formal registration and compliance with trade regulations to project legitimacy and avoid enforcement risks (Landau, 2018; Wood & Cooke, 2023). Some engage in selective partnership with South African businesses to navigate procurement systems and municipal licensing (Khosa & Kalitanyi, 2015). These relational strategies highlight how immigrant entrepreneurs cultivate institutional legibility and social recognition by adapting their business practices to align with evolving regulatory requirements and community expectations. While such adaptations are uneven, they underscore the active role of immigrant entrepreneurs in negotiating their embeddedness, not merely as economic actors but as social participants.

Technology and digital innovation have further enhanced the capacity of immigrant entrepreneurs to adapt in the face of infrastructural and security challenges. Across African and Asian groups, entrepreneurs have integrated mobile money, e-commerce platforms and social media marketing into daily operations, increasing business visibility and improving customer relations (Fatoki, 2014; Fubah & Moos, 2022). Somali and Nigerian traders have used point-of-sale apps and airtime-based credit systems to maintain sales in informal settlements with limited infrastructure (Crush & Tawodzera, 2024; Peberdy & Rogerson, 2000). Pakistani and Chinese retailers have employed inventory management software and web-based ordering systems to streamline supply chains, enhancing efficiency and reducing losses from theft or delays (Landau, 2018; Wood & Cooke, 2023). These technological tools not only facilitate growth but offer a layer of protection in environments marked by violence, exclusion and volatility. The rise of hybrid online-offline business models during and after the COVID-19 pandemic further demonstrates entrepreneurial agility in the face of systemic disruption (Misago & Landau, 2022). These strategies affirm the entrepreneurial ingenuity of immigrant communities and their capacity to innovate under constraint.

Zimbabwe's informal economy and transnational trade: immigrant entrepreneurs as key players

Zimbabwe's informal economy plays a pivotal role in sustaining livelihoods amid persistent economic instability, currency depreciation and high unemployment. Within this environment, immigrant entrepreneurs have become central actors, driving trade, facilitating access to goods and supporting urban and peri-urban markets through diverse business models. Their enterprises operate across informal retail, services and logistics sectors, linking local demand with regional supply networks and contributing to grassroots economic activity (Crush & Skinner, 2015). By integrating Zimbabwe into broader Southern African trade corridors, particularly through connections with South Africa, Mozambique and Zambia, immigrant entrepreneurs reinforce regional commercial flows and strengthen market integration (Nshimbi & Moyo, 2017). Although immigrant businesses are increasingly visible in Zimbabwe's urban economies, systematic academic analysis of their evolving roles remains limited (Crush & Skinner, 2015; Kademaunga, 2017). This analysis examines Chinese and Nigerian immigrant entrepreneurs, whose prominence in urban markets and transnational trade highlights the intersections of migration, informality and regional economic development.

Gated economy: structural and social barriers to immigrant entrepreneurship in Zimbabwe

Immigrant entrepreneurs in Zimbabwe face structural barriers that undermine the stability and expansion of their businesses. High import duties, unpredictable trade policies and customs inefficiencies significantly restrict business operations and profitability (Crush & Skinner, 2015). Chinese entrepreneurs, particularly active in retail and manufacturing, frequently contend with inconsistent border regulations and systemic corruption, which delay shipments and inflate transaction costs (Gukurume, 2020). Similarly, Nigerian entrepreneurs in Zimbabwe's urban markets are affected by opaque licensing processes and exclusion from formal business registration, which prevents access to credit and government support schemes (Hamish & Vupenyu, 2020). As a result, many are forced into the informal economy, exposing them to police harassment and legal precarity (Kademaunga, 2017). These institutional challenges are compounded by limited access to utilities and basic infrastructure, which increase operational risks for immigrant-led businesses. While Zimbabwe's informal sector provides short-term flexibility, it also institutionalises exclusion, locking many immigrant entrepreneurs into a cycle of precarity and limiting their ability to scale or transition into formal entrepreneurship (Crush & Skinner, 2015).

Social exclusion and xenophobic hostility further compound the institutional challenges faced by immigrant entrepreneurs in Zimbabwe. Nigerian entrepreneurs often face suspicion and social hostility in urban commercial spaces, where they are accused of displacing local traders and dominating informal markets (Hamish & Vupenyu, 2020). These tensions are inflamed by persistent narratives portraying immigrant entrepreneurs as economic threats, reinforcing public resentment and occasionally escalating into violence, such as the 2019 xenophobic attacks in Harare (Mushonga & Makwara, 2023). Chinese entrepreneurs, although less directly affected by violence, face cultural alienation and growing friction with local traders who accuse them of flooding markets with low-cost goods and avoiding integration into local commerce networks (Gukurume, 2020; Hodzi, 2019). Both groups are hindered by language barriers and a lack of institutional support for integration, which obstructs opportunities for collaboration and limits their legitimacy in the eyes of host communities. These social dynamics are not only disruptive but also diminish the long-term sustainability of immigrant enterprises, discouraging reinvestment and perpetuating mistrust in cross-cultural business relations (Crush & Skinner, 2015).

Zimbabwe's fragile infrastructure and macroeconomic volatility introduce further operational constraints for immigrant entrepreneurs. Frequent power outages, limited access to reliable transport and erratic telecommunications increase the cost and risk of doing business (Kademaunga, 2017). Chinese entrepreneurs, dependent on global supply chains, struggle to maintain inventory and meet customer expectations when ports and roads are congested, or fuel is scarce (Gukurume, 2020). Nigerian entrepreneurs face similar logistical hurdles in running small retail and service businesses, where delays and inflation compromise pricing strategies and undermine consumer trust (Hamish & Vupenyu, 2020). Zimbabwe's fluctuating exchange rates and hyperinflation complicate profit forecasting, necessitating continuous adjustments in pricing strategies, cost management and financial planning to maintain business viability. During the COVID-19 pandemic, these challenges intensified, particularly for immigrant businesses with limited access to state assistance (Mushonga & Makwara, 2023). In this unstable environment, immigrant entrepreneurs, including Chinese and Nigerian entrepreneurs are disproportionately affected due to their limited integration into formal safety nets, forcing them to rely on self-financing and community support to navigate persistent volatility (Crush & Skinner, 2015).

Resilient innovators: adaptive strategies of immigrant entrepreneurs in Zimbabwe

Despite these barriers, immigrant entrepreneurs in Zimbabwe have developed robust adaptive strategies that enable business survival and innovation. Chinese entrepreneurs utilise transnational networks to maintain strong supply chains and gain access to bulk purchasing options, which improve efficiency and competitiveness (Gukurume, 2020). These networks are bolstered by structured business associations in cities like Harare that provide financing, logistical support and legal guidance (Haifang, 2018). Nigerian entrepreneurs similarly rely on dense co-ethnic networks for operational resilience. These networks facilitate informal lending systems and cooperative resource sharing, especially in densely populated urban neighbourhoods (Hamish & Vupenyu, 2020). Nigerian community associations provide essential capital and mentoring to new entrants, supporting their transition into Zimbabwe's informal economy. Although these strategies promote business continuity, they also reinforce ethnic segmentation, limiting wider integration into formal or mainstream sectors (Mushonga, 2022).

Strategic collaboration and social engagement are also key to immigrant entrepreneurial adaptation. In response to widespread xenophobia, some Nigerian entrepreneurs have invested in local community outreach and neighbourhood security to build social legitimacy and reduce exposure to violence (Hamish & Vupenyu, 2020). These efforts include hiring local employees and participating in community events to foster goodwill. Chinese entrepreneurs have also sought to ease local tensions by initiating joint ventures with Zimbabwean partners and supporting informal community development initiatives, though such partnerships remain limited in scope (Gukurume, 2020). Both groups navigate social exclusion by balancing cultural preservation with strategic integration, though these efforts are often hindered by mistrust and limited institutional support. Nevertheless, immigrant entrepreneurs continue to negotiate their positions through calculated social and economic alliances, reinforcing their presence in local markets while managing risk and protecting their businesses from disruption (Crush & Skinner, 2015).

Digital innovation and technology use further exemplify immigrant entrepreneurs' adaptive ingenuity in Zimbabwe. Chinese entrepreneurs increasingly employ mobile payment systems and digital inventory platforms to navigate infrastructure challenges and broaden their customer base beyond physical stores (Gukurume, 2020). Similarly, Nigerian entrepreneurs leverage platforms like WhatsApp and Facebook to promote products, manage orders and sustain customer engagement, allowing them to operate across formal and informal channels (Hamish & Vupenyu, 2020). These digital strategies were accelerated during the COVID-19 pandemic, which prompted many immigrant businesses to shift towards hybrid models combining in-person and virtual transactions (Mushonga & Makwara, 2023). These technological adaptations mitigate the effects of infrastructural gaps, enhance operational efficiency and increase resilience in a volatile economic context. By harnessing digital tools, immigrant entrepreneurs, including Chinese and Nigerian entrepreneurs demonstrate strategic flexibility, positioning themselves as indispensable actors in Zimbabwe's informal economy and regional trade ecosystem (Crush & Skinner, 2015).

Comparative synthesis: immigrant entrepreneurship in West and Southern Africa

Across West and Southern Africa, immigrant-led enterprises operate within fragmented institutional environments shaped by exclusion, informality and regulatory inconsistency. In cities across both subregions, entrepreneurs contribute to trade, services and regional integration while navigating policy volatility and contested belonging. Despite local variation, structural barriers related to finance, governance and legitimacy consistently shape how ventures are established and sustained. These barriers reflect systemic institutional weaknesses rather than isolated challenges. Table 9.1 presents key dimensions of immigrant entrepreneurship in West and Southern Africa, highlighting shared patterns and contextual distinctions across the two subregions.

TABLE 9.1 Key comparative dimensions of immigrant entrepreneurship in West and Southern Africa

Category	*West Africa*	*Southern Africa*
Immigration policy framework	Fragmented and inconsistent immigration policies; investment regulations often restrict sectoral access for non-citizens.	Restrictive immigration and business regulations limit formal entry; informalisation is widespread due to legal and administrative barriers.
Institutional ecosystem	Institutional support is limited and uneven; engagement with immigrant entrepreneurs varies across localities and sectors.	Weak institutional integration and inconsistent support; immigrant enterprises often operate outside formal development strategies.
Financial access and inclusion	Formal financial systems are largely inaccessible; entrepreneurs depend on informal savings groups, diaspora remittances and rotating credit schemes.	Exclusion from banking and credit systems is widespread; reliance on informal lending, remittances and community-based finance remains essential.
Regulatory environment	Policy shifts, licensing ambiguity and customs inefficiencies hinder formalisation; enforcement is selective and unpredictable.	Regulatory environments marked by xenophobic enforcement, corruption and administrative opacity; pathways to formalisation remain narrow.
Community and social networks	Dense co-ethnic networks facilitate access to capital, labour and information but often remain disconnected from national business ecosystems.	Strong co-ethnic and transnational networks support enterprise operations; however, social exclusion and xenophobia restrict broader integration.
Transnational strategies	Entrepreneurs leverage diaspora ties and regional trade networks to sustain supply chains and mitigate institutional instability.	Transnational trade, digital tools and diaspora relationships enable operational resilience amid infrastructural and institutional breakdowns.
Cultural identity and market positioning	Cultural identity is mobilised to build trust, assert legitimacy and navigate exclusion; however, perceptions of foreignness may constrain market access.	Identity is strategically employed to gain visibility and customer trust, though local hostility complicates efforts to establish brand legitimacy.

Strategic policy interventions for Sub-Saharan Africa

Immigrant entrepreneurship remains under-recognised in Sub-Saharan African policy frameworks, despite its central role in sustaining local markets and transnational trade. Table 9.1 illustrates how legal precarity, fragmented institutions and limited financial access intersect with race, gender, class and migration status to shape unequal entrepreneurial outcomes. In response, entrepreneurs mobilise informal capital, community networks and transnational ties to sustain their businesses and navigate exclusion. These strategies reflect the interaction of agency and constraint at the heart of the MEF (Kloosterman et al., 1999) while also underscoring the role of informality in Sub-Saharan African contexts. As Anthias (2013) and Essers & Benschop (2007) note, identity operates as a relational and strategic resource shaped by structural inequality. The following section outlines five targeted measures grounded in the lived experiences of immigrant entrepreneurs across Sub-Saharan Africa.

Harmonising regulatory access through one-stop registration platforms

Immigrant entrepreneurs across Sub-Saharan Africa face fragmented and exclusionary regulatory regimes that hinder formalisation, deter compliance and constrain long-term planning. In Nigeria, ambiguous investment policies and bureaucratic delays impede market entry, particularly for Chinese and Lebanese entrepreneurs reliant on high-volume imports (Ovie-D'Leone & Esuga, 2024; Zhou et al., 2023). In Ghana, the enforcement of the GIPC Act bars immigrants from participating in small-scale retail, limiting business scalability and market access (Marfo, 2012; Yendaw, 2022). In South Africa, complex licensing systems and restrictive immigration laws exclude African immigrant entrepreneurs from formal procurement and zoning frameworks (Crush & Tawodzera, 2024; Tengeh, 2013). In Zimbabwe, opaque customs procedures and informal border controls further marginalise immigrant traders and entrench informality (Gukurume, 2020).

To address these barriers, governments should establish digital one-stop registration platforms tailored to immigrant entrepreneurs. These platforms should offer mobile-based applications, multilingual support and integrated trade licensing, while linking with local chambers of commerce and aligning with African Continental Free Trade Area (AfCFTA) protocols to facilitate transnational business mobility. In settings such as Zimbabwe and Nigeria, this approach would reduce informal gatekeeping and improve regulatory transparency. Policy success should be measured by a 35% increase in formal business registrations by immigrant entrepreneurs within three years. Embedding inclusive registration infrastructure is essential to enable equitable market participation and institutional legitimacy.

Expanding inclusive finance through diaspora bonds and credit cooperatives

Access to finance remains one of the most persistent challenges for immigrant entrepreneurs in Sub-Saharan Africa. In Ghana and Nigeria, Chinese and Lebanese entrepreneurs depend on informal credit systems due to collateral requirements and the non-recognition of alternative financial histories (Liu, 2019; Malki, 2013). In South Africa, banks often exclude immigrant entrepreneurs, particularly African migrants, due to documentation barriers and systemic bias (Fatoki & Patswawairi, 2012; Griffin-EL & Olabisi, 2018). In Zimbabwe, both Chinese and Nigerian entrepreneurs rely on peer-to-peer lending, which constrains growth and increases exposure to risk (Gukurume, 2020; Hamish & Vupenyu, 2020).

Governments and regional institutions should develop inclusive finance initiatives that incorporate diaspora bonds, mobile banking platforms and immigrant-led credit cooperatives. These programmes must recognise informal savings groups, peer guarantees and rotating credit as valid proxies for creditworthiness. Delivery should be co-designed with fintech firms and immigrant business associations to ensure accessibility and trust. A 30% increase in successful loan disbursements to immigrant entrepreneurs over five years should serve as the primary metric of effectiveness. Redefining financial legitimacy to reflect lived entrepreneurial realities is key to fostering sustainable and investment-ready immigrant enterprises.

Building intercultural market infrastructure through cross-sector mentorship

The absence of structured mentorship opportunities limits immigrant entrepreneurs' ability to grow, diversify and connect with broader economic ecosystems. In South Africa, Somali and Nigerian entrepreneurs often operate in isolation from formal support systems, relying on insular ethnic networks (Khosa & Kalitanyi, 2015; Misago & Landau, 2022). In Ghana and Nigeria, Lebanese and Chinese entrepreneurs face legitimacy gaps and limited engagement with local trade bodies despite their longstanding economic presence (Akyeampong, 2004; Liu, 2022). In Zimbabwe, the informal status of many immigrant-led ventures impedes access to institutional mentorship and further entrenches marginalisation (Hamish & Vupenyu, 2020).

To address this, national and municipal governments should establish cross-sector mentorship hubs in key cities such as Lagos, Johannesburg, Accra and Harare. These hubs should provide multilingual coaching, sector-specific advisory and structured peer exchange platforms that connect immigrant and local entrepreneurs. Designed in collaboration with diaspora business associations and local chambers of commerce, these programmes would help dismantle enclave dynamics while building inclusive business networks. A 25% increase in mentorship participation within three years should be used to assess success. Developing relational infrastructure is vital to fostering entrepreneurial inclusivity and sustained cross-cultural collaboration.

Institutionalising gender-inclusive enterprise support

Across Sub-Saharan Africa, female immigrant entrepreneurs face overlapping barriers shaped by gender, migration status and exclusion from formal economic systems. These challenges are particularly visible in trade, food services and home-based enterprises, where access to credit, legal protections and institutional support is limited. In Nigeria, South Asian female entrepreneurs working in informal markets encounter restricted financial access and systemic marginalisation within male-dominated regulatory environments (Nwajiuba et al., 2016). In South Africa, African female immigrants are disproportionately affected by xenophobic violence and insecure legal status, constraining business operations (Crush & Ramachandran, 2010). In Ghana, women engaged in care-oriented or home-based ventures are often excluded from enterprise programmes due to rigid eligibility criteria (Yendaw, 2022). These dynamics highlight the urgent need for structural reforms that address the intersection of gender, informality and migration.

To advance inclusive entrepreneurship, governments must integrate gender-responsive strategies into national economic and migration policies. Priority actions include micro-franchising models, digital training platforms and accessible childcare support for female entrepreneurs. Programmes should adopt flexible delivery formats and engage immigrant women's associations to ensure cultural relevance. A 30% increase in registered female immigrant-led businesses over five years should serve as a measurable outcome. Recognising gender as a fundamental structural issue is essential to building inclusive entrepreneurial ecosystems across the continent.

Enhancing digital resilience through regional innovation hubs

Digital exclusion remains a major constraint on immigrant entrepreneurs' ability to scale, compete and integrate into regional markets. In Ghana, many immigrant-owned businesses lack access to stable broadband, secure payment systems and logistics software (Lam, 2015). In South Africa, infrastructural disparities in immigrant-dense communities restrict digital uptake (Wood & Cooke, 2023). In Zimbabwe, although mobile payment systems like EcoCash provide some financial access, broader digital literacy and infrastructure gaps persist (Gukurume, 2020).

To close these gaps, governments and private-sector actors should invest in regional innovation hubs located within immigrant business corridors. These hubs should offer subsidised broadband, mobile-first e-commerce platforms and training in fintech, branding and logistics. Programmes must prioritise sectors with high immigrant participation and link businesses to regional supply chains and AfCFTA-aligned trade platforms. A 35% increase in digital business launches or platform integration by immigrant entrepreneurs within three years should be the primary policy metric. Positioning digital inclusion as a core component of national economic strategy will enhance competitiveness and build resilient, future-ready entrepreneurial ecosystems.

Conclusion

This chapter demonstrates that immigrant entrepreneurship is a key driver of economic resilience across Sub-Saharan Africa, despite persistent barriers including financial exclusion, bureaucratic uncertainty and social hostility. Through comparative analysis of Nigeria, Ghana, South Africa and Zimbabwe, it shows how immigrant entrepreneurs mobilise transnational supply chains, informal credit systems and digital innovation to adapt to fragmented institutional environments. By applying the RMEF, the chapter advances a clearer understanding of how structural barriers, identity-driven strategies and informal networks interact to shape entrepreneurial outcomes. The framework proves analytically valuable for capturing the complexity of entrepreneurial practice in contexts where informality and institutional volatility are central, not peripheral, features of economic life. In addition to these theoretical contributions, the chapter offers targeted policy recommendations aimed at strengthening regulatory frameworks, expanding financial inclusion, supporting digital infrastructure and promoting gender-responsive enterprise development. Future research should prioritise empirical testing of the RMEF across diverse Sub-Saharan African contexts. Advancing this research agenda is critical to building more inclusive, contextually grounded and theoretically robust accounts of immigrant entrepreneurship.

References

Adebayo, P. (2010). Transnational networks of the Lebanese-Nigerian diaspora. Middle East Institute. https://www.ndu.edu.lb/lerc/publications/Transnational%20Networks%20of%20the%20Lebanese-Nigerian%20Diaspora.pdf

Adegbite, E., & Adesina, K. (2021). Regulatory complexities and business adaptation strategies in Nigeria. *Journal of African Business, 22*(1), 15–34. https://doi.org/10.1080/15228916.2020.1838834

Adepoju, A. (2005). Patterns of migration in West Africa. In T. Manuh (Ed.), *At home in the world? International migration and development in contemporary Ghana and West Africa* (pp. 24–54). Sub-Saharan Publishers.

Agbim, K. C. (2018). Emotional intelligence and immigrant entrepreneurship development: A correlation analysis of the Lebanese family entrepreneurships in Nigeria. *International Journal of Small and Medium Enterprises, 1*(2), 26–42.

Akinyoade, A., Dietz, T., & Uche, C. U. (2017). *Entrepreneurship in Africa* (Vol. 15). Brill. https://doi.org/10.1163/9789004351615

Akyeampong, E. K. (2004). Memories of place and belonging: Identity, citizenship, and the Lebanese in Ghana. *Ghana Studies, 7*(1), 25–42.

Akyeampong, E. K. (2006). Race, identity and citizenship in Black Africa: The case of the Lebanese in Ghana. *Africa, 76*(3), 297–323. https://doi.org/10.3366/afr.2006.0033

Aluko, O., & Adetola, B. O. (2021). Xenophobia and its impact on immigrant businesses in Lagos, Nigeria. *Journal of African Migration, 12*(2), 56–75.

Anthias, F. (2013). Intersectional what? Social divisions, intersectionality and levels of analysis. *Ethnicities, 13*(1), 3–19. https://doi.org/10.1177/1468796812463547

Ayertey, S., Laryeafio, M. N., Panditharathna, R., & Banor, M. A. (2024). Investigating the macro and micro perspectives on Chinese migrant entrepreneurs in Ghana: A qualitative study. In D. Hyams-Ssekasi & E. Daskalaki (Eds.), *Migration and Entrepreneurship in the Global Context: Case Studies, Processes and Practices* (pp. 149–182). Palgrave Macmillan. https://doi.org/10.1007/978-3-031-34067-3_7

Chen, Y. (2021). 'Africa's China': Chinese manufacturing investment in Nigeria and channels for technology transfer. *Journal of Chinese Economic and Business Studies, 19*(4), 335–358. https://doi.org/10.1080/14765284.2021.1943184

Charman, A., & Piper, L. (2012). Xenophobia, criminality and violent entrepreneurship: Violence against Somali shopkeepers in Delft South, Cape Town, South Africa. *South African Review of Sociology, 43*(3), 81–105. https://doi.org/10.1080/21528586.2012.727550

Crush, J. (2022). Xenophobia denialism and the global compact for migration in South Africa. In K. T. Geiger & I. Segatti (Eds.), *Governing migration for development from the Global South* (pp. 133–158). Brill Nijhoff.

Crush, J., & Ramachandran, S. (2010). Xenophobia, international migration and development. *Journal of Human Development and Capabilities, 11*(2), 209–228. https://doi.org/10.1080/19452821003677327

Crush, J., & Ramachandran, S. (2014). *Xenophobic violence in South Africa: Denialism, minimalism, realism* (SAMP Migration Policy Series No. 66). Southern African Migration Programme. https://samponline.org/wp-content/uploads/2016/10/Acrobat66.pdf

Crush, J., & Skinner, C. (2015). *Informal migrant entrepreneurship and inclusive growth in South Africa, Zimbabwe and Mozambique*. African Books Collective.

Crush, J., & Tawodzera, G. (2024). Informal pandemic precarity and migrant food enterprise in South Africa during COVID-19. *Global Food Security, 43*, 100804. https://doi.org/10.1016/j.gfs.2024.100804

Dandago, K. I., & Ango, Y. U. I. (2015). The impact of ethnicity on entrepreneurship: A global review and lessons for Nigeria. In M. Manimala & K. P. M. Wasdani (Eds.), *Entrepreneurial Ecosystem: Perspectives from Emerging Economies* (pp. 91–107). Springer. https://doi.org/10.1007/978-81-322-2086-2_3

Dankwah, K. O., & Amoah, P. A. (2018). Gauging the dispositions between indigenes, Chinese and other immigrant traders in Ghana: Towards a more inclusive society. *Asian Ethnicity, 20*(1), 67–84. https://doi.org/10.1080/14631369.2018.1490173

Dankwah, K. O., & Valenta, M. (2019). Chinese entrepreneurial migrants in Ghana: Socioeconomic impacts and Ghanaian trader attitudes. *The Journal of Modern African Studies, 57*(1), 1–29. https://doi.org/10.1017/S0022278X18000678

de Sardan, J. P. O. (2006). *Everyday corruption and the state: Citizens and public officials in Africa*. Zed Books.

Dubinsky, I. (2022). Lebanese in Anglophone West Africa. In *Oxford Research Encyclopedia of African History*. Oxford University Press. https://doi.org/10.1093/acrefore/9780190277734.013.987

Essers, C., & Benschop, Y. (2007). Enterprising identities: Female immigrant entrepreneurs of Moroccan or Turkish origin in the Netherlands. *Organisation Studies, 28*(1), 49–69. https://doi.org/10.1177/0170840606068256

Falola, T. (1990). Lebanese traders in Southwestern Nigeria, 1900–1960. *African Affairs, 89*(357), 523–553. https://doi.org/10.1093/oxfordjournals.afraf.a098331

Fatoki, O. (2014). Immigrant entrepreneurship in South Africa: Current literature and research opportunities. *Journal of Social Sciences, 40*(1), 1–7.

Fatoki, O., & Patswawairi, T. (2012). The motivations and obstacles to immigrant entrepreneurship in South Africa. *Journal of Social Sciences, 32*(2), 133–142.

Fofack, H. (2018). *Afreximbank: Economic integration in Africa and the AfCFTA.* International Monetary Fund. https://www.imf.org/en/Publications/fandd/issues/2018/12/afcfta-economic-integration-in-africa-fofack

Fubah, C. N., & Moos, M. N. (2022). Immigrant entrepreneurship in South Africa: A review and research agenda. *The Journal for Transdisciplinary Research in Southern Africa, 18*(1), 1160. https://doi.org/10.4102/td.v18i1.1160

Gadzala, A. W. (2015). *Africa and China: How Africans and their governments are shaping relations with China*. Rowman & Littlefield.

Ghana Investment Promotion Centre. (2013). *Ghana Investment Promotion Centre Act, 2013 (Act 865)*. Government of Ghana. https://www.gipc.gov.gh/wp-content/uploads/2023/04/GHANA-INVESTMENT-PROMOTION-CENTRE-GIPC-ACT-865.pdf

Gordon, S. L. (2020). Xenophobia and the South African State. *African Affairs, 119*(476), 1–22. https://doi.org/10.1093/afraf/adaa005

Griffin-EL, E. W., & Olabisi, J. (2018). Breaking boundaries: Exploring the process of intersective market activity of immigrant entrepreneurship in the context of high economic inequality. *Journal of Management Studies, 55*(3), 457–485. https://doi.org/10.1111/joms.12327

Gukurume, S. (2018). Chinese migrants and the politics of everyday life in Zimbabwe. In O. Hodzi (Ed.), *Chinese in Africa: "Chineseness" and the complexities of identities* (pp. 85–102). Routledge/Taylor & Francis. https://doi.org/10.4324/9780367815714-6

Guzman, J., & Kacperczyk, A. O. (2019). Gender gap in entrepreneurship. *Research Policy, 48*(7), 1666–1680. https://doi.org/10.1016/j.respol.2019.03.012

Haifang, L. (2018). Associations as social capital of 'new Chinese migrants' in Africa: Empirical investigations of Ghana, Zimbabwe, Tanzania, and South Africa. In E. H. O. Asante & M. P. van Dijk (Eds.), *Migration and agency in a globalizing world: Afro-Asian encounters* (pp. 69–90). Palgrave Macmillan.

Hamish, M. R., & Vupenyu, D. (2020). In pursuit of being and belonging: Migrant associations and the integration of Nigerian migrant entrepreneurs in Harare. *African Human Mobility Review, 6*(1), 116–134. https://www.scielo.org.za/scielo.php?pid=S2410-79722020000100006&script=sci_arttext

Hodzi, O. (2019). Chinese in Africa: 'Chineseness' and the complexities of identities. *Asian Ethnicity, 20*(1), 1–7.

Kademaunga, M. (2017). Thriving Chinese migrant entrepreneurship in a deteriorating socio-economic environment in Zimbabwe. In C. Nshimbi & I. Moyo (Eds.), *Migration, transnational trade and development in Africa: Exploring the role of non-state actors in the SADC region* (pp. 99–124). Palgrave Macmillan.

Khosa, R. M., & Kalitanyi, V. (2015). Migration reasons, traits and entrepreneurial motivation of African immigrant entrepreneurs: Towards an entrepreneurial migration progression. *Journal of Enterprising Communities: People and Places in the Global Economy*, *9*(2), 132–155.

Khosa, R. M., & Kalitanyi, V. (2016). Challenges in operating informal businesses: Evidence from African immigrant entrepreneurs in Cape Town, South Africa. *Mediterranean Journal of Social Sciences, 7*(1), 77–85.

Kloosterman, R. C, Van Der Leun, J., & Rath, J. (1999). Mixed embeddedness:(in) formal economic activities and immigrant businesses in the Netherlands. *International Journal of Urban and Regional Research, 23*(2), 252–266. https://doi.org/10.1111/1468-2427.00194

Lam, K. N. (2015). Chinese adaptations: African agency, fragmented community and social capital creation in Ghana. *Journal of Current Chinese Affairs, 44*(1), 9–41. https://doi.org/10.1177/186810261504400102

Landau, L. B. (2018). Xenophobia in South Africa: Why it's time to unsettle narratives about migrants. *The Conversation,* https://theconversation.com/xenophobia-in-south-africa-why-its-time-to-unsettle-narratives-about-migrants

Liu, S. (2019). China town in Lagos: Chinese migration and the Nigerian state since the 1990s. *Journal of Asian and African Studies, 54*(6), 783–799. https://doi.org/10.1177/0021909619845015

Liu, S. (2022). *The history of Chinese presence in Nigeria (1950s–2010s): Factories, commodities, and entrepreneurs*. Taylor & Francis.

Malki, I. X. (2013). Productive Aliens: Economic planning and the Lebanese in Ghana, c. 1930–1972. *Mashriq & Mahjar: Journal of Middle East and North African Migration Studies, 1*(1), 1–25.

Mambula, C. J. (2010). Characteristics of migrant entrepreneurs as agents of direct investment in sub-Saharan Africa: An observation of the Lebanese in Nigeria. *World Journal of Entrepreneurship, Management and Sustainable Development, 6*(3), 190–210. https://doi.org/10.1108/20425961201000019

Marfaing, L., & Thiel, A. (2011). Chinese commodity imports in Ghana and Senegal: Demystifying Chinese business strength in urban West Africa (No. 180). *GIGA Working Papers.*

Marfaing, L., & Thiel, A. (2013). The impact of Chinese business on market entry in Ghana and Senegal. *Africa, 83*(4), 646–669. https://doi.org/10.1353/afr.2013.0050

Marfo, S. O. (2012). *Immigrant businesses in Ghana: A study of the Lebanese in Accra* (Doctoral dissertation, University of Ghana).

Meagher, K. (2010). *Identity economics: Social networks and the informal economy in Nigeria* (Vol. 25). Boydell & Brewer.

Mickiewicz, T., & Olarewaju, T. (2020). New venture evolution of migrants under institutional voids: Lessons from Shonga Farms in Nigeria. *International Small Business Journal, 38*(5), 404–423. https://doi.org/10.1177/0266242619896266

Misago, J. P., & Landau, L. B. (2022). 'Running them out of time:' Xenophobia, violence, and co-authoring spatiotemporal exclusion in South Africa. *Geopolitics, 28*(4), 1611–1631. https://doi.org/10.1080/14650045.2022.2078707

Misztal, B. (2002). *Informality: Social theory and contemporary practice*. Routledge.

Mushonga, R. H. (2022). Performing conviviality in diverse and precarious urban spaces: Everyday experiences of Nigerian migrant entrepreneurs in Downtown, Harare. *Urban Geography, 45*(2), 161–178. https://doi.org/10.1080/02723638.2022.2150424

Mushonga, R. H., & Makwara, F. (2023). 'Locked down but not locked out': Everyday experiences of migrant traders during the COVID-19 pandemic era in Harare, Zimbabwe. *Journal of Asian and African Studies, 58*(5), 1–15. https://doi.org/10.1177/00219096231197770

Nazareno, J., Zhou, M., & You, T. (2019). Global dynamics of immigrant entrepreneurship: Changing trends, ethnonational variations, and reconceptualisations. *International Journal of Entrepreneurial Behaviour & Research, 25*(5), 780–800. https://doi.org/10.1108/IJEBR-03-2018-0141

Ngota, B. L., Rajkaran, S., & Mang'unyi, E. E. (2019). African immigrant entrepreneurs in South Africa: Exploring their economic contributions. *Entrepreneurial Business and Economics Review, 7*(4), 33–55.

Nkongolo-Bakenda, J. M., & Chrysostome, E. V. (2013). Engaging diasporas as international entrepreneurs in developing countries: In search of determinants. *Journal of International Entrepreneurship, 11*(1), 30–64. https://doi.org/10.1007/s10843-012-0098-1

Nshimbi, C., & Moyo, I. (2017). *Migration, transnational trade and development in Africa*. Palgrave Macmillan.

Nwajiuba, C., Harkiolakis, N., Thurman, P., Halkias, D., & Caracatsanis, S. M. (2016). Nigeria: Female immigrant entrepreneurship in Western Africa. In D. Halkias, P. W. Thurman, N. Harkiolakis, & S. M. Caracatsanis (Eds.), *Female Immigrant Entrepreneurs: The economic and social impact of a global phenomenon* (pp. 101–112). Routledge.

Okafor, E. (2022). Family business practices among Lebanese entrepreneurs in Nigeria. *International Journal of Entrepreneurship and Small Business, 47*(1), 99–115. https://doi.org/10.1504/IJESB.2022.124456

Oladejo, M. T. (2021). Ibadan market women and Lebanese traders in Southwest Nigeria, 1900–1960. *African Identities, 21*(3), 603–618. https://doi.org/10.1080/14725843.2021.1954878

Olaniyan, A. (2017). The Lebanese community of Ibadan: A portrait of successful entrepreneurship. In *Mobility between Africa, Asia and Latin America* (pp. 72–88). Bloomsbury Academic. https://doi.org/10.5040/9781350221406.ch-004.

Oladele, S., & Bamkole, P. (2024). *Transitional challenges in Lagos' (Nigeria) entrepreneurial ecosystem: A multi-level analysis*. In *Exploring entrepreneurship: Unpacking the mosaic of entrepreneurship across Africa* (pp. 433–463). Cham: Springer Nature Switzerland.

Ovie-D'Leone, A. I., & Esuga, F. (2024). Chinese diasporic transnationalism and economic sustainability in Nigeria. *Adeleke University Journal of Business and Social Sciences, 4*(1), 66–89.

Peberdy, S. (2016). International migrants in Johannesburg's informal economy. In M. Crush, A. Chikanda, & C. Skinner (Eds.), *Mean streets: Migration, xenophobia and informality in South Africa* (pp. 123–140). Cape Town: Southern African Migration Programme (SAMP).

Peberdy, S., & Rogerson, C. (2000). Transnationalism and non-South African entrepreneurs in South Africa's small, medium and micro-enterprise (SMME) economy. *Canadian Journal of African Studies/Revue canadienne des études africaines, 34*(1), 20–40. https://doi.org/10.1080/00083968.2000.10751189

Raimi, L., & Aslani, B. (2019). Exploring the contributions of informal ethnic entrepreneurship to economic development in Nigeria. In *Informal ethnic entrepreneurship: Future research paradigms for creating innovative business activity* (pp. 179–193). Springer.
Tengeh, R. K. (2013). Advancing the case for the support and promotion of African immigrant-owned businesses in South Africa. *Journal of Sociology and Social Anthropology, 4*(1–2), 1–12.
Tengeh, R. K., & Nkem, L. (2017). Sustaining immigrant entrepreneurship in South Africa: The role of informal financial associations. *Sustainability, 9*(8), 1396. https://doi.org/10.3390/su9081396
Wood, G., & Cooke, F. L. (2023). Transient entrepreneurs?: Chinese migrant small commercial businesses in South Africa. *Journal of International Management, 29*(6), 101094. https://doi.org/10.1016/j.intman.2023.101094
World Bank. (2019). *Leveraging economic migration for development: A briefing for the World Bank Board.* World Bank. https://documents.worldbank.org/en/publication/documents-reports/documentdetail/461021574155945177/leveraging-economic-migration-for-development-a-briefing-for-the-world-bank-board
Xiao, A. H. (2015). In the shadow of the states: The informalities of Chinese petty entrepreneurship in Nigeria. *Journal of Current Chinese Affairs, 44*(1), 75–105. https://doi.org/10.1177/186810261504400104
Xiao, A. H. (2018). Exploring social interactions between Chinese immigrants and corruption in Nigeria. In A. O. Akinola (Ed.), *Africa now!: Emerging issues and alternative perspectives* (pp. 189–210). Palgrave Macmillan.
Xiao, A. H., & Liu, S. (2021). "The Chinese" in Nigeria: Discursive ethnicities and (dis)embedded experiences. *Journal of Contemporary Ethnography, 50*(3), 368–394. https://doi.org/10.1177/0891241620986838
Yendaw, E. (2022). Driving factors and sources of capital for immigrant entrepreneurs in Ghana. *Journal of Global Entrepreneurship Research, 12*(1), 53–69. https://doi.org/10.1007/s40497-022-00321-5
Zhou, W., Raja, R., & Wen, G. (2023). Influence of "Primary Groups" on New Chinese Immigrant Entrepreneurship in Africa. *International Migration Review, 57*(4). https://doi.org/10.1177/01979183231190891

10

CONCLUSION

The future of immigrant entrepreneurship

This concluding chapter synthesises the key findings presented across the regional case studies, drawing together patterns of structural barriers, adaptive strategies and emerging opportunities that characterise immigrant entrepreneurship globally. It reflects on the analytical value of the reconceptualised mixed embeddedness framework (RMEF), demonstrating how entrepreneurial identity (EI) mediates access to resources, legitimacy and opportunity within diverse institutional contexts. The chapter identifies areas of global convergence as well as context-specific divergences, highlighting how legal frameworks, gender dynamics and spatial configurations shape entrepreneurial experiences differently across regions. It also discusses the theoretical and practical implications of these findings, outlines long-term policy directions for supporting immigrant entrepreneurship and issues a call to action for building inclusive entrepreneurial futures. Together, these discussions position immigrant entrepreneurs as central agents of economic transformation and resilience in an increasingly complex global economy.

Key findings on immigrant entrepreneurship across regional and institutional contexts

This section draws on comparative case evidence from secondary sources to highlight cross-cutting patterns and regional variations that have significant theoretical and policy implications. The RMEF provided an analytical lens for understanding EI as a dynamic, relational mechanism for negotiating exclusion and accessing opportunity. To structure the discussion of these findings, three thematic areas are developed: (1) global convergences, (2) context-specific divergences and (3) the negotiating role of identity within embedded institutional environments.

Global convergences

Across all examined regions, immigrant entrepreneurs consistently demonstrate remarkable adaptability in the face of structural adversity. Despite significant variation in national policies, migration histories, economic infrastructures and institutional maturity, a clear pattern emerges.

DOI: 10.4324/9781003605072-12

Immigrant entrepreneurs frequently establish ventures in environments where access to formal systems is restricted, regulatory frameworks are exclusionary and public support mechanisms are limited or absent.

In both developing economies such as Brazil, Mexico, Ghana and Zimbabwe and high-income countries such as the United States (U.S.), Canada, the United Kingdom (UK), Germany and the United Arab Emirates (UAE), immigrant-owned businesses often operate within informal or semi-formal sectors. These ventures contend with persistent constraints, including licensing restrictions, documentation challenges and limited access to formal credit markets. This global pattern confirms that informality is not a temporary or peripheral stage of immigrant entrepreneurship; it is a structural condition embedded in the socio-economic realities of cities across the Global North and Global South (United Nations Conference on Trade and Development [UNCTAD], 2018).

In response to these barriers, immigrant entrepreneurs mobilise co-ethnic networks, transnational connections and community-based knowledge systems. These networks provide more than material resources; they offer legitimacy, mentorship, cultural continuity and support in the face of systemic exclusion. Informal financial mechanisms such as rotating savings clubs, collective remittances and familial lending arrangements are common across diverse settings. Examples include African women's cooperative lending circles in New York (Oloke & Halkias, 2020), Bangladeshi rotating savings and credit associations (ROSCAs) in London (George & Dhaliwal, 2025), Afro-Brazilian savings groups in Rio de Janeiro (de Queiroz Falcão et al., 2020), Chinese lending cooperatives in Mexico City (Martínez Rivera, 2024), Pakistani credit associations in South Africa (Fubah & Moos, 2022) and capital pooling among South Asian entrepreneurs in Dubai (Yasin, 2022). These systems function as practical alternatives to formal banking, particularly for entrepreneurs who lack credit histories, collateral or legal residency. Through these relational strategies, entrepreneurs secure trust, financial resources and labour, maintaining continuity in exclusionary contexts. Informal economies therefore emerge as complex arenas of resource exchange, cultural affirmation and entrepreneurial agency (Barrett et al., 1996).

Digital technologies represent a third pattern of global convergence, expanding market access and operational flexibility for immigrant entrepreneurs while helping them navigate spatial and institutional constraints (Duan et al., 2020). These tools extend EI and network reach into digital spaces, reducing reliance on restrictive formal systems, though their uptake is shaped by exclusions tied to race, gender, migration status and class. In Zimbabwe, Chinese and Nigerian entrepreneurs use mobile platforms and informal credit to manage volatility while facing xenophobia and regulatory risks (Crush & Skinner, 2015; Hamish & Vupenyu, 2020). In South Africa, African immigrant and Asian entrepreneurs rely on mobile technology amid systemic marginalisation (Crush & Tawodzera, 2024; Fubah & Moos, 2022). In Nigeria, Chinese, Lebanese and South Asian women entrepreneurs leverage mobile banking, logistics and social media to overcome infrastructural and gendered barriers (Nwajiuba et al., 2016; Zhou et al., 2023). In Dubai, Chinese and African entrepreneurs adopt digital commerce to navigate opaque regulations and spatial marginalisation, often operating in legally ambiguous contexts (Pelican, 2014; Wang, 2019).

Across these varied contexts, digital entrepreneurship is not merely a technical shift but a strategic practice that reshapes access, asserts legitimacy and redefines belonging in exclusionary urban economies.

Context-specific divergences

While immigrant entrepreneurs across global contexts exhibit adaptability and resilience, the case studies also highlight significant divergences shaped by institutional design, legal frameworks and access to regulation. In cities such as Harare, Lagos and Guadalajara, ventures often operate within informal systems marked by inconsistent or absent state enforcement. Here, entrepreneurs secure permits, credit and commercial space through relational negotiation rather than formal channels, navigating legitimacy through embedded networks (Artasu & Niglio, 2019; Hamish & Vupenyu, 2020; Raimi & Aslani, 2019).

In contrast, cities such as Berlin, Toronto and London enforce highly codified regulations and institutional gatekeeping, restricting market entry, particularly for those with precarious legal status or limited financial history (Schmiz & Räuchle, 2020; Sepulveda et al., 2011; Zhuang, 2021). In Dubai, entrepreneurs contend with discretionary inspections, nationality-based restrictions and sponsorship dependencies, which selectively limit access under a façade of openness (Pelican, 2014; Wang, 2019; Yasin, 2022). These differentiated legal regimes underscore the institutional burdens faced by immigrant entrepreneurs and echo organisation for economic co-operation and development (OECD) (2021) calls for more inclusive regulatory frameworks and support for informal-to-formal transitions.

Public narratives and social perceptions further entrench these institutional divides by shaping who is recognised as a legitimate economic actor. In parts of Africa, such as Ghana and South Africa, immigrants are often portrayed as economic threats, reinforcing xenophobic enforcement and regulatory hostility (Dankwah & Valenta, 2019; Fubah & Moos, 2022). In Israel, African asylum seekers are frequently labelled as infiltrators, leading to exclusionary policies and public antagonism (Barak-Bianco & Raijman, 2015). In contrast, across much of North America, Oceania and Western Europe, immigrant entrepreneurs are publicly celebrated as contributors to economic dynamism, even as structural barriers remain entrenched. In the U.S., for example, immigrants represented 19% of new business owners in 2023 while accounting for just 14% of the population (Tremper, 2024). In Australia and Germany, immigrant contributions are often acknowledged, yet access to finance, markets and institutional legitimacy continues to be constrained (Collins, 2003; Schmiz & Räuchle, 2020). These contrasting public discourses directly affect access to state support, institutional trust and public visibility.

Gender further mediates these divergences, producing unequal entrepreneurial pathways. In Latin America, Africa and the Middle East, immigrant women are disproportionately concentrated in informal sectors, often without institutional support, which limits their scalability and financial inclusion (Dionisio, 2024; Mushonga & Makwara, 2023; Yaseen, 2013). In Israel's Triangle region, Arab women entrepreneurs face compounded barriers related to patriarchal norms, spatial exclusion and limited mobility (Abu-Asbah & Heilbrunn, 2011). These experiences differ from those in cities such as New York, Vancouver and Tel Aviv, where gender-responsive programmes offer structured support through training, mentoring and development initiatives. Nonetheless, disparities persist, shaped by intersections of race, legal status and social capital (Oloke & Halkias, 2020; Said & Vyas, 2025; Teixeira & Salinas, 2024). As noted by UNCTAD (2018), addressing gendered exclusion requires tailored interventions that reflect the specific legal, financial and social barriers facing women in informal and transitional economies.

Finally, transnational networks and spatial configurations further intensify these divergences. In North America and Europe, formal diaspora institutions and remittance systems provide structured platforms for transnational finance and trade (Ram et al., 2008; You & Zhou, 2019). In contrast, Latin American and African entrepreneurs often rely on informal associations and rotating credit systems, which offer adaptability but remain vulnerable to disruption and precarity (Dankwah & Valenta, 2019; Dionisio, 2024). In the Middle East, especially in Dubai and Tel Aviv, legal uncertainty and racialised urban governance constrain formal transnational activity, compelling entrepreneurs to operate through diasporic channels under conditions of limited legal recognition (Pelican, 2014; Said & Vyas, 2025). Spatially, fragmented governance in cities like São Paulo and Johannesburg creates district-level regulatory variation, forcing entrepreneurs to adapt to hyper-local demands (Choi, 2022; Misago & Landau, 2022). In smaller cities such as Accra and Guadalajara, dense commercial zones foster integration through embeddedness but also heighten surveillance and competitive gatekeeping (Artasu & Niglio, 2019; Dankwah & Amoah, 2020). These spatial and transnational dynamics shape how immigrant entrepreneurs perform identity, secure opportunity and negotiate visibility within uneven urban environments.

The negotiating role of identity within embedded institutional environments

By positioning identity as both shaped by and constitutive of embedded institutional environments, the RMEF reframes immigrant entrepreneurship as a process of strategic negotiation within dynamic and uneven structures, rather than passive adaptation. EI functions as a relational and situational construct that mediates access to institutional resources, legitimacy and opportunity (Essers & Benschop, 2007). Within this framework, intersectionality highlights how race, gender, migration status and class intersect to shape differentiated entrepreneurial trajectories (Anthias, 2013). Institutional theory explains how actors engage with the formal and informal rules that structure economic participation (Scott, 2008), while transnationalism reveals how identity is mobilised across borders to navigate constraints and expand access to opportunity (Vertovec, 2004). Together, these perspectives provide a more dynamic understanding of embeddedness, placing identity at the centre of how immigrant entrepreneurs negotiate structures, build legitimacy and pursue agency within uneven institutional contexts.

Entrepreneurs respond to exclusion and regulatory complexity by managing how they present themselves and engage with institutions. In London and Dubai, markets are segmented by race, legal status and migration histories. In London, African entrepreneurs use cultural familiarity and community networks to address systemic barriers and adapt to a fragmented policy landscape shaped by post-Brexit uncertainty (Ojo, 2021). In Dubai, entrepreneurs from Chinese, South Asian and African backgrounds rely on diasporic ties and adopt outward-facing identities that fit state narratives, while using informal networks to navigate behind-the-scenes bureaucracy (Pelican, 2014; Wang, 2019; Yasin, 2022). These examples show that institutional access is not evenly distributed and that entrepreneurs often rely on informal mechanisms and strategic self-presentation to maintain business operations (Bruni et al., 2004; Essers & Benschop, 2007).

Access to finance, markets and legitimacy also varies according to how different identity markers intersect. In São Paulo, Afro-Brazilian women rely on mutual lending circles and informal partnerships because formal systems exclude them from credit and training opportunities (Dionisio, 2024). In Ghana, Chinese entrepreneurs reduce exposure to inconsistent enforcement by working through cooperative organisations and regional supply chains (Dankwah & Amoah, 2020; Lam, 2015). In West Africa, Lebanese family firms use intergenerational wealth, kin-based networks and diaspora legitimacy to maintain transnational business continuity (Agbim, 2018; Malki, 2013). These cases show that institutional barriers are experienced differently depending on an entrepreneur's position within social hierarchies.

The framework also highlights how embeddedness is affected by geography and time. Entrepreneurs operate in multiple markets and must respond to changing economic conditions, legal shifts and political instability. In Mexico City, Chinese entrepreneurs use regional distribution networks to keep businesses running despite policy unpredictability (Martínez Rivera, 2024). In Ghana, Lebanese businesses draw on long-established diaspora institutions to secure financing and regulatory legitimacy (Malki, 2013). During the COVID-19 pandemic, immigrant entrepreneurs in Brazil, Zimbabwe and Canada moved their operations online, using digital tools to adapt to market closures, supply chain disruptions and shifting consumer behaviour (Dionisio, 2024; Mushonga & Makwara, 2023; Zhuang, 2021). These cases demonstrate that embeddedness is not static but constantly reconstituted through a dynamic interplay between institutional structures, social relationships and external disruptions.

Theoretical and practical implications

This book advances the study of immigrant entrepreneurship by building on recent theoretical developments that position identity not as a static trait but as a relational and strategic resource. The RMEF moves beyond foundational frameworks such as the mixed embeddedness framework (MEF) (Kloosterman et al., 1999), institutional theory (Scott, 2008) and theories of capital (Bourdieu, 1986), which tend to emphasise structure and resources over identity dynamics. By integrating EI into the core of analysis, this approach shows how immigrant entrepreneurs navigate barriers, build legitimacy and engage with institutional and market contexts in differentiated ways. This contributes to a more nuanced understanding of how identity work intersects with access to opportunity, aligning with research that views identity as performative, situated and embedded in power relations (Bruni et al., 2004; Essers & Benschop, 2007). The framework therefore offers both a theoretical advancement and a practical tool for analysing entrepreneurial agency within complex socio-institutional environments.

The framework also refines the concept of capital by showing that economic, social and cultural resources do not operate independently of identity. The ability to convert resources into business outcomes depends on how EI is recognised, interpreted and validated within specific institutional contexts. For example, Afro-Brazilian women in São Paulo, Chinese entrepreneurs in Mexico City and Cameroonian women in Dubai gain financing and customer trust not solely through formal qualifications or collateral but by drawing on shared cultural practices and aligning with informal norms (Dionisio, 2024; Martínez Rivera, 2024; Pelican, 2014). These examples illustrate that capital is shaped by social hierarchies and that access to resources is often negotiated through interpersonal relationships and community-based recognition. This supports critiques by Collins (1998) and recent OECD (2021) work on unequal access to opportunity.

This approach also contributes to institutional theory by highlighting how entrepreneurs are not passive recipients of formal rules. Instead, they negotiate and respond to institutional conditions through identity-based strategies. In Dubai, African and South Asian entrepreneurs build credibility by branding their ventures in line with state discourses on innovation and diversity while relying on informal partnerships to navigate opaque regulatory systems (Malit & Oliver, 2013; Yasin, 2022). In Berlin, Syrian women access funding and public visibility through engagement with solidarity-based networks that emphasise resilience and cultural familiarity (Hartmann & Schilling, 2019). These cases show that institutional structures are experienced differently depending on how identity is situated within local systems of recognition and exclusion.

The framework also accounts for how entrepreneurial practice is shaped by both long-term social positions and immediate changes in context. Identity-based constraints do not operate in isolation from other variables such as gender, religion, class or generational status. Lebanese family businesses in Ghana benefit from elite status and established networks that allow them to operate with relative institutional security (Malki, 2013). In contrast, Syrian women in Rio de Janeiro combine cultural production with social enterprise to gain visibility and local support in more marginalised contexts (de Queiroz Falcão et al., 2020). Entrepreneurs also modify their strategies in response to sudden disruptions. During the COVID-19 pandemic, business owners in Brazil, Zimbabwe and Canada adopted digital tools to maintain operations, adapting their business models to meet both economic constraints and shifting social expectations (Dionisio, 2024; Gukurume, 2020; Machado et al., 2021). These examples reinforce the idea that entrepreneurial embeddedness is shaped by evolving conditions and that identity plays a continuous role in mediating access to opportunity.

These findings have several practical implications. For entrepreneurs, recognising identity as a strategic asset can support differentiation, trust-building and market engagement. In Toronto and Accra, entrepreneurs have developed branding strategies that combine cultural references with professional standards to attract diverse clients and gain institutional legitimacy (Ayertey et al., 2024; Zhuang, 2021). For incubators and civil society organisations, the framework suggests that entrepreneurship support should account for intersecting identities rather than treating ethnicity or nationality as stand-alone categories. Programmes that provide culturally responsive mentoring, gender-aware finance and community-based training, as demonstrated in Vancouver, should be extended and embedded in broader policy frameworks (Teixeira & Salinas, 2024).

The framework also offers important implications for policy design. Rather than relying on broad deregulation or generic access initiatives, policy must address the structural conditions that shape entrepreneurial inclusion. Identity should not be seen as a constraint but as a factor that influences how entrepreneurs engage with markets, institutions and regulatory systems. Recognising these dynamics is essential for building support systems that reflect the diverse realities of immigrant entrepreneurs. The RMEF provides a basis for developing targeted, evidence-informed policy strategies, which are outlined in the following section.

Long-term policy directions

Equitable and sustainable immigrant entrepreneurship requires policy approaches that move beyond short-term initiatives and address the structural conditions that shape entrepreneurial opportunity. This includes institutional, legal, financial and informational factors that continue to constrain the development and scalability of migrant-led ventures. The following four areas outline key priorities for long-term policy reform aimed at enabling immigrant entrepreneurs to contribute meaningfully to inclusive economic growth.

Institutional support for immigrant ventures

Many entrepreneurship support programmes are built around assumptions that do not reflect the conditions under which immigrant entrepreneurs operate. These programmes often target formally educated, native-born entrepreneurs who possess legal documentation and have established credit histories. As a result, immigrant entrepreneurs who start businesses in informal or necessity-driven contexts frequently lack access to relevant support.

Public institutions should revise these systems to reflect the realities of migrant entrepreneurship. This includes providing multilingual advisory services, training staff in intercultural communication and creating accessible entry points to business information, mentorship and regulatory assistance. Governments and international agencies should fund intermediary organisations that maintain close relationships with migrant communities. These organisations can act as trusted links between immigrant entrepreneurs and formal systems. Public-private partnerships should also include immigrant-led associations as active participants in the design and delivery of entrepreneurship initiatives. These measures would move immigrant entrepreneurship from the margins of support systems to a recognised position within national economic development strategies.

Reforming access to capital

Financial exclusion remains a major obstacle for many immigrant entrepreneurs. Standard lending models based on employment history, asset ownership or domestic credit scores systematically exclude individuals without formal documentation or prior integration into host-country systems. This limits their ability to grow or stabilise their businesses.

Financial reform should focus on expanding alternative evaluation methods that recognise the creditworthiness of entrepreneurs operating in informal or transitional settings. Governments can support the adoption of community-based credit scoring, peer guarantees and trust-based lending models. Development banks and financial regulators can lower institutional risk by offering partial loan guarantees, matching grant schemes and diaspora-linked financing instruments. Commercial banks and microfinance providers can be encouraged to adopt these tools without sacrificing financial stability. At the same time, digital financial platforms, including mobile banking and identity verification technologies, can increase access for those who are unbanked or undocumented. Financial inclusion should be integrated into national economic planning, not treated as a secondary concern.

Aligning legal status with entrepreneurship policy

In most countries, immigration policy is primarily oriented towards employment and family reunification. Entrepreneurship is rarely considered a core pathway within migration frameworks. This creates a policy gap in which entrepreneurs with uncertain legal status face exclusion from business registration, licensing and state support.

Legal frameworks should be updated to formally recognise entrepreneurship as a legitimate route to economic integration. This includes expanding visa categories for business creation, providing legal regularisation options for undocumented entrepreneurs with demonstrated economic activity and eliminating residency-based restrictions that block access to institutional resources. At the regional level, transnational agreements should permit mobility for migrant entrepreneurs, particularly within blocs such as the European Union (EU), Economic Community of West African States (ECOWAS), Southern African Development Community (SADC) or Association of Southeast Asian Nations (ASEAN). Legal certainty is essential for investment, formalisation and long-term strategic planning. Recognising the role of entrepreneurship in legal pathways is critical to sustainable economic participation.

Improving data and representation in policymaking

Many immigrant entrepreneurs operate outside formal registries and national datasets, making their contributions difficult to measure and support. This invisibility reduces the effectiveness of policy and reinforces misleading narratives about economic dependency. At the same time, migrant entrepreneurs are often excluded from the decision-making bodies that shape economic development.

National statistical agencies and international organisations should develop data collection systems that capture the diversity of immigrant entrepreneurship. These systems should disaggregate data by legal status, business type, gender, sector and transnational activity. Such information is essential for targeted programme design and resource allocation. In parallel, immigrant business owners and associations should be directly involved in policy advisory boards, entrepreneurship councils and economic development initiatives. Representation strengthens institutional accountability and ensures that policy reflects the needs and realities of migrant communities.

By addressing institutional support, capital access, legal status and knowledge systems, policymakers can replace fragmented efforts with coordinated frameworks that support the long-term viability of immigrant entrepreneurship. These businesses should not be viewed as peripheral to national economies, but as integral to their resilience, innovation and inclusive growth.

A call to action: building inclusive entrepreneurial futures

The future of entrepreneurship depends on whether inclusion is treated as a foundational principle rather than an optional goal. Immigrant entrepreneurs are reshaping economic landscapes across global cities and peripheral regions. They generate employment, diversify markets and sustain communities, yet their contributions are often constrained by institutional systems that do not fully reflect their lived realities. These entrepreneurs are not merely adapting to exclusion; they are creating opportunity under conditions of systemic barrier. Ensuring meaningful inclusion requires more than recognising their persistence. It demands systemic changes that position migrant-led entrepreneurship as a core component of national and regional economic strategies.

Achieving this vision requires renewed engagement across research, practice and policy. Researchers must move beyond static conceptions of entrepreneurial integration to interrogate the dynamic institutional and social conditions that shape opportunity structures. Greater attention is needed to regions where vibrant entrepreneurial activity remains under-documented and where informal, translocal and digital strategies redefine economic participation. Practitioners, including incubators, educators and non-governmental organisations, must design support systems that build on cultural knowledge, community networks and relational strategies rather than imposing assimilationist models. Entrepreneurial education must equip migrants not simply to navigate exclusion but to participate in reshaping economic systems themselves. These efforts must prioritise regulatory literacy, digital inclusion, intercultural communication and community-driven finance as foundational to inclusive practice.

Policy responses must also evolve beyond the extension of existing frameworks. Inclusive entrepreneurship requires coordination across migration governance, financial regulation and economic development planning. Immigrant entrepreneurs must be recognised not as marginal beneficiaries but as active agents who reconfigure the institutional environments in which they operate. Building flexible, adaptive systems that reflect the realities already being constructed through migrant entrepreneurship is essential. Supporting entrepreneurial futures cannot rely on integrating migrants into pre-existing structures; it requires designing systems that respond to and are transformed by migrant agency and innovation.

The case studies presented in this book illustrate how immigrant entrepreneurs develop embedded, relational strategies to address exclusion and build new forms of opportunity. Drawing from these patterns, models such as social entrepreneurship and cross-sector collaboration offer particularly promising avenues for fostering broader inclusion and systemic transformation. While such models were not always explicitly articulated in the case studies, the underlying dynamics of community-based innovation, resilience building and informal partnership provide strong foundations upon which these approaches can be further developed. Immigrant entrepreneurs demonstrate that inclusion can be achieved not merely through market participation but through ventures that actively challenge and reshape exclusionary structures. Future collaborations that combine immigrant entrepreneurs' transnational reach with local institutional linkages may further amplify their contributions to economic and social systems.

Ultimately, building inclusive entrepreneurial futures demands recognising immigrant entrepreneurs as transformative agents within dynamic, relational and evolving structures. Their practices, rooted in adaptation, innovation and collective agency, point towards more equitable, resilient and adaptive economies. Supporting these trajectories is not simply an economic imperative; it is essential for realising futures in which entrepreneurship becomes a vehicle for social inclusion, institutional transformation and collective resilience.

References

Abu-Asbah, K., & Heilbrunn, S. (2011). Patterns of entrepreneurship of Arab women in Israel. *Journal of Enterprising Communities: People and Places in the Global Economy, 5*(3), 184–198. https://doi.org/10.1108/17506201111156661

Agbim, K. C. (2018). Emotional intelligence and immigrant entrepreneurship development: A correlation analysis of the Lebanese family entrepreneurships in Nigeria. *International Journal of Small and Medium Enterprises, 1*(2), 26–42.

Anthias, F. (2013). Intersectional what? Social divisions, intersectionality and levels of analysis. *Ethnicities, 13*(1), 3–19. https://doi.org/10.1177/1468796812463547

Artasu, M. C., & Niglio, O. (2019). *Italianos en México: Arquitectos, ingenieros, artistas entre los siglos XIX y XX.* Aracne Editrice.

Ayertey, S., Laryeafio, M. N., Panditharathna, R., & Banor, M. A. (2024). Investigating the macro and micro perspectives on Chinese migrant entrepreneurs in Ghana: A qualitative study. In *Migration and Entrepreneurship in the Global Context: Case Studies, Processes and Practices* (pp. 149–182). Springer International Publishing. https://doi.org/10.1007/978-3-031-53688-5_8

Barak-Bianco, A., & Raijman, R. (2015). Asylum seeker entrepreneurs in Israel. *Economic Sociology: The European Electronic Newsletter, 16*(2), 4–13. https://hdl.handle.net/10419/156049

Barrett, G., Jones, T., & McEvoy, D. (1996). Ethnic minority business: Theoretical discourse in Britain and North America. *Urban Studies, 33*(4–5), 783–809. https://doi.org/10.1080/00420989650011825

Bourdieu, P. (1986). The forms of capital. In J. G. Richardson (Ed.), *Handbook of theory and research for the sociology of education* (pp. 241–258). Greenwood Press.

Bruni, A., Gherardi, S., & Poggio, B. (2004). Doing gender, doing entrepreneurship: An ethnographic account of intertwined practices. *Gender, Work & Organisation, 11*(4), 406–429. https://doi.org/10.1111/j.1468-0432.2004.00240.x

Choi, W. (2022). Ethnic resources reviving: The case of the Korean ethnic economy in Bom Retiro, São Paulo. *Korea Journal, 62*(4), 78–102. https://doi.org/10.25024/kj.2022.62.4.78

Collins, J. (2003). Cultural diversity and entrepreneurship: Policy responses to immigrant entrepreneurs in Australia. *Entrepreneurship & Regional Development, 15*(2), 137–149. https://doi.org/10.1080/0898562032000075168

Collins, P. H. (1998). It's all in the family: Intersections of gender, race, and nation. *Hypatia, 13*(3), 62–82. https://doi.org/10.1111/j.1527-2001.1998.tb01370.x

Crush, J., & Skinner, C. (2015). *Informal migrant entrepreneurship and inclusive growth in South Africa, Zimbabwe and Mozambique*. African Books Collective.

Crush, J., & Tawodzera, G. (2024). Informal pandemic precarity and migrant food enterprise in South Africa during COVID-19. *Global Food Security, 43*, 100804. https://doi.org/10.1016/j.gfs.2024.100804

Dankwah, K. O., & Valenta, M. (2019). Chinese entrepreneurial migrants in Ghana: Socioeconomic impacts and Ghanaian trader attitudes. *The Journal of Modern African Studies, 57*(1), 1–29. https://doi.org/10.1017/S0022278X18000678

de Queiroz Falcão, R. P., Cruz, E. P., Piccoli, D. A. C., & Mancebo, R. C. (2020). Self-employment of Syrian refugees: Unveiling social networks and human capital of food stall owners in Rio de Janeiro. *Revista da Micro e Pequena Empresa, 14*(2), 100–124.

Dionisio, M. (2024). Analysing the transformational role of Black women entrepreneurs in the Brazilian beauty sector. *Social Enterprise Journal, 20*(5), 750–765. https://doi.org/10.1108/SEJ-12-2023-0154

Duan, C., Kotey, B., & Sandhu, K. (2020). *Digital entrepreneurship for immigrants: Motivations, strategies, ecosystems, and performance*. In L. M. Camarinha-Matos, M. Boucher, & H. Afsarmanesh (Eds.), *Leadership, management, and adoption techniques for digital service innovation* (pp. 164–187). IGI Global. https://doi.org/10.4018/978-1-7998-2799-3.ch009

Essers, C., & Benschop, Y. (2007). Enterprising identities: Female immigrant entrepreneurs of Moroccan or Turkish origin in the Netherlands. *Organisation Studies, 28*(1), 49–69. https://doi.org/10.1177/0170840606068256

Fubah, C. N., & Moos, M. N. (2022). Immigrant entrepreneurship in South Africa: A review and research agenda. *The Journal for Transdisciplinary Research in Southern Africa, 18*(1), 1160. https://hdl.handle.net/10520/ejc-transd_v18_i1_a1160

George, R., & Dhaliwal, S. (2025). *Navigating uncertainty: Challenges faced by Bangladeshi female entrepreneurs in East London, UK. The Journal of Entrepreneurship, 33*(4), 839–861. https://doi.org/10.1177/09713557241309481

Gukurume, S. (2020). Chinese migrants and the politics of everyday life in Zimbabwe. In *Chinese in Africa* (pp. 85–102). Routledge.

Hamish, M. R., & Vupenyu, D. (2020). In pursuit of being and belonging: Migrant associations and the integration of Nigerian migrant entrepreneurs in Harare. *African Human Mobility Review, 6*(1), 116–134. https://www.scielo.org.za/scielo.php?pid=S2410-79722020000100006&script=sci_arttext

Hartmann, C., & Schilling, K. (2019). Cham Saar: The first Syrian-German cheese manufacturer. In S. Heilbrunn, J. Freiling, & A. Harima (Eds.), *Refugee entrepreneurship* (pp. 51–70). Palgrave Macmillan. https://doi.org/10.1007/978-3-319-92534-9_3

Kloosterman, R. C, Van Der Leun, J., & Rath, J. (1999). Mixed embeddedness:(In) formal economic activities and immigrant businesses in the Netherlands. *International Journal of Urban and Regional Research, 23*(2), 252–266. https://doi.org/10.1111/1468-2427.00194

Lam, K. N. (2015). Chinese adaptations: African agency, fragmented community and social capital creation in Ghana. *Journal of Current Chinese Affairs, 44*(1), 9–41. https://doi.org/10.1177/186810261504400102

Machado, M. M., Falcão, R. P. Q., Cruz, E. P., & Hossein, C. S. (2021). The Canadian experience from the perspective of Brazilian entrepreneurship in Toronto. *Iberoamerican Journal of Entrepreneurship and Small Business, 10*(3), Article e1963. https://doi.org/10.14211/regepe.e1963

Malit, F. T., & Oliver, T. (2013). *Labor migration and deskilling in the United Arab Emirates: Impacts on Cameroonian labour migrants*. Cornell University, ILR School. https://ecommons.cornell.edu/items/29cf5521-41f4-4e06-a639-f9c2042340ec

Malki, I. X. (2013). Productive Aliens: Economic planning and the Lebanese in Ghana, c. 1930–1972. *Mashriq & Mahjar: Journal of Middle East and North African Migration Studies, 1*(1), 1–25.

Martínez Rivera, S. (2024). Constructing Chinese spaces in Mexico City: The case of the Viaducto Piedad neighbourhood. *Journal of Current Chinese Affairs, 53*(1), 111–129. https://doi.org/10.1177/18681026241242488
Misago, J. P., & Landau, L. B. (2022). 'Running them out of time:' Xenophobia, violence, and co-authoring spatiotemporal exclusion in South Africa. *Geopolitics, 28*(4), 1611–1631. https://doi.org/10.1080/14650045.2022.2078707
Mushonga, R. H., & Makwara, F. (2023). 'Locked down but not locked out': Everyday experiences of migrant traders during the COVID-19 pandemic era in Harare, Zimbabwe. *Journal of Asian and African Studies, 58*(5), 1–15. https://doi.org/10.1177/00219096231197770
Nwajiuba, C., Harkiolakis, N., Thurman, P., Halkias, D., & Caracatsanis, S. M. (2016). Nigeria: Female immigrant entrepreneurship in Western Africa. In D. Halkias, P. W. Thurman, N. Harkiolakis, & S. M. Caracatsanis (Eds.), *Female Immigrant Entrepreneurs: The economic and social impact of a global phenomenon* (pp. 101–118). Routledge.
OECD. (2021). *Entrepreneurship policies through a gender lens (OECD Studies on SMEs and Entrepreneurship)*. OECD Publishing. https://doi.org/10.1787/71c8f9c9-en
Ojo, S. (2021). Black African perceptions of entrepreneurial outcomes in the UK. *Society and Business Review, 16*(2), 278–305. https://doi.org/10.1108/SBR-06-2020-0087
Oloke, T., & Halkias, D. (2020). Nigerian female immigrant entrepreneurs within the service industry in New York City, USA: An integrative literature review. *SSRN*. https://doi.org/10.2139/ssrn.3529631
Pelican, M. (2014). Urban lifeworlds of Cameroonian migrants in Dubai. *Urban Anthropology and Studies of Cultural Systems and World Economic Development, 43*(1/2/3), 255–309. https://www.jstor.org/stable/24643112
Raimi, L., & Aslani, B. (2019). Exploring the contributions of informal ethnic entrepreneurship to economic development in Nigeria. In In V. Ramadani, L.-P. Dana, V. Ratten, & A. Bexheti (Eds.), *Informal Ethnic Entrepreneurship: Future Research Paradigms for Creating Innovative Business Activity* (pp. 179–193). Springer. https://doi.org/10.1007/978-3-319-99064-4_12
Ram, M., Theodorakopoulos, N., & Jones, T. (2008). Forms of capital, mixed embeddedness and Somali enterprise. *Work, Employment and Society, 22*(3), 427–446. https://doi.org/10.1177/0950017008093479
Said, I. S., & Vyas, V. (2025). Intersectionality of place and race: Entrepreneurial performance of Arab citizens of Israel. *International Journal of Entrepreneurial Behaviour & Research, 31*(1), 53–79. https://doi.org/10.1108/IJEBR-07-2022-0615
Schmiz, A., & Räuchle, C. (2020). Migrantische Ökonomie als Teil der lokalen Ökonomie. In S. Henn, M. Behling, & S. Schäfer (Eds.), *Lokale Ökonomie – Konzepte, Quartierskontexte und Interventionen* (pp. 1–17). Springer. https://doi.org/10.1007/978-3-662-57780-6_5
Scott, W. R. (2008). *Institutions and organisations: Ideas and interests* (3rd ed.). Sage Publications.
Sepulveda, R. L., Syrett, S., & Lyon, F. (2011). Population superdiversity and new migrant enterprise: The case of London. *Entrepreneurship & Regional Development, 23*(7–8), 469–497. https://doi.org/10.1080/08985620903420211
Teixeira, C., & Salinas, A. L. (2024). Mexican entrepreneurs in the Greater Vancouver Area (GVA), Canada. In *Immigrant Entrepreneurship: Challenges and Opportunities* (pp. 289–322). Springer Nature Switzerland.
Tremper, N. (2024). *Immigrants started nearly 1 in 5 new businesses in 2023.* Gusto. https://gusto.com/company-news/2024-immigrant-entrepreneur-report
UNCTAD. (2018). *Harnessing the potential of migrant entrepreneurship* (UNCTAD/DIAE/2018/2). United Nations Conference on Trade and Development. https://unctad.org/system/files/official-document/diae2018d2_en.pdf
Vertovec, S. (2004). Migrant transnationalism and modes of transformation. *International Migration Review, 38*(3), 970–1001. https://doi.org/10.1111/j.1747-7379.2004.tb00226.x
Wang, Y. (2019). Making Chinese spaces in Dubai: A spatial consideration of Chinese transnational communities in the Arab Gulf states. *Journal of Arabian Studies, 9*(2), 269–287. https://doi.org/10.1080/21534764.2019.1762313

Yaseen, Z. K. (2013). Women entrepreneurs: Challenges and opportunities in the Arab world, UAE case. *Business & Entrepreneurship Journal, 2*(1), 43–48. https://www.scienpress.com/Upload/BEJ/Vol%20 2_1_4.pdf

Yasin, N. (2022). Cold grass or hot sands? A comparative study of immigrant Punjabi–Pakistani entrepreneurs in London and Dubai. *Strategic Change, 31*(4), 387–396. https://doi.org/10.1002/jsc.2511

You, T. L., & Zhou, M. (2019). Simultaneous embeddedness in immigrant entrepreneurship: Global forces behind Chinese-owned nail salons in New York City. *American Behavioural Scientist, 63*(2), 166–184. https://doi.org/10.1177/0002764218793684

Zhou, W., Raja, R., & Wen, G. (2023). Influence of "primary groups" on new Chinese immigrant entrepreneurship in Africa. *International Migration Review, 57*(4). https://doi.org/10.1177/01979183231190891

Zhuang, Z. C. (2021). The impact of immigrant entrepreneurship on city building: Learning from Toronto. In C. Y. Liu (Ed.), *Immigrant entrepreneurship in cities* (pp. 185–206). The Urban Book Series. Springer. https://doi.org/10.1007/978-3-030-50363-5_9

GLOSSARY

Adaptive strategies Innovative practices developed by immigrant entrepreneurs to overcome financial, legal and cultural barriers in host countries.

Administrative opacity The lack of clarity, consistency and accessibility in bureaucratic procedures, creating barriers to business registration and formalisation for immigrant entrepreneurs.

Agency The capacity of immigrant entrepreneurs to strategically navigate structural barriers, mobilise resources and adapt to diverse institutional environments.

Asylum-seeker entrepreneur Individuals waiting for a decision on their asylum application who start small businesses to survive, often without full legal working rights.

Bicultural Relating to or having proficiency in two distinct cultures, enabling individuals to navigate and integrate the norms, values and practices of both.

Bonding social capital Trust-based ties within close-knit ethnic or community groups that provide access to initial resources such as financing, labour and customer bases.

Bridging social capital Connections beyond ethnic or community boundaries, linking immigrant entrepreneurs to broader markets, institutions and opportunities.

Community-based collaboration The pooling of resources, knowledge and labour among immigrant entrepreneurs within local or ethnic networks to overcome systemic barriers.

Cultural branding The strategic use of cultural heritage, traditions and identity narratives to differentiate immigrant-owned businesses in competitive markets.

Cultural capital Socially valued knowledge, skills, and dispositions, including cultural familiarity with consumer behaviour and business norms, that influence entrepreneurial success.

Cultural entrepreneurship The creation of businesses that embed cultural traditions and identities into products, services or branding to engage both ethnic and mainstream markets.

Cultural heritage The traditions, practices, knowledge and artefacts passed down through generations that shape a community's identity and values.

Cultural segmentation The confinement of immigrant-owned businesses to ethnically defined markets, which can limit broader commercial integration.

Diaspora The movement of people away from their original homeland. They often maintain cultural connections while living in new countries.

Diaspora capital Financial, social and symbolic resources mobilised through transnational community ties that support immigrant entrepreneurship.

Diaspora entrepreneurs Entrepreneurs who serve diaspora communities while simultaneously integrating into the wider host economy.

Diasporic networks Cross-border social and economic ties that immigrant entrepreneurs leverage for knowledge, resources and market expansion.

Diasporic solidarity Mutual aid and trust-based practices within diaspora communities that foster entrepreneurship and resilience under conditions of exclusion.

Digital entrepreneurship Entrepreneurial activity conducted via digital platforms, e-commerce and online networks, often allowing immigrant entrepreneurs to bypass traditional institutional barriers.

Embedded Deeply rooted within or strongly connected to a particular system, structure or community.

Embedded agency The ability of immigrant entrepreneurs to strategically mobilise community networks, cultural resources and institutional knowledge to navigate and reshape exclusionary environments.

Embedded financial practices Informal financial methods, such as rotating savings associations and family lending, that immigrant entrepreneurs use when excluded from formal systems.

Embedded transnationalism Maintaining strong business, social and cultural ties across national borders while operating primarily in the host country.

Entrepreneurial identity (EI) The self-concept and market positioning of entrepreneurs shaped by race, migration status, gender and cultural norms and strategically performed to access legitimacy and opportunity.

Entrepreneurial mobility nexus The connection between migration, business creation and economic adaptation, showing how moving across countries shapes entrepreneurial activities and opportunities.

Ethnic economies Ecosystems where immigrant-owned businesses primarily serve co-ethnic communities, offering mutual support but sometimes limiting broader market expansion.

Ethnic enclaves Urban spaces or sectors densely populated by immigrant businesses serving co-ethnic clientele.

Ethnic entrepreneur Entrepreneurs who belong to an ethnic minority group (whether immigrants or born in the host country) and build businesses based on cultural identity, community ties and ethnic markets.

Ethnic entrepreneurship Entrepreneurial activities rooted in ethnic community networks, often relying on intra-community trust, labour and capital.

Ethnic networks Community-based business and social networks among immigrants that facilitate financing, mentorship, workforce recruitment and emotional support.

Financial exclusion The systemic denial or restriction of immigrant entrepreneurs' access to formal banking, credit and investment mechanisms based on race, migration status or socioeconomic factors.

First-generation immigrants People who are born in another country and move to a new one, often starting businesses out of necessity due to limited job opportunities, discrimination or restrictive immigration policies.

Forced entrepreneurship Starting a business out of economic necessity when formal employment is difficult to access, commonly observed among first-generation immigrants facing labour market barriers.

Formal institutions Established legal and regulatory systems that shape entrepreneurial opportunities and barriers, such as business licensing, immigration laws and financial policies.

Forms of capital The four essential resources—economic, social, cultural and human capital—that immigrant entrepreneurs mobilise to navigate opportunities and constraints.

Fragmented governance The disjointed and inconsistent regulation and support from public institutions that immigrant entrepreneurs must navigate, often leading to reliance on informal systems.

Guanxi A Chinese concept of cultivating interpersonal relationships based on trust, mutual obligation and reciprocity, often critical for immigrant entrepreneurs accessing resources and opportunities.

Human capital Skills, education, work experience and knowledge that influence entrepreneurs' adaptability, opportunity recognition and business success.

Identity-based market positioning The strategic use of cultural, ethnic or national identity by immigrant entrepreneurs to build trust, differentiate offerings and access niche or broader markets.

Identity-based strategies Entrepreneurial tactics that mobilise aspects of identity (race, ethnicity and gender) to navigate exclusion, build legitimacy and access new opportunities.

Immigrant entrepreneur People who have moved to a new country and started businesses there, using resources from both their home and host countries to overcome challenges and create economic opportunities.

Immigrant entrepreneurship Entrepreneurial activity carried out by individuals who have migrated to a new country, shaped by migration-specific factors such as legal status, cultural adaptation and social networks.

Informal economy Economic activities operating outside state regulation, often providing immigrant entrepreneurs with pathways to business formation and survival.

Informal finance Non-institutional financial practices such as rotating savings groups, family loans and community lending, offering alternatives to formal credit systems.

Informal institutions Unwritten rules, norms and social practices that influence business activities outside formal regulatory systems.

Institutional barriers Formal legal and regulatory obstacles that restrict immigrant entrepreneurs' ability to establish or grow businesses.

Institutional embeddedness The degree to which immigrant entrepreneurs are influenced by and interact with formal and informal institutions in the host society.

Institutional exclusion The marginalisation of immigrant entrepreneurs from formal support structures like finance, licensing and business development services.

Institutional fragmentation The lack of cohesive, coordinated and accessible support for immigrant entrepreneurship across public and private sectors.

Institutional literacy Knowledge and understanding of regulatory, legal and financial systems necessary for business establishment and success.

Intersectional exclusion The compounding effects of multiple marginalised identities (e.g., race, gender, migration status) that shape entrepreneurial barriers and opportunities.

Intersectionality An analytical framework examining how race, gender, class and migration status interact to shape experiences of opportunity and exclusion.

Language barriers Limited proficiency in the host country's language, restricting immigrant entrepreneurs' ability to access markets, services and regulatory processes.

Legal precarity A state of insecure or unstable legal status that limits access to rights, protections, and formal economic opportunities, increasing vulnerability to exclusion and exploitation.

Legal status The official classification of migrants under immigration law (e.g., asylum seeker, refugee and temporary migrant), shaping their entrepreneurial opportunities.

Marginalisation The process by which certain groups are pushed to the edges of society, limiting their access to resources, opportunities and full participation in economic, social or political life.

Minority A group or individual distinguished by ethnic, racial or social identity, often facing systemic barriers to full economic, political or social participation.

Mixed Embeddedness Framework (MEF) A theoretical model explaining immigrant entrepreneurship through the intersection of market conditions, institutional structures and ethnic social networks.

Multidimensional Involving multiple factors or layers such as social, economic, cultural and institutional aspects that influence a situation or outcome.

Multi-scalar An approach that looks at how different levels (local, national and global) interact to shape immigrant entrepreneurs' experiences, opportunities and barriers.

Narrative-based branding Using personal or community storytelling to build market visibility, challenge stereotypes and establish entrepreneurial legitimacy.

Opportunity structure The social, economic and institutional conditions that shape what business opportunities are available or restricted for entrepreneurs.

Proxy ownership An informal arrangement where immigrants operate businesses legally owned by citizens or permanent residents to bypass restrictive laws.

Reconceptualised Mixed Embeddedness Framework (RMEF) A theory that explains immigrant entrepreneurship by combining identity, agency and transnational strategies, showing how entrepreneurs navigate both ethnic ties and wider economic systems.

Refugee entrepreneur Migrants who have been granted refugee status and start businesses to rebuild their lives, often relying on external support like non-governmental organisations and microfinance.

Regulatory complexity The multilayered and often opaque legal and administrative frameworks that create significant challenges for immigrant entrepreneurs.

Relational Concerning the way individuals or groups connect, interact and build relationships with each other.

Returnee entrepreneurs Immigrants who return to their country of origin to start businesses using skills, networks and capital acquired abroad.

Rotating savings and credit associations (ROSCAs) Informal financial cooperatives where members contribute regular savings into a shared pool distributed cyclically, providing vital capital.

Second-generation immigrants People born in the host country to immigrant parents who typically pursue broader, innovation-driven opportunities beyond ethnic communities and have better access to education and formal resources.

Skilled/investor migrant entrepreneur Migrants who enter a country through skilled worker or investor visa programmes and launch businesses, often with strong financial backing and access to growth opportunities.

Social capital Resources embedded in networks of relationships, providing immigrant entrepreneurs access to financing, information and markets.

Social entrepreneurship Business ventures focused on addressing societal needs while also generating economic value, commonly deployed by immigrant entrepreneurs.

Social exclusion The process by which individuals or groups are marginalised and denied full access to economic, social and political opportunities.

Spatial inequality The unequal distribution of economic opportunities, infrastructure and resources across urban and rural spaces.

Stereotyping The act of assigning fixed, oversimplified traits to individuals or groups, often leading to misunderstanding, discrimination or exclusion.

Start-Up Visa A government programme that offers immigrant entrepreneurs a pathway to residency by supporting the creation of innovative new businesses.

Strategic identity work The conscious and deliberate use of ethnic, racial or gender identities to build entrepreneurial legitimacy, navigate exclusion and expand market opportunities.

Structural barriers Institutional, economic and societal obstacles that limit immigrant entrepreneurs' access to resources and markets.

Structural exclusion The systemic denial of immigrant entrepreneurs' access to resources, legitimacy and market participation.

Super-diversity The intense diversification of urban populations across ethnicity, migration status, language, and cultural practices, influencing entrepreneurial strategies.

Symbolic exclusion The marginalisation of immigrant entrepreneurs through cultural stereotypes and lack of mainstream recognition.

Temporary migrant entrepreneur Migrants on short-term visas who start businesses but face limits on business growth and long-term planning due to visa restrictions.

Translocal agency The ability to act across multiple spatial contexts (local, national and transnational) simultaneously to build entrepreneurial resilience.

Transnational Something that operates or connects across national borders, involving people, businesses or ideas in multiple countries.

Transnational embeddedness The deep connection and active involvement of businesses or people across several countries, maintaining ties, operations and resources.

Transnational entrepreneurs Entrepreneurs who operate simultaneously in both their home and host country markets using cross-border networks and strategies.

Transnational entrepreneurship Business activities that span national boundaries, involving the mobilisation of resources, networks and opportunities across multiple countries.

Transnational social fields Overlapping spaces where immigrants maintain economic, social and cultural ties across borders.

Undocumented entrepreneur Migrants without legal residency or work permits who run businesses informally, often facing legal risks and relying on community support networks.

Urban citizenship Informal belonging and participation in the host city's economic, social and cultural life, often through entrepreneurship.

Urban economy The economic activities, industries and markets concentrated within cities, shaped by factors such as population density, infrastructure and spatial inequality.

Venture capital (VC) Investment funding provided to high-growth start-ups in exchange for equity, which immigrant entrepreneurs often face barriers in accessing.

Voluntary entrepreneurship Starting a business by choice, often to pursue innovation and growth opportunities, increasingly seen among second-generation immigrants who are better integrated into mainstream economic systems.

Workforce optimisation Strategic use of co-ethnic labour to minimise costs, ensure cultural alignment and boost operational efficiency.

Xenophobia Institutional and social hostility targeting immigrant entrepreneurs based on their nationality or perceived foreignness.

INDEX

Note: **Bold** page numbers refer to **tables**.

For Product Safety Concerns and Information please contact our EU
representative GPSR@taylorandfrancis.com
Taylor & Francis Verlag GmbH, Kaufingerstraße 24, 80331 München, Germany

www.ingramcontent.com/pod-product-compliance
Ingram Content Group UK Ltd.
Pitfield, Milton Keynes, MK11 3LW, UK
UKHW050229200926
475702UK00020B/2937
* 9 7 8 1 0 3 2 9 9 6 0 8 0 *